A SPIRITUAL STRATEGY

FOR COUNSELING
AND PSYCHOTHERAPY

A SPIRITUAL STRATEGY

FOR
COUNSELING
AND
PSYCHOTHERAPY

SECOND EDITION

P. SCOTT RICHARDS
AND
ALLEN E. BERGIN

AMERICAN PSYCHOLOGICAL ASSOCIATION
Washington, DC

Published by
American Psychological Association
750 First Street, NE
Washington, DC 20002
www.apa.org

To order
APA Order Department
P.O. Box 92984
Washington, DC 20090-2984
Tel: (800) 374-2721
Direct: (202) 336-5510
Fax: (202) 336-5502
TDD/TTY: (202) 336-6123
Online: www.apa.org/books/
E-mail: order@apa.org

In the U.K., Europe, Africa, and the Middle East, copies may be ordered from
American Psychological Association
3 Henrietta Street
Covent Garden, London
WC2E 8LU England

Typeset in Goudy by World Composition Services, Inc., Sterling, VA

Printer: Port City Press, Inc., Baltimore, MD
Cover Designer: Minker Design, Bethesda, MD
Project Manager: Debbie Hardin, Carlsbad, CA

The opinions and statements published are the responsibility of the authors, and such opinions and statements do not necessarily represent the policies of the American Psychological Association.

Library of Congress Cataloging-in-Publication Data

Richards, P. Scott
    A spiritual strategy for counseling and psychotherapy / P. Scott Richards and Allen E. Bergin.—2nd ed.
        p. cm.
    Includes bibliographical references and index.
    ISBN 1-59147-254-7
    1. Psychotherapy—Religious aspects. 2. Mental health counseling—Religious aspects. 3. Psychotherapy patients—Religious life. 4. Spirituality. I. Bergin, Allen E., 1934-   II. Title.

RC489.S676R53   2005
616.89—dc22   2004031072

British Library Cataloguing-in-Publication Data
A CIP record is available from the British Library.

Printed in the United States of America
Second Edition

Dedicated to
Sir John Marks Templeton,
whose ideals and philanthropy have
ushered in a new era of faithful
scholarship in science and religion.

And in memory of
David B. Larson, MD
(1947–2002).

CONTENTS

PREFACE

We are pleased that religious and spiritual issues have become a prominent topic of concern for researchers, clinicians, and theorists in recent years. Any reader of popular or professional literature becomes rapidly aware of a burgeoning interest in spirituality, a breathtaking diversity of representation, and the need for rigor in discerning the substantial from the insubstantial.

Likewise, we are gratified by the positive reception accorded to the first edition of this book. In this second edition we concentrate on clearly and thoroughly laying out the foundations, rationale, and methods for a new psychotherapy strategy we call *theistic psychotherapy*. We invite mental health professionals who believe in God and spiritual realities to join with us in bringing this therapeutic tradition into the professional and academic mainstreams.

In this edition we also provide an extensive update of the burgeoning empirical and clinical literature on spiritually oriented psychotherapies and treatment methods. We expand our discussions of the philosophical and theoretical foundations of our theistic spiritual strategy. We more fully describe a theistic view of science and scholarship. We also discuss progress that has been made in this domain during the past decade and discuss tasks that lie ahead in the quest to bring theistic perspectives and approaches more fully into the mainstream of mental health professions.

This edition also constitutes a continuing effort to link advances in scholarship with recommendations for practice among clients who need interventions adapted to their beliefs and lifestyles. We are pleased to be part of a movement of colleagues who are bridging the gap between professional expertise and the multicultural contexts from which mental health clientele come.

Furthermore, we are encouraged by the continuing development of official support for programs of inquiry, training, and relevant ethical standards by the major mental health professions. This marks a significant change in the orientation of these clinical fields toward a formerly neglected domain of phenomena. We are excited by the keen interest that is occurring in the practical areas in universities, and we anticipate that the years ahead will be marked by advances and innovations that merit professional acceptance and public appreciation of a spiritually oriented approach to psychotherapy. Ultimately, we believe that integrating theistic spiritual perspectives and interventions into psychological practice will bring greater healing and increased health to individuals throughout the world.

ACKNOWLEDGMENTS

We are grateful to Susan Reynolds, our acquisitions editor at the American Psychological Association (APA), for her encouragement and patience during the lengthy process of revising and updating the first edition. We are also grateful to Susan Herman, our development editor at the APA, for her helpful feedback on drafts of the book manuscript. We also express gratitude to Edward P. Shafranske for his helpful suggestions.

We thank several talented students at Brigham Young University who provided valuable assistance on the book: Jeremy Bartz, Adam Froerer, Kari O'Grady, Justin Poll, and Coral Richards. The book is much better as a result of their insightful feedback, suggestions, and enthusiastic support.

We acknowledge several professional colleagues who have greatly influenced our thinking about spirituality and psychotherapy in recent years, particularly Michael E. Berrett, Randy K. Hardman, Lisa Miller, and Brent D. Slife. We also thank our colleagues and friends in Division 36 (Psychology of Religion) of the APA and in the Association of Mormon Counselors and Psychotherapists. We have learned much from their research and clinical wisdom.

Finally, we will remain forever grateful to our wives, Marcia Richards and Marian Bergin. Their love and support give us inspiration, joy, and strength.

I
INTRODUCTION

PROLOGUE

No single volume can do justice to the range and depth of human faith in and devotion to religious and spiritual phenomena; nor can the potential they hold for healing be described in full. We have been humbled by the greatness of this subject and by our inadequacy truly to comprehend and explain it. We are deeply conscious of our limitations and of the biases inherent in exploring from our own cultural context a world of spiritual experience that is universal, and more varied and complex, than anyone can grasp.

We know that our theistic perspective will touch only a portion of the world's people; nevertheless, we have begun a task that has proved to be deeply rewarding. It has brought us in touch with a literature and a variegated group of perceptive thinkers and practitioners who have stretched our boundaries and enriched our lives. We believe that this work has taken us a step beyond existing writings and that it is creating a synergy with the work of similarly motivated colleagues. A momentum has clearly been created, and a critical mass of intellectual and clinical effort is leading us in new directions that are promising and hopeful. Our own ability to help other people has been strengthened, and we believe that the synergy being created will lead to clinical innovations of profound significance.

Fundamental to all of this is a renewed and deepened appreciation for the diversity of human spirituality. It is a multiform manifestation of inwardly real experiences that are not readily categorizable in the standard languages of social science. Despite this diversity, there is much commonality. We have tried hard to reach for those threads of common humanity that bind us together as a human family existing in one world under a divine order that people perceive dimly but fervently. The potential of the commonalities to improve the human condition by blessing each other in multiple ways seems endless, and are, we think, pleasing to God.

On the other hand, we are also deeply pained by the way cultural traditions and categorizations have led to divisions, intolerance, discrimination, coercion, and even warfare. We see such themes justified by ideologies and played out clinically in the social–emotional abuses that occur in relationships and families. To derive hatred and violence from spiritual conviction is high tragedy. Such are alien to the spirit of God, even if rationalized by religious precepts. Many modern world problems grow out of deeply held but erroneous beliefs. Sadly, most traditions carry a measure of conceptual baggage that lends itself to unrealities, limitations on human possibilities, and, ultimately, the undermining of people's sense of worth and motivation for growth. We cannot begin to propose solutions for all of these problems, but they do stand as a warning that the labels *spiritual* or *religious* do not automatically identify something good. The same is true when the label *psychotherapy* is applied to a technique. Not all psychotherapy is therapeutic!

Despite such problems, we are encouraged by the fact that there is a large group of spiritually dedicated, intelligent people of good will who stand together on behalf of human welfare. Drawing on this benevolent base, our perspective begins with a theistic position and accompanying assumptions. We state these as openly and clearly as we can so they can be evaluated further by us and by others. Such evaluations can be both empirical and spiritual, objective and subjective, and qualitative and quantitative. By defining a viewpoint and being open to evaluation, we hope that new theoretical and clinical integrations of the spiritual domain will occur within professional mental health approaches.

Although we adhere to a tradition within the Judeo–Christian framework, we are sincerely and emotionally committed to an ecumenical perspective of respect and appreciation for the varied world cultures of belief, including spiritual humanism and individualized religiosity. Also, despite a tendency among Western intellectuals to ignore or demean Asian, African, Native American, and other traditions, we believe it is essential to embrace the ennobling graces of these spiritual schemes in an ecumenically sophisticated psychology of religious therapeutics. We pursue these goals in this book and in our *Handbook of Psychotherapy and Religious Diversity* (P. S. Richards & Bergin, 2000) and *Casebook for a Spiritual Strategy in Counseling and Psychotherapy* (P. S. Richards & Bergin, 2004).

1

THE NEED FOR A THEISTIC
SPIRITUAL STRATEGY

We are not human beings having a spiritual experience;
We are spiritual beings having a human experience.
                                          —Teilhard deChardin

The end of the 20th century and dawn of the new millennium was characterized by a resurgence of interest in spiritual issues and faith within the American population. Leading mainstream news magazines and newspapers such as *Time*, *Newsweek*, and *U.S. News and World Report* featured cover stories on these issues (e.g., Kalb, 2003; Kaplan, 1996; Kluger & Chu, 2004; Wallis, 1996; Woodward & Underwood, 1993). Hundreds of popular books and many TV specials focused additional attention on spiritual and religious matters. Thousands of World Wide Web sites about religion and spirituality were created. Many organizations and research institutes were founded to promote and study faith and spirituality. Millions of Americans sought a clearer understanding of how faith and spirituality could assist them in their daily lives (Moyers, 1996).

But not all was positive concerning religion. Global events such as the religiously motivated terrorist attacks on September 11, 2001; the violence and wars between Muslims, Christians, and Jews in Afghanistan, Iraq, Israel and Palestine; and the sexual abuse of children by clergy were all stark reminders of the dark side of religion (Turner, 2002). Despite these tragic events, religion and spirituality remain important to the majority of people in the United States. Recent polls have found that over 95% of Americans profess belief in God, 65% are members of a church, 60% say

5

that religion is very important in their lives, and 62% believe that religion can answer all or most of today's problems (Gallup, 2003).

The continuing widespread public interest in religion and spirituality has created a powerful cultural demand for psychotherapists to become more aware of and sensitive to the spiritual values and needs of their clients. However, this has not been an easy task for many professionals. Because of the alienation that has existed historically between the behavioral sciences and religion, the spiritual concerns of clients have long been neglected in the psychotherapy profession (Bergin, 1980a; Jones, 1994). Many psychotherapists have not been adequately trained for or prepared to deal effectively with spiritual issues, and their personal secular views or lack of experience with religion can create barriers to meeting the spiritual needs of their clientele (Bergin, 1991; P. S. Richards & Bergin, 2000; Shafranske, 2000). Fortunately, this situation is changing.

During the past decade, hundreds of articles on religion, mental health, spirituality, and psychotherapy have been published in professional journals. Mainstream publishers have also published many books on these topics. Opportunities for continuing education concerning religious and spiritual issues in health and psychotherapy have become more widely available. All of the major mental health organizations now explicitly acknowledge in their ethical guidelines that religion is one type of diversity that professionals need to respect (American Psychological Association, 2002; P. S. Richards & Bergin, 2000; Shafranske, 1996). Increasing numbers of graduate training programs in psychology are giving attention to religious and spiritual aspects of diversity (Brawer, Handal, Fabricatore, Roberts, & Wajda-Johnston, 2002). Many psychotherapists now believe that therapy may be more successful if clients' spiritual issues are addressed sensitively and capably along with their other concerns (P. S. Richards & Bergin, 2000, 2004; Sperry & Shafranske, 2005).

The rise of a more spiritually open *Zeitgeist*[1] or *spirit of the times* in the behavioral sciences has been favorable to the development of spiritually and religiously accommodative treatment approaches (McCullough, 1999; W. R. Miller, 1999; P. S. Richards & Bergin, 1997, 2000, 2004; Sperry & Shafranske, 2005). These approaches encourage psychotherapists to address clients' spiritual concerns when relevant, and to use language and interventions that show respect for and honor the healing potential of their clients' faith. Buddhist, Hindu, Christian, Jewish, and Muslim psychotherapy approaches have been outlined (e.g., Collins, 1988; Epstein, 1995; Hedayat-

---

[1] *Zeitgeist* is a German term popularized in psychology by Boring (1950), meaning "spirit of the times" or "habits of thought that pertain to a culture."

Diba, 2000; McMinn, 1996; Rabinowitz, 1999, 2000; Rubin, 1996; Sharma, 2000; Spero, 1985). Spiritual approaches based on Jungian, transpersonal, psychodynamic, cognitive, interpersonal, humanistic, and multicultural psychologies have also been described (e.g., Boorstien, 2000; Elkins, 1995; Faiver, Ingersoll, O'Brien, & McNally, 2001; Griffith & Griffith, 2002; Helminiak, 1996; Judy, 1996; Kelly, 1995; Lovinger, 1984; Nielsen, Johnson, & Ellis, 2001; Sperry, 2001; Sperry & Shafranske, 2005; Swinton, 2001; Vaughan, Wittine, & Walsh, 1996; West, 2000).

We think that the adaptation of a variety of psychotherapy approaches to culturally diverse religious and spiritual beliefs and practices in the world is a positive trend (Keller, 2000; P. S. Richards & Bergin, 2000). This trend parallels the growth of clinical strategies adapted to many other dimensions of human diversity (e.g., Ponterotto, Casas, Suzuki, & Alexander, 1995; D. W. Sue & Sue, 1990). The small amount of comparative research to date has shown that spiritually oriented and religiously accommodative therapy approaches are as effective as secular ones (McCullough, 1999; Worthington, Kurusu, McCullough, & Sandage, 1996; Worthington & Sandage, 2001a). On the grounds of effectiveness, client preference, and cultural compatibility, such approaches may often be the treatment of choice for religious clients. We hope that practitioners and researchers from diverse spiritual traditions will continue to develop and evaluate spiritual therapeutic approaches.

Although we think there is great value in the diversity of spiritual treatment approaches, this book focuses specifically on efforts we and others have made during the past 25 years to develop a theistic spiritual strategy[2] for mainstream professionals (Bergin, 1980a, 1991; P. S. Richards & Bergin, 1997, 2000, 2004). Given the fact that in the Western hemisphere and Europe more than 80% of the population professes adherence to one of the major theistic world religions[3] (Judaism, Christianity, and Islam), we think a theistic strategy is needed in mainstream psychotherapy to provide a culturally sensitive framework for theistic clients, particularly for those who are devout (Bergin, 1980a; P. S. Richards & Bergin, 2000). In addition, there is much healing potential in the theistic world religions (Benson, 1996; P. S. Richards & Bergin, 1997). We think that the spiritual resources found in the theistic religious traditions, if more fully accessed by psychotherapists, could help enhance the efficacy of psychological treatment.

---

[2]Consistent with Liebert and Liebert (1998), we use the term *strategy* to refer to a broad theoretical orientation or framework (e.g., psychoanalytic, dispositional, environmental, representational), which provides perspectives regarding personality theory and therapeutic change, assessment and measurement, interventions for psychological treatment, and research philosophy and methodology.
[3]See Table 1.1 for more complete religious demographic statistics in the United States and Table 4.1 for worldwide statistics.

TABLE 1.1
Religious Adherents in the United States (Mid-2000)

Adherents	Number	Percentage
Christians	235,742,000	84.7
Affiliated	191,828,000	68.9
Protestants	64,570,000	23.2
Roman Catholics	58,000,000	20.8
Evangelicals	72,363,000	27.5
Anglicans	2,400,000	0.9
Orthodox	5,762,000	2.1
Multiple affiliation	27,534,000	9.9
Independents	78,550,000	28.2
Marginal	10,080,000	3.6
Evangelicals	*40,640,000*	*14.6*
evangelicals	*98,662,000*	*35.4*
Unaffiliated	43,914,000	15.8
Baha'is	753,000	0.3
Buddhists	2,450,000	0.9
Chinese folk religionists	78,500	0.0
Ethnic religionists	435,000	0.2
Hindus	1,032,000	0.4
Jains	7,000	0.0
Jews	5,621,000	2.0
Muslims	4,132,000	1.5
Black Muslims	1,650,000	0.6
New religionists	811,000	0.3
Shintoists	56,200	0.0
Sikhs	234,000	0.1
Spiritists	138,000	0.1
Taoists	11,100	0.0
Zoroastrians	52,700	0.0
Other religionists	577,000	0.2
Nonreligious	25,078,000	9.0
Atheists	1,149,000	0.4
Total population	278,357,000	100.0

Note. Reprinted with permission from *Britannica Book of the Year*, Copyright 2004 by Encyclopedia Britannica, Inc. This table extracts and analyzes a microcosm of the world religion table. It depicts the United States, the country with the largest number of adherents to Christianity, the world's largest religion. *Structure:* Vertically the table lists 30 major religious categories. The major religions in the United States are listed with largest (Christians) first. Indented names of groups in the "Adherents" column are subcategories of the groups above them and are also counted in these unindented totals, so they should not be added twice into the column total. Figures in italics draw adherents from all categories of Christians above and so cannot be added together with them. Figures for Christians are built on detailed head counts by churches, often to the last digit. Totals are then rounded to the nearest 1,000. Because of rounding, the corresponding percentage may sometimes not total exactly 100%. *Christians:* All persons who profess publicly to follow Jesus Christ as Lord and Savior. This category is subdivided into *Affiliated Christians* (church members) and *Unaffiliated* (nominal) *Christians* (professing Christians not affiliated with any church). *Evangelicals/evangelicals:* These two designations—italicized and enumerated separately here—cut across all of the six Christian traditions or ecclesiastical megablocs listed above and should be considered separately from them. *Evangelicals* are mainly Protestant churches, agencies, and individuals calling themselves by this term (for example, members of the National Association of Evangelicals); they usually emphasize 5 or more of 7, 9, or 21 fundamental doctrines (salvation by faith, personal acceptance, verbal inspiration of Scripture, depravity of man, Virgin Birth, miracles of Christ, atonement, evangelism, Second Advent, etc.). The *evangelicals* are Christians of evangelical conviction from all traditions who are committed to the evangel (gospel) and involved in personal witness and mission in the world—alternatively termed Great Commission Christians. *Jews:* Core Jewish population relating to Judaism, excluding Jewish persons professing a different religion. *Other categories:* Definitions as given in chapter 4 of this volume, in Table 4.1.

Consider the following case examples:

Case 1: Mary and John

Mary and John were both 34 years old and had been married for 10 years. Mary was a member of the Roman Catholic Church, and John was a member of the Lutheran Church-Missouri Synod. The couple was treated at a private psychotherapy practice located at a Roman Catholic church in the upper Midwest region of the United States. Mary and John's presenting problems included unresolved hurts, excessive anger toward each other manifested in daily verbal fighting, and poor communication skills. Mary and John often fought about their religious difference and John's resentment over Mary's efforts to convert him to Roman Catholicism. Mary and John acknowledged that their main motivation for keeping the marriage together was their two children, an 8-year-old daughter and 3-year-old son.

After completing a thorough assessment, their therapist, Dr. Mark J. Krejci, a Roman Catholic, concluded that, despite their differences, Mary's and John's spiritual lives could be a positive area in which they could interact. Both had a deep, genuine belief in God and wanted to share this faith in the family context, but they did not know how to do this.

With the couple's consent to work on spiritual issues, Dr. Krejci encouraged them to engage in a number of spiritual practices together, which included praying for each other, participating in a nondenominational Bible study group, giving altruistic gifts to one another, attending church services at each other's churches, and sharing conversations with one another about their personal spiritual journeys. Dr. Krejci also helped Mary and John to recognize the need and gain the desire to forgive each other for past hurts and offenses. He presented to them a theistic biblical model of forgiveness. In addition to considering forgiveness as a cognitive and emotional process, this model of forgiveness considers images of God's forgiveness to be powerful resources in the change process.

Forgiveness played an important role in improving the couple's communication skills and in reducing their angry feelings toward one another. Instead of using insults and raised voices, Mary and John learned to handle disagreements with what they called "Christian love." Forgiveness and mutual sharing of their spiritual lives resulted in the couple developing a stronger, more enjoyable marriage. They were also able to generalize positive emotions that they had developed from forgiveness and spiritual exchanges to other areas of their relationship. Such positive change via forgiveness, of course, does not have to be rooted in religious belief and practice, but it is our hypothesis that religious conviction, context, and feelings deepen such a process and make it more enduring. (P. S. Richards & Bergin, 2004)

Case 2: Renee

Renee was a 16-year old Black woman who was 5 months' pregnant and depressed. She sought assistance from Dr. Lisa Miller, a Jewish woman who leads an interpersonal psychotherapy group (with a theistic spiritual emphasis) for pregnant teenagers in a public high school in Harlem, New York. Renee's mother had died during the last year, leaving her without a family or a home. Renee's biological father refused to have anything to do her after he found out she was pregnant and that she would not submit to an abortion. Renee's boyfriend, the father of her child, also refused to see her any more after she refused to have an abortion. Despite abandonment by her father and boyfriend, Renee continued to assert, "I am not going to kill my baby. This is my child!"

Dr. Miller supported Renee's decision on spiritual grounds to not have an abortion, affirming that the preservation of the child's life was a legitimate decision. Dr. Miller also affirmed that Renee had been brave in protecting her child under such unsupportive conditions. The other group members also supported Renee's decision and affirmed her courage. As the group therapy proceeded over 12 weeks, Renee had opportunities to realistically examine the challenges that lay before her as a young, unwed mother without familial support. Although the path before her appeared daunting, Renee also had opportunities to explore and affirm her belief that motherhood is a spiritual calling that she wished to honor. She also discussed her belief that her deceased mother was watching over her and that her mother approved of her decision to give birth to the child.

By the time treatment ended, Renee had qualified for a government-sponsored program that provided her with an apartment and child care while she completed her final year of high school and 4 years of college. She was able to build a world far away from her old neighborhood and the people who might harm her child—a world in which her youth and poverty did not prevent her from being a loving and effective mother. Although Renee was not involved in a religious community or denomination, her Christian upbringing and her nondenominational personal spirituality served as an anchor and source of strength as she prepared for motherhood. Dr. Miller's own belief in the grace and spiritual power of motherhood allowed her to empathize with and support Renee in her emotional and spiritual journey toward motherhood. (P. S. Richards & Bergin, 2004)

As can be seen, John, Mary, and Renee each had spiritual issues that were inextricably intertwined with their presenting problems. In the complete case reports, published in our *Casebook for a Spiritual Strategy in Counseling and Psychotherapy* (P. S. Richards & Bergin, 2004), it is apparent that the treatment of these clients could not have been completely successful without addressing their spiritual beliefs and issues. Furthermore, the case reports make clear that the clients' and therapists' faith in God, as well as the theistic spiritual interventions that were used, promoted healing and enhanced treatment outcomes.

The purpose of this volume is to describe concepts and interventions that will help mental health professionals implement a theistic psychotherapy approach in their practices. We also hope that the book will help psychotherapists, regardless of their theoretical orientations and personal religious backgrounds, to become more attuned to the spiritual issues in the lives of their clients so that they can assist them more effectively. This book is intended for practitioners, graduate students, and academicians in mainstream clinical and counseling psychology, psychiatry, clinical social work, and marriage and family therapy who wish to augment their secular training and skills with a spiritual framework and approach.

BACKGROUND AND OVERVIEW

Introducing spiritual content into mainstream theory, research, and practice is a formidable challenge. Strong forces of historical inertia resist this effort, but worldwide cultural and intellectual trends that are affecting modern thought propel it forward. For good reasons, the leading minds in the development of science, including psychology, have deliberately excluded spiritual content from their theories, laws, principles, and technical procedures. Some of these leading thinkers were themselves religiously devout, whereas others were neutral or antagonistic; however, there was a general acquiescence to excluding theological ideas and denominational biases for the sake of making a discipline a science. For many (e.g., Isaac Newton), the scientific project in itself was a way of revealing the designs of God in nature. Excluding the spiritual was thus a practical decision rooted in the methodological and conceptual assumption that things that cannot be observed, measured, or reliably described pertain to a different realm than science.

Assertions concerning faith in the existence of God, the spirit of God, divine intelligence, redemption through Christ, the spiritual essence of humans, the possibility of spiritual regulators of behavior, or the influence of God on the mind or body were thus ruled out of scientific discourse. Faith in science became an alternative to traditional faith. Theologians and, to a degree, philosophers, lost the prominent place they had once held in the world of scholarship.

The movement broadly defined as "scientific modernism" gained momentum and eventual ascendancy. The choice to become objective, empirical, and, when possible, experimental and quantitative, succeeded beyond the expectations of even the most gifted scholars' visions of the future. The marvels of the modern world and the pace of new development in science and technology stand as a testament to the insight of the originators and promoters of modern science. These successes have been most evident in the physical and biological fields, but scientific approaches to knowledge and application have spread broadly and have influenced nearly all fields of inquiry, including the behavioral sciences.

We have substantial admiration for this way of comprehending and managing the world, including its use in many areas of experimental psychological science. As students of personality and therapeutic change, however, we have regularly confronted obstacles to effective application of this way of thinking to the clinical phenomena we observe. Our frustration is widespread, and it is why so many individuals and groups have split off from mainstream psychological science over the years. Dozens of great people have grappled with the gap between modernist scientific psychological models or methods and the personal and clinical phenomena with which they have dealt. Some of these efforts managed to keep the less tangible aspects of humanity close to standard scientific procedures, whereas others broke entirely from the tradition in which they had been trained and had faith. This long, hard trial of history is marked by some of the pioneers in the field, including Gordon Allport, Robert Coles, Erik Erikson, Viktor Frankl, William James, Carl Jung, George Kelly, Rollo May, Abraham Maslow, Hobart Mowrer, M. Scott Peck, Carl Rogers, Joseph Rychlak, and Irvin Yalom.

In the spirit of these pioneers' efforts, we propose an alternative perspective, influenced by but departing in degrees from them. The humanistic, existential, cognitive, agentive, and spiritual themes they espoused touched on and opened the door for considering a theistic dimension within the psychological domain. Our effort goes farther to build on the works of insightful and courageous creators of theistic, spiritual perspectives in human personality and psychotherapy. Some of them have been only marginally noted in the mainstream psychology literature, because much of their work has been disparate from that literature. Some of the prominent contributors to this effort include Herbert Benson, Peter Benson, Gary R. Collins, Robert Emmons, James W. Fowler, Richard L. Gorsuch, Ralph W. Hood, Stanton L. Jones, Eugene Kelly, Harold G. Koenig, David B. Larson, Jeffery Levin, Robert J. Lovinger, H. Newton Malony, John Martin, Michael E. McCullough, Mark R. McMinn, Lisa Miller, William R. Miller, David Myers, Bruce Narramore, Kenneth I. Pargament, L. Rebecca Propst, Carol R. Rayburn, Edward P. Shafranske, Melvin Spero, Len Sperry, Bernard Spilka, Merton B. Strommen, Siang Yang Tan, Alan C. Tjeltveit, William West, Everett L. Worthington, and David Wulff. Although these and other courageous theistic scholars and practitioners have influenced our approach, this book is our personal synthesis and program.

A Theistic Spiritual Strategy

Our theistic spiritual strategy is a comprehensive orientation that includes a theistic conceptual framework, a body of religious and spiritual therapeutic interventions, and guidelines for implementing theistic perspectives and interventions (P. S. Richards & Bergin, 2004). The foundational assumptions of our theistic strategy are that "God exists, that human beings are the creations of God, and that there are unseen spiritual processes by which the link between God and humanity is maintained" (Bergin, 1980a, p. 99). We also assume that people who have faith in God's power and draw on spiritual resources during treatment will have added strength to cope, heal, and grow. No other mainstream tradition has adequately incorporated theistic spiritual perspectives and practices into its approach, and so this orientation fills a void in the field. Obviously, theistic clinical perspectives are neither original nor unique to our work; however, we have formulated a position that expresses our own viewpoint but also embraces the substantial contributions of many others.

Figure 1.1 demonstrates that the conceptual framework of our theistic strategy includes (a) theological premises that are grounded in the theistic worldview, (b) philosophical assumptions that are consistent with the theistic worldview, (c) a theistic personality theory, and (d) a theistic view of psychotherapy. These conceptual foundations provide a rationale that embraces the necessity for spiritual interventions in psychotherapy, what types may be useful, and when they might appropriately be implemented. Thus, in various places in this book, we offer recommendations for psychotherapists to consider when implementing spiritual perspectives and interventions during treatment. We include guidelines concerning (a) adopting ecumenical and denominational therapeutic stances; (b) establishing a spiritually open and safe therapeutic relationship, (c) setting spiritual goals in psychotherapy, (d) conducting religious and spiritual assessments, (e) attending to ethical concerns in spiritual psychotherapy, and (f) implementing spiritual interventions appropriately in therapy.

We describe a variety of spiritual practices and interventions that may contribute to therapeutic change, including but not limited to prayer, contemplation and meditation, reading of sacred writings, forgiveness and repentance, worship and ritual, fellowship and service, quest for spiritual direction, and moral instruction and clarification. Our theistic conceptual framework does *not*, however, tell psychotherapists specifically *how* to implement spiritual interventions in treatment, nor does it tell them how to integrate such interventions with mainstream secular perspectives and interventions. Hence, as illustrated by the rectangle in Figure 1.1 labeled *Theistic Psychotherapy Approaches*, we recognize that our theistic strategy can be applied in practice in numerous ways, as illustrated in the recent *Casebook*

```
┌─────────────────────────────────────────┐
│       THEISTIC PSYCHOTHERAPY            │
│            APPROACHES                   │
│        Theistic–Integrative            │
│        Theistic–Interpersonal          │
│       Theistic–Family Systems          │
│         Theistic–Cognitive             │
│         Theistic–Humanistic            │
│        Theistic–Psychodynamic          │
└─────────────────────────────────────────┘
                    ⇑
┌─────────────────────────────────────────┐
│          THEISTIC VIEW OF              │
│           PSYCHOTHERAPY                 │
│        Meta-Empathy, Inspiration       │
│          Therapeutic Valuing           │
│   Spiritual Practices and Techniques   │
│         Spiritual Assessment           │
│           Spiritual Goals              │
│      Ecumenical and Denominational     │
└─────────────────────────────────────────┘
                    ⇑
┌─────────────────────────────────────────┐
│      THEISTIC PERSONALITY THEORY       │
│     Marriage, Family, and Community    │
│           Benevolent Power             │
│    Inspired Integrity, Faithful Intimacy│
│       Agency, Moral Responsibility     │
│  Eternal Spiritual Identity, Spirit of Truth│
└─────────────────────────────────────────┘
                    ⇑
┌─────────────────────────────────────────┐
│   THEISTIC PHILOSOPHICAL FOUNDATIONS   │
│      Theistic Holism, Contextuality    │
│      Altruism, Theistic Relationism    │
│        Moral Universals, Agency        │
│  Scientific Theism, Methodological Pluralism│
└─────────────────────────────────────────┘
                    ⇑
┌─────────────────────────────────────────┐
│    THEISTIC WORLDVIEW OR THEOLOGY      │
│           Life after Death             │
│            Good and Evil               │
│     Spiritual Communication with God   │
│        Humans are creations of God     │
│              God exists                │
└─────────────────────────────────────────┘
```

Figure 1.1. Theological, philosophical, theoretical, and applied foundations of a theistic spiritual strategy.

for a *Spiritual Strategy in Counseling and Psychotherapy* (P. S. Richards & Bergin, 2004).

We have formulated the conceptual framework for our theistic strategy broadly with the hope that it will be suitable for mental health professionals from a variety of theistic religious traditions, including many branches within Judaism, Islam, and Christianity. This is most appropriate for an orientation that emerges from the professional mainstream. It must appeal to a broad range of practitioners and clients and not be too denominationally specific. This will make it usable in the wide spectrum of training programs and clinical facilities that serve a diverse but mainly theistic public. Denominational (subcultural) specificity can be developed within this broad orientation and be practiced appropriately in parochial settings by qualified clinicians.

An Invitation to Theistic Mental Health Professionals

Most psychotherapists do not use the term *theistic* to describe their therapeutic orientation, possibly because it has not previously been offered as an option for mainstream professionals. We wish to offer it as a valid option now. We propose the term *theistic psychotherapy* as a general label for psychotherapy approaches that are grounded in the theistic worldview (cf. P. S. Richards & Bergin, 2004; Sperry & Shafranske, 2005). *Theistic psychotherapy* refers to a global psychotherapy orientation or tradition, such as the psychodynamic, humanistic, and cognitive traditions, not to the psychotherapy of a specific denomination, such as Christian, Jewish, or Islamic therapies. We also use the term *theistic psychotherapy* to describe approaches that begin with a theistic foundation but also absorb and integrate interventions from mainstream secular approaches.

We propose the term *theistic psychotherapist* to refer to psychotherapists who believe in God and who incorporate theistic perspectives and interventions to some degree into their therapeutic approach. Because surveys have shown that approximately 30% to 50% of psychotherapists are members of one of the theistic world religions, believe in God, and use spiritual interventions in their professional practices (e.g., Ball & Goodyear, 1991; Bergin & Jensen, 1990; P. S. Richards & Potts, 1995b; Shafranske, 2000; Shafranske & Malony, 1990), many therapists could appropriately be called *theistic psychotherapists*; they might at least include the term *theistic* in describing their approach.

We assume that most if not all *theistic psychotherapists* will integrate theistic perspectives and interventions with one or more of the mainstream secular psychotherapy traditions. Thus psychotherapists who combine theistic concepts and interventions with psychodynamic ones might wish to describe their therapeutic approach as *theistic–psychodynamic* (e.g.,

Shafranske, 2005). Those who combine theistic and cognitive perspectives and interventions could describe their approach as *theistic–cognitive* (e.g., Johnson, 2004; Nielsen, 2004; Tan & Johnson, 2005); those who combine theistic and interpersonal perspectives and interventions could describe their approach as *theistic–interpersonal* (e.g., L. Miller, 2004, 2005); and those who combine the theistic with several mainstream secular traditions could describe their approach as *theistic–integrative* (P. S. Richards, 2005).

By using the terms *theistic psychotherapy* and *theistic psychotherapist* broadly, we hope to bring some unity and strength to a diversity of practitioners who have faith that God's spiritual influence can assist clients and therapists in their journeys of healing and growth.

We do not think therapists must incorporate all of our conceptual framework or process guidelines into their psychotherapy approach in order to be regarded as theistic psychotherapists. In our view, counselors and psychotherapists who believe in God in a manner that is generally consistent with the theistic world religions, and whose beliefs appreciably influence their theoretical perspective and therapeutic approach, are theistic psychotherapists, regardless of what mainstream secular perspectives and interventions they select. A therapist who responds "yes" to all or most of the following questions fits our definition of a theistic psychotherapist:

1. Do you believe in God or a Supreme Being?
2. Do you believe that human beings are creations of God?
3. Does your theistic worldview influence your view of human nature and personality theory?
4. Do your theistic beliefs influence your ideas about human dysfunction and therapeutic change?
5. Do your theistic beliefs have any impact on your relationship with, assessment of, or intervention with your clients?
6. Do you believe that God, or the spirit of God, can enhance the therapeutic process?

Characteristics of Theistic Psychotherapy

To be viable in the mainstream mental health professions, we assume that a theistic, spiritual strategy for psychotherapy needs to be empirical, integrative, and ecumenical; it must also accommodate denominationally specific applications (Bergin & Payne, 1991; P. S. Richards, 2005).

Empirical

By using the term *empirical,* we mean that the claims of a theistic strategy regarding human nature, the change process, and treatment effectiveness can and should be evaluated rigorously with careful research. It is widely recognized that psychotherapy is not simply an applied technology but is an intuitive, artistic enterprise. Nevertheless, there is a commitment within the mental health professions that the field of psychotherapy must examine its practices and claims with empirical research to advance as a field and maintain its credibility (Bergin & Garfield, 1994; Lambert, 2004). The practices and claims of theistic psychotherapy must also be submitted to such scrutiny.

Without reasonable harmony with the findings of other researchers, theistic psychotherapy will not advance or influence mainstream mental health professionals. This is not to say that we endorse a narrow view of what science should be. Rather, we support the notion of "methodological pluralism" (Kazdin, 1994; Slife & Gantt, 1999). We value traditional experimental and quantitative research paradigms, but we also believe that qualitative, phenomenological, and experiential approaches can contribute much to the understanding of human personality and psychotherapy (see chap. 12, this volume).

Integrative

By saying that our strategy is *integrative*, we recommend that theistic therapists should not use spiritual interventions exclusively or in a "cookbook" fashion, but as part of a flexible, multidimensional, integrative treatment approach that includes mainstream secular perspectives and interventions. During the past few decades, therapists have moved away from allegiance to a single school of thought and toward a multidimensional approach (Bergin & Garfield, 1994; Lambert, 2004; Norcross & Goldfried, 1992; Stricker & Gold, 1993). The majority now uses an integrative approach (Jensen, Bergin, & Greaves, 1990), seeking to tailor treatment and interventions to the unique characteristics and needs of each client. Even those who advocate careful outcome studies on single approaches have acknowledged that ordinary practice is an art of progressively integrating multiple approaches as the therapist proceeds to adapt strategies to the individual client.

Consistent with this trend, we encourage psychotherapists to integrate perspectives and interventions from other therapeutic traditions into their theistic approach according to their own preferences. We do not believe that a theistic orientation supersedes the need for psychodynamic, behavioral, cognitive, humanistic, and systemic perspectives or for necessary medication or hospitalization. Rather, by complementing these therapeutic traditions it uniquely enriches understanding of human personality and therapeutic change. An integrative theistic orientation allows therapists the flexibility to choose the religious and spiritual interventions that seem to best match the needs of a given client. We consider this flexibility a means to tap into the resources of a spiritual dimension that may be a major aspect of the client's life (Bergin, 1988, 1991).

We recognize that there are major conceptual and technical inconsistencies within secular therapy traditions, as well as between secular and theistic frameworks (Bergin, 1991; Slife & Reber, 2001; Slife & Williams, 1995). The process of developing a conceptually consistent and sound theistic orientation is not necessarily easy. This challenge will be developed further in subsequent chapters, particularly in chapter 6. Our point here is that psychotherapists need to be open to many possible resources in the change process. We endorse experimentation with and evaluation of efforts to use theistic psychotherapy, both alone and in combination with other orientations with which clinicians are familiar and comfortable. Obviously, this will be easier with some combinations than with others.

Ecumenical

When we say our theistic strategy is *ecumenical,* we mean that its philosophical and spiritual assumptions are reasonably accommodating to the worldviews of the major religious and spiritual traditions that modern therapists are most likely to encounter in North America. Thus, psychotherapists from a variety of backgrounds may use its theoretical perspectives, clinical guidelines, and therapeutic interventions. By identifying common aspects of the theistic spirituality of clients, an ecumenical theistic strategy enables therapists to avoid getting tangled in the theological conflicts of divergent theistic religious traditions and to intervene sensitively and effectively regardless of a client's particular theistic religious affiliation and spiritual beliefs.

Without an ecumenical strategy, theistic treatment approaches would consist only of denominationally specific ones (e.g., for Catholics, Protestants, Jews, Muslims, Latter-Day Saints, etc.). Although denominationally specific perspectives and interventions are needed, a unifying ecumenical theistic orientation is also needed to avoid the fragmentation and incoherence that currently characterizes this domain of psychotherapy, and to allow perspectives and interventions grounded in the theistic world religions to influence mainstream psychotherapy practice.

Denominationally Specific

When we say that our theistic strategy accommodates and facilitates *denominationally specific* applications, we mean that it is flexible and contains guidelines to help therapists use denominationally specific concepts and interventions sensitively and effectively. Bergin and Payne (1991) pointed out that clients from different religious traditions "present different needs embedded in languages and lifestyles that demand technical content adapted to their needs" (p. 208). Our theistic orientation helps therapists honor and fully utilize the unique religious beliefs and spiritual resources available to clients who belong to a particular denomination or tradition (Kelly, 1995; Lovinger, 1984). Having attained a general spiritual understanding, therapists may develop the skills needed to use denominationally specific interventions with clients from their own background or religious traditions of which they have acquired an in-depth understanding. Thus psychotherapists can "learn how to function both in the broader ecumenical world and in the fine texture" (Bergin & Payne, 1991, p. 208) of one or more specific theistic religious traditions.

Unique Contributions of a Theistic Spiritual Strategy

We have grounded our orientation in the theistic worldview for a number of reasons. First, we believe in God and in spiritual realities. We think that the naturalistic–atheistic worldview on which all of the traditional mainstream psychotherapy traditions have been grounded does not adequately account for the complexities and mysteries of life and of the universe. We agree with scholars who have argued that spiritual perspectives are needed to enrich scientific understanding of human beings, of the origins and operations of the universe, and of health and human welfare (Barbour, 1990; Griffin, 2000; Jones, 1994). Although we do not endorse all of the teachings and practices advocated by the theistic world religions, we find much therapeutic potential in these traditions.

Second, we think the theistic worldview provides a more adequate foundation than the naturalistic worldview on which to construct theories of human nature, personality, and therapeutic change. A number of scholars have suggested that the naturalistic–atheistic worldview is philosophically and empirically problematic (Bergin, 1980a; Griffin, 2000; Slife, 2004; Slife, Hope, & Nebeker, 1999). For example, Griffin (2000) argued not only that this worldview provides an impoverished view of human nature, but that it is inconsistent with the empirical evidence and with beliefs that are "inevitably presupposed in practice" by both laypersons and scientists (p. 99).

The theistic view of human nature and of the world, in contrast, has profound positive implications for personality theory, psychotherapy, and the processes of healing and change (Bergin, 1988, 1991). This perspective contributes uniquely to psychology and psychotherapy by providing (a) a theistic conception of human nature and personality (see chaps. 4 and 5); (b) a moral frame of reference for guiding and evaluating psychotherapy (see chaps. 6 and 7); and (c) a body of spiritual techniques and interventions (see chaps. 8–10). It also provides a theistic view of scientific discovery and the research process (see chap. 11).

Third, we prefer the theistic worldview because the majority of people in North America believe in it and derive their values from it. Most psychotherapists are much more likely to encounter clients who approach life with a theistic worldview rather than other worldviews. From the standpoint of numbers only, there is a pressing need for such an approach. Mainstream psychological theories and treatment approaches based on naturalistic assumptions "are not sufficient to cover the spectrum of values pertinent to human beings and the frameworks within which they function" (Bergin, 1980a, p. 98).

Caveats

We recognize that some of our perspectives and recommendations may be controversial. Basing our theistic framework on the belief that there is a Supreme Being who guides and influences human beings may be objectionable to some professionals. We address this concern at various points throughout the book, but particularly in chapters 2 through 5. Our view that it is possible—and even desirable—for therapists and clients to seek guidance and inspiration from a divine source to assist them in the healing process might also seem controversial. So might our recommendation that therapists use various spiritual interventions, such as praying for their clients, using imagery with spiritual content, and encouraging clients to seek blessings and spiritual guidance from their religious leaders.

We hope that professionals who find such perspectives and recommendations objectionable will not "throw the baby out with the bath water" and conclude that there is nothing of value for them in this book. Those who feel negatively about a specific perspective or intervention can certainly disregard it. They may still find considerable value in the overall strategy we describe, discovering that it aids them in working more sensitively and effectively with their theistic clients and with the increasing number of mental health practitioners whose orientations are similar to ours.

We recognize that we are embarking on much new ground. Some of our ideas have not been tested empirically, so there is much room for discussion, debate, and revision in the years ahead. We do not present our ideas dogmatically; we offer them openly and with a hope that they will prove helpful to researchers and practitioners of diverse theoretical and spiritual perspectives.

In basing our spiritual strategy on a theistic worldview, we are not endorsing all theistic religions or their practices. We recognize that there has been, and still is, much harm done in the name of religion. For example, the oppression of minority groups and women, as well as acts of violence, terrorism, and war, have been waged in the name of religion (Ellis, 1986; Meadow, 1982; Shrock, 1984; Turner, 2002). We deplore the use of religion for such destructive purposes. We endorse in the theistic world religions only that which is healthy and beneficial to all of humankind. In chapter 5 we discuss in some detail our views about how theistic, spiritual beliefs and institutions can contribute powerfully to a healthy personality, mental health, and harmonious social relations.

Definitions of "Religion" and "Spirituality"

As we approach this topic, it may be helpful to clarify what we mean by the words *religion* and *spirituality*. During the last decade much debate and discussion has occurred over the meaning of these words. Surveys of social scientists, clergy, nurses, and college students, as well as content analyses of social scientific writings, have shown numerous and diverse definitions (Pargament, Sullivan, Balzer, Van Haitsma, & Raymark, 1995; Zinnbauer, Pargament, & Scott, 1999). Most scholars and lay persons agree, however, that although the terms overlap and are similar in many regards, they are not identical (Zinnbauer et al., 1999).

The recent trend among social scientists and the public has been to (a) define *religion* as a narrow construct and *spirituality* as more encompassing; (b) polarize and differentiate *religion* and *spirituality*; (c) define *religion* as external, institutional, static, and substantive, and *spirituality* as personal, relational, dynamic, and functional; and (d) view *religion* as negative and *spirituality* as positive (Zinnbauer et al., 1999). Several scholars have argued that such polarization can "yield only a limited understanding of the two constructs" (Zinnbauer et al., 1999, pp. 899, 903; see also Pargament, 1999). We agree with this concern.

It is beyond the scope of this book to review or resolve the controversies regarding the terms *religion* and *spirituality*. Here we simply wish to help readers understand what we mean when we use the terms in this book. We consider it a serious mistake to view religion as "bad" and spirituality as "good." We also feel that to polarize or completely differentiate these terms tends to oversimplify and distort their meaning. Clearly the constructs overlap a great deal—they have many shared meanings and characteristics. Nevertheless, given the empirical finding that most people differentiate these terms in their minds to some degree, it seems important to explain how we consider them to differ.

Although we agree with those who have argued that polarizing *religion* as an institutional activity and *spirituality* as a private or individual expression is an oversimplification (Pargament, 1999), studies have shown that these are the main criteria that many people use to distinguish between these terms. Furthermore, when people refer to themselves as spiritual but not religious, they often mean they are not affiliated with an organized religion, but they do feel connected with God or other sacred things (Zinnbauer et al., 1999). Given this, we think there is some value in partially distinguishing between the terms *religion* and *spirituality* in this manner, as long as it is remembered that "virtually every major religious institution is quite concerned with spiritual matters" and that "every form of religious or spiritual expression occurs in a social context" (Pargament, 1999, p. 9).

When we use the terms *religion* and *religiousness* in this book, therefore, we are referring to theistic religious beliefs, practices, and feelings that are often, though not always, expressed institutionally and denominationally (e.g., church attendance, participating in public religious rituals, reading sacred writings). But we agree with those who have argued that *religion* includes much more than church attendance and other institutional expressions of belief. Religious beliefs and behaviors can be very personal, private, and sacred (Pargament, 1999).

When we use the term *spiritual* in this book, we are referring to invisible phenomena associated with thoughts and feelings of enlightenment, vision, harmony with truth, transcendence, and oneness with God (cf. James, 1902/1936). These have often been correlated with but are not synonymous with objective and visible mental, emotional, and biological measures (Chadwick, 1993; Hood, 1995; Koenig, McCullough, & Larson, 2001; Larson & Larson, 1994; Levin, 1995). We define *spirituality* as a state of being attuned with God or the Divine Intelligence that governs or harmonizes the universe. Pargament (1999) defined *spirituality* as "a search for the sacred" (p. 12). We like his definition and would expand it from our perspective to include "a search for *and harmony with* God and the sacred." Accordingly, the most essential characteristics of spiritual people are that they enjoy loving and genuine closeness, harmony, and connection with God and spiritual realities. In our view, therefore, if a religious practice or experience helps a person feel more closeness and connection with God, then that practice or experience is spiritual. Without this personal connection, the practice or experience may be religious, but not spiritual.

We assume that *spirituality* is a unique domain and cannot be subsumed by other domains such as cognitions, emotions, social systems, and so on. The spiritual is a unique reality that has not been articulated well in behavioral science and practice. We have made it our task to participate in initiating that articulation, as we try to bring the ineffable yet powerful dimension of spirituality into the practical realities of the experience and resolution of emotional distress.

Plan of This Volume

In chapters 2 through 5 we present the historical, philosophical, and theoretical foundations of a theistic spiritual strategy. Practitioners who want to begin with the clinical applications of the strategy should go to chapter 6, which begins with a discussion of the psychotherapy process and methods. We hope that readers will then return to chapters 2 through 5, because the rationale and justification for a spiritual strategy presented in these chapters is essential.

In chapter 2 we briefly discuss the historical neglect of religious and spiritual issues in the mainstream mental health professions. We assert that, in attempting to establish their theories as "scientific," the early leaders of psychology and psychiatry adopted many of the philosophical assumptions of 19th-century Newtonian and Darwinian science. We briefly define these assumptions and discuss why their influence has led to the exclusion of spiritual perspectives. A major addition to chapter 2 in this edition is an expanded discussion of "The Age of Science" and a new section that considers some of the philosophical and empirical problems with atheistic naturalism.

In chapter 3 we discuss the new *Zeitgeist* of science generally and of the behavioral sciences, including psychotherapy, which is much more compatible with religious and spiritual worldviews. We treat the major influences on the development of this spiritual *Zeitgeist*. The most significant additions to chapter 3 in this edition are discussions of recent contributions to a spiritual *Zeitgeist* in science and psychology, including the science–religion dialogue; the spirituality and medicine movement; the positive psychology movement; and the development of spiritually oriented psychotherapy approaches.

In chapter 4 we discuss the importance of a *Weltanschauung*, or worldview, in personality development, mental health, and psychotherapy. We present the theological and philosophical foundations of our framework, with detailed explanation of the Western or theistic worldview, and brief contrasts to the worldviews of the Eastern spiritual traditions and modern-day naturalistic science. A major addition to chapter 4 in this edition is a discussion of the major metaphysical, axiological, and epistemological underpinnings of a theistic approach to psychology and psychotherapy (e.g., scientific theism, theistic holism, agency, moral absolutism, altruism, theistic relationism, and contextuality).

In chapter 5 we describe some of the major assumptions of a theistic, spiritual view of human personality and therapeutic change. We briefly summarize empirical research findings that religious and spiritual influences are often, but not always, positively related to physical and mental health. We also discuss qualitative and quantitative evidence for theistic spiritual realities, including reports of death-related visions, mystical and spiritual experiences, and spiritual and anomalous healing experiences.

In chapters 6 through 11 we present the clinical application of our theistic framework. In chapter 6 we discuss the implications of a theistic worldview for the understanding of psychotherapy, beginning with the major goals of theistic psychotherapy and moving into the major roles and tasks of therapists who implement this approach, including relationships, assessment, and intervention. We also discuss the client's role in theistic psychotherapy. An important addition to this chapter is how therapists can integrate theistic perspectives and interventions into their therapy approach in a conceptually informed and consistent manner.

In chapter 7 we consider ethical questions and dangers that may arise when therapists implement theistic spiritual perspectives and interventions in treatment. These include (a) developing dual relationships, or blurring boundaries between professional and religious roles; (b) displacing or usurping religious authority; (c) imposing religious values on clients or, equally offensive, being insensitive to their values; (d) violating work setting (church–state) boundaries; and (e) practicing outside the boundaries of professional competence. We also identify contraindications for spiritual interventions and offer general process suggestions regarding their use.

In chapter 8 we describe a rationale and approach for conducting a religious and spiritual assessment in theistic psychotherapy. We describe clinically important religious and spiritual dimensions that therapists should assess. We then present a multilevel, multidimensional assessment approach that considers all major systems in clients' lives: for example, physical, social, behavioral, cognitive, educational–occupational, psychological–emotional, and religious–spiritual. An important addition to this chapter is our review of current developments in the spiritual assessment domain, along with their relevance for theistic practitioners and researchers.

In chapter 9 we describe a variety of religious and spiritual practices that have endured for centuries among members of the world's theistic religious traditions: e.g., prayer, rituals, meditation and contemplation, and reading of scriptures and sacred writings. We cite research that supports the potential healing properties of these spiritual practices, and we offer suggestions for using them in theistic psychotherapy. In this chapter we have added information about repentance and atonement and have updated references to recent scholarship about spiritual practices.

In chapter 10 we review the variety of spiritual interventions that theistic psychotherapists have used to date, along with available research evidence on efficacy. We describe several spiritual treatment package approaches that have been reported in the literature. We explore the use of spiritual interventions in marital and family therapy, group therapy, and child and adolescent therapy, with a variety of clinical populations.

In the first edition, chapter 11 expanded on chapter 10 by providing a variety of case examples. With the advice of our editors, a companion volume entirely devoted to case material, *Casebook for a Spiritual Strategy in Counseling and Psychotherapy* (P. S. Richards & Bergin, 2004), has replaced that chapter. The new chapters 11 and 12 cover a variety of topics pertinent to the future of a theistic, spiritual strategy. In chapter 11 we discuss the implications of the theistic worldview for our understanding of scientific discovery and research processes. We suggest a theistic view of epistemology and scientific discovery, exploring the role of intuition and inspiration in the scientific discovery process. We briefly outline some of the major quantitative and qualitative research designs or methodologies that have potential for advancing spiritual strategies in personality theory and psychotherapy. Important additions to chapter 11 are expanded and updated discussions titled "Scientific Theism," "Methodological Pluralism" and "A Theistic View of the Scientific Process."

In chapter 12 we have updated our discussion of some of the needs and directions for the future advancement of a theistic strategy. In particular, we discuss needs and directions for theory and research, multicultural education and clinical training, and several professional practice domains, including psychotherapy, behavioral medicine and health psychology, public health education, community psychology, and pastoral counseling.

II
HISTORICAL PERSPECTIVES

2

THE ALIENATION BETWEEN RELIGION AND PSYCHOLOGY

Many worlds of consciousness exist . . . which have a meaning for our life . . . the total expression of human experience . . . invincibly urges me beyond the narrow "scientific" bounds. Assuredly, the real world is of a different temperament—more intricately built than physical science allows.

—William James

During the later part of the 20th century, many writers acknowledged that religious and spiritual issues had traditionally been neglected in the mainstream mental health professions (e.g., Bergin, 1980a, 1980b; Campbell, 1975; Collins, 1977; Lovinger, 1984; Strommen, 1984). For example, Collins (1977), a clinical psychologist, pointed out that

> During the course of its history, psychology has never shown much interest in religion. General psychology books tend to give the topic scant if any attention. Apart from a few classic studies like those of James, Freud, and Allport (James, 1902/1936; Freud, 1927; Allport, 1950), the topic of religious behavior has been largely ignored by psychological writers. (p. 95)

A survey of introductory psychology texts by Spilka and colleagues clearly documented this neglect (Spilka, Comp, & Goldsmith, 1981; Spilka, Hood, & Gorsuch, 1985). Spilka et al. (1981) found that about 40% of introductory psychology texts published in the 1950s included something about religion. This number dropped to 27.5% for texts published in the 1970s. Citations were mostly to well-known figures such as Freud, James, and Jung and to philosophers and theologians. Research in the psychology of religion generally was ignored (Spilka et al., 1985).

Strommen, a psychology of religion expert and editor of *Research on Religious Development: A Comprehensive Handbook* (Strommen, 1971), observed that religion was neglected in psychological research as well:

> Let me begin by drawing your attention to a most ironic situation—one that seems strange for a discipline that prides itself on its objectivity. For the past one-half century, the dimension of life—a religious faith—that occasioned the name *psychology* has been ignored systematically as an important variable in the pursuit of understanding human behavior. This, in spite of the fact that religious beliefs and values [we have found] are among the best predictors of what people will say or do. (Strommen, 1984, p. 151)

Thus, theoretical literature and research provided very little treatment of religion and spirituality as a dimension of human experience and basic existence. Bergin (1983) pointed out that religious and spiritual issues also were also neglected in graduate training programs:

> Training in the clinical professions is almost bereft of content that would engender an appreciation of religious variables in psychological functioning. Race, gender, and ethnic origin now receive deserved attention, but religion is still an orphan in academia. (p. 171)

Surveys of mental health training programs suggest this situation has not significantly changed. For example, Kelly's (1994) survey of heads of counseling programs documented that only 25% of the programs offered significant training in spiritual and religious issues. More recently, Schulte, Skinner, & Claiborn (2002) sent surveys to training directors or representatives of member programs of the Council of Counseling Psychology Training Programs (CCPTP). Thirty-one percent of the respondents said that spiritual and religious issues are regularly discussed in their training programs. Only 10% stated that faculty members in the program are expected to be knowledgeable about various religious and spiritual traditions.

Given that religious and spiritual issues have been neglected in psychological and clinical theory, research, and training, it is not surprising that psychotherapists have also tended to neglect them in working with clients (Bergin, 1980a, 1983; Collins, 1977; Henning & Tirrell, 1982). In a national survey of psychotherapists conducted in the mid 1980s, Jensen and Bergin (1988) found that only 29% of the therapists considered religious matters to be important in treatment of all or many of their clients. Henning and Tirrell (1982) observed that

> There has traditionally been much counselor resistance on professional and personal grounds to examining spiritual concerns. . . . Most counselors feel free to openly examine occupational, family, sexual and interpersonal issues. . . . Religious issues, however, are frequently viewed with apprehension. (p. 92)

Why is it that religious and spiritual concerns were so long excluded from the mainstream mental health professions? There is not a simple answer to this. The relationships among religion, psychological thought, and psychotherapy are long and complex. Historical, philosophical, and theoretical influences all seem to have contributed to this alienation from spirituality during the 20th century (Appleyard, 1992; Barbour, 1990; Beit-Hallahmi, 1974; Bergin, 1980a; Collins, 1977; Fuller, 1986; Hearnshaw, 1987; Karier, 1986; Lovinger, 1984; Lundin, 1985; Murray, 1988; Strunk, 1970). It is beyond the scope of this book to provide a chronological history of these influences (see Vande Kemp, 1996). Instead, we briefly describe the context within which modern-day behavioral science developed and note some of the historical and philosophical influences that contributed to the alienation of psychology and religion.

THE AGE OF SCIENCE

Although the Middle Ages (approximately A.D. 500 to 1300) of Western civilization were significantly influenced by Islamic civilization, they were characterized mainly by centuries of intellectual domination and control by medieval Christianity. In Europe, the Middle Ages were followed by the Renaissance in the early modern period of Western history (approximately A.D. 1300 to 1600). During this time the domination and control of medieval Christianity were being challenged philosophically (by humanism), theologically (by the Protestant Reformation), and scientifically (by Copernicus' and Galileo's heliocentric, or sun-centered, universe). The early beginnings of psychological and clinical thought can be traced to religious and philosophical ideas of this early modern period of Western civilization, to the Age of Reason (1700s to 1800s) that followed, and to the rise of modern science (1600 to the present; Hearnshaw, 1987; Murray, 1988; Ronan, 1982). The modern period, or the Age of Science, has been a culmination of these historical trends. It was during this time that what is now often referred to as *modern* or *modernistic science* rose to unprecedented influence (e.g., Bertens, 1995; Griffin, 1989; Griffin, Cobb, Ford, Gunter, & Ochs, 1993).

Philosophical Assumptions of 19th-Century (Modernistic) Science

During the rise of modernistic science, a number of philosophical assumptions became influential within the philosophical and scientific communities, including naturalism, determinism, universalism, reductionism, atomism, materialism, mechanism, ethical relativism, ethical hedonism, classical realism, positivism, and empiricism. We will briefly define each of these philosophical assumptions and then discuss how they came to be associated so closely with the scientific worldview.

Metaphysical Assumptions

Metaphysics is the branch of philosophy that is concerned with the nature of reality and with "the origin and nature of space and time, the nature of change and causality, the nature of the human person, freedom and determinism, the existence of God, and the problem of evil" (Percesepe, 1991, p. 20). *Naturalism* is the metaphysical belief that "natural laws and/ or principles ultimately govern the events of nature, including our bodies, behaviors, and minds" (Slife, 2004, p. 45). Metaphysical naturalism posits that "the universe is self-sufficient, without supernatural cause or control, and that in all probability the interpretation of the world given by the sciences is the only satisfactory explanation of reality" (Honer & Hunt, 1987, p. 225). *Methodological naturalism,* on the other hand, makes no ontological claims about the nature of the universe or God, but nevertheless requires that scientific explanations must "refrain from invoking any special action of God" (Griffin, 2000, p. 56). Thus, scientists who accept metaphysical naturalism, methodological naturalism, or both assume that human beings and the universe can be understood and eventually fully explained without including God or divine influence in the scientific theories or in the interpretation of research findings. *Atheism*, which is similar to the philosophy of naturalism, is the "positive belief that God does not exist" (Percesepe, 1991, p. 469). *Agnosticism,* also closely related to the philosophy of naturalism, claims that it "is not possible to know whether there is a God or a Supreme Being" (Honer & Hunt, 1987, p. 97).

Determinism is the belief that "every event in the universe is completely dependent on and conditioned by its cause or causes" (Honer & Hunt, 1987, p. 219). According to Percesepe (1991), *hard determinism* is the belief that "every event has a sufficient natural cause; nothing is left to chance. The same laws of causality that govern nature govern human actions as well" (p. 403). *Universalism* is the "notion that natural laws—because they are lawful—do not change in time or space. . . . A law should work universally; otherwise, it only applies to one point in time and space and thus is not lawful (or truthful)" (Slife, Hope, & Nebeker, 1999, p. 60).

Reductionism is the belief that "a whole can be completely understood by an analysis of its parts" (Honer & Hunt, 1987, p. 216). Closely related to reductionism are the philosophies of atomism, mechanism, and materialism. *Atomism* is "the notion that the material objects of our observation and knowledge can themselves be separated and divided into variables, constructs, and laws that are smaller and presumably more basic than their larger counterparts" (Slife et al., 1999, p. 62). *Mechanism* is the belief that human beings, the world, and the universe are "like a machine, that is, . . . composed of smaller pieces working smoothly together, the working of the whole being lawfully determined and necessary" (Slife & Williams, 1995, pp. 134–135). *Materialism* "is the view that matter is the fundamental reality in the world, and whatever else exists is dependent upon matter. In its most extreme form, materialism holds that whatever exists is physical" (Percesepe, 1991, p. 316).

Griffin (2001) pointed out that the term *materialism* is used in at least two ways. The most common meaning of materialism is "the view that there are no actual things other than material ones" (Griffin, 2001, p. 42). Another meaning of materialism posits that

> The ultimate units of nature are bits of matter, with "matter" understood to mean things that are *vacuous actualities*, in the sense of being entirely devoid of experience. Such bits of matter can have only *external* relations with one another, meaning that relations to other things cannot be internal to (constitutive of) them. The only kind of motion that can be attributed to them, furthermore, is *locomotion*, meaning motion from one place to another, as opposed to any sort of *internal* becoming. This view . . . is also called the "mechanistic" view of nature. (Griffin, 2001, pp. 41–42)

Axiological (Ethical) Assumptions

Axiology is the "branch of philosophy that deals with value theory" (Percesepe, 1991, p. 20). Ethics is the discipline within axiology "that attempts to establish rational grounds for right conduct" (Percesepe, 1991, p. 21) and that "attempts to determine what is good for people and what is right for them to do" (Honer & Hunt, 1987, p. 221). *Ethical relativism* is the axiological belief that "there are no universally valid principles, since all moral principles are valid relative to cultural or individual choice" (Percesepe, 1991, p. 572). In other words, "whatever a culture or society [or individual] holds to be right is therefore right or, at least, 'right for them'" (Solomon, 1990, p. 235). *Ethical hedonism* is the belief that "we always ought to seek our own pleasure and that the highest good for us is the most pleasure together with the least pain" (Honer & Hunt, 1987, p. 222).

Epistemological Assumptions

Epistemology is the "branch of philosophy that studies the nature, sources, validity, and limits of knowledge" (Percesepe, 1991, p. 18). Science embraces *positivism*, which is the belief that "knowledge is limited to observable facts and their interrelations and, hence, that the sciences provide the only reliable knowledge" (Honer & Hunt, 1987, p. 226). According to positivism, scientific theories can be "shown to be true on the basis of evidence" (Bechtel, 1988, p. 18). Positivists believe that it is possible for scientists to be objective, value-free observers and that through empirical observation the verification of scientific facts and theories will provide a complete understanding of reality. Positivism is associated with a belief in classical (or naive) realism. *Classical realism* posits that the universe is real, existing independently of human consciousness, and through experience with it, human beings can eventually perceive and understand it accurately (Barbour, 1990; Lincoln & Guba, 1985).

Positivism and classical realism are also associated with *empiricism*, the epistemological belief "that [what] our sense experience—seeing, touching, hearing, smelling, tasting—provides us with reliable knowledge of the world" (Percesepe, 1991, p. 19). Empiricism assumes that "knowledge has its source and derives all its content from experience. Nothing is regarded as true save what is given by sense experience or by inductive reasoning from sense experience" (Honer & Hunt, 1987, p. 220). Empiricism is related to the philosophy of *sensationism*, which says that "we have no mode of perception except sensory perception," or in other words, that "we can perceive things beyond our bodies only by means of our physical sense organs" (Griffin, 2000, pp. 14, 38).

The Adoption of Scientific Naturalism by Modernistic Science

Although not all scientists are atheistic or agnostic, most scientists during the past century have adopted scientific naturalism as the primary underlying assumption of their theories and research. Naturalism is "the oldest and deepest of science's substantive commitments" (Leahey, 1991, p. 378), for without the belief that the happenings of the universe can be explained in natural terms, it was feared that science would become obsolete. Scientific explanations of the universe would be no more tenable than religious, mystical, and superstitious ones. As stated by Leahey (1991), naturalism is "science's central dogma, without which it could not function" (p. 379). Some scientists have adopted both metaphysical and methodological naturalism as grounding assumptions, whereas others have accepted methodological naturalism as a way of doing science, even though they retained a personal belief in God. In either case, God was not considered in scientific theories, research, and discourse.

Griffin (2000) has documented and provided a helpful explanation of how scientific naturalism in its atheistic form came to be the virtually unquestioned dogma or foundational assumption of modernistic science. He explained that scientific naturalism grew out of the legal–mechanical tradition of the 17th century. The legal–mechanical tradition was a combination of the mechanism that originated from the Greek atomists and the legal ideas of nature (i.e., the order of nature is entirely due to divinely imposed laws) based on voluntarist theologians such as Calvin. This tradition emerged dominant in the conflict of worldviews during the 17th century against the Aristotelian worldview and the less well-known neo-Platonic–magical–spiritualist tradition.

Theistic scientists of the 17th century, such as Sir Isaac Newton, favored the legal–mechanical worldview because they believed it was more in harmony with and would help support the Christian view of the universe. Newton "asserted that his system, built upon the idea of matter devoid of the power to move itself or exert influence at a distance, pointed to the existence not only of a divine being, but also of one with the power to ordain, reveal, and enforce rules" (Griffin, 2000, p. 122). Thus the mechanistic scientific worldview was accepted not because of empirical evidence or because of its theoretical coherence, but because it "supported theism of a particular sort" (Griffin, 2000, p. 126).

The attempt to combine the mechanistic view of nature with a supernaturalistic version of Christianity into the scientific worldview "began to unravel almost as soon as it was established, due to various problems" such as the world's evil and "the growing distaste" among scientists "for the idea of supernatural interruptions of the laws of nature" (Griffin, 2000, pp. 27–28). Theistic scientists then attempted to combine a supernaturalistic theology with a naturalistic doctrine of nature by retreating to a deistic view that God had created the universe but no longer intervened in the world. According to Griffin (2000), this "deistic compromise between naturalism and supernaturalism, accordingly, proved primarily to be a halfway house to complete atheism . . . this transition from supernaturalism to atheism via deism . . . also involved a shift from dualism to materialism . . ." (pp. 28–29). The influence of Darwin's theory of evolution in the 19th century helped to complete the transition from deistic naturalism to atheistic naturalism because it provided an explanation regarding the origins of human life that did not require an appeal to God. Since that time, naturalism has dominated science and has become *the* scientific worldview.

As the central dogma of science, scientific naturalism received relatively little critical scrutiny during the 20th century; however, a number of scholars have carefully examined this worldview and have found it wanting (e.g., Griffin, 2000, 2001; Jones, 1994; Plantinga, 1991a, 1991b, 1993; Whitehead, 1925/1967, 1929/1968). Scientific naturalism carries with it a number of philosophical commitments that are problematic for science, including sensationism, materialism, and atheism. These philosophies are problematic because they prevent "the scientific community from providing rational explanations for a wide range of phenomena" (Griffin, 2000, p. 36). They are also inconsistent with empirical evidence and with "hard-core common sense beliefs," or in other words, beliefs that are "inevitably pre-supposed in practice" by both laypersons and scientists (Griffin, 2000, pp. 36, 99).

Sensationism is problematic for science because it provides no basis for scientists' belief in causation, induction, and the uniformity of nature (Griffin, 2001). This problem has been ignored or minimized by many scientists, but philosophers have argued that an acceptance of sensation-ism undermines the rationality of science (e.g., Kuhn, 1970; Polanyi, 1962; Whitehead, 1925/1967). The practice of science also presupposes several other notions that are not grounded in sensory perception, including (a) the idea of truth and its importance, (b) the reality of mathematical and logical truths, and (c) the importance of moral, aesthetic, ethical, and religious ideals (Griffin, 2001). If sensationism is accepted, such notions must be excluded from science and the cognitive domain because they are unempirical, not being rooted in sensory perceptions (Griffin, 2001).

Materialism is problematic for science because it fails to adequately account for several concepts in physics, including gravitation, time, and physical causation (Griffin, 2001; Whitehead, 1938/1968). It is also inconsis-tent with the theory of evolution, fails to account for the emergence of mind or consciousness, is irreconcilable with human freedom or agency, and rules out the possibility of rational activity (Griffin, 2001; Whitehead, 1925/1967). As explained by Griffin (2001),

> The problem of how conscious experience could have emerged out of wholly insentient matter is insoluble in principle, as an increasing number of both dualists and materialists have acknowledged. . . . as long as science presupposes the materialistic view of the ultimate units of nature, it will make itself incapable of making sense of the feature of the world of which we are most certain, our own experience. This inherited view of nature, in other words, makes science incapable of making rational sense of the existence of scientists. (p. 45)

Atheism is also problematic for science. Griffin (2001) argued that a science that excludes God and divine influence from the universe and from human existence and activity will remain unable to give satisfactory explanations for the "basic order of the world, the upward trend of the evolutionary process, the novelty that has appeared in this process, the world's "excessive" beauty, and the objectivity of normative ideals and other ideal (nonfactual) entities, such as those of mathematics and logic" (p. 48). Atheism, when combined with sensationism and materialism, also leads to a deterministic, relativistic and nihilistic worldview in which life has no ultimate meaning (Griffin, 2000). These philosophical commitments also logically lead to several other problematic philosophical positions, including reductionism, atomism, mechanism, positivism, and ethical hedonism (Griffin, 2000). Thus many philosophers and scientists agree that scientific naturalism provides an impoverished view of human nature and does not adequately account for the complexities and mysteries of life and of the universe (e.g., Barbour, 1990, 2000; Dembski, 2004; Eccles & Robinson, 1984; Griffin, 2000, 2001; Whitehead, 1925/1967, 1929/1968).

Psychology's Adoption of Modernistic Assumptions: An Alternative Faith

Modern-day psychology and psychiatry developed during the late 19th and early 20th centuries, a time when modern science was successfully challenging religious authority and tradition as the dominant worldview and source of truth (Appleyard, 1992; Barbour, 1990; Bergin, 1980a; Burns & Ralph, 1974; Collins, 1977; Hearnshaw, 1987; Karier, 1986; Lucas, 1985). The Newtonian "clocklike" view of the physical universe dominated the scientific world at this time, giving rise to deterministic and mechanistic thought (Appleyard, 1992; Barbour, 1990; Hearnshaw, 1987; Lucas, 1985; Slife, 1993). Many scientists "believed that humanity was . . . a part of the all-encompassing world machine, whose operation could be explained without reference to God. Such a materialistic world held no place for consciousness or inwardness except as subjective illusions" (Barbour, 1990, p. 220). Charles Darwin's theory of evolution was also rapidly gaining scientific acceptance as an explanation for the origin of life (Appleyard, 1992; Barbour, 1990; Lucas, 1985; Mason, 1962). The prestige and technological successes of science, combined with the lack of persuasive response from religious institutions, contributed to the decline in status and influence of religious explanations for the origins and nature of the universe and human beings (Appleyard, 1992; Lucas, 1985). Many people at this time believed that science, not religion, would unlock all the mysteries of the universe.

To escape religious contamination and establish psychology and psychiatry as respected sciences, Sigmund Freud, along with early founders of the behavioral tradition (i.e., Watson, Thorndike, Skinner) and other early leaders of the behavioral sciences, accepted the prevailing scientific philosophies of the day (Karier, 1986; Wertheimer, 1970). Although it was not always done explicitly or even deliberately, they built their theories on faith in the worldview and philosophical assumptions of scientific naturalism (Karier, 1986; Leahey, 1991). Their foundational axiom of faith was that human behavior could be explained naturalistically: i.e., without resorting to spiritual or transcendent explanations. At least some of these leaders were also atheistic (Karier, 1986). For example, both Freud and Watson rejected the religious faiths of their parents and replaced those beliefs with their own naturalistic, atheistic psychological faith (Karier, 1986). Numerous other leaders in the field, such as Skinner, Hull, Wolpe, Bandura, and Rogers, did likewise.

Perhaps because of their personal beliefs about religion, and perhaps because science in the late 19th and early 20th centuries was vigorously challenging religious authority and tradition, psychoanalytic and behavioral scientists developed theories that portrayed religious beliefs and behaviors in negative ways. For example, in the *Future of an Illusion*, Freud stated that religious ideas "are illusions, fulfillments of the oldest, strongest and most urgent wishes of mankind" (Freud, 1927/1961, p. 30). He also said that religion is "the universal obsessional neurosis of humanity" (Freud, 1927/1961, p. 43). Freud also compared religious beliefs to a "sleeping draught" and said that "the effect of religious consolations may be likened to that of a narcotic" (Freud, 1927/1961, p. 29).

Watson basically ignored spiritual behavior, but when he did mention it in his writings, he revealed his bias against religion. For example, in his book *Psychology From the Standpoint of a Behaviorist*, Watson said that "psychology, up to very recent times, has been held so rigidly under the dominance both of traditional religion and of philosophy—the two great bulwarks of medievalism—that it has never been able to free itself and become a natural science" (Watson, 1924/1983, p. 1). This clearly reflects the aim of early psychologists to situate psychology firmly within the sharp lines of science and as far away from the "fuzzy" and anachronistic areas of religion and philosophy as possible.

In arguing why psychology should not concern itself with studying consciousness, Watson wrote that "'states of consciousness,' like the so-called phenomena of spiritualism, are not objectively verifiable and for that reason can never become data for science" (Watson, 1924/1983, p. 1). According to Leahey (1991), Watson "linked introspective psychology to religion and railed against both" (p. 239). Karier (1986) observed that "Watson . . . made the quantum leap between the animal and human kingdoms" and then went farther and "quickly proceeded to deny soul, mind, consciousness, or any unique status for man or his mental or spiritual experiences" (p. 129). Skinner and a long line of behaviorists adopted similar views (Viney & King, 1998; Wulff, 1991).

The early leaders of psychology also adopted as underlying assumptions deterministic, reductionistic, atomistic, materialistic, and mechanistic views of human beings. Freud theorized that human behavior is determined by unconscious intrapsychic instincts and drives and by psychosexual events that occur during the first 5 or 6 years of life (Hillner, 1984; Lundin, 1985). Freud's theory was deterministic, reductionistic, atomistic, and mechanistic in the sense that Freud believed that early childhood psychosexual events and intrapsychic forces explain and control human motivations (especially pathological ones) and behavior (Hillner, 1984; Lundin, 1985). Early behaviorists (e.g., Watson) believed that behavior is determined by environmental influences (Hillner, 1984; Lundin, 1985; Watson, 1924/1983). The early behavioral theory was also reductionistic, atomistic, materialistic, and mechanistic in the sense that it was believed that human behavior could be explained and reduced to stimulus–response connections and that only observable behavior was considered real (Hillner, 1984; Lundin, 1985; Watson, 1924/1983). A human being was a materialistic "machine" that was completely controlled by environmental influences (Krasner, 1962).

The early leaders of psychology also adopted the assumptions of ethical relativism and ethical hedonism. The influence of Darwin's theory of evolution led Freud and the early behavioral leaders to theorize that human beings by nature are highly similar to the rest of the animal kingdom (Hillner, 1984; Lundin, 1985; Watson, 1924/1983). They theorized that humans are basically hedonistic or reward-seeking, and they advocated that human beings should be more accepting of these tendencies (Hillner, 1984; Lundin, 1985; Watson, 1924/1983). They rejected the notion that there are transcendent moral and ethical principles that can or should optimize human behavior and social relations.

The early psychologists also adopted the assumptions of classical realism, positivism, empiricism, and universalism. They believed that they were establishing respectable scientific theories of human behavior by following the lead of physical and biological science (Hillner, 1984; Lundin, 1985; Watson, 1924/1983). They considered their theories and research to describe and verify universal laws of human behavior and functioning. They claimed that their theories were grounded in empirical observations and would be proved true on the basis of empirical evidence (Hillner, 1984; Lundin, 1985; Watson, 1924/1983). As stated by Karier (1986), "While Freud considered himself a scientist akin to Darwin, he also saw himself as the creator of a new science, one that would effect the crossover from the world of the poetic artist to that of the empirical scientist" (p. 214). Watson (1924/1983) stated that "for the behaviorist, psychology is that division of natural science which takes human behavior—the doings and sayings, both learned and unlearned, of people as its subject matter" (p. 4) and that "[b]ehavioristic psychology attempts to formulate, through systematic observation and experimentation, the generalizations, laws and principles which underlie man's behavior" (p. 5).

Some Caveats

For many years, naturalistic assumptions greatly influenced theory and research, the content of textbooks, the criteria by which submitted journal articles were judged, the nature of graduate education, and the types of recognition provided by professional societies (Bergin, 1980a, 1980b; Slife & Williams, 1995). It would, however, be incorrect to imply that these assumptions were overpowering in the behavioral sciences.

During this period of strong "scientism," there was a continuing, but not entirely effective, opposition by a movement called *humanistic–existential psychology* (Maslow, 1971; May, Angel, & Ellenberger, 1958; Rogers, 1951, 1961; Yalom, 1980). Although it was influenced by naturalism, this approach was opposed to the deterministic, reductionistic, and mechanistic views that prevailed. This movement gave hope to those who viewed human behavior as being more complex and potentially agentive, as reflecting the potential for actualization espoused in the aspirations of idealistic religions. This movement opened the way for alternative conceptions of human functioning, although it retained many of the naturalistic and relativistic themes of the dominant scientific tradition.

Similarly, the cognitive movement in psychology developed parallel to the more deterministic trends but did not break through as a substantial influence until the late 1960s. This movement also created a space for serious discussion of agency and self-control, in contrast to control by biology or environment, yet it suffers to a degree from lingering reductionistic and mechanistic influences that led to machine or computer models of intelligent functioning that, with "inputs" and "outputs," resembled scientism in many ways. See Gardner (1985) for a historical and philosophical analysis of the rise of science and the emergence of the cognitive revolution.

Concurrently there was a third ongoing counterculture: writers who wrote frankly about religion, including one of the founders of modern psychology, William James (1902/1936), and psychoanalysts such as Jung (1938), social psychologists such as Allport (1950), psychiatrists such as Frankl (1959), and the continuously developing pastoral counseling movement. However, this religiously open counterculture did not begin to significantly influence the mainstream behavioral sciences until the 1970s and 1980s, as we discuss in more detail in chapter 3.

In addition to the humanistic–existential, cognitive, and spiritual trends that challenged the dominant traditions over the years, there was considerable variety within the behavioral and psychodynamic traditions that resulted in considerable debate and richness. Not only did Jung oppose classical psychoanalysis, but Adler, Anna Freud, Fromm, Horney, Sullivan, Erikson, Winnicott, and others contributed to ego psychology and social interactionism in human dynamics, providing for controversy and latitude in thinking about human behavior (Hall & Lindzey, 1978; Hall, Lindzey, & Campbell, 1998). These trends were particularly important in the clinical fields, as the change process noted by clinicians often evidenced many phenomena that could not be construed within the classical mechanistic perspective. In addition, the behavioral movement was laced with criticisms and oppositions such as those by Tolman and other early cognitive behaviorists, a trend documented powerfully by Koch (1959–1963). This trend was greatly accentuated and enlarged by Bandura (1969, 1986, 1997) and others who followed his work.

It is interesting that despite the opposing trends, with their potential for latitude in thought and practice, even some of the most radically dissenting psychologists had difficulty avoiding the domination of the naturalistic and mechanistic worldview. For instance, Carl Rogers, who was one of the strongest advocates of human agency and potential, independent of conditioning and unconscious processes, wrote and spoke in somewhat deterministic ways (e.g., Rogers, 1957, 1959). After trying to apply the dominant paradigm to the clinical phenomena he dealt with, he ultimately was frustrated and went in new directions (Coulson & Rogers, 1968; Rogers, 1980). In these efforts, Rogers, as others like him, adopted radically different views of what science is, what knowledge is, and how truth should be sought (Koch, 1981).

PROBLEMS OF SCIENTIFIC NATURALISM
FOR PSYCHOTHERAPISTS

The scientific naturalistic worldview is not only problematic for natural and behavioral scientists, but in our view adopting it in the clinical situation poses insoluble problems for contemporary mental health practitioners and researchers (Bergin, 1980a; Griffin, 2000, 2001; P. S. Richards & Bergin, 1997; Slife, 2004; Slife et al., 1999). For example, scientific naturalism provides an impoverished view of human nature upon which it is difficult to build theories of personality and therapeutic change (Griffin, 2000, 2001). Scientific naturalism also constrains, biases, and ultimately forecloses many conceptual and clinical options that would otherwise be open to therapists and researchers (Slife, 2004; Slife et al., 1999). Finally, scientific naturalism conflicts with the worldviews of the major theistic world religions, and thereby fails to provide a culturally sensitive psychotherapy framework for religious clients who seek assistance from mental health professionals (Bergin, 1980a). We discuss each of these problems in more detail in the following sections. Table 2.1 provides a summary of the philosophies of scientific naturalism; some of the problems for personality theory, psychotherapy, and positive human development are noted as well.

Naturalism Provides an Impoverished View of Human Nature

If mental health professionals accept scientific naturalism, to be logically consistent, they must accept the other problematic viewpoints

TABLE 2.1
Philosophical Assumptions and Problems of Scientific Naturalism for Contemporary Mental Health Practitioners and Researchers

Assumptions of scientific naturalism	Problems for mental health professionals
Naturalism and atheism: There is no Supreme Being or transcendent spiritual influence.	Provides an impoverished view of human nature; conflicts with the spiritual worldviews of the vast majority of psychotherapy clients
Determinism: Human behavior is completely caused by forces outside of human control.	Denies the reality of human agency and responsibility, both of which are presupposed in practice by the majority of therapists and clients
Naturalistic universalism: Natural laws, including laws of human behavior, are deterministic and context-free; they apply deterministically across time, space, and persons. A phenomenon is not real if it is not generalizable and repeatable.	Denies the importance of unique contextual influences and personal agency required in human adjustment and change; can lead to "cookbook" treatment approaches that downplay the importance of treatment tailoring and client uniqueness
Reductionism and atomism: All of human behavior can be reduced or divided into smaller parts or units. In addition, the "qualities of each individual are understood as originating from the individual— from the self" (Slife, 2004, p. 65).	Encourages therapists to adopt fragmented views of their clients (e.g., in terms of their intrapsychic dynamics, reinforcement histories, or biochemistry); downplays the importance of cultural and relationship influences
Materialism and mechanism: Human beings are like machines composed of material or biological parts working together.	Dehumanizes clients; denies the reality of human agency, rationality, and responsibility; creates an insoluble mind–body dilemma; leads to the view that consciousness is simply a by-product (epiphenomenon) of brain physiology; contributes to the biologization of mental health disorders and treatment
Ethical relativism: There are no universal or absolute moral or ethical principles. Values are culture-bound. What is right and good varies across social and individual situations.	Provides no basis from which to evaluate whether clients' values and lifestyles are healthy or unhealthy, socially benevolent or socially destructive, or moral or immoral; conflicts with what all therapists presuppose in practice, that is, all therapists endorse and promote values during therapy even if in theory they endorse ethical relativism

Ethical hedonism: Human beings always seek rewards (pleasure) and avoid punishments (pain). This is the basic valuing process built into human behavior.	Promotes the view that "therapists and clients are capable only of a sophisticated selfishness" (Slife, 2004, p. 47); leads to treatment goals and approaches that are concerned only about individual pleasure, gratification, and self-fulfillment, even at the expense of familial and societal welfare
Classical realism and positivism: The universe is real and can be accurately perceived and understood by human beings. Science provides the only valid knowledge. Scientific theories can be proved true on the basis of empirical evidence.	Promotes an unrealistic, grandiose view of the validity, power, and scope of the scientific method; denies the role of human influences and limitations in the scientific enterprise (e.g., the value-laden nature of science, political and social influences in scholarship, limitations of scientific methods for collecting data about the world, and limitations in the ability of human beings to accurately perceive, observe, and interpret reality)
Sensationism, empiricism, and objectivism: Sensory experience provides human beings with the only reliable source of knowledge. Nothing is true or real except that which is observable through sensory experience or measuring instruments. It is possible to observe and measure the world in an objective, nonbiased manner.	Denies the reality or importance of additional ways of apprehending the world, for example, through intuition and inspiration; denies the reality of nonmaterial realities that are not knowable through sensory experience or measuring instruments (e.g., mathematical forms, logical arguments, thoughts, emotions, spiritual experiences, etc.); denies the now widely recognized fact that all therapists and researchers have values, biases, and assumptions that influence their professional work

commonly linked to the modern scientific worldview, including sensationism, mechanism, materialism, determinism, and reductionism (Griffin, 2000; Slife, 2004; Slife et al., 1999). The implications of this worldview for a view of human nature were clearly stated by William Provine, a historian of science (as cited in Griffin, 2000, p. 32):

> [First, m]odern science directly implies that the world is organized strictly in accordance with deterministic principles or chance . . . . There are no purposive principles whatsoever in nature. There are no gods and no designing forces that are rationally detectable . . . .
>
> Second, modern science directly implies that there are no inherent moral or ethical laws.
>
> Third, human beings are marvelously complex machines. The individual human becomes an ethical person by means of only two mechanisms: deterministic heredity interacting with deterministic environmental influences. That is all there is.
>
> Fourth, we must conclude that when we die, we die and that is the end of us . . . . There is no hope of life everlasting.
>
> [F]ree will, as traditionally conceived, the freedom to make uncoerced and unpredictable choices among alternative possible course of action, simply does not exist . . . . [T]he evolutionary process cannot produce a being that is truly free to make choices.
>
> The universe cares nothing for us . . . . Humans are as nothing even in the evolutionary process on earth . . . . There is no ultimate meaning for humans.

We agree with Provine, Griffin, and others who have argued that scientific naturalism provides an impoverished view of human nature. We think that this view of human nature is one of the major reasons, along with economic and historical influences, for much of psychology's negative focus and limited social influence during the past century (M. E. P. Seligman, 2002).

The psychology and psychiatry professions have been widely criticized over the years for the negative views of human nature they have promoted (e.g., Bergin, 1980a, 1980b; Campbell, 1975; M. E. P. Seligman, 2002). For example, human beings have been portrayed in psychodynamic and behavioral theories as passive victims of unconscious psychic forces and instincts, childhood conflicts, or environmental stimuli and responses. Other theories view human behavior as motivated by "self-interest, aggressiveness, territoriality, class conflict, and the like" (M. E. P. Seligman, 2002, p. 8). Psychology and psychiatry have also been preoccupied with disease, abnormality, and maladjustment (Maddux, 2002). Many psychological practitioners have adopted a disease model of mental illness and have focused on "repairing damage: damaged habits, damaged drives, damaged childhood, and damaged brains" (M. E. P. Seligman, 2002, p. 4).

During the past several decades there has been a movement away from negative perspectives toward more positive, holistic, agentive, and morally responsible views of human beings (Emmons, 1999; Jensen & Bergin, 1988; Pargament, 1997; M. E. P. Seligman, 2002; Shafranske, 1996). Surveys indicate that many behavioral scientists and psychotherapists also believe that God exists, that life has ultimate meaning and purpose, and that life continues after death (Bergin & Jensen, 1990; Shafranske, 2000).

Many behavioral scientists and psychotherapists have rejected the negative view of human nature provided by scientific naturalism because they recognize, either rationally or intuitively, that it is inadequate. It denies or trivializes much of what is most important and distinctive about human beings, including mind, consciousness, agency, morality, responsibility, love, relationships, creativity, intuition, meaning, purpose, and faith in God (Bergin, 1980a; M. E. P. Seligman, 2002). The view of human nature offered by scientific naturalism is inadequate for a science about human beings, especially for helping professionals who wish to help them heal, develop, and grow.

Naturalism Constrains Alternative Conceptual and Clinical Options

When behavioral scientists and psychotherapists ground their work in the philosophy of scientific naturalism, they close the door to other conceptual and clinical options—options that could lead to a more valid human science and more effective forms of treatment. Slife (2004) described five major assumptions of naturalism pertaining to the behavioral sciences and psychotherapy: objectivism, materialism, hedonism, atomism, and universalism.

> *Objectivists* assume that the logic inherent in the methods and techniques of science and therapy can be relatively free of systematic biases and values. *Materialists* assume that most, if not all psychological disorders will eventually be shown to have observable and biological bases. *Hedonists* assume that the chief goal of life (and therapy) is some form of happiness, fulfillment, or well-being. *Atomists* assume that the qualities of people are contained within the self, so the basic unit of therapy is the individual. And finally, *Universalists* assume that true knowledge and valid methods are fundamentally unchangeable across time and space, whether in therapy or in science. (Slife, 2004, p. 46)

According to Slife (2004), these naturalistic assumptions "constrain not only what is thought to be the desired outcome of research and therapy but also what is viewed as the desired process" (Slife, 2004, p. 75). Naturalism assumes that the desired *outcome* of research and therapy is a generalizable, observable, objective benefit to the individual client; the desired *process* is to isolate and manipulate observable and value-free variables to find the natural laws or theoretical principles (Slife, 2004). Slife (2004) argues that the pervasive influence of naturalism contributes to several of the current controversies and problems in psychotherapy practice and research, including the controlling hand of managed care, the biologization of disorders and treatment, and the push for empirically supported treatments and brief therapies at the expense of therapy innovation and longer-term treatment approaches.

Slife (2004) explained that when naturalistic assumptions are accepted without examination as if they are reified truths, behavioral scientists and psychotherapists are prevented from considering alternative perspectives, such as continental philosophy, holism, altruism, contextualism, and hermeneutics. These alternative perspectives lead to different conceptions about desirable outcomes and processes of therapy and research. For example, continental philosophy embraces therapists' and clients' values as inescapable, valuable resources for treatment and healing. Holism affirms the importance of nonmaterial influences such as agency and spirituality. Altruism considers altruistic motivations and a willingness to sacrifice for others as healthy and worthwhile, rather than viewing self-satisfaction as the sole criterion of health. Contexualism emphasizes the influences of context and relationships in treatment and research. Hermeneutics considers the "changeable . . . at least as fundamental as the unchangeable" and values contextual patterns in experiences, meaning, and relationships (Slife, 2004, p. 48).

Naturalism Conflicts With the Beliefs and Values of Religious Clients

Another major problem with scientific naturalism is that it conflicts with the spiritual and cultural beliefs and values of the large number of people in North America who believe in God and who are religiously committed. It is easy to see how Freud's naturalistic view that religiosity is an illusion or an obsessional neurosis and the behavioral view that religious behavior is simply a conditioned response conflict starkly with a theistic spiritual conception of the world. The theistic world religions teach that there is a Supreme Being who was involved in the creation of the world and who continues to influence the lives of human beings. These religions also describe religious and spiritual beliefs and behaviors as being essential for optimal human growth and fulfillment (Bergin, 1980a).

The deterministic, reductionistic, atomistic, mechanistic, and materialistic views of human behavior conflict with the views of both the Western and Eastern world religions, which assert that human beings are responsible agents and inherently different from the conception of humans as machines. The world religions also affirm that there are nonmaterial, spiritual realities that are not physical or material. The world religions view human beings as multidimensional, both spiritually and holistically, thereby disagreeing with reductionistic and atomistic beliefs that the behavior and emotions of human beings are simply the product of primitive biological drives or environmental stimuli and responses.

Several writers have pointed out that the philosophies of ethical relativism and hedonism also conflict with the teachings of the major world religious traditions (e.g., Bergin, 1980a, 1980b; Campbell, 1975), most of which describe human beings as being more ethically and spiritually advanced than other living organisms. These religions teach that human beings can choose to control and transcend their hedonistic tendencies in order to experience spiritual fulfillment. Humans can also transcend self-interest and altruistically promote the welfare of others. These world religions teach that there are moral universals that God has revealed, or that are built into the universe, that should guide human behavior and social relations (Smart, 1983).

Although many religious traditions of the world do not reject empirical ways of knowing, or even the possibility that scientific theories might be supported by empirical evidence, they do reject the belief that empirical knowledge is the only valid source of truth or that empiricism alone can lead to a completely accurate knowledge of the universe. They teach that some experiences are contextual, invisible, and private (i.e., spiritual and transcendent) and cannot necessarily be empirically observed, accurately replicated, or publicly verified (Slife, Hope, & Nebeker, 1996). The world religions also teach that there are spiritual ways for human beings to learn and know truth about the realities of the universe (e.g., inspiration, enlightenment, spiritual harmony, and revelation).

Many religious people, including religious leaders, distrust mainstream, secular mental health professions, including psychotherapy (P. S. Richards & Bergin, 2000; Worthington, 1986). Their suspicion may be rooted in an awareness that many psychologists and psychotherapists during the past century have endorsed naturalistic, mechanistic, hedonistic, relativistic, and atheistic values and practices, which conflict with those of most traditional religious communities (Bergin, 1980a; Campbell, 1975; Jones, 1994; P. S. Richards & Bergin, 1997). In addition, some prominent leaders of psychology and psychotherapy have been openly critical of religion and religious believers (e.g., Ellis, 1971, 1980; Freud, 1927). Several studies have confirmed that devoutly religious persons prefer to work with therapists from their own faith, or at least with religious therapists because they fear that secular therapists will misunderstand or seek to undermine their religious beliefs (Weaver, Koenig, & Larson, 1997; Worthington, Kurusu, McCullough, & Sanders, 1996).

CONCLUSION

Scientific naturalism has had a major and long-lasting impact on mainstream psychology and psychotherapy (Bergin & Garfield, 1994; Matarazzo, 1985). The adoption of scientific naturalism as a grounding assumption for the behavioral sciences and mental health professions by the early leaders led to enduring philosophical and theoretical biases against spiritual perspectives. These conceptual biases became deeply embedded in psychological and clinical thought during the first half of the 20th century and have a continuing influence. The lingering effect of these assumptions is that theistic spiritual perspectives have not yet been more fully integrated into the modern-day, mainstream mental health professions. Although many religious psychotherapists reject naturalistic philosophical assumptions, when asked to state their theoretical orientation they often profess allegiance to mainstream traditions that are grounded in such assumptions (Jensen & Bergin, 1988; Slife, 2004; Slife & Williams, 1995).

Many behavioral scientists and mental health professionals continue to adhere to scientific naturalism and to theories grounded in its assumptions because they believe this is the only scientifically respectable option. However, increasing numbers of behavioral scientists and mental health professionals have convincingly questioned the basis for and validity of this viewpoint. On the grounds of its inconsistency with empirical evidence, its philosophical incoherence, its incompatibility with beliefs that are inevitably presupposed in practice, and its impoverished view of human nature, we think scientific naturalism is not only inadequate, but detrimental as a foundation for the behavioral sciences and mental health professions. It appears that many scientists and scholars agree with us. As we discuss in chapter 3, a more spiritually open *Zeitgeist* now exists and continues to grow in the natural, health, and behavioral sciences.

3

THE NEW *ZEITGEIST*

Something unbelievable has occurred in these last years. For the first time in its history, modern science and its practitioners have begun to grapple with the fundamental questions of human existence. From the United Nations to the Catholic Church, from Castel Gondolfo to Geneva, from computer specialists in Bangalore to spiritualists in Berkeley, the barriers between science, ethics and religion have been falling. Like the students from East and West who sat on the Berlin Wall that November night in 1989, scientists and theologians are celebrating the resumption of an interrupted dialogue.

—Philip Clayton

Although the naturalistic–atheistic faith adopted by the early leaders of psychology and psychiatry had a long and powerful impact on the mental health professions, the influence of this belief system has gradually weakened. Discoveries in physics and the recent growth of the science–religion dialogue have softened formerly hardened beliefs in materialistic, mechanistic, atheistic, and deterministic views of the universe. Developments in philosophy have challenged the adequacy of naturalism and other modernistic philosophical assumptions. Medical research on the mind–body connection has undermined reductionistic and materialistic views of human beings and has stimulated interest in the role of faith and spirituality in physical healing. Renewed societal and public interest in spirituality has stimulated researchers and scholars to seek to understand a phenomenon that affects such a large proportion of the world's population.

Challenges to naturalistic assumptions have also come from within the professions of psychology and psychotherapy. Research on religion and mental health and on the positive psychology movement has undermined negative views of religion that prevailed in psychology for most of the 20th century. The development of alternative psychotherapy traditions such as the humanistic–existential and cognitive approaches, the movement toward psychotherapy integration, the movement toward multicultural counseling, the recognition of the importance of values in psychotherapy, and the development of spiritually oriented treatment approaches have challenged naturalistic, deterministic, relativistic, and hedonistic views of human nature and methods of therapeutic change. The purpose of this chapter is to briefly describe these trends and to discuss how they are contributing to the development of a theoretical *Zeitgeist* within both the natural and behavioral sciences that is more in harmony with a spiritual worldview and a theistic strategy for psychotherapy than the *Zeitgeist* of the 19th and early 20th centuries (Barbour, 1990; Bergin, 1980a, 1991; Jones, 1994).

CHANGES IN PHYSICS

At the end of the 19th century, the view of the universe provided by Newtonian science was realistic, positivistic (objective), deterministic, mechanistic, linear, and reductionistic (Slife, 1993). However, the 19th-century Newtonian view of the universe as "an elaborate clockwork mechanism, utterly logical and predictable in its operations" began to crumble in the early 20th century (Lucas, 1985, p. 166) as Albert Einstein's theory of relativity, Max Planck's quantum theory, and other scientific discoveries and viewpoints developed (Paul, 1992). Theories that directly challenged the clockwork view of the world, such as Heisenberg's uncertainty principle, Bohr's complementarity principle, and Bell's theorem revolutionized the conception of the universe (Appleyard, 1992; Barbour, 1990; Lucas, 1985; Paul, 1992).

Instead of realism and positivism, the findings of modern-day physics suggest that scientific theories and observations are only "partial representations of limited aspects of the world as it interacts with us" (Barbour, 1990, p. 99). The process of observation itself may alter the nature and properties of the object being observed, and the ability to perceive or observe reality accurately may be fundamentally limited (Barbour, 1990; Lucas, 1985; Mason, 1962). Instead of a deterministic universe, the findings of modern physics suggest that "there is a complex combination of law and chance. . . . Nature is characterized by both structure and openness. The future cannot be predicted in detail from the past" (Barbour, 1990, p. 220). Instead of mechanism and reductionism, modern views suggest that "nature . . . is relational, ecological, and interdependent. Reality is constituted by events and relationships rather than by separate substances or separate particles. . . . Distinctive holistic concepts are used to explain the higher-level activities of systems, from organisms to ecosystems" (Barbour, 1990, p. 221). Templeton and Herrmann (1994), citing the physicist Paul Davies, further documented the notion of a nonmechanical, creative universe that is nonlinear and not subject to reductionism (cf. Davies, 1988, 1992).

The findings of 20th-century physics called into question the assumptions of determinism, mechanism, reductionism, classical realism, and positivism; they have also reopened the door to the recognition of spiritual realities in the universe (Templeton & Herrmann, 1994). At the end of the 19th century, many scientists believed that religious and spiritual views of the universe would soon be extinct. During the past two decades, however, growing numbers of physicists and other scientists have acknowledged that the view of the universe provided by modern physics is surprisingly compatible with religious and spiritual views of reality (Appleyard, 1992; Barbour, 1990; Brush, 1988; Capra, 1983; Davies, 1992; Lucas, 1985; Peacocke, 2001; Polkinghorne, 1990; Templeton & Herrmann, 1994; Tipler, 1994; Weidlich, 1990). Thus current research in physics has not denied the existence of God or of spiritual realities, but has placed such beliefs well within the realm of rational plausibility. This realization has helped to fuel a growing dialogue between scientists and theologians concerning the compatibility of scientific and religious views of reality (e.g., Davies, 1992; Griffin, 2000; Peacocke, 2001).

THE SCIENCE AND RELIGION DIALOGUE

The alienation of science and religion during most of the 20th century prevented widespread organized dialogue among scientists and theologians (Clayton, 2003). This situation changed dramatically during the late 1990s and early 2000s as increasing numbers of natural scientists and theologians began to explore the connections between science, religion, and spirituality. One significant catalyst for the growth in this dialogue developed when Robert Russell, the founder and director of the Berkeley-based Center for Theology and the Natural Sciences (CTNS), created a program called "Science and the Spiritual Quest." With financial support from Sir John Templeton, this program "assembled leading scientists from around the world in private workshops, organized public conferences and telecasts, published books and articles and drew media attention to questions of science-and-religion" (Clayton, 2003, p. 2). The resurgence of interest in the science–religion dialogue also attracted critics, many of whom argued that such dialogue is unnecessary and counterproductive (e.g., Clayton, 2003; Giberson, 2003).

Despite its critics, the science–religion dialogue continues to flourish (Giberson, 2003). Since its inception in 1999, the monthly publication *Research News and Opportunities in Science and Theology* has documented much of the growth of this movement by informing readers of a seemingly endless variety of events, centers, books, research reports, and academic courses concerning the science–religion dialogue. This dialogue expanded to include scholars from many of the natural sciences, including astronomy, biology, biochemistry, chemistry, evolution, and physics. Philosophers, theologians, and religious scholars also participate (Polkinghorne, 2002).

The growth in the breadth and depth of the science–religion dialogue has led to rigorous discussions about a variety of issues. For example, theistic scientists have written much regarding the theory of evolution, discussing possible conflicts and compatibility with theistic understandings of the origin and progression of life on earth (Dembski, 2001, 2004; Giberson & Yerxa, 2002; Griffin, 2000; Hunter, 2003; K. R. Miller, 1999; Peacocke, 2001; Schroeder, 2001). Theistic interpretations of the "big bang" theory and other explanations for the origin of the universe have also received attention (e.g., Davies, 1999; Peacocke, 2001; Polkinghorne, 1998; Schroeder, 2001). Many "scientific" issues have been explored from theistic and other spiritual perspectives, including genetics, artificial intelligence, and ethics in technology and science. The growth of the science–religion dialogue in recent years has contributed to, and is part of, the new more spiritually open *Zeitgeist* that now exists in both the natural and behavioral sciences. This new intellectual climate has helped to enable the consideration of theistic perspectives in science, psychology, and psychotherapy.

PHILOSOPHICAL INFLUENCES

During the late 19th and early 20th centuries, classical realism, positivism, and empiricism were the most widely accepted and influential epistemological assumptions in the philosophy of science (Edwards, 1967). However, during the second half of the 20th century, studies in both the history and philosophy of science led to a reappraisal and decline of these premises (e.g., Hesse, 1980; Kuhn, 1970; Laudan, 1984; Lincoln & Guba, 1985; Polanyi, 1962; Toulmin, 1962). This examination and reevaluation by science historians and philosophers has stimulated, and has been stimulated by, an intellectual movement called *postmodernism*.

Postmodernism is a family of perspectives and philosophies that contend that "there are no metaphysical absolutes; no fundamental and abstract truths, laws, or principles that determine what the world is like and what happens in it" (Slife & Williams, 1995, p. 54). Postmodern philosophers have challenged, or attempted to deconstruct, the deterministic, reductionistic, mechanistic, and positivistic assumptions of mainstream science and psychology (Faulconer & Williams, 1985; Gergen, 1982, 1985; Messer, Sass, & Woolfolk, 1988; Packer, 1985; Slife, 1993; Slife & Williams, 1995).

Postmodernists favor a worldview that centers on a person's involvement with the world. Human behavior is seen as meaningful only within the contexts or relationships in which it occurs. Human behavior is contextual; it cannot be "objectified" by artificially removing it from that which gives it significance. Postmodern theory holds that all meaning comes from the relationships between individuals and their world, their culture, their language, and each other. This renders concepts of knowledge and truth to be the interpretive creations of sets of people who share a common language, culture, and view of the world. Postmodernists therefore reject positivistic science and "empiricism and rationalism as universal ways of knowing that supposedly apply to all or most situations" (Slife & Williams, 1995, p. 77). According to postmodernists, all knowledge and "our interpretations of our world, are socially constructed" (Slife & Williams, 1995, p. 80).

The foregoing historical and philosophical critiques of science have competed with and to some extent undermined 19th- and early 20th-century views of science. Belief that the universe can be perceived by human beings objectively and accurately has been replaced by the general view that people's ability to accurately perceive reality is limited. *Critical realism,* the belief that the universe exists independent of people's observations but cannot be completely or accurately perceived by human beings, is now more widely accepted than *classical realism* (Barbour, 1990; Manicas & Secord, 1983). Thus the common perception is that people are always approximating reality or truth rather than having a completely accurate picture of it. Some philosophers and scientists have also pointed out that the observations themselves may influence and change the nature of that which is observed (e.g., Heisenberg's "uncertainty principle"; Barbour, 1990; Fennema & Paul, 1990). This may be especially true in the behavioral sciences.

In contrast to the belief that scientists are objective, value-free observers, it is now widely recognized within science and psychology that all scientists have values and biases that influence and limit their observations (Howard, 1985; Jones, 1994). Scientific observations are viewed as value- and theory-laden, and it is understood that scientific theories cannot be proved true in an absolute sense, nor can they be easily falsified (Brush, 1988; Kuhn, 1970; Lakatos & Musgrave, 1970; Polanyi, 1962). Science is now understood by many philosophers of science as a "social activity in which disciplines develop their own rules of practice" and where "knowledge is a social and historical product" (Kuhn, 1970; Manicas & Secord, 1983, p. 401). Again, these limitations are thought to be more pronounced in the social and behavioral sciences than in the natural sciences.

In contrast to the positivistic belief that the only way to gain knowledge and understanding of the world is through rigorous application of traditional quantitative and experimental empirical methodologies, many scholars now endorse epistemological and methodological pluralism (e.g., Slife & Gantt, 1999; Denzin & Lincoln, 1994; Greenberg, Elliott, & Lietaer, 1994; Kirk & Miller, 1986; Reichardt & Cook, 1979). Rational and intuitive ways of knowing are being reconsidered, and more subjective, exploratory, and qualitative methodologies have been advocated and used (Denzin & Lincoln, 1994; Lincoln & Guba, 1985).

Although many of these trends are controversial, and we do not agree with the relativistic extremes to which they sometimes extend, this broadening of our ideas about the nature of science has helped to break down some of the boundaries, distinctions, and alienation between science and religion. It is more widely recognized that science and religion are more epistemologically compatible than was once thought (Barbour, 1990; Jones, 1994). As summarized by Barbour (1990),

> There are many parallels between science and religion; the interaction of data and theory (or experience and interpretation); the historical character of the interpretative community; the use of models; and the influence of paradigms or programs. In both fields there are no proofs, but there can be good reasons for the judgments rendered by the paradigm community. There are also important differences between science and religion, but some of them turn out to be differences in emphasis or degree rather than the absolute contrasts sometimes imagined. We have traced a number of polarities in which the first term was more prominent in science and the second in religion, but both were found to be present in both fields: objectivity and subjectivity; rationality and personal judgment; universality and historical conditioning; criticism and tradition; and tentativeness and commitment. (p. 65)

The recognition of this greater epistemological compatibility has enabled consideration of the ways in which religious and spiritual perspectives may validly contribute to the understanding of the scientific process, of human beings, and of the universe. A growing number of philosophers and scholars no longer view metaphysical and methodological naturalism as necessary or helpful to the scientific enterprise—some of them have argued that it is time to make philosophical and methodological space for God and divine action in science (e.g., Dembski, 2001, 2004; Griffin, 2000, 2001; Slife, 2004; Slife, Hope, & Nebeker, 1999).

SOCIETAL AND PUBLIC INFLUENCES

At the dawn of the 20th century, it was widely believed in society that religious and spiritual beliefs were completely separate from, and even inferior to, scientific thought (e.g., Freud, 1927/1961). The supposed triumphs of science over medieval religious doctrines and traditions led many to place their faith in science. They viewed science as the new hope for humanity, with its impressive discoveries and technological successes. During this period, strong belief in religion and spirituality seemed to be on the decline. A variety of studies seemed to support this trend, and some observers confidently predicted that the influence of religion would continue to decline even to its extinction (e.g., Beckwith, 1985).

However, these predictions were wrong. During the past two decades a renewed interest in religion and spirituality has been evident in the world, particularly in North America (e.g., Antoun & Hegland, 1987; Kantrowitz et al., 1994; Sheler, 2002; Shine, 1996; Taylor, 1994). Popular manifestations of this spiritual renewal can be seen in the print, audio, and visual media (e.g., Kalb, 2003; Kantrowitz et al., 1994; Moyers, 1996; Sheler, 2002; Taylor, 1994). The signs of change are also evident in the surge of religious music, the growth of religious revivalism in public venues and on college campuses (Shine, 1996), the search for moral guidelines both within and outside of traditional religious institutions, and increases in religious orthodoxy. Morality- and value-oriented literature has become popular, along with preoccupation with spiritual phenomena (e.g., near-death experiences, angelic visitations, other visions, etc. (Antoun & Hegland, 1987; Kantrowitz et al., 1994; Taylor, 1994). Thus, in the popular culture, dissatisfaction with the back-seat role of spirituality has become pervasive.

Many factors have contributed to this increased interest in spirituality. For example, many people have lost faith in the ability of science to provide solutions to all of humanity's problems (Bergin, 1980a). Many people experience anxiety and fear as they observe street violence, crime, war, family disintegration, and social upheaval, all of which test people's sense of meaning and coherence in the world today. Whatever the reasons may be, society's renewed interest in spiritual issues has influenced the field of psychology, effecting a greater openness to the consideration of religious and spiritual perspectives in mainstream psychology and psychotherapy.

INFLUENCES FROM THE MEDICAL PROFESSION

Throughout much of recorded history, religion and medicine have been closely intertwined (Koenig, McCullough, & Larson, 2001). For thousands of years, physical and mental illnesses were largely understood in religious terms (Koenig et al., 2001; Zilboorg & Henry, 1941). In many religions and cultures, priests, monks, nuns, and other religious leaders have also been medical practitioners and nurses, and religious organizations have built and staffed many early and contemporary medical and mental hospitals (Koenig et al., 2001).

The rise of modern, naturalistic science during the 18th and 19th centuries, however, contributed to a schism between medicine and religion. Thus during much of the 20th century, most mainstream medical researchers and physicians focused exclusively on biological causes and cures of disease.

The possible influences of the mind and spirit on health and healing were neglected (Benson, 1996; Koenig et al., 2001). Few medical training programs provided training about faith or spirituality, and most practicing physicians believed that they should avoid discussing these topics with their patients (Koenig et al., 2001; Larson & Larson, 1994; Puchalski, Larson, & Lu, 2000).

This situation began to change during the latter part of the 20th and early years of the 21st centuries as increasing numbers of medical researchers and physicians became interested in understanding how the mind and spirit may influence disease and health (Kalb, 2003; Koenig et al., 2001). For example, in the 1970s, Herbert Benson and his colleagues at Harvard Medical School launched what was to become a four-decade, systematic research and training program in mind–body medicine. Their research demonstrated that spiritual practices (e.g., repetitive prayer and chants, meditation, etc.) and faith in God can elicit the *relaxation response,* which has been helpful in treating a number of diseases, including hypertension, cardiac rhythm irregularities, chronic pain, insomnia, infertility, and the symptoms of cancer and AIDS (Benson, 1996). In 1988, Benson founded the Mind/Body Institute, Inc., which offers clinical programs to over 9,000 patients each year, including teachers and students, corporate executives and employees, and the general public (Chausse, 2003). Benson and his colleagues at the Mind/Body Institute and Harvard Medical School Department of Continuing Education also provide training in mind–body medicine and spirituality and healing to health care professionals from around the world.

Another pioneer in the movement to bring spirituality back into the medical profession is the late David B. Larson. During the 1980s and 1990s, Larson published a number of systematic review articles that documented the fact that religion and spirituality had been sorely neglected as variables in medical and psychiatric research (e.g., Larson, Pattison, Blazer, Omran, & Kaplan, 1986; Larson et al., 1992). Larson also authored and coauthored several books, monographs, and training guides, and he played a prominent role in the effort to have spirituality included as a part of medical and psychiatric training programs (e.g., Larson & Larson, 1994; Larson, Swyers, & McCullough, 1997; Larson, Lu, & Swyers, 1997). Larson also founded the National Institute for Healthcare Research (NIHR), which was later renamed the International Center for the Integration of Health and Spirituality (ICIHS). NIHR/ICIHS served as a think tank and resource center for scholars and practitioners interested in spirituality and health. It did much during the 1990s to raise professional and public awareness of the role of faith and spirituality in health and healing.

Two other prominent contributors in the movement to integrate spirituality into the medical profession are Harold G. Koenig and Cristina M. Puchalski. Koenig is an associate professor of psychiatry and medicine at

Duke University Medical Center in North Carolina and the founder of Duke's Center for the Study of Religion/Spirituality and Health. He has published prolifically about spirituality and health and is heavily involved in training and continuing education on this topic (e.g., Koenig et al., 2001; Koenig, 1998, 1999). Puchalski is the founder and director of the George Washington Institute for Spirituality and Health (GWish). She is also an assistant professor in the departments of Medicine and Health Care Sciences at the George Washington University School of Medicine in Washington, D.C. She has worked to bring courses about spirituality into medical schools and to encourage medical students to engage in compassionate caregiving (e.g., Puchalski & Larson, 1998; Puchalski et al., 2000).

The efforts of Benson, Larson, Koenig, Puchalski, and increasing numbers of health care professionals throughout the world are having an impact on the medical profession. Ten years ago, only a few medical schools offered courses in spirituality and healing. Now over half of U.S. medical schools have such courses (Puchalski et al., 2000). Many medical researchers and practitioners now regard faith and spirituality as important resources in physical health and healing and are willing to discuss spiritual issues with patients. The movement to include spiritual perspectives and resources in medicine has been stimulated by, and has helped stimulate, a more spiritually open *Zeitgeist* in the mental health professions.

RESEARCH ON THE BRAIN, COGNITION, AND CONSCIOUSNESS

In the late 19th and early 20th centuries, relatively little was known about the human brain in relation to cognition and consciousness. Early attempts to study these relationships proved unfruitful, and interest in studying mental phenomena was declining because of the scathing criticisms of early leaders of the behavioral psychology movement (e.g., Watson, 1924/1983). The reductionistic view that all mental phenomena are fully caused and controlled by chemical and electrical events within the brain also preempted researchers' interest in mental events (R. W. Sperry, 1988). Thus, cognition and consciousness were viewed as inappropriate subject matter for hard-nosed (i.e., respectable) behavioral scientists.

During the 1960s and 1970s, dissatisfaction with anti-mentalist perspectives, the rising interest in computers and artificial intelligence, and the development of new technologies for studying the human brain contributed to a renewed interest in the study of brain biology, cognition, and consciousness (Karier, 1986; R. W. Sperry, 1988). This revolution led to impressive advances in the understanding of consciousness and the human brain. As described by R. W. Sperry (1988),

By the mid-1970s, mainstream psychology had also revised its earlier views concerning consciousness and the subjective, replacing long dominant behaviorist theory with a new mentalist or cognitive paradigm. This changeover, impelled by a large complex of cognitive, linguistic, computer, and related theoretic and sociologic developments . . . has now legitimized the contents of inner experience, such as sensations, percepts, mental images, thoughts, feelings, and the like, as ineliminable causal constructs in the scientific explanation of brain function and behavior. (p. 607)

R. W. Sperry and other leading brain researchers (e.g., Eccles & Robinson, 1984; Popper, 1972; Popper & Eccles, 1977) also have argued that "conscious mental states . . . interact functionally at their own level and also exert downward causal control over brain physiology in a supervenient sense . . . subjective mental qualities of inner experience . . . play an active, causal control role in conscious behavior and evolution" (R. W. Sperry, 1988, p. 607). Although not all of these researchers believe in God or in transcendent spiritual phenomena (e.g., R. W. Sperry, 1988, 1995), they are in agreement that such understandings of human consciousness and the brain are more compatible with spiritual views of human nature than were the earlier anti-mentalist, reductionistic views (e.g., Eccles & Robinson, 1984; Popper & Eccles, 1977; R. W. Sperry, 1988, 1995).

Contemporary understandings of the brain and consciousness have motivated some theistic researchers and philosophers to attempt to harmonize research findings with theological interpretations of the body, mind, and spirit. For example, after rigorously discussing research on brain functioning and physiology, Eccles and Robinson (1984) concluded that

Since materialist solutions fail to account for our experienced uniqueness, we are constrained to attribute the uniqueness of the psyche or soul to a supernatural spiritual creation. To give the explanation in theological terms: Each soul is a Divine creation, which is "attached" to the growing fetus at some time between conception and birth. (p. 43)

More recently, Griffin (2000), a theistic philosopher, rejected dualistic or supernatural explanations of the human mind or spirit, but advocated for a perspective of theistic *nondualistic interactionism* of mind and body. Griffin (2000) explained,

Because the mind is distinct from the brain, but not ontologically different in kind from the cells making up the brain, our presupposition about their interaction—that the body influences our conscious experiences and these experiences in turn influence our bodies—is not unintelligible. Because the mind at any moment is a full-fledged actuality—as actual as the brain cells and their constituents—we can take at face value our assumption that our decisions are not fully determined by causal forces coming up from the body, but that they are truly "decisions" in which our minds exercise genuine self-determination. (p. 174)

Griffin (2000, 2001) argued that this position, which is in harmony with empirical findings, allows for interaction between the mind and body, affirms the reality of human agency or self-determination, makes plausible the possibility of life after death, and leaves room for faith in God and divine influence in the world.

In conclusion, research on the brain, cognition, and consciousness has seriously undermined reductionistic, materialistic accounts, leading to a rigorous and promising dialogue concerning compatibilities between spiritual and scientific views of the mind, body, and spirit. Some scholars believe that the historic mind–body riddle that has plagued philosophers and scientists for centuries could be resolved—making theistic perspectives of the human mind and spirit more plausible and easier to understand (Griffin, 2000, 2001; Peacocke, 2001).

RESEARCH ON RELIGION AND MENTAL HEALTH

Although more than 75 years have passed since religious beliefs were first renowned in mainstream psychiatry and psychology as unhealthy and unproductive, this viewpoint, or versions of it, have persisted until recent years (Bergin, 1980a, 1980b, 1983, 1991; Ellis, 1980; Jensen & Bergin, 1988). For example, in 1980 Albert Ellis, one of the most influential of contemporary psychologists, stated that "religiosity . . . is in many respects equivalent to irrational thinking and emotional disturbance . . . . The elegant therapeutic solution to emotional problems is to be quite unreligious and have no degree of dogmatic faith that is unfounded or unfoundable in fact" (Ellis, 1980, p. 637). Such views persisted in mainstream psychology despite the fact that research investigating the relationship between religion and health was surprisingly sparse, and perhaps because early reviews of what research there was were negative and carried over from older anti-religious *Zeitgeist* (Dittes, 1971; Sanua, 1969).

In the 1980s and 1990s, however, this view began to change. Hundreds of studies have now been done about religion and health. Overall, the findings have not supported the "religiosity–emotional disturbance" hypothesis but, to the contrary, have provided evidence that religion and spirituality are positively associated with many indicators of mental health (Gartner, Larson, & Allen, 1991; Koenig, 1998; Koenig, McCullough, & Larson, 2001; Payne, Bergin, Bielema, & Jenkins, 1991; Plante & Sherman, 2001). We summarize these findings in more detail in chapter 5.

Research on religion and mental health has contributed to a reevaluation by many mainstream mental health professionals regarding the role of religious and spiritual beliefs in psychotherapy, a reevaluation that was clearly manifested in a national survey of four professional groups of therapists (Jensen & Bergin, 1988). Even Ellis (1996; Nielson, Johnson, & Ellis, 2001) revised his views in this regard. Religious beliefs and behavior can no longer be viewed simply as a neurosis or irrelevant response to be ignored or extinguished. To the contrary, a majority of mainstream psychotherapists now consider such beliefs and behaviors to be resources for promoting therapeutic change (Bergin, 1991; Nielsen et al., 2001; P. S. Richards & Potts, 1995b; Shafranske, 1996).

THE POSITIVE PSYCHOLOGY MOVEMENT

At the end of World War II, when the Veterans Administration and the National Institute of Mental Health were created, "practicing psychologists found they could make a living treating mental illness . . . and academic psychologists discovered they could get grants for research on mental illness" (M. E. P. Seligman, 1998, p. 1). According to M. E. P. Seligman (1998), with the creation of these two organizations, psychologists became preoccupied with mental illness and adopted the disease model of human functioning. Accordingly, for the remainder of the 20th century, mainstream psychologists largely neglected the study of human strengths and virtues, leaving mental health professionals ill-equipped to facilitate normal human development or engage in effective prevention (M. E. P. Seligman, 2002).

After becoming president of the American Psychological Association in 1997, M. E. P. Seligman (2002) shifted his focus from studying mental illness to understanding human strengths and virtues. He coined the term "positive psychology" and called on psychologists to change their focus "from a preoccupation only with repairing the worst things in life to also building the best qualities in life" (p. 3). He also asserted,

> We have discovered that there are human strengths that act as buffers against mental illness: courage, future-mindedness, optimism, interpersonal skill, faith, work ethic, hope, honesty, perseverance, the capacity for flow and insight, to name several. Much of the task of prevention in this new century will be to create a science of human strength whose mission will be to understand and learn how to foster these virtues in young people. (M. E. P. Seligman, 2002, p. 5)

Psychologists and other health professionals have responded with enthusiasm to Seligman's call to develop a positive psychology. Since 1998, numerous journal articles and book chapters have been published on the topic, as well as several books (e.g., Emmons & Crumpler, 2000; Gillham & Seligman, 1999; McCullough, Pargament, & Thoresen, 2000; Peterson,

2000; M. E. P. Seligman & Csikszentmihalyi, 2000; Snyder & Lopez, 2002). Professional conferences have been held and grant funding has been made available to promote research in this domain.

The rapid growth of interest in positive psychology has occurred in the context of the more spiritually open *Zeitgeist* that has existed in the mainstream mental health professions during the past 20 years (P. S. Richards & Bergin, 1997). The great religious traditions of the world have long been concerned with understanding and promoting human virtues and strengths (L. Miller, Richards, & Keller, 2000; Park, 2003). Furthermore, religious organizations and leaders have historically focused their efforts more on facilitating normal human development and preventing problems than on remedying them (Pargament, 1997).

Even before Seligman's call to develop a positive psychology, many scholars with interests in spirituality and the psychology of religion were already conducting research about human virtues and strengths, including forgiveness, spirituality, gratitude, ultimate concerns and spiritual strivings, hope, faith, love, and humility (e.g., Emmons, 1999; Emmons & Shelton, 2002; McCullough & Worthington, 1999; Pargament & Mahoney, 2002; Park, 2003; Worthington, 1998). Thus many behavioral scientists with interests in religion and spirituality have resonated to Seligman's desire to develop a psychology that focuses more on human strengths and virtues than on mental illness (Park, 2003). It appears, therefore, that the positive psychology movement has been supported and stimulated by the current professional interest in spirituality. But the positive psychology movement has also stimulated additional interest in religion and in the study of human virtues and strengths that have been traditionally associated with religion.

ALTERNATIVE THERAPEUTIC TRADITIONS

Even as psychoanalysis and behavioral psychology rose to prominence during the early 20th century, dissenters began to criticize and challenge the assumptions of these theories. Several of Freud's early followers eventually broke from the tenets of psychoanalytic theory to establish their own approaches. For example, Adler and Jung rejected Freud's reductionistic views of human nature (Kaufmann, 1989; Mosak, 1989). As noted in Bandura's (1986) review, behavioral psychology also quickly attracted critics, especially for its dogmatic denial of both mental processes and consciousness, and for its rigid adherence to strict empiricism and positivism. Although behavior therapy was built on the philosophical foundations of early behavioral psychology, the attempt to design a behavioral technology has been essentially displaced by the cognitive–behavioral movement, which is more agentive in perspective (see Bandura, 1969, 1986, 1997).

During the 1950s and 1960s, major alternatives to psychoanalysis and behaviorism arose (Leahey, 1991). One of these became the "third force" in psychology: the humanistic–existential tradition (Leahey, 1991; May, Angel, & Ellenberger, 1958). Rogers (1961, 1980) and Maslow (1968, 1970, 1971), two leaders of humanistic–existential thought, challenged the deterministic and reductionistic views of human beings promoted by the psychoanalytic and behavioral traditions. They argued that human beings cannot be reduced to simple biological drives or environmental stimulus–response connections and that humans have the capacity to transcend their circumstances, thus actualizing their innate human potential through positive choices. Rogers, Maslow, and others challenged psychology's commitment to strict experimental empiricism and positivism by way of their phenomenological emphasis and their willingness to describe emotions, purpose, values, and other nonobservable phenomena (see Rychlak, 1981).

The cognitive and systemic philosophies were also developing during the 1950s and 1960s, although it was not until the 1970s that these two traditions emerged as major influences within the field. The leaders of the cognitive psychotherapy tradition raised questions about the validity of deterministic and reductionistic views of human beings by their emphasis on the interdependence of cognition, affect, and behavior, along with their belief that human beings can change the way they feel and behave by changing their thinking (Beck, 1976; Burns, 1980; Ellis, 1973; Meichenbaum, 1977). The leaders of the systemic tradition also questioned deterministic and reductionistic views of human beings by emphasizing complex systemic influences on human behavior. Such theorists assume that human beings are not simply passive recipients of systemic influences but are agents who have the capacity to actively modify their family systems to bring about change (Gurman & Kniskern, 1981). Both the cognitive and systemic traditions contributed to an increased appreciation of the complexity of human behavior and emotions, thereby raising further doubts about the positivistic claim that human behavior can be truly understood and therefore predicted through empirical observation and linear causality.

A related development has been Joseph Rychlak's critiques of the assumptions and trends in traditional psychology, especially as they affect personality theory and psychotherapy (Rychlak, 1981). His creative proposals favor an agentive view of human nature and seek to replace experimental psychology's Newtonian causality with an empirically based human teleology called *Logical Learning Theory* (Rychlak, 1979, 1994). In his 1994 volume Rychlak asserts and provides data to support the idea that "if we begin with a technical language that is intentional rather than mechanistic, we can end with a perfectly valid, experimentally proven view of human behavior" (Rychlak, 1994, p. xix). Rychlak's influence continues in part through the work of former students such as Brent Slife (1993) and Richard Williams (1992).

Thus, during the first 75 years of the 20th century, five major therapeutic traditions rose to prominence in mainstream psychotherapy: the psychoanalytic, behavioral, humanistic–existential, cognitive, and systemic strategies (Matarazzo, 1985). The assumptions of determinism, reductionism, classical realism, and positivism were rejected or questioned to some degree by the early leaders of the humanistic, cognitive, and systemic traditions. By the 1970s and early 1980s, even leaders within the psychodynamic and behavior therapy traditions seemed to be adopting views that were less deterministic and reductionistic. Contemporary psychoanalytic thinking is more open to the legitimacy of the spiritual domain (e.g., Spero, 1992), and behavioral therapy even acquired the new designation of "cognitive–behavioral" (Beck, 1976; Garfield & Bergin, 1986; Meichenbaum, 1977).

THE MOVEMENT TOWARD ECLECTICISM OR PSYCHOTHERAPY INTEGRATION

During the past 15 years, a new movement has risen to prominence: the eclectic or integrative approach (Bergin & Garfield, 1994; Norcross, 1986; Norcross & Goldfried, 1992). According to a national survey by Jensen, Bergin, and Greaves (1990), a majority of psychotherapists are now using integrative and multidimensional philosophies in their approach to psychotherapy. Perhaps it is not surprising that the techniques used most often are a combination of the psychodynamic, behavioral, cognitive, humanistic–existential, and systemic traditions (Jensen et al., 1990). Thus, the five major therapeutic traditions remain, in an integrative fashion, the most influential in mainstream psychotherapy. Spiritual techniques are also beginning to find their way into this broad clinical perspective (Payne, Bergin, & Loftus, 1992).

With its emphasis on treatment tailoring, client and therapist choice, holism, and integration, the integrative tradition has further contributed to a rejection by many psychotherapists of the assumptions of determinism and reductionism. The acknowledgment by the integrative tradition of the great complexity of human personality and therapeutic change seems to have further highlighted for many the limitations of strictly empirical and positivistic epistemological claims.[1]

---

[1]We agree with Slife and Williams (1995), who have argued that although the contemporary psychodynamic, behavioral, humanistic, cognitive, systemic, and integrative traditions appear to have laid aside determinism, reductionism, and positivism at the applied level, at deeper philosophical and

THE MULTICULTURAL COUNSELING MOVEMENT

During the first half of the 20th century, the majority of influential contributors to theory, research, and practice in mainstream psychology and psychotherapy were White, middle- to upper-class men. Little attention was given to the issues and concerns of women or minority group members (D. W. Sue, 1981; D. W. Sue & Sue, 1990). When women and minority group members were included in psychological theories or research, they were often portrayed as deficient or pathological (Gilligan, 1982; Sue & Sue, 1990). Most psychotherapists seemed to believe that their therapeutic approaches could be applied equally effectively to all clients, regardless of the client's gender, race, religion, or lifestyle.

During the turbulent decades of the 1960s and 1970s, culturally encapsulated views of women and minority groups received widespread criticism (D. W. Sue & Sue, 1990). The civil rights and feminist movements challenged and began to break down many of the prevailing stereotypes. Within the psychotherapy profession, the cross-cultural or multicultural movement gained momentum and became a major force. During the 1980s and 1990s, numerous articles and books that discussed the importance of multicultural sensitivity were published (e.g., Ibrahim, 1985, 1991; Ponterotto, Casas, Suzuki, & Alexander, 1995; Ponterotto, Suzuki, & Meller, 1996; D. W. Sue, 1981; D. W. Sue & Sue, 1990; S. Sue, Zane, & Young, 1994). Many professional associations incorporated guidelines regarding respect for diversity and sensitivity to multicultural issues into their ethical and training standards (e.g., American Counseling Association, 1995; American Psychological Association, 1981, 1992).

The multicultural movement of the 1980s and 1990s helped mainstream mental health professionals become more aware and more tolerant of the great diversity that exists in the world. Although most multicultural scholars during this time period focused primarily on aspects of diversity related to race, ethnicity, gender and lifestyle, their research and writings helped to create a space for mental health professionals to begin to consider the religious aspects of diversity (P. S. Richards & Bergin, 2000). Although once declared "an orphan in academia" (Bergin, 1983, p. 171), religion received much more attention in mainstream psychology and psychotherapy during the 1990s.

Religion is now explicitly recognized as one type of diversity in the American Psychological Association's ethical guidelines (APA, 2002a) and in the APA's *Guidelines on Multicultural Education, Training, Practice, and*

---

theoretical levels such assumptions often remain unexamined and may continue to influence the processes and outcomes of therapy.

Organizational Change for Psychologists (APA, 2002b). Prominent multicultural scholars have also acknowledged in recent years that spirituality is a basic condition of human existence and that a "psychology that fails to recognize this aspect of human existence is a spiritually and emotionally bankrupt discipline" (D. W. Sue, Bingham, Porche-Burke, & Vasquez, 1999). In harmony with this perspective, several multicultural books published in recent years have devoted considerable attention to the religious and spiritual aspects of diversity (Fukuyama & Sevig, 1999; P. S. Richards, Keller, & Smith, 2003; T. B. Smith & Richards, 2002, 2005). Thus, the multicultural movement and the recognition of the importance of spiritual diversity within the multicultural field have helped to create a space for a theistic spiritual strategy in psychology and psychotherapy.

RECOGNIZING THE IMPORTANCE OF VALUES

As psychology and psychotherapy developed, early leaders believed that values could be kept out of psychological theory, research, and practice (Patterson, 1958). These leaders assumed that a therapist could be a "blank slate:" an objective, scientific technician, or a nonjudgmental, nonevaluative listener. Yet, as early as the late 1940s and continuing into the 1960s and 1970s, the belief that values could be kept out of psychotherapy was challenged theoretically and empirically (Beutler, 1972; Kessell & McBrearty, 1967; Patterson, 1958). Several writers have argued persuasively that psychotherapy is a value-laden process (Bergin, 1980a, 1980b; 1980c; Campbell, 1975; R. F. Kitchener, 1980a, 1980b; London, 1964, 1986; Lowe, 1976; Tjeltveit, 1999). It is now widely accepted in mainstream psychotherapy that therapists cannot remain value-free as they work with their clients and that psychotherapy research also is influenced by the researcher's values (Bergin & Garfield, 1994).

Ethical relativism and ethical hedonism continue as influential within the profession of psychotherapy (e.g., Ellis, 1980). However, even these assumptions have been challenged by behavioral scientists and psychotherapists in recent years (e.g., Barbour, 1990; Bergin, 1980a, 1980b, 1983, 1985, 1991; Collins, 1977; Doherty, 1995; Jones, 1994; Tjeltveit, 1999). Several writers have specifically criticized psychology's and psychiatry's long-standing promotion of ethical hedonism. For example, in his 1975 presidential address to the American Psychological Association, Campbell said,

> A major thesis of this address is that present-day psychology and psychiatry in all their major forms are more hostile to the inhibitory messages of traditional religious moralizing than is scientifically justified . . . . The religions of all ancient urban civilizations . . . taught that many aspects of human nature need to be curbed if optimal social coordination is to

be achieved, for example, selfishness, pride, greed, dishonesty, covetousness, lust, wrath. Psychology and psychiatry, on the other hand, not only describe man as selfishly motivated, but implicitly teach that he ought to be so. They tend to see repression and inhibition of individual impulse as undesirable, and see all guilt as a dysfunctional neurotic blight created by cruel child rearing and a needlessly repressive society. They further recommend that we accept our biological and psychological impulses as good and seek pleasure rather than enchain ourselves with duty. (pp. 1103–1104)

Campbell (1975) further commented that "on these issues, psychology and psychiatry cannot yet claim to be truly scientific and thus have special reasons for modesty and caution in undermining traditional belief systems" (p. 1103).

Several writers have also criticized psychology and psychiatry for promoting ethical relativism (Bergin, 1980c, 1985; Doherty, 1995; R. F. Kitchener, 1980a). For example, R. F. Kitchener (1980a) offered the following:

Why has relativism been so influential and popular among social and behavioral scientists? Why has it seemed to be a logical conclusion that inevitably had to be drawn? I could give several reasons, but an obvious one is the following. In looking around at different individuals and cultures, one of the most striking features is the obvious fact that people value different things [cultural relativism] . . . . Even if this were true (and there are reasons to think it is not), it would not show that psychological relativism and cultural relativism are true. It does not follow that what ought to be valued differs from individual to individual (ethical relativism). (pp. 5–6)

Commenting on R. F. Kitchener's article, Bergin (1980c) stated,

Kitchener (1980[a]) properly identifies inconsistencies in the philosophies and between the philosophies and actions of behavior therapists. This state of the art is not, however, confined to the behavioral position, but is true of most approaches to therapy and to applied behavioral science in general. It is interesting to observe professional change agents who believe in a relativistic philosophy and simultaneously assert dogmatically the virtue of the therapeutic goals they promote . . . . Kitchener correctly identifies such inconsistency [ethical relativism] as a dilemma for therapists who wish to logically justify the positions they take with respect to therapeutic goals. (p. 11)

There is now evidence that the majority of therapists do believe that certain values promote mental health and that these values should be endorsed and used to guide therapy (Bergin, 1985; Jensen & Bergin, 1988). Although the specific values therapists should use to guide and evaluate psychotherapy are subject to question and debate, the majority of therapists (with notable exceptions, such as Ellis, 1980) no longer seem to concur with relativistic or hedonistic moral philosophies. Instead, many endorse personal responsibility, family commitment, humility before God, self-control, self-sacrifice, forgiveness, and honesty (Doherty, 1995; Jensen & Bergin, 1988; see also chaps. 5 and 6, this volume). Thus current perspectives within the psychotherapy profession concerning values are more in harmony with religious and spiritual worldviews than were the value-free, ethically relativistic, and hedonistic beliefs of the early leaders of psychiatry and psychotherapy (Bergin, Payne, & Richards, 1996).

DEVELOPMENT OF SPIRITUALLY ORIENTED PSYCHOTHERAPY APPROACHES

Because the dominant psychotherapy traditions all excluded theistic spiritual perspectives and interventions from their theories and treatment methods (Bergin, 1980a) for much of the 20th century, few resources were available for mainstream mental health practitioners who wished to include religion and spirituality as part of treatment. This situation began to change, however, in the late 1970s and early 1980s, when articles and books about religiously accommodative and spiritually oriented psychotherapy approaches were provided by mainstream publishers with increasing frequency (e.g., Bergin, 1980a; 1985; 1988; Collins, 1977; Lovinger, 1984; Propst, 1988; Spero, 1985; Worthington et al., 1996). During the 1990s and early 2000s, the proliferation of such articles and books has continued. Many writers have described multicultural psychotherapy approaches that advocate respect for religious and spiritual diversity (e.g., Faiver, Ingersoll, O'Brien, & McNally, 2001; Frame, 2003; Griffith & Griffith, 2002; Kelly, 1995; Lovinger, 1990; G. Miller, 2003; Sperry, 2001; Swinton, 2001; West, 2000). Treatment approaches based on Jungian, transpersonal, cognitive, and humanistic psychologies have also been proposed (Elkins, 1995; Helminiak, 1996; Nielsen et al., 2001; Vaughan, Wittine, & Walsh, 1996). Approaches grounded in Buddhist, Hindu, Christian, Jewish, and Muslim spiritual thought have also been described (Epstein, 1995; Hedayat-Diba, 2000; Rabinowitz, 2000; Rubin, 1996; Sharma, 2000; Worthington, 1990).

The development of numerous spiritual and religiously accommodative psychotherapy approaches has been stimulated by, and has helped to stimulate, the more spiritually open *Zeitgeist* in the mainstream mental health professions. Although the majority of training programs in the mental health professions still neglect religious and spiritual issues (Brawer, Handal, Fabricatore, Roberts, & Wajda-Johnston, 2002; P. S. Richards & Bergin, 2000;

Shafranske, 2000; Yarhouse & Fisher, 2002), many resources are now available for practitioners and graduate students. For example, books, articles, continuing education workshops, Web sites, professional conferences, professional organizations, and an expanding network of mental health professionals with expertise in spiritual diversity are now available to assist those who wish to incorporate spiritual perspectives into their professional identities and practices. Psychotherapists need no longer feel constrained to strictly adhere to secular, naturalistic theories and methods of therapeutic change.

CONCLUSION

The scientific, philosophical, and social influences discussed in this chapter have eroded the credibility and influence of the philosophies of determinism, reductionism, empiricism, classical realism, positivism, ethical relativism, and ethical hedonism. The changes in the philosophical and theoretical climate that have occurred during recent decades laid the foundation for a reconsideration of naturalism, psychology's and psychiatry's most deeply and rigidly held philosophical assumption.

A number of mental health professionals have called for the restoration of spiritual, theistic perspectives in the profession of psychotherapy (e.g., Bergin, 1980a, 1988, 1991; Collins, 1977; Jones, 1994). For example, Jones (1994), citing the philosopher Alvin Plantinga (1984; Plantinga & Wolterstorff, 1983), argued that

> there is no compelling reason for individuals who believe in God not to include the existence of God among the fundamental worldview assumptions brought to the scholarly, scientific task . . . . Albert Ellis and B. F. Skinner, among others, have explicitly made naturalism . . . a part of the fundamental commitments they bring to the scientific task. If disbelief in the supernatural can suitably be among the control beliefs of some scientists, it would seem that belief in God and related beliefs about human persons could be allowable for others as part of their control beliefs. (p. 195)

Consistent with this idea, Bergin (1980a) stated that

> other alternatives are . . . needed . . . . The alternative I wish to put forward is a spiritual one. It might be called theistic realism. . . . The first and most important axiom [of theistic realism] is that God exists, that human beings are the creations of God, and that there are unseen spiritual processes by which the link between God and humanity is maintained. (p. 99)

Because of the changes in philosophical and theoretical climate that have occurred in science, philosophy, and psychology during recent decades, theistic perspectives are being considered and accepted by many main-stream personality theorists and psychotherapists (Shafranske, 1996; Worthington, Kurusu, McCullough, & Sandage, 1996). The spiritually open *Zeitgeist* that now exists in the natural and behavioral sciences has created space for a theistic framework and approach in mainstream psychology and psychotherapy.

III

THEOLOGICAL, PHILOSOPHICAL, AND THEORETICAL PERSPECTIVES

4

THEOLOGICAL AND PHILOSOPHICAL ASSUMPTIONS OF THEISTIC PSYCHOTHERAPY

There is something strikingly new in modern spirituality. . . . The world's diversity of religious traditions . . . has come home to us in a quite literal way . . . the . . . presence of so many people of once-alien traditions . . . is . . . requiring a degree of accommodation and respect that was earlier unknown.

—David Wulff

The first purpose of this chapter is to describe the Western or theistic worldview, because it provides the theological foundation on which our theistic strategy is structured. We describe the history, demographics, and core metaphysical beliefs (i.e., views of deity, human nature, purpose of life, spirituality, morality, and life after death) of the five theistic world religious traditions: Judaism, Christianity, Islam, Zoroastrianism, and Sikhism. We also show that the theistic worldview is in harmony with the beliefs of a large proportion of the world's population, including the majority of psychotherapy clients. Although we do not expect all psychotherapists and mental health professionals to agree with this view, we argue that it is important for them to attempt to understand and appreciate it more fully, as many of their clients approach life with this perspective. We also briefly compare and contrast the theistic worldview with the Eastern and scientific naturalistic worldviews.

The second purpose of this chapter is to describe the philosophical foundations of our theistic strategy, including the philosophies of scientific theism, theistic holism, agency, moral universalism, theistic relationism, altruism, and contextuality. Contemporary views in science, the philosophy of science, and psychology are now much more compatible with theistic philosophical assumptions than in previous decades (Griffin, 2000, 2001; Jones, 1994; P. S. Richards & Bergin, 1997; Slife, 2004). Theistic assumptions starkly conflict with the naturalistic, deterministic, and relativistic assumptions adopted by scientists and behavioral scientists in the late 19th and early 20th centuries, and thus they provide a radically different philosophical foundation for personality theory and psychotherapy.

We assume that all psychotherapy traditions are grounded in a particular theology and philosophy even though many psychotherapists may not explicitly or consciously think about or acknowledge it (Slife & Richards, 2001).[1] Because we believe that it is impossible for psychotherapists to escape their theological and philosophical assumptions, in this chapter we seek to be explicit about ours.

THE IMPORTANCE OF A *WELTANSCHAUUNG*

During the past few decades, a number of writers have pointed out how important it is for psychotherapists and mental health professionals to understand their clients' worldviews. For example, Ibrahim (1985) stated,

> A lack of understanding of one's own and one's clients' world views results in frustration and anxiety for both the helper and the client. Goals and processes considered appropriate by the helper may be antithetical and meaningless for the client. In such an instance, the appropriate course for the helper is to establish clearly how the client views the world. (pp. 629–630)

A *Weltanschauung*, or worldview, according to Wilhelm Dilthey, a 19th century German philosopher and pioneering contributor to the understanding of worldviews (Dilthey, 1978), is composed of beliefs a person holds about the universe and the nature of reality that attempt "to resolve the enigma of life" (Kluback & Weinbaum, 1957, p. 25). Worldviews "furnish answers to the largest questions that human beings can ask about their condition" (Wagar, 1977, p. 4).

The deepest questions human beings can ask about the nature of reality and about their own existence are metaphysical and existential questions. For example, How did the universe and the earth come into existence?

---

[1] The mainstream psychotherapy traditions are grounded in the theology of scientific naturalism. We regard scientific naturalism as a theology because, like all religions and worldviews, it makes certain ontological claims about the nature of God and reality (Dixon, 2002). As we discuss in chapter 2 of this volume, scientific naturalism also carries with it a number of philosophical assumptions and commitments.

How did life, particularly human life, come to exist? Is there a Supreme Being or Creator? What is the purpose of life? How should people live their lives in order to find happiness, peace, and wisdom? What is good, moral, and ethical? What is undesirable, evil, and immoral? How do people live with the realities of suffering, grief, pain, and death? Is there life after death, and, if so, what is the nature of the afterlife? Such questions have concerned religious leaders, artists, philosophers, writers, and scientists throughout the history of humankind (Kluback & Weinbaum, 1957).

During the past few decades, numerous scholars have written about the importance of worldviews and have pointed out that worldviews have a major impact on human relationships, societies, and cultures (e.g., Horner & Vandersluis, 1981; Koltko-Rivera, 2004; Kluback & Weinbaum, 1957; C. Kluckhohn, 1951, 1956; F. R. Kluckhohn & Strodtbeck, 1961; Sarason, 1981; Sire, 1976; Wagar, 1977). For example, Sarason (1981), a clinical psychologist, stated that "one's view of the universe is interwoven with one's view of people. However one conceives of the universe, it is connected to how one sees oneself in relation to other people, the social world" (pp. 47–48). Wagar (1977) asserted that the "cultural life of all societies takes form and direction from . . . [their] world views" (p. 4).

A person's worldview may also have a significant influence on physical and mental health and on interpersonal relationships (Koltko-Rivera, 2004). Traditionally, psychologists and psychiatrists have tended to ignore worldviews and values, limiting their research, theory, and practice to a consideration of what is "objectively" observable: behaviors, relationships, and physical and mental health. Fortunately, this has begun to change in recent years. As illustrated in Figure 4.1, a person's metaphysical worldview influences values and goals, which influence lifestyle and behavior, which influence physical and mental health and, in turn, interpersonal relationships.

The following example helps to clarify this point. John is a devout Latter-Day Saint who believes in God and believes that God has revealed a health code that emphasizes care of the physical body as the "temple of one's spirit." Those who follow this code are promised both health and wisdom. This is part of John's metaphysical worldview. In keeping with this principle, John sets a goal early in life to abide by its admonition against alcohol and tobacco. John's goals and values influence his lifestyle and behavior, and he avoids drinking parties, bars, and cigarettes. Because of his religious beliefs, John remains abstinent from alcohol and tobacco throughout his life and thus avoids the negative effects of tobacco use and the potential of alcohol abuse. His physical and mental health and his interpersonal relationships are free of the damaging effects of these substances. Perhaps his mental processes are also clearer and his judgment wiser than they otherwise might have been.

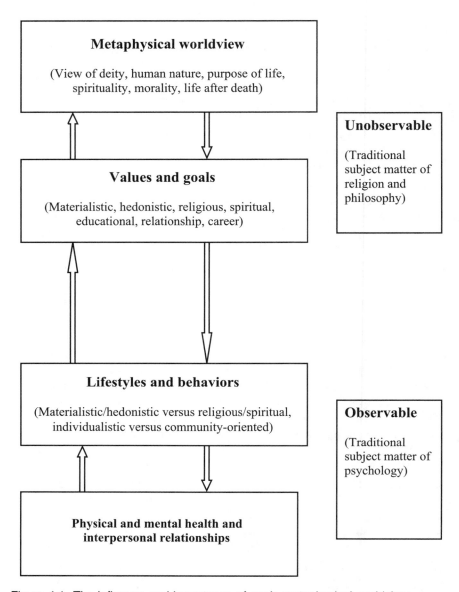

Figure 4.1. The influence and importance of one's metaphysical worldview.

If John's metaphysical worldview did not include a belief that God had commanded him to abstain from tobacco and alcohol, he might not have set a goal to abstain, and he may have decided that he enjoyed and valued drinking and smoking. Smoking and drinking might have become part of his lifestyle, and ultimately he would have suffered the health consequences of such behaviors, including, for example, the possibility of cancer or alcoholism and all of the emotional and relationship problems associated with them.

There is not, of course, a one-to-one relationship between people's worldviews and their physical and mental health and interpersonal relationships. People's values and goals are not always consistent with their worldviews, nor are their lifestyles and behaviors always consistent with their values and goals. In addition, many other factors potentially affect a person's physical and mental health and relationships, such as genetic vulnerabilities, disease, aging, and accidents. Nevertheless, a worldview is one important influence on physical and mental health and relationships.

Multicultural writers in the psychotherapy and mental health professions have, in recent years, drawn attention to the ways that people from various races and cultures differ in their worldviews (e.g., Horner & Vandersluis, 1981; Ibrahim, 1985, 1991; Speight, Myers, Cox, & Highlen, 1991; D. W. Sue, 1978; D. W. Sue & Sue, 1990). For example, D. W. Sue (1978; see also D. W. Sue & Sue, 1990) proposed a two-dimensional locus of control–locus of responsibility model that he believed would be helpful for understanding how minority and majority group clients differ in their worldviews. Building on the value orientation theory of Kluckhohn (1951, 1956; F. R. Kluckhohn & Strodtbeck, 1961), Ibrahim (1985) proposed a five-dimensional (i.e., human nature, person and nature, time–sense, activity, and social relations) value orientations model and illustrated how this model could help therapists to understand how clients from different cultural and racial backgrounds differ in their worldviews.

Multicultural scholars have made an important contribution to the understanding of worldviews and have illustrated how important it is for psychotherapists to understand each client's unique perspective. However, as valuable as these worldview models have been, they are somewhat limited in scope and have not provided an adequate understanding of the spiritual dimension in the major metaphysical perspectives of humankind.

THREE MAJOR METAPHYSICAL WORLDVIEWS

According to Wilhelm Dilthey, although there is great variety in the philosophical and religious belief systems in the world, there are only three major types of metaphysical worldviews: naturalism, idealism of freedom, and objective idealism (Ermarth, 1978; Kluback & Weinbaum, 1957; Rickman,

1976, 1979).[2] In discussing Dilthey's typology of worldviews, Wagar (1977) described the core differences between them concisely:

> Naturalism, apprehends reality as a physical system accessible to sense experience. . . . Idealism of freedom, takes a subjective view of reality, discovering in man a will independent of nature and grounded in a transcendental spiritual realm. . . . Objective idealism, shrinks from the dualism implicit in the second. It proclaims the unity and divinity of all being. . . . The naturalist . . . defines the good life as the pursuit of happiness or power, the subjective idealist . . . defines it as obedience to conscience or divine will, and the objective idealist . . . sees it as a midpoint between the two extremes. . . . The naturalist . . . tends to subscribe to a mechanistic determinism that undercuts freedom of will, whereas the subjective idealist . . . upholds moral freedom, and the objective idealist . . . unites determinism and indeterminism. (pp. 5–6)

Examples of philosophies or worldview subtypes that can be classified within Dilthey's *naturalistic worldview* are rationalism, positivism, Marxism, existentialism, and secular humanism (Wagar, 1977). The Western, or monotheistic, world religious traditions: Judaism, Christianity, Islam, Zoroastrianism, and Sikhism are major representations of the *idealism of freedom, or subjective idealistic, worldview*. The Eastern world religious traditions (i.e., Buddhism, Hinduism, Jainism, Shintoism, Confucianism, and Taoism) are major examples of the *objective idealistic worldview*. According to Dilthey, these three major types of worldviews have coexisted during the past several millennia and have rivaled each other by providing alternate answers to the major metaphysical and existential questions of life (Ermarth, 1978; Kluback & Weinbaum, 1957; Rickman, 1976, 1979, Wagar, 1977). Of course, we emphasize that although most worldviews ultimately may be classifiable into one of Dilthey's three types, there is much individual variation in specific worldviews. Many people undoubtedly combine elements from all three worldview types, and others "may also elaborate idiosyncratic world views that draw upon the reigning orthodoxies and in some measure transcend them" (Wagar, 1977, p. 4).

As we discuss in chapter 2, the naturalistic worldview has dominated the psychotherapy and mental health professions during the past century, and religious and spiritual perspectives have been excluded from theory, research, and practice deliberately. As a result, most psychotherapists and mental health professionals are well acquainted with the naturalistic worldview, but they have less understanding and appreciation of the two major

---

[2] The Russian American sociologist Sorokin (1957) proposed a similar typology as the basis for a theory of comparative world cultures.

religious and spiritual worldviews: the Western, or monotheistic, worldview and the Eastern (polytheistic or pantheistic) spiritual worldview.

THEOLOGICAL FOUNDATIONS OF THEISTIC PSYCHOTHERAPY: THE THEISTIC WORLDVIEW

There are five major monotheistic religious traditions in the world: Judaism, Christianity, Islam, Zoroastrianism, and Sikhism (Palmer & Keller, 1989). As can be seen in Table 4.1, approximately one half of the world's people belong to one of the monotheistic world religions. Judaism, Christianity, and Islam are the major monotheistic religions of the Western world (Smart, 1994). Zoroastrianism and Sikhism are monotheistic religions as well; the majority of their followers live in India. These religions all believe in *theism*: that is, the belief that "God exists transcendent to the world as the Creator who gives to the world its original existence and sustains it in existence" (Honer & Hunt, 1987, p. 231). They also believe in monotheism, the belief that there is one Supreme Being or Supreme God (Honer & Hunt, 1987).

Judaism

The roots of Judaism can be traced to the early patriarchs of the ancient Middle East—Abraham, Isaac, and Jacob—in the second millennium B.C. (Nielsen et al., 1988; Palmer & Keller, 1989; Smart, 1994). Many scholars and Jewish people view the prophet Moses and his brother Aaron as the founders of Judaism (Palmer & Keller, 1989; Smart, 1994). In approximately 1,300 B.C., Moses led the descendents of Jacob out of bondage in Egypt to Mount Sinai. During the period in Sinai, Moses communicated with God on Mount Sinai and was called to be a leader and prophet to his people. Today Moses is still considered the prophetic basis of Jewish law and practice.

After wandering in the wilderness for 40 years, the Jewish people settled in their "Promised Land" (the land of Canaan where they built the City of Jerusalem). Eventually, the Jewish people were exiled from the Promised Land and scattered throughout the Middle East, North Africa, Europe, and other parts of the world (Palmer & Keller, 1989). After centuries of exile, the State of Israel was founded in 1948, and many Jewish people began to gather again in their ancient Promised Land.

Today there are approximately 14.5 million Jewish people in the world: about 6 million in North America, 4.5 million in Asia, and 2.5 million in Europe (D. B. Barrett & Johnson, 2002). There are now numerous subdivisions

TABLE 4.1
Adherents of All Religions by Continental Areas (Mid-2001)

Religion	Africa	Asia	Europe	Latin America	North America	Oceania	World	Percentage	Number of countries
Christians	368,244,000	317,759,000	559,359,000	486,591,000	261,752,000	25,343,000	2,019,052,000	32.9	238
Affiliated	342,819,000	312,182,000	536,588,000	481,132,000	213,038,000	21,600,000	1,907,363,000	31.1	238
Roman Catholics	123,467,000	112,086,000	285,554,000	466,226,000	71,391,000	8,327,000	1,067,053,000	17.4	235
Protestants	90,989,000	50,718,000	77,497,000	49,008,000	70,164,000	7,478,000	345,855,000	5.6	232
Orthodox	36,038,000	14,219,000	158,375,000	564,000	6,400,000	718,000	216,314,000	3.5	134
Anglicans	43,524,000	735,000	26,628,000	1,098,000	3,231,000	5,428,000	80,644,000	1.3	163
Independents	85,476,000	157,605,000	25,850,000	40,357,000	81,032,000	1,536,000	391,856,000	6.4	221
Marginal	2,502,000	2,521,000	3,606,000	6,779,000	10,747,000	468,000	26,623,000	0.4	215
Unaffiliated	25,425,000	5,577,000	22,771,000	5,459,000	48,714,000	3,743,000	111,689,000	1.8	232
Baha'is	1,779,000	3,538,000	132,000	893,000	799,000	113,000	7,254,000	0.1	218
Buddhists	139,000	356,533,000	1,570,000	660,000	2,777,000	307,000	361,985,000	5.9	126
Chinese folk religionists	33,100	385,758,000	258,000	197,000	857,000	64,200	387,167,000	6.3	89
Confucianists	250	6,277,000	10,800	0	0	24,000	6,313,000	0.1	15
Ethnic religionists	97,762,000	129,005,000	1,258,000	1,288,000	446,000	267,000	230,026,000	3.8	140
Hindus	2,384,000	813,396,000	1,425,000	775,000	1,350,000	359,000	819,689,000	13.4	114
Jains	66,900	4,207,000	0	0	7,000	0	4,281,000	0.1	10
Jews	215,000	4,476,000	2,506,000	1,145,000	6,045,000	97,600	14,484,000	0.2	134
Muslims	323,556,000	845,341,000	31,724,000	1,702,000	4,518,000	307,000	1,207,148,000	19.7	204
New religionists	28,900	101,065,000	160,000	633,000	847,000	66,900	102,801,000	1.7	60
Shintoists	0	2,669,000	0	6,900	56,700	0	2,732,000	0.0	8
Sikhs	54,400	22,689,000	241,000	0	535,000	18,500	23,538,000	0.4	34
Spiritists	2,600	2,000	134,000	12,169,000	152,000	7,100	12,466,000	0.2	55
Taoists	0	2,658,000	0	0	11,200	0	2,670,000	0.0	5
Zoroastrians	910	2,519,000	670	0	79,100	1,400	2,601,000	0.0	22
Other religionists	67,300	63,100	238,000	99,600	605,000	9,500	1,082,000	0.0	78
Nonreligious	5,170,000	611,876,000	105,742,000	16,214,000	28,994,000	3,349,000	771,345,000	12.6	236
Atheists	432,000	122,408,000	22,555,000	2,787,000	1,700,000	369,000	150,252,000	2.5	161
Total population	802,150,000	3,730,168,000	728,270,000	525,878,000	311,877,000	30,164,000	6,128,512,000	100.0	238

Note. Reprinted with permission from the *Britannica Book of the Year*, copyright 2004 by Encyclopedia Britannica, Inc. Additional information from *Names of Continents:* These follow current United Nations demographic terminology, which now divides the world into the six major areas shown in the table heading. Note that "Asia" includes the former Soviet Central Asian states, and "Europe" includes all of Russia extending eastward to Vladivostok, the Sea of Japan, and the Bering Strait. *Countries:* The last column enumerates sovereign and nonsovereign countries in which each religion or religious grouping has a numerically significant and organized following. *Christians:* Followers of Jesus Christ affiliated with churches (Church members, including children: 1,907,363,000, shown divided among the six standardized ecclesiastical megablocs), plus persons professing in censuses or polls to be Christians though not so affiliated. Figures for subgroups of Christians do not add up to the totals in the first line, because some Christians adhere to more than one denomination. *Independents:* This term here denotes members of churches and networks that regard themselves as postdenominationalist and thus independent of historic, organized, institutionalized, denominationalist Christianity. *Marginal Christians:* Members of denominations on the margins of organized mainstream Christianity (e.g., Church of Jesus Christ of Latter-Day Saints, Jehovah's Witnesses, and Christian Science). *Buddhists:* 56% Mahayana, 38% Theravada (Hinayana), 6% Tantrayana (Lamaism). *Chinese folk religionists:* Followers of traditional Chinese religion (local deities, ancestor veneration, Confucian ethics, universalism, divination, some Buddhist and Taoists elements). *Confucianists:* Non-Chinese followers of Confucius and Confucianism—mostly Koreans in Korea. *Ethnic Religionists:* Followers of local, tribal, animistic, or shamanistic religions, with members restricted to one ethnic group. *Hindus:* 70% Vaishnavites, 25% Shaivites, 2% neo-Hindus and reform Hindus. *Jews:* Adherents of Judaism. *Muslims:* 83% Sunnites, 16% Shi'ites, 1% other schools. Up to 1990, the Muslims in the former Soviet Union who had embraced Communism were not included as Muslims in this table. After the collapse of Communism in 1990–1991, these Muslims were once again enumerated as Muslims if they had returned to Islamic profession and practice. *New religionists:* Followers of Asian 20th century new religions, new religious movements, radical new crisis religions, and non-Christian syncretistic mass religions, all founded since 1800 and most since 1945. *Other Religionists:* Including a handful of religions, quasi-religions, pseudoreligions, parareligions, religious or mystic systems, and religious and semireligious brotherhoods of numerous varieties. *Nonreligious:* Persons professing no religion, nonbelievers, agnostics, free thinkers, uninterested, or dereligionized secularists who are indifferent to all religion but not militantly so. *Atheists:* Persons professing atheism, skepticism, disbelief, or irreligion, including the militantly antireligious (opposed to all religion). *Total population:* United Nations medium variant figures for mid-2001.

within Judaism; the major ones are Reformed Judaism, Conservative Judaism, and Orthodox Judaism (Palmer & Keller, 1989; Smart, 1994).

Christianity

The roots of Christianity are embedded clearly in Judaism, but Christianity emerged as a separate world faith because of the life and teaching of Jesus of Nazareth (Nielsen et al., 1988; Palmer & Keller, 1989; Smart, 1994). Jesus was born in Bethlehem of Judea sometime between 6 B.C. and A.D. 6 (Nielsen et al., 1988). Jesus was raised in the Jewish faith. At the age of about 30, he was baptized by his cousin (John the Baptist) and began his public ministry. Jesus taught about the Kingdom of God and preached a message of love, peace, service, and forgiveness. In addition, he claimed to be the Son of God, the Messiah, or the Anointed One and bore witness that he had been sent to Earth by God, his Father in Heaven, commissioned to redeem humankind from sin and death. In approximately A.D. 33, Jesus was put to death by crucifixion. According to early Christian writings (the New Testament in the Bible), three days after his death, Jesus was resurrected from the dead and appeared to his followers. Jesus commissioned his followers (apostles) to go into all of the world preaching his message.

There are approximately two billion Christians in the world today, or approximately one third of the world's population (D. B. Barrett & Johnson, 2002). The majority of Christians live in the Western world (i.e., North and South America and Europe); however, Christians can be found throughout the world. There are approximately 260 million Christians in North America (close to 85% of the population). There are numerous divisions within Christianity today. The largest denomination is the Roman Catholic Church, which makes up nearly half of the world's Christians (D. G. Barrett, 1996). Eastern and Oriental Orthodox churches number about 216 million (D. B. Barrett & Johnson, 2002). Another major division in Christianity is Protestantism, which had its beginnings in the Reformation. Many denominations fall within Protestantism, including the Episcopalian, Methodist, Lutheran, Presbyterian, Congregational, Mennonite, Unitarian, and Baptist denominations (Palmer & Keller, 1989). Followers of newer denominations that are Christian but differ in some respects from mainstream Christianity include Mormons, Jehovah's Witnesses, and Seventh-Day Adventists.

Islam

The roots of Islam, like those of Judaism, can be traced to Abraham, but Islam originated as a new world faith because of the life and teachings of the prophet Muhammad (Farah, 1994; Nielsen et al., 1988; Palmer & Keller, 1989; Smart, 1994). Muhammad was born in A.D. 570 in Mecca.

In A.D. 610, according to tradition, Muhammad was praying and engaging in religious devotions in the hills above Mecca when he had a vision of the angel Gabriel (Farah, 1994; Nielsen et al., 1988; Palmer & Keller, 1989; Smart, 1994). Muhammad had other revelatory experiences that started him on his mission as a messenger of God (Allah). Muslims also believe that God's eternal speech and words were revealed to the prophet Muhammad and are recorded in the Qur'an, the Muslim holy book. Although Muhammad's message at first found little acceptance in Mecca, after establishing a following elsewhere (the city of Medina), Muhammad eventually returned to Mecca and became its leader (Farah, 1994; Nielsen et al., 1988; Palmer & Keller, 1989; Smart, 1994).

There are approximately 1.2 billion Muslims in the world (D. B. Barrett & Johnson, 2002). The major population centers of Islam are in North Africa (e.g., Morocco, Algeria, Libya, Egypt), Asia (e.g., Turkey, Iran, Iraq, Jordan, Kuwait, Saudi Arabia, Pakistan), and Indonesia (Palmer & Keller, 1989; Smart, 1994). There also are approximately 4.5 million Muslims in North America (D. B. Barrett & Johnson, 2002). There are numerous subdivisions or traditions within Islam; however, the two major traditions today are orthodox, or Sunni Islam, and Shi'ah, or Shi'ite Islam (Farah, 1994; Nielsen et al., 1988).

Zoroastrianism

Zoroastrianism originated in ancient Persia, the geographical area today known as Iran (Nigosian, 1994). Zarathustra, also known by his Greek name Zoroaster, was the prophet–founder. Zarathustra was born, it is believed, sometime before 600 B.C. According to tradition, Zarathustra had a vision in which he was met by a supernatural messenger who led him into the presence of the Supreme God, where he was given a commission to preach his message for the benefit of all humankind (Boyce, 1979, 1984).

Today there are about 2.6 million Zoroastrians in the world (D. B. Barrett & Johnson, 2002). Zoroastrianism is practically unknown in the world outside of India—only approximately 79,000 adherents live in North America (D. B. Barrett & Johnson, 2002). Although Zoroastrianism is a small religion in terms of numbers, it is an important world religion in the sense that, according to some scholars, in ancient times it influenced the beliefs of Judaism, Christianity, and Islam (Boyce, 1979; Palmer & Keller, 1989; Smart, 1994).

Sikhism

Sikhism was founded in northern India, not far from present-day Lahore, Pakistan, in the 15th century A.D. by Guru Nanak. At the age of

30, Nanak experienced a life-changing vision in which he reported that he was carried up to God's presence and was told that there was "neither the Hindu nor Muslim" (R. R. Keller, personal communication, May 8, 1996; Nielsen et al., 1988; Palmer & Keller, 1989). At this point Nanak became a guru (i.e., one who drives away darkness and preaches enlightenment; Nielsen et al., 1988). The religious teachings of Sikhism parallel the Sant tradition within Hinduism. Sikhism also has significant similarities with Islam. Guru Nanak rejected many of the teachings of popular Hinduism and "urged his followers to meditate, worship God, and to sing hymns" (Nielsen et al., 1988, p. 362).

Today there are approximately 23.5 million Sikhs in the world (D. B. Barrett & Johnson, 2002). About 85% to 90% of Sikhs live in the Indian state of Punjab in Asia. Large groups of Sikhs live in Delhi and other parts of India. Approximately 240,000 Sikhs live in Europe, and approximately 535,000 live in North America (D. B. Barrett & Johnson, 2002).

Commonalities

Table 4.2 summarizes the core metaphysical beliefs of the major monotheistic world religions. Although there is a great deal of variation between (and within) them concerning specific religious doctrines and practices, at a more general level there is surprising harmony among them concerning their global *Weltanschauung*.

In general, the worldview of all of the major monotheistic world religions includes the belief that there is a God, a Supreme Being, who created the world and the human race. Human beings were placed on the Earth by the Creator for a divine purpose. Each has a spiritual essence or soul, which continues to exist after death. Human beings can receive spiritual guidance and strength from God through prayer, meditation, and other spiritual practices.

The monotheistic world religions all believe that although there is much that is evil, materialistic, and spiritually destructive on the Earth, human beings have agency and can choose to overcome and transcend these influences. God has revealed moral truths and principles to human beings to guide their personal behavior and social relations. Spiritual growth and progression are both desirable and possible, and they can lead to enlightenment and fulfillment. The human soul and personality do not cease to exist at the death of the mortal body but continue to live in some type of an afterlife. Human beings will someday be judged by God for how they lived their mortal lives. The reward or position human beings will receive in the afterlife is influenced by their obedience to God's teachings and by their spiritual growth and progression in this life.

TABLE 4.2

Metaphysical Beliefs of the Major Western (Monotheistic) Religious Traditions

Worldview dimension	Judaism	Christianity	Islam	Zoroastrianism	Sikhism
View of deity	There is one Supreme Being. God, also called Elohim or Jehovah, is the creator of all things. God is eternal, all-powerful, and all-knowing. Most modern Jews believe God does not have a physical body, but they believe God is real. God revealed Himself and His law through Moses, as recorded in the Torah (the Pentateuch, or first five books of the Old Testament).	Most Christians believe in the Holy Trinity: God the Father, God the Son, and God the Holy Ghost. Some Christians believe that the Holy Trinity is one in essence, but other Christians believe they are one in purpose but not in essence. God is a personal God. He is the creator of all things. God is eternal, all-powerful, all-knowing, and all-loving. God has revealed Himself and His words in Jesus Christ, of whom the Bible bears witness as the Son of God.	God, called Allah, is the only true God or Supreme Being. Allah is the creator of the universe and of human beings. God is all-powerful, all-seeing, all-hearing, all-speaking, and all-knowing. God does not have a body but is real. God is eternal. God has revealed His eternal speech and words to human beings in the Qur'an (the holy book of scripture).	There is one supreme God, called Ahura Mazda. There are also six lesser immortal beings who work in concert with God. In the view of some, Ahura Mazda is an anthropomorphic God. God is just and benevolent. God has revealed Himself to human beings in the Avesta (sacred books of Zoroastrianism).	There is one God, called 1 Oankar or Satnam. God is the creator and sustainer of all things. God is formless but is a personal God. God is immanent in His creations and transcendent. God is eternal. God has revealed Himself through the 10 gurus in the Guru Granth Sahib (a body of sacred scriptures that are viewed as an "embodiment of God").

(continued)

TABLE 4.2 (Continued)

Worldview dimension	Judaism	Christianity	Islam	Zoroastrianism	Sikhism
View of human nature	Human beings are made in God's image; humans are the high point of God's creations. Human beings have a spiritual soul that is immortal. People have free will and have the agency to obey God's laws.	Human beings were created by God. Humans have a body and an immortal spirit or soul. Most Christians believe that human beings have free will—the power to choose good over evil. Many Christians believe that there is something basically evil in human nature because of the fall of Adam and Eve, which can be corrected only by God's grace, and that people's own self-effort cannot free them from sin.	Human beings are God's creations. People have both a body and an immortal soul. Some controversy exists in Islam over the question of free will. Some believe God determines human actions, whereas others say that humans have agency to choose, particularly those actions on which they are judged.	Human beings are the creations of God. They have a body and an immortal spirit. Human beings have the power to choose between good and evil.	Human beings are the creations of God. They have an immortal spirit. Human beings are free to choose between good and evil and to show devotion to God.
Purpose of life	The Jewish people are God's chosen people and have a mission to help make the world a better place morally and spiritually. Individually, each person needs to obey God's commandments to develop morally and to qualify to live in a place of peace and eternal progress in the world to come.	God wishes to have a relationship with human beings. God created people to enjoy His divine presence forever. Human beings are to glorify God by having faith in Jesus Christ and by repenting of their sins and following the teachings of Jesus. Those who do so will receive God's grace, be forgiven, and be welcomed into God's presence in the hereafter (Heaven).	Human beings must learn to submit to God's will, obey His law, and do good. They must give up worldly things and overcome their vices. Those who do so will be rewarded in the hereafter (Heaven).	Human beings may have lived in a spiritual existence before mortal life. They must learn to choose between good and evil and to obey and serve God. The faithful must cooperate in defeating the powers of evil. The righteous will be rewarded with peace, happiness, and immortality.	The ultimate purpose of life is to obtain spiritual liberation from the cycle of rebirth and to achieve union with God and to receive spiritual insight in this life. People must learn to choose good over evil and develop love, faith, and humility.

View of spirituality	Obedience to God's laws and worshipping Him leads to character development (acquisition of qualities such as goodness, humility, and holiness). Humans can communicate with God through prayer and worship. God responds to people reaching out to Him.	Accepting Jesus Christ as Savior will lead one to good works, a moral life, and devotion and worship. This will allow one to receive the influence of the Holy Spirit and partake of other fruits of the spirit (e.g., love). Through prayer and the influence of the Holy Spirit, human beings can communicate with God and receive God's help, influence, and grace.	Obeying God's law as revealed in the Qur'an and "giving up" worldly things allows people to grow spiritually. The path of spiritual growth involves overcoming vices such as arrogance, greed, and dishonesty. This leads to higher levels of religious experience and union with God. Humans can communicate with God through prayer, meditation, and repetition of set phrases or the name of God.	Choosing good over evil, prayer, and meditation will help people on the pathway to spiritual growth. Human beings can communicate with God through prayer.	Through dependence on God, human beings can overcome their ego and pride and achieve spiritual liberation and growth and a mystical union with God. Spiritual growth leads one to the qualities of love, faith, mercy, and humility. Humans can communicate with and worship God, particularly through prayer and singing.
View of morality	God revealed His law at Sinai. There are 613 commandments or religious duties (Mitzvat). Charity, good deeds, respect for human dignity, humility, truthfulness, controlling one's anger, and not being envious are examples of other morally good behaviors and qualities.	There are both good and evil in the world. Human beings must learn to choose good over evil. Accepting Jesus as Savior and following His teachings is the path to righteousness and morality. Morality includes behaviors and qualities such as love, service, honesty, family devotion, and moral-ity includes behaviors such as drunkenness, adultery, and fornication.	God has revealed His law in the Qur'an. Those who worship Allah and obey His laws are good. There are five classes of moral actions: those that are obligatory, recommended, prohibited, disapproved, and indifferent. Examples of prohibited behaviors include drinking of alcohol and immodesty of dress. Fasting and prayer, payment of alms, and devotion to the family are examples of morally good behaviors.	There are two basic powers in the world: truth versus the lie. There is an adversary (a "Hostile Spirit"). Having children is good, but practices such as adultery and prostitution are evil.	There are five evil passions: lust, anger, covetousness, attachment to worldly things, and pride. From these five passions comes all violence and falsehood. A number of behaviors are considered immoral (e.g., gambling, theft, smoking, cutting one's hair, marital infidelity).

(continued)

TABLE 4.2 (Continued)

Worldview dimension	Judaism	Christianity	Islam	Zoroastrianism	Sikhism
View of life after death	The souls of human beings live on in a spirit world after mortal death. Eventually the bodies of the dead will be resurrected, although many Jews believe only in the immortality of the soul. There will also be a judgment in which people will be judged for what they did with their lives. The righteous will go to a place of peace, where they will continue to progress and enjoy a nearness to God. Those who were evil will not enjoy this state.	The spirits or souls of human beings continue to exist after mortal death. Someday there will be a judgment and a resurrection of the body and spirit (or at least a spiritual resurrection). Those who have accepted and followed Jesus will be accepted into God's presence to enjoy Him forever. Those who have done evil and who have not accepted Jesus will be banished to hell, outer darkness, or extinction.	The souls of human beings do not cease to exist at mortal death. There will be a judgment at the final hour of the world. The dead will be resurrected. The wicked will be punished by God by being sent to hell, and the good will be rewarded in heaven.	The spirits of those who die hover near their earthly body for 3 days and nights before passing to an initial individual judgment. The spirit and the body will be joined at the time of the resurrection, or "Final Renovation." Good people will be rewarded with immortality. The spirits of the wicked have no such assurance.	Followers believe in reincarnation. Devotion to God leads to spiritual liberation and a release from the cycle of birth and rebirth. Such a release allows human beings to enter into a realm of infinite and eternal bliss and union with God. Those who are evil obtain adverse karma, which endlessly protracts the cycle of reincarnation.

Note. Sources consulted: Boyce (1984); Carmody and Carmody (1989); Farah (1994); Jacobs (1984); Nielsen et al. (1988); Nigosian (1994); Palmer and Keller (1989); and Smart (1994).

THEISTIC WORLDVIEW CONTRASTED
WITH EASTERN SPIRITUALITY
AND SCIENTIFIC NATURALISM

There are six major Eastern world religious traditions: Hinduism, Buddhism, Jainism, Shintoism, Confucianism, and Taoism (Palmer & Keller, 1989; Smart, 1993). Approximately one fourth of the world's population adheres to one of these religions (D. G. Barrett, 1996). Most adherents to the Eastern religious traditions believe in either polytheism or pantheism, although some are atheistic or agnostic. *Polytheism* is the belief that "there is a multitude of personal gods, each responsible for a different sphere of life" (Percesepe, 1991, p. 469). *Pantheism* is the belief that "God is identical with nature; all is God, and God is all. . . . Everything exists ultimately in God" (Percesepe, 1991, p. 469).

Hinduism

The roots of Hinduism can be traced back to the second millennium B.C. to the arrival of a cultural group called the Aryans in India, who mingled with the Dravidians, the prehistoric inhabitants of India (Nielsen et al., 1988; Palmer & Keller, 1989). The religious beliefs of these two groups of people became intermingled and contributed to the formation of classical Hinduism (Nielsen et al., 1988; Palmer & Keller, 1989). Hinduism has no personal founder, and it does not have a central authority or structured organization. The beliefs and practices of individual Hindus tend to be highly diverse, because Hinduism has assimilated much from other religions in the world (Palmer & Keller, 1989). For example, some Hindus believe in many deities, including nature deities such as Indra (the atmospheric god) and Agni (the god of fire), whereas other Hindus believe in only one God. Ultimately, most Hindus believe that there is one absolute reality, or Brahman-Atman (i.e., that "everything in the universe is one"; Nigosian, 1994, p. 85).

Despite this diversity in belief, or perhaps because of it, Hinduism "has provided a framework for the life of most Indians for well over two thousand years. . . . Hinduism continues to be the dominant religious tradition of India" (Nielsen et al., 1988, p. 132). There are approximately 819 million Hindu people in the world today (D. B. Barrett & Johnson, 2002). Approximately 80% of the people in India consider themselves to be Hindus. A substantial minority of the people in Bangladesh are Hindus. There are approximately 1.3 million Hindus in North America and approximately 1.4 million in Europe (D. B. Barrett & Johnson, 2002).

Buddhism

Buddhism originated in India in the fifth century B.C. Its founder was Siddhartha Gautama, who was born, it is believed, in 563 B.C. in Lumbini, India. According to Buddhist tradition, Siddhartha Gautama achieved enlightenment and became the Buddha (the Awakened One). In so doing, Buddha rejected the Hindu gods and preached a doctrine of enlightened equality. Buddha did not consider his message to be a divine revelation, nor did he advocate dependence on a group of gods or on a Supreme Being (Nielsen et al., 1988; Palmer & Keller, 1989).

There are approximately 362 million Buddhists in the world (D. B. Barrett & Johnson, 2002), with the majority of them living in Asia. In North America there are approximately 2.8 million Buddhists and in Europe approximately 1.6 million (D. B. Barrett & Johnson, 2002). There are three main schools of Buddhism: Theravada Buddhism (meaning "Way of the Elders"), Mahayana Buddhism (meaning "The Greater Vehicle"), and Vajrayana Buddhism (meaning "Vehicle of the Thunderbolt;" Nielsen et al., 1988; Palmer & Keller, 1989). Theravada Buddhism is today the dominant religion in Ceylon (Sri Lanka) and much of mainland Southeast Asia (Nielsen et al., 1988). Mahayana Buddhism is found chiefly in China, as well as Taiwan, Korea, Vietnam, and Japan (Nielsen et al., 1988). Vajrayana Buddhism, "which can be treated as an aspect of Mahayana" (Palmer & Keller, 1989, p. 53), is "found mainly in Tibet and Mongolia, but also in Japan, where it is known as Shingon" (Nielsen et al., 1988, p. 203).

The schools of Buddhism differ somewhat in their understanding of concepts such as the existence of deities and the nature of nirvana (one's release from mortal existence). For example, Theravada Buddhism is functionally atheistic because it accepts that, although some "gods may exist, they cannot help others gain the release from the wheel of rebirth" (Palmer & Keller, 1989, p. 54). Mahayana Buddhism teaches that there are many deities and helping beings to worship and adore (Palmer & Keller, 1989). However, most Buddhists in Eastern countries practice their religion within the context of native beliefs, folklores, and superstitions that existed long before Buddhist teachings (Palmer & Keller, 1989). Therefore, there is a difference between Buddhist philosophy and popular Eastern Buddhism. Several schools of Buddhism also have spread to North America, including Zen Buddhism and Nyingma Tibetan Buddhism (Palmer & Keller, 1989).

Jainism

Jainism originated in the fifth century B.C. in northeastern India. Its founder was Vardhamana Mahavira (Nielsen et al., 1988; Nigosian, 1994; Palmer & Keller, 1989). Mahavira, according to legends and traditions, spent his youth in luxury and then left his home at age 30 to seek salvation through self-denial. At the age of 42, after wandering as a naked ascetic, he found full enlightenment and became a "conqueror" (a *jina*; Nielsen et al., 1988; Nigosian, 1994; Palmer & Keller, 1989). Mahavira did not believe in a Supreme Being or other deities; he believed that the universe is eternal and uncreated (Nielsen et al., 1988). There are approximately 4.3 million Jains in the world (D. B. Barrett & Johnson, 2002). Most Jains are "concentrated in the northern states of Rajasthan, Gujarat, and Maharashtra, and in central India" (Palmer & Keller, 1989, p. 35). There are approximately 7,000 Jains in North America (D. B. Barrett & Johnson, 2002).

Shinto

Shinto is the native religion of the people of Japan. The origins of Shinto are unknown, as is a possible founder. It is believed that the formative years of Shinto were during the third to the sixth centuries A.D. Shinto has been the religion of the common people and has been passed on in their daily lives. Shintoists do not believe in a Supreme Being or transcendent deities, although there are a variety of deities that are not omnipotent or transcendent. There are many different Shinto groups, including Shrine Shinto, Sectarian Shinto, Pure Shinto, Confucian Shinto, Mountain Shinto, Purification Shinto, Redemptive Shinto, and Folk (Popular) Shinto (Nigosian, 1994). Many of these Shinto groups are composed of subgroups. There are approximately 2.7 million Shintoists in the world, with the majority of them living in Asia (D. B. Barrett & Johnson, 2002). Shinto today has more adherents in Japan than does any other religion (Nigosian, 1994). There are approximately 57,000 Shintoists in North America (D. B. Barrett & Johnson, 2002).

Confucianism

Confucianism originated in the fifth century B.C. (Nielsen et al., 1988; Nigosian, 1994; Palmer & Keller, 1989). Its founder, Confucius, was born in the present-day Shantung peninsula of China. Confucius sought political office for many years but never achieved this goal. Later in life, Confucius resumed teaching, studying, writing, and editing. He died at the age of 72. Before his death, the number of his followers had grown steadily and continued to grow after his death. Confucius thought of himself as a devoted student of antiquity and a transmitter of the wisdom of the past. Confucius was generally not interested in metaphysical questions, and his writings did not contain teachings about a Supreme Being or other deities, although there is evidence that he believed in a personal heaven (Palmer & Keller, 1989). Confucianism is primarily a social and political philosophy, although it does have some moral and religious dimensions in that it states that human beings need to learn to live with inner virtue and proper conduct. For the past 2,000 years, "the teachings of Confucius have had a great influence on the thought, government institutions, literature, arts, and social customs of China" (Nielsen et al., 1988, p. 272). Confucianism has also been influential in Japan, Korea, and Vietnam (Nielsen et al., 1988; Nigosian, 1994; Palmer & Keller, 1989). There are approximately 6.3 million Confucians in the world today, with almost all of them living in Asia (D. B. Barrett & Johnson, 2002).

Taoism

Taoism originated in the fifth century B.C. in China (Nielsen et al., 1988; Nigosian, 1994; Palmer & Keller, 1989), founded by Lao Tzu. Tzu, it is said, worked in government circles in Loyang, the Chinese imperial capital. Eventually, he became disillusioned with political and government service and left it. Before leaving Loyang, Tzu wrote a book titled the *Tao Te Ching* (meaning "The Way of the Tao," or "The Wisdom of Tao"; Palmer & Keller, 1989). According to some scholars, Tzu was a contemporary of Confucius and disagreed with him about a number of beliefs. Tzu did not believe in a Supreme Being or in deities of any kind, although he believed in the Tao, or "Way" (an impersonal principle that gives order and harmony to the universe; Nigosian, 1994; Palmer & Keller, 1989). Religious Taoism came into existence some time around the second or first century B.C. and moved away from a purely philosophical belief system to become a "widely accepted cult whose members practiced divination, exorcism, healing and sorcery"; they believed in some deities and in immortality (Palmer & Keller, 1989, p. 71). There are approximately 2.7 million Taoists in the world today, with almost all of them living in Asia (D. B. Barrett & Johnson, 2002).

Commonalities

There is much diversity in belief among the six Eastern religious traditions, more so than among the five monotheistic world religions. Because of this diversity, it is difficult to find commonalities among the Eastern religions. Nevertheless, some broad generalizations are possible. First, for the most part the Eastern religions do *not* teach that there is a transcendent or Supreme God or Creator. Instead, Hinduism, Mahayana Buddhism, Jainism, Shinto, and Religious Taoism teach that there are many gods or deities (polytheism) that, along with all of nature and humanity, are all ultimately One. These religions do concern themselves with metaphysical and mystical questions. Confucianism and philosophical Taoism do not concern themselves with gods or deities and could perhaps be thought of as atheistic or agnostic. All the Eastern religious traditions either explicitly or implicitly affirm that human beings have free will and the capacity to choose how to live their lives. All of these religions also reject ethically hedonistic philosophies. Instead, they teach that there are moral paths, or ways of living one's life, that are desirable, ethical, moral, and honorable and that following these paths will lead to enlightenment, peace, happiness, honor, and ideal relationships.

The major purpose of life, according to the polytheistic Eastern traditions, is to gain freedom from the constraints of the flesh and society and to achieve harmony and union with the divine (S. J. Palmer, personal communication, June 5, 1996). Another major purpose of life is to learn to live in harmony with the moral or ethical path or way. Although most of the Eastern religions reject the idea that spiritual assistance and communication with a transcendent God is possible, the polytheistic ones do believe that assistance from deities or helping beings is available. Most of the Eastern religions also reject the idea that personal identity continues in an afterlife. They teach that individual identity eventually ceases either in extinction or in some type of spiritual enlightenment or unity with the impersonal and eternal divine essence, or the One.

Table 4.3 compares and contrasts the core metaphysical beliefs of the theistic worldview with the Eastern and scientific naturalistic worldviews. In such a brief table, it is necessary, of course, to oversimplify the metaphysical beliefs of each of these major positions. Nevertheless, Table 4.3 does provide some insight into the similarities and differences between them. The Western theistic worldview and the naturalistic, scientific worldviews differ the most dramatically. Their metaphysical beliefs across all six worldview dimensions are almost diametrically opposed, although there is some agreement about the notions that pursuing truth, harmonious relationships, and the betterment of humanity is desirable and that there are some moral or ethical principles that if followed can promote healthy social and interpersonal relations. The Western and Eastern spiritual worldviews have some similarities, including the general notions that (a) some sort of harmony with an eternal principle or essence (with God or an impersonal One) is possible; (b) human beings have free will; (c) there are moral or ethical principles or laws with which human beings should seek to live in harmony; and (d) there are paths or ways that lead to personal and social harmony, enlightenment, growth, peace, and happiness.

The discrepancies between the Eastern spiritual worldview and the naturalistic, scientific worldview are less dramatic than are the differences between the Western spiritual worldview and the naturalistic, scientific worldview. The Eastern and naturalistic worldviews tend to be in agreement

TABLE 4.3

Comparison of the Theistic Worldview With the Eastern Spiritual and Scientific–Naturalistic Worldviews

Worldview	View of deity	View of human nature	Purpose of life	View of spirituality	View of morality	View of life after death
Western (monotheistic)	There is a God, a Supreme Being, who created the universe, the Earth, and human beings. God is eternal, omnipotent, and all-knowing. God loves and assists human beings.	Human beings are creations of God. Human beings have an eternal soul or spirit. Human beings have free will and the capacity to choose good over evil and to obey God's commandments.	There is a transcendent, divine purpose to life. Human beings are here on Earth to learn to be obedient to God's will, to choose good over evil, and to prepare to live in a joyful and peaceful afterlife.	Human beings can communicate with God through prayer and meditation. People grow spiritually as they obey God's will, worship Him, and love and serve their fellow human beings.	God has revealed laws and commandments to guide human behavior. Obedience to God's laws promotes spiritual growth, harmonious social relations, and personal happiness, and prepares people for rewards in the afterlife.	The spirits or souls of human beings continue to exist after mortal death. There is an afterlife of peace and joy for those who live righteously in mortal life. In the afterlife the wicked are punished or suffer for their sins.
Eastern	There is no Supreme Being or God. There may be nature deities or helping beings, but they are not all-powerful and all-knowing. There may be an eternal, impersonal, universal essence, or One.	Human beings may or may not have an eternal soul. Individual identity eventually ends either in extinction or in mystical unity with the eternal, universal One. Human beings do have free will and the capacity to choose a path that leads to enlightenment and harmonious relationships.	The purpose of life is to learn to follow a path to enlightenment and harmony, to live an ethical and moral life so that one can obtain release from endless rounds of rebirth, or at least so that one can enjoy honor, peace, and ideal relationships in this life.	Spiritual enlightenment comes from living in harmony with the ethical path and through meditation and self-denial. Enlightenment leads to insight into the true nature of the universe and of reality.	A variety of notions exist about what is moral and desirable behavior. There tends to be agreement that a moral path or way does exist and that following it leads to enlightenment and to personal and social harmony.	Considerable variety regarding beliefs about the afterlife, including belief that people cease to exist at death, that they are immortal but no longer have individual identity and are part of the universal One, or that some type of individual soul persists after death.

Naturalistic, scientific	There is no God or Supreme Being, nor are there any supernatural gods or transcendent forces of any kind. The universe was produced and is maintained by natural forces, processes, and laws (e.g., the big bang, organic evolution).	Human beings are the end product of millions of years of evolutionary processes, as theorized by Charles Darwin and evolutionary scientists. Life originated on this Earth through natural processes; there was no God or transcendent force involved in the creation of life. Human beings do not have an immortal spirit or soul. Human consciousness can be completely accounted for with biological and physiological explanations. Human beings may or may not have free will depending on the particular naturalistic theory.	There is no transcendent purpose or meaning in life. The only purpose or meaning in life is that which human beings construct or invent for themselves. Pursuing truth and knowledge and contributing to the betterment and welfare of humanity are seen as meaningful purposes for science.	Spirituality is just another word for naturalistic phenomena (i.e., psychological, physiological, and cognitive processes). There are no transcendent spiritual realities. Human beings cannot communicate with a God because there is no God to communicate with.	There are no moral absolutes or universals. Societies and groups may construct moral and ethical guidelines to help regulate social functioning and to protect the welfare of individuals, but such moral and ethical guidelines are relativistic and may be suitable for that particular society or group.	There is no life after death. When human beings die, they cease to exist.

that there is no transcendent God or Supreme Being, although the naturalistic worldview rejects the idea of polytheism. The Eastern notion that there is some type of mystical eternal One is not totally compatible with the naturalistic worldview, although this notion is easier to reconcile with the naturalistic worldview than the monotheistic belief in a transcendent Supreme Being.

Because the Eastern spiritual traditions (particularly Theravada Buddhism, Shinto, Confucianism, and Philosophical Taoism) say less about questions regarding the "world to come"—such as whether there is an immortal soul, a final judgment, and an afterlife—than do the monotheistic religious traditions, the naturalistic worldview conflicts less with the Eastern worldview than with the Western view. Of course, an exception is the Buddhist, Hindu, and Jain beliefs in reincarnation, which are incompatible with the naturalistic worldview. The emphasis of the Eastern traditions on living in harmony with the universe and following an ethical path that promotes good social relations seems compatible with some of the humanistic currents within the contemporary naturalistic, scientific worldview.

The naturalistic (scientific), subjective idealist (Western or monotheistic), and objective idealistic (Eastern) worldviews continue to compete for the cognitive and emotional allegiance of human beings throughout the world. Adherents to each of these three major perspectives can be found among intelligent, rational, good people throughout the world. In our global society, where communication and cultural barriers are rapidly breaking down, these views conflict more frequently and more directly than in past centuries. Unfortunately, these clashes of cultures and worldviews create anxiety, tension, and intrapsychic and interpersonal conflict for many people. Distrust, suspicion, and violent confrontations between people of different races, cultures, and religions are widespread in the world and can be attributed, in part at least, to differences in beliefs. We hope that understanding and tolerance of conflicting worldviews will increase so that peace and harmony will eventually prevail.

We believe that both the Western and Eastern spiritual worldviews have much of value to contribute to mainstream psychotherapy. They can enrich the understanding of human personality, the practice of psychotherapy, and the processes of healing and change. At the least, a better understanding and appreciation of the Western and Eastern spiritual perspectives should help psychotherapists and mental health professionals to work more sensitively with clients who approach life with these belief systems. In this book we explore how the theistic worldview can contribute to theories of personality and psychotherapy. Without prejudice, we leave the task of exploring the contributions of the Eastern spiritual traditions to other scholars (e.g., Epstein, 1995; Rubin, 1996).

PHILOSOPHICAL FOUNDATIONS
OF THEISTIC PSYCHOTHERAPY

The postmodern challenges to modernistic science and philosophy during the past several decades have made space for alternative philosophies that are more compatible with the theistic worldview. Our theistic framework for psychotherapy is grounded in a number of philosophical assumptions about human nature, ethics, and epistemology, including *scientific theism, theistic holism, human agency, moral universalism, theistic relationism, altruism,* and *contextuality* (see Table 4.4). To fully discuss all of these assumptions and their implications is beyond the scope of this book; this has been done more fully elsewhere (e.g., Bergin, 1980a, 1985; Howard & Conway, 1986; Jones, 1994; Slife, 2004; Slife & Gantt, 1999; Slife, Hope, & Nebeker, 1999; Slife & Williams, 1995; Williams, 1992). Our purpose here is to briefly introduce readers to these assumptions and to mention why we think they provide a more viable foundation for a theistic strategy than do naturalistic assumptions.

Scientific Theism

The resurgence of humanistic–existential thought, the emergence of the cognitive revolution, and the postmodern movements in support of hermeneutics, narratives, qualitative research, and social constructivism have created a logical space for a spiritual strategy in science. We agree with the changes in philosophy of science associated with these movements that affirm human agency versus determinism, humanism versus naturalism, and probability versus mechanism (Neimeyer & Mahoney, 1995). However, we build on these trends by adding explicitly religious and spiritual content, and we use the term *scientific theism* as the label for our viewpoint.

The most important axiom of scientific theism is that God exists and can communicate with human beings through spiritual means (Bergin, 1980a). Scientific theism also assumes that God is the creator of the universe, the Earth, and life. Scientific theism, therefore, rejects *scientific naturalism* in its atheistic form (Griffin, 2000). We think it is unnecessary to exclude God from scientific theories or from the scientific discovery process. Ultimately, the most useful scientific theories and interpretations will provide insight into the role of divine intelligence in the origins and operations of the universe. In these ways, our scientific theism is similar to other perspectives of theistic science that have been proposed, including Johnson's and Plantinga's *theistic realism* (P. E. Johnson, 1993; Plantinga, 1991a, 1991b) and Griffin's and Whitehead's *naturalistic theism* (Griffin, 2000, 2001). We recognize that there are important differences between various theistic perspectives of

TABLE 4.4
Philosophical Foundations of Theistic Psychology and Psychotherapy

Philosophical perspective	Strengths for behavioral scientists and psychotherapists
Scientific theism: God is the ultimate creative and controlling force in the universe and the ultimate reality. Human beings can understand God and the universe, although this knowledge will always be incomplete and distorted. Scientific (rational and empirical) methods can discover some aspects of reality, but spiritual ways of knowing (intuition and inspiration) are also needed. Epistemological and methodological pluralism are endorsed.	Provides a richer, more positive view of the world and human nature than scientific naturalism; in harmony with the spiritual worldviews of most people, the majority of psychotherapy clients; leaves room for common realities that most people presuppose in practice, including agency, responsibility, meaning and purpose, genuine love and altruism, and invisible realities such as spiritual communion with God
Theistic holism: Humans are holistic spiritual beings and cannot be reduced simply to biology, mind, or relationships. They are composed of an eternal spirit or soul. The human spirit interacts with and influences other dimensions of reality, including the physical, cognitive, emotional, interpersonal, and cultural. Humans cannot be adequately understood by reducing or dividing them into smaller units or by ignoring the spiritual dimension.	Affirms the spiritual worth and unlimited potential of human beings; affirms the eternal nature of the human soul and personality; avoids dehumanizing people into smaller, mechanistic, deterministic parts; provides a positive view of human nature—a view that may help lead to a more "positive psychology" in the mainstream behavioral sciences
Agency: Human beings have moral agency and the capacity to choose and regulate their behavior. Human behavior has antecedents, such as biological and environmental influences that may limit a person's choices in some situations, but not their agency. Choices have consequences.	Affirms the reality of human agency, choice, responsibility and accountability, and thus is consistent with beliefs that are presupposed in practice by virtually all psychotherapists and clients; acknowledges that agency is not absolute and that all events, including human actions and emotions, have meaningful antecedents (e.g., biological realities, environmental influences, unconscious processes, childhood experiences) that can set some limits on human choices
Moral universalism: There are universal moral principles or values that influence healthy psychological and spiritual development, although the application of these values may vary depending on the time, context, and other competing values. Some values are more healthy and moral than others.	Affirms the importance of values and lifestyle choices in human development and functioning; provides a moral and ethical framework or rationale that therapists and clients can use to evaluate whether values and lifestyle choices are healthy; helps therapists and clients avoid the incoherency of ethical relativism, which differs from cultural relativism

Theistic relationism: Human beings are inherently relational. Humans can be understood through the study of their relationships with other human beings and with God.	Helps therapists and clients avoid a narrow, individualistic focus that can lead to preoccupation with self and alienation from others; affirms the importance of relationships and community and encourages social conscience and connection with others and with God
Altruism: Human beings often forgo their own rewards (pleasure) for the welfare of others. Responsibility, self-sacrifice, suffering, love, and altruistic service are valued above personal gratification.	Affirms the value of self-sacrifice and service to others and thereby helps promote love and relationships; promotes treatment goals and interventions that are concerned with familial and societal welfare
Contextuality: At "least some of the properties and qualities of things . . . come from outside the thing—in its context" (Slife, 2004, p. 48). There are real phenomena that are contextual, unique, and private—phenomena that are not necessarily empirically observable, generalizable, or repeatable (e.g., transcendent spiritual experiences).	Reminds therapists about the importance of context and culture in treatment; affirms the importance of tailoring treatment interventions to fit the unique issues and characteristics of each client; reminds therapists, clients, and researchers that nonobservable, infrequent, and private experiences may be real and important

science, but it is beyond the scope of this book to consider them (see Griffin, 2000).

The notion that God, in person, in spirit, and in intelligence, is behind part of or sustaining of all existence is fundamental. We want to be clear that our references to spiritual realities are not occult, pantheistic, or part of numerous popular spiritualistic movements. Our view is distinctly theistic and generally in the Western tradition that dominates in North American culture; however, we embrace some aspects of spiritual humanism and Eastern spirituality that seem to be consistent with newer developments in philosophy and science and that can also be in harmony with theism. We are also integrative in that we assume that honest and flexible searches for truth and understanding, whether in philosophy, the sciences, humanities, arts, or theologies—which are disciplined and subjected to critique—have something significant to offer our picture of how and why the Creator works and what part we have in the grander scheme (Gorsuch, 2002; Rayburn & Richmond, 2002).

In their provocative review of trends in the biological and physical sciences as they relate to the major existential questions, Templeton and Herrmann (1994) pointed to mind-stretching possibilities. They concluded their chapter on the search for reality with the following statements, which reflect their perception of prominent themes in the work of many of the most acclaimed thinkers and researchers in the natural sciences:

> Here is a world in which novelty and order are intertwined . . . [God's] action can be mediated both through the interaction of law and chance . . . through . . . new form and direction at the infinity of starting points and branching points in nonlinear chaotic processes.
>
> All that we have said seems to shout for a God of marvelous creativity who mediates in a world in dynamic flux, a world moving in the direction of ever more complex, more highly integrated form—form set free to dance . . . .
>
> Molecules, organisms, species are not fixed states of being, but rather stages of becoming. The current perspectives on reality of both science and theology seem to grasp dimly the edges of this grand paradigm of becoming. Perhaps in the end it is only God who expresses this ceaseless progression toward the highest integration and the greatest complexity. Perhaps in the end the only reality is God. (Templeton & Herrmann, 1994, pp. 162–163)

Templeton and Herrmann describe scientific theism well; however, there is more to it than metaphors from biology and physics can embrace. We think that scientific theism will eventually show how the power of God is manifested in human existence, in personal spirituality, and in positive change processes.

There are several other important themes we wish to mention here. First, scientific theism is pluralistic in that it embraces multiple "ways of knowing," including authority (both scientific and religious authority), sensory experience (empirical observation), reason, intuition and divine inspiration. Scientific theism affirms the reality and value of intuitive and inspirational ways of knowing, assuming that in the scientific process many great ideas, creations, and discoveries are given as insights to scientists through divine inspiration during or after diligent effort by the scientist (Bergin, 1979; Bergin & Strupp, 1972, p. 453; O'Grady & Richards, 2004). One implication of this view is that scientists may improve their work by more consistently exercising faith in God and by humbly seeking for enlightenment in their endeavors. A number of religious scholars, past and present, have done this, and we have received personal communications from some of them (e.g., O'Grady & Richards, 2004). This has generally been a sacred and private matter, too precious to speak of in public. Nevertheless, such inspirational processes do exist, and with proper respect and reverence they can be studied and better understood (O'Grady & Richards, 2004).

The pluralistic viewpoint of scientific theism also leads logically to the acceptance of methodological pluralism, which is the practice of using a wide range of research designs and paradigms, including quantitative and qualitative inquiry (Kazdin, 1994; Slife & Gantt, 1999). We recognize that quantitative and qualitative research traditions are based on different and often conflicting assumptions about the nature of reality and epistemology (Lincoln & Guba, 1985; Slife et al., 1999) and that these assumptions may limit or distort what researchers may study and discover, including what they are able to learn about the nature of faith and spiritual realities (Slife et al., 1999). We agree with those who have encouraged researchers to consider the assumptions of the research paradigms they are using and to be aware of the conceptual costs and benefits of these paradigms (Slife, 2004; Slife et al., 1999). We think there are advantages and disadvantages associated with each research tradition, and so we advocate the thoughtful use of both, depending on the focus of the research questions and the nature of the subject matter.

The qualitative study of personal experience, phenomenology, and constructive alternativism and the use of hermeneutic interpretations are critical, but the relativism inherent in the postmodern notion that all science is subjective is, we think, unfortunate. No matter how "new" the philosophy may be or how pluralistic research methodologies become, it would be a mistake to give up the quest for procedures that establish the reliability of observation and thus forfeit a clear means for checking one's perceptions against those of other observers. If behavioral scholarship focuses exclusively on postmodern methods, the time-tested sources of knowledge are lost. Thus, we affirm that our task is to develop spiritual models of humans that are harmonious with both qualitative descriptions and quantitative methods.

At the same time, we acknowledge that modern and postmodern strategies are currently based on opposing assumptions about human nature and opposing procedures for ascertaining knowledge about that nature (Slife & Williams, 1995; Wann, 1964). No one has theoretically reconciled these incompatibilities, but we prefer not to reject one or the other. While the debate continues, we think there are advantages to supporting both of these "ways of knowing" in the pluralistic quest to understand human experiences and phenomena.

We also acknowledge that all modes of inquiry and theory building are based on faith and "biases," including our own. All scientific and scholarly modes are culture-bound, rooted in unprovable assumptions and expressible only within contexts and by selected invented languages. The choice of how to proceed and the criteria for judging results are personal. We therefore invite readers to "come and see" whether our perspective seems promising and fruitful.

In keeping with the themes argued in chapters 1, 2, and 3 of this volume, we reject the "classical realism" that reflects strong, if not singular, commitment to a naturalistic and materialistic view of the universe. We also reject idealism and solipsism, which question whether a world independent of human perception and cognition exists or can be known (Howard, 1986; Manicas & Secord, 1983). Critical realism and postmodernism have opened scholarly pathways in directions that make our task easier, but we do not fully endorse either one. We use the term *theistic realism* to refer to our view that it is possible for scientists to gain valid understanding and knowledge about the world and about spiritual realities, although this knowledge will always be incomplete and somewhat limited and distorted by their methods, culture, and context. Nevertheless, by using multiple ways of knowing and by seeking inspiration in their scientific endeavors, scientists can advance our ability to know truth and understand the world, spiritual realities, and God (O'Grady & Richards, 2004). This is not to say that we think the existence of God or spiritual realities can be proved in a positivistic sense through science. We agree with Shafranske (2005), who suggested that clinicians and scholars might affirm the possibility of the actuality of God and spiritual realities without demanding empirical proof for them.

Theistic Holism

Holism is "the notion that many qualities of things arise only in relation to other things . . . . Holistic wholes . . . cannot be reduced to their component parts without losing their original qualities" (Slife et al., 1999, p. 66).

In fact, some holists suggest that "the parts themselves depend on the whole for their very existence" (Slife et al., 1999, p. 75). Holism is different from the assumption of atomism in that "atomism assumes that the properties of each part originate . . . from the individual part's self-contained properties. Atomistic wholes can thus be reduced to their constituent components" (Slife et al., 1999).

We agree with other scholars who have suggested that a holistic view of human beings is more compatible with theistic spiritual views of human nature than are the atomistic and reductionistic views associated with scientific naturalism (e.g., Slife et al., 1999). We prefer the term *theistic holism* to affirm the reality of the divinely created soul, something that naturalistic versions of holism have overlooked or denied. Human beings cannot be reduced to merely physiology, biology, or environment. They are composed of an eternal spirit or soul that was created by God (see chap. 5, this volume). This reflects a fundamental reality of human beings.

The human spirit interacts with and influences other dimensions of existence, including physiological, biological, cognitive, emotional, interpersonal, and cultural systems. Attempting to reduce or divide human beings into smaller units, thus ignoring their spiritual essence, cannot provide an accurate or complete understanding of human nature or human personality.

Agency

Agency is the capacity human beings have to choose and to exercise their wills in regulating their thoughts, feelings, and behaviors. Agency is different from the assumption of radical determinism, which is based on a naturalistic, mechanistic ontology and assumes that human behavior is completely determined by forces outside of human control, such as genetic, intrapsychic forces, or environmental stimuli (Slife & Williams, 1995; Williams, 2005).

God has endowed humans with agency, giving them ultimate control over their choices. However, every human is part of a specific context of possibilities. Our bodies, environments, past choices, and knowledge provide us with possibilities that vary from individual to individual. Thus, humans are free to choose from the various possibilities that surround them; however, they are not free to dictate every possibility that surrounds them. An example of how one's context can affect his or her world of possibilities without detracting from his or her agency can be illustrated with the phenomenon of addiction. If a man is predisposed to alcoholism, before taking his first drink he is free to drink alcohol or to abstain. Before his first drink he also has the possibility to live without cravings for alcohol. After choosing to consume alcohol, he is still just as free to choose whether to drink; however, as a consequence of his choice, he loses the possibility to live without alcohol cravings, at least for a time.

We agree with Williams (2005), who stated that "[a]ll events (and other things, including human actions) have meaningful antecedents, absent which the events (or things) would not occur or would not be what they are" (p. 160). In accepting this view, we reject indeterminism, the view that events and human actions are essentially random.

An agentive view is more compatible with the theistic worldview than is determinism, because it gives humans responsibility before God for their actions and justifies the consequences that God and nature may impart to them. An agentive conceptualization also leads to a more positive view of human nature in at least two important ways. First, it restores meaning to human experience. For example, if a decision to engage in a romantic relationship is caused solely by the emission and reception of pheromones, there is no real romantic love, merely chemical reactions. If a child's decision to obey his or her parents is solely the result of operant conditioning, then there is no such thing as loyalty to parents but merely reinforcement histories. If, however, individuals can make choices based on the desires of their hearts, those choices become far more meaningful.

We also see an agentive explanation of human behavior as more positive in that it gives individuals more responsibility for and control over their actions. As Slife (2004) has pointed out, assuming a deterministic cause of psychological disorders leads to deterministic treatments of such disorders, when in fact more agentive treatments may be helpful. For example, if mental health professionals assume that obsessive–compulsive disorders (OCDs) are caused solely by problems in brain physiology, they may be inclined to look solely to medications as a treatment. Alternatively, professionals who believe in the efficacy of human agency may consider alternative treatment options. Schwartz and his colleagues recently found that a volitional approach to treatment of OCD is effective, actually altering the metabolism of the brain (Schwartz, 1999).

Moral Universalism

Ethical or moral objectivism affirms the "universal validity of some moral principles" (Pojman, 1999, p. 369). Moral absolutism, the most radical form of moral objectivism, asserts that there is only one right answer to every moral or ethical situation. A more moderate form of moral objectivism, what we prefer to call *moral universalism*, sees some "moral principles as universally valid but not always applicable" (Pojman, 1999, p. 369). For example, a moral principle such as honesty could be overridden in some situations by the moral principle of the need to preserve human life. Moral objectivism differs from ethical relativism, which asserts that there are no universal moral or ethical principles—whatever an individual or society decides is moral is therefore by definition moral.

Moral universalism is a moderate version of moral objectivism (not moral absolutism), which we think is consistent with the theistic spiritual worldview. According to Ninian Smart (1983), a respected world religion scholar, "The major faiths have much in common as far as moral conduct goes. Not to steal, not to lie, not to kill, not to have certain kinds of sexual relations—such prescriptions are found across the world" (p. 117). The theistic religious traditions also agree that human beings can and should transcend hedonistic and selfish tendencies in order to grow spiritually and to promote the welfare of others.

Such universal moral principles form part of our framework. Additional values consistent with the major religions also specifically promote mental health, harmonious relationships, and spiritual growth: for example, personal and social responsibility, family commitment, self-control, marital fidelity, humility, self-sacrifice, forgiveness, interpersonal sensitivity, and honesty (Jensen & Bergin, 1988). However, the application and prioritization of these values may vary somewhat depending on the time, context, and other competing values (P. S. Richards, Rector, & Tjeltveit, 1999). Our theistic theory of personality posits that living in congruence with moral values is essential for optimal human development and well-being. Moral development, therefore, is intertwined with healthy personality and spiritual development and functioning.

The moral nature of humans has been an ongoing topic of study and debate in the field of psychology. Theorists have framed moral development in terms of cognitive-based justice reasoning (Kohlberg, 1981), relationship-based caring (Gilligan, 1982), emotion-based empathy (Eisenberg & Miller, 1987), identity-based moral narratives (Day & Tappan, 1996), and biologically evolved, culturally influenced intuitive processes (Haidt, 2001). Collectively, these theories view moral growth as involving the development of more complex and expansive perspectives of other people and the world, which allows humans to see beyond themselves to be concerned about the welfare of others. Although the various models and vast research on moral development provide helpful insights relative to the human capacity for goodness, we think that theistic perspectives offer additional understanding of this capacity.

Specifically, we posit that exercising faith in God and having spiritual experiences help humans to gain expanded, deeper, and spiritually inspired meanings and perspectives of themselves, other people, and the world, thus enabling greater goodness and morality. According to Tillich (1963), true morality is grounded in the universal spiritual nature of humans, as well as in contextual spiritual influences from God. Thus humans are seen as engaging in moral acts appropriate to any given situation by responding to their own inherent nature in concert with divine grace. William James (1947) also conveyed a perspective of morality that calls for more inclusion of the spiritual.

Theistic Relationism

Relationism is the notion that relationships are a fundamental aspect of existence. According to this view, human beings and life itself are inherently relational in nature (Slife, 2004). Relationism contrasts with individualism, which asserts that " the basic unit of human reality is the individual person, who is assumed to exist and have determinate characteristics prior to and independent of his or her social existence" (Richardson & Zeddies, 2001, p. 152). We agree with those who have suggested that rigid individualistic views create societal and personal conflict and indifference, while relational views allow for interpersonal cooperation and commitment (e.g., Clark, 1998; Etzioni, 1994).

We prefer the term *theistic relationism* to describe our theistically informed understanding about the importance and role of relationships in human development and functioning. From our perspective, true relationships involve interactions between human beings and between human beings and a living God. All of the theistic world religions emphasize the importance of relationships and community, including relationships with God (Smart, 1994). Theistic perspectives about relationships challenge the psychological view of humans as innately selfish and separate beings who focus on personal survival.

In his classic work *I and Thou*, Buber (1923/1996) argued that true relationships entail the active and reciprocal encounter of whole beings rather than the objective and possessive interaction of persons fragmented into traits or processes. Thus, individuals who engage in true relationships recognize the interdependence of their identity and the identities of others and do not attempt to compartmentalize others or themselves as categorized entities incapable of change or choice. Buber suggested that similar relationships may be experienced with God. Human encounters with God and other humans are mediated, according to Buber (1923/1996), by an enabling "spirit," which he defined as existing "not in the I but between I and You . . . not like the blood that circulates in you but like the air in which you breathe" (p. 89). It is through this spirit and through whole and reciprocal relations with God that truly genuine and loving relationships with other persons are possible. According to this view, all relationships, whether person-to-person or person-to-God, are mediated by an enabling love or spirit.

C. S. Lewis (1960/1991) also emphasized the relational nature of human beings and, specifically, the reciprocal effects of interactions with

God and other persons. Lewis asserted that God enables and ennobles individuals' loving relationships with other humans: all true forms of friendship, romantic love, and altruism. Further, he detailed how honest engagement in such earthly love encourages intimate relationships with God. In the largest religious sense, human beings, as the creations of God, are brothers and sisters. Humanity is then a family, the "Family of God."

Altruism

Altruism is the ability that humans have to forgo their own rewards (pleasure) for the welfare of others. Human beings possess the ability and inclination to act for the sake of others with the well-being of others as their ultimate motive. Empirical studies have shown that altruism is positively associated with improved interpersonal and social relations (Batson et al., 1993), and that it may also be a curative influence in psychotherapy (Yalom, 1995).

Altruism contrasts with the assumption of hedonism in that the latter assumes that human beings always seek pleasure and avoid pain—that this is their most basic and fundamental motivation (Slife, 2004). According to hedonism, true altruism is not possible. Many psychological theories have portrayed altruism as hedonism wrapped in the guise of good deeds. For example, Freudian theory assumed that all human behavior is motivated by the pleasure principle; behaviorism claimed that the universal law of reinforcement determines humans to act only in ways that induce pleasure while avoiding pain; humanistic theories advocated that individuals should be authentic to their own needs above all else. These hedonistic theories tend to view seemingly altruistic acts as accidental, maladaptive, or ultimately grounded in self-interest.

We think that the assumption of altruism is more in harmony with a theistic view of human nature than the assumption of hedonism. According to the theistic world religions, true altruism is possible. Humans can care about one another, not just superficially or accidentally, but sincerely and meaningfully. Responsibility, self-sacrifice, suffering, love, and altruistic service can be valued above personal gratification.

Altruistic love must be balanced with self-love, or it could lead to unhealthy self depreciation. Self-love is the healthy concern for one's personal well-being and happiness, not to be confused with selfishness: the state of being "concerned excessively or exclusively with oneself" (Merriam-Webster, Inc., 2003, p. 1128). Selfishness is the antithesis of altruism, and we believe it to be detrimental to one's spiritual, social, and psychological well-being (Bergin, 2002).

Jesus Christ is recognized by Christians as the transcendent exemplar of altruism in that he willingly suffered temporally and spirituality to an infinite degree in behalf of all of God's children. Great contributions to human welfare have been inspired by his example (e.g., Martin Luther King Jr., Mahatma Ghandi). Central to the highest forms of altruism is the principle of self-sacrifice, the opposite of the destructive narcissism that pervades modern society. Sacrifice is prominent in the doctrine and practice of many religions (Smart, 1983, 1994). Despite its distortion into grotesque extremes in human history, this principle is basic to enduring, constructive relationships. When it is undergirded by sound theology and healthy spirituality, altruism has a unique healing power.

Contextuality

Contextuality is the notion that at "least some of the properties and qualities of things . . . come from outside the thing—in its context" (Slife, 2004, p. 48). Contextualists reject the notion that a phenomenon is not real if it is not generalizable and repeatable, suggesting that the "changeable is at least as fundamental as the unchangeable" (Slife, 2004, p. 48). Contextualism contrasts with naturalistic universalism, which assumes that natural laws are context-free and apply across time, space, and persons (Slife & Williams, 1995).

We agree with scholars who have argued that contextualism may be more consistent with theistic, spiritual views of reality, especially realities about human development and relationships. According to Slife and his colleagues,

> spirituality . . . takes into account a person's unique, subjective meaning and situation. This unique meaning and situation—what we have termed context—is different from modernism's universalism because universalism implies that the general and the lawful, instead of the particular and the exceptional, are ultimately real. (Slife et al., 1999, p. 67)

We agree that contextualism is more open to the consideration of spirituality in behavioral science research and psychotherapy practice because it does not insist that phenomena be empirically observable, generalizable, and repeatable. Contextualism invites researchers and practitioners to take seriously emotional and spiritual experiences—experiences that are often contextual, invisible, private, unique, and nongeneralizable (Slife et al., 1999). Contextualism is also more consistent with theistic perspectives of reality in that it rejects the idea that there are natural or universal psychological laws that completely and deterministically control human behavior and relationships. In this sense, contextualism is also consistent with agentive and spiritual perspectives of human beings.

CONCLUSION

Contemporary views in science, the philosophy of science, and psychology are more compatible with both the theistic worldview and the philosophical assumptions we have described than were the prevailing philosophies of previous decades (Griffin, 2000, 2001; Jones, 1994; P. S. Richards & Bergin, 1997; Slife, 2004). We think the theistic worldview and philosophies such as *scientific theism, theistic holism, human agency, moral universalism, theistic relationism, altruism,* and *contextuality* provide a rich foundation on which to build theories of personality and psychotherapy. Jones (1994) argued that religious worldviews might contribute to the progress of psychological science and practice "by suggesting new modes of thought . . . and new theories" (p. 194). We agree with this. We think that the theistic worldview, in particular, contributes important insights into previously neglected aspects of human nature, personality, therapeutic change, and the practice of psychotherapy.

In chapter 5 we discuss the theoretical foundations of theistic psychotherapy, focusing on some of the major implications of the theistic worldview for personality theory. In subsequent chapters we describe the clinical applications of our theistic psychotherapy framework. When possible, we point out how theistic personality and psychotherapy concepts might be suitable for psychotherapists and clients who do not believe in this view. There is much that is ecumenical about the approach we describe, and we hope to build bridges wherever we can with psychotherapists and clients with diverse perspectives.

5

THEORETICAL AND EMPIRICAL FOUNDATIONS OF THEISTIC PSYCHOTHERAPY

I do believe there is some kind of transcendent organizing influence in the universe which operates in man as well. ... My present, very tentative, view is that perhaps there is an essential person which persists through time, or even through eternity.

—Carl R. Rogers

A theistic spiritual perspective has direct implications for the ways clinicians conceptualize human personality and the change processes that characterize growth, development, and healing. Integrating such content into mainstream clinical theory, research, and practice is a formidable undertaking. The reasons for proceeding have been outlined in the overview of history and new trends provided in the previous four chapters. In this chapter, we set forth additional concepts and observations that establish the scholarly rationale for the clinical applications that will follow in the subsequent chapters. This rationale is rooted in standard, modernist methods and results, as well as in newer trends in theory and research. Beyond this, and fundamental to our purpose, we attempt to integrate these with spiritual traditions and literature, including our own specific perspectives.

THEORETICAL FOUNDATIONS OF THEISTIC PSYCHOTHERAPY: A THEISTIC PERSONALITY THEORY

All mainstream psychotherapy traditions are grounded in a theory of human personality. Personality theories provide a framework and rationale for assessment and treatment with their *view of human nature*, *view of human development and functioning*, and *view of therapeutic change and healing*. We address each of these global issues in our theistic personality theory, some of the main concepts and distinguishing features of which are summarized in Exhibit 5.1.

View of Human Nature

Our view of human nature is grounded in the worldview of the theistic world religions and in the philosophical assumptions described in chapter 4. This theistic view of human nature may be summarized in broad terms that we hope will prove useful to an ecumenical array of theistically oriented clinicians and clients:

1. God exists; is humankind's creator; embodies love, goodness, and truth; and acts on people's behalf and for their sakes.
2. Humans are beings of body and spirit, both temporal and spiritual. They are the offspring of God, created in the image of God, and they carry within them the germ or seed of divinity.
3. Human existence is sustained through the power of God.
4. Human beings are able to communicate with God by spiritual means, such as prayer and prophetic revelation, and this inspired communication can positively influence their lives.
5. There is spiritual evil that opposes God and human welfare. Humans also can communicate with and be influenced by evil to their detriment and destruction.
6. Good and evil can be spiritually discerned through the *Spirit of Truth*.
7. Humans have agency and are responsible to both God and humanity for the choices they make and the consequences of those choices.
8. Because theistic, spiritual influences exist, their application in people's lives should be beneficial to their well-being.
9. God's plan for people is to use the experiences of this life to choose good—no matter how painful life may be—to learn wisdom and develop their potential to become more in harmony with or like God.

We assume that human nature includes spiritual capacities—that is, ways of responding to, harmonizing with, or acting on the promptings and enlightenment from God or the *Spirit of Truth*. We use the term *Spirit of Truth* as the generic label for God's spirit and divine influence in the world with the hope that it will facilitate communication across diverse perspectives. Commonly used terms such as *conscience*, *inspiration*, and *revelation* also are

EXHIBIT 5.1
Key Concepts of a Theistic Personality Theory

View of human nature	View of healthy functioning	View of unhealthy functioning	View of therapeutic change
People have free will or agency, although both environmental and biological factors can limit agency. Agency expands or contracts by the choices we make. Human beings are multisystemic organisms (i.e., biological, social, cognitive, psychological, and spiritual). Human beings have a spirit or soul that is eternal in nature. Spiritual processes exist that allow human beings to communicate with a Supreme Being. Human beings have great potential for growth and can realize their potential by seeking spiritual awareness and growth. Human beings can also follow a path of deterioration by neglecting their spiritual growth and choosing evil.	Biological, social, psychological, and spiritual factors all influence personality development. People who believe in their eternal spiritual identity, follow the influence of God's spirit, and live in harmony with universal moral principles are more likely to develop in a healthy manner socially and psychologically. Spiritually healthy people have the capacity to enjoy loving, affirming relationships with others, have a clear sense of identity and values, and their external behavior is in harmony with their value system. They also feel a sense of closeness and harmony with God and experience a sense of strength, meaning, and fulfillment from their spiritual beliefs.	Psychological disturbance and symptoms can be caused by a variety of influences, including physiological (e.g., neurotransmitter depletions), familial (e.g., abuse, marital conflict) social (e.g., prolonged work-related stress), cognitive (e.g., irrational thinking), and spiritual (e.g., moral transgressions) problems. People who neglect their spiritual growth and well-being or who consistently choose to ignore the Spirit of Truth and do evil are more likely to suffer poor mental health and disturbed, unfulfilling interpersonal relationships.	Therapeutic change and healing can be facilitated through a variety of means, including physiological (e.g., medications), familial (e.g., improving communication), social (e.g., prevention, education), cognitive (e.g., modifying irrational beliefs), and spiritual (e.g., prayer, repentance, meditation). At its core, healing and change is a spiritual process through which the mortal overlay is penetrated to reveal and affirm the person's eternal spiritual identity, worth, and agentive powers. Psychological, relational, and even physical healing is facilitated, and is more profound and lasting, when people heal and grow spiritually.

embraced within this concept. This perspective is readily accessible in the world's religious, spiritual, poetic, and mystical literature. For instance, we find the following in the biblical Book of Job: "There is a spirit in man [humans]: and the inspiration of the Almighty giveth them understanding" (Job 32:8; Church of Jesus Christ of Latter-Day Saints, 1979).

Our view of human nature is based on a belief in a personal, sympathetic, compassionate, dependable, and active God—one who acts providentially in history and in the lives of human beings (McGrath, 1999; Polkinghorne, 1998). We believe that humans experience divine providence in many ways, including but not limited to the experience of miracles. Miracles are "special providences" that occur in a specific way and time and that often provide insights into the divine purpose and meanings of life. They usually instill awe and love of the divine in the individual who witnesses them (Peacocke, 2001; Polkinghorne, 1998). Miracles are generally considered to be extraordinary, or "parapsychological," but they are not necessarily disruptive of the natural order of the universe (Griffin, 2001).

We believe that communication with God takes place via a shared experience that transcends the observable senses (Peacocke, 2001). The exchange of thoughts and feelings between God and humans can be viewed as a form of telepathy or influence at a distance (Griffin, 1989). In such communion, God does not coerce humans, but rather lovingly persuades and entices them with full respect for their agency (Griffin, 1989, 2001). In our view, God, or the Spirit of Truth, invites and entices human beings to choose good over evil and to bring their lives into harmony with universal moral truths or laws of living, such as personal and social responsibility, family commitment and kinship, marital fidelity, humility, self-sacrifice, forgiveness, honesty, integrity, and respect for life (Bergin, 1985; Jensen & Bergin, 1988; L. Miller, 2005; P. S. Richards, Rector, & Tjelveit, 1999).

We assert that there is a spiritual essence to human personality. Personality is influenced by a variety of systems and processes, but the eternal spirit is an essential aspect of identity and a regulator of conduct. Personality development and functioning are optimized when people are able to affirm their eternal spiritual identity; follow the influence of the Spirit of Truth; regulate their behavior, feelings, and thoughts in harmony with universal principles and values; and engage in congruent and loving relationships with other human beings and with God. In addition to these premises, religious literature, history, and scripture identify other conceptual themes and bipolar behavioral themes that we describe below, which lay the basis for the beginnings of our theistic theory of personality development and functioning.

By introducing a spiritual aspect into personality theory, we do not intend to subsume all other aspects of personality via a single dominating perspective, as some theories have attempted. Our view is more integrative. We endorse some (but not all) major themes of other perspectives, such as psychoanalysis (unconscious dynamics and insight), behaviorism (conditioned emotional reactions), cognitive theories (deficient schemas, rationality, and self-regulation), humanistic and experiential views (incongruent experiencing of self and self-actualization), and interpersonal and familial systems theory (triangulation and balance). Spiritual aspects of people's lives may be influenced by any of these, and vice versa. We believe that human personality operates according to a complex variety of principles and that an adequate theory of change must be comprehensive and multifaceted.

View of Human Development and Functioning

Spiritual personality theory, integrated with secular knowledge, may be further outlined in the following eight psychospiritual themes or tasks. The list of bipolar constructs in Exhibit 5.2 was inspired in part by Erikson (1963), but it is also compatible with Gilligan's (1982) notion of women's life cycle and with studies of women's spirituality (Randour, 1987). It derives mainly from studies of religion and mental health, from sacred texts, from studies of religious and spiritual experiences reported by college students we have studied, and from attempts to integrate ideas from these with current secular research, theory, and practice. We make no attempt to sketch a stage-like developmental scheme. Rather, the list is hierarchical, progressing from the core of individual personality to the complexity of interpersonal and communal interactions. Also note that these opposite poles are endpoints that represent continuous dimensions. People may be at various points along the dimension between the polar opposites. Obviously, each of these bipolar topics deserves its own chapter. This is the focus of another book that expresses a more specifically Latter-Day Saint theological context (Bergin, 2002).

These themes describe psychospiritual tasks or challenges that people confront as they develop and experience life. Spiritually and psychologically

EXHIBIT 5.2
Psychospiritual Themes in a Theistic View of Personality
and Therapeutic Change

I.	Eternal identity	vs.	Mortal overlay
II.	Agency	vs.	Impairment
III.	Moral responsibility	vs.	Relativism and uncertainty
IV.	Integrity	vs.	Deception
V.	Benevolent power	vs.	Authoritarianism
VI.	Faithful intimacy	vs.	Infidelity and self-focus
VII.	Marriage, family, and community	vs.	Alienation and isolation
VIII.	Growth and change	vs.	Stagnation

mature people move toward the positive ends of the poles in each of the themes. The closer people move toward the positive ends of the dichotomies, the fewer their pathologies and the more benevolent their influence on others. People who move toward the negative ends of the poles experience poorer psychological and spiritual health, and their interpersonal relationships tend to be more disturbed and transient. Their eternal potentialities also are impaired or obstructed (Bergin, 2002). Therefore, these psychospiritual themes provide a conceptual schema, which adds to our ordinary secular understanding of healthy and unhealthy human development and functioning.

It may seem that these topics are not obvious derivatives from theistic spiritual traditions, in which one might expect to consider topics such as faith, love, truth, repentance, grace, forgiveness, revelation, reconciliation, redemption, commandments, doctrines, obedience, sacrifice, service, witnessing, and so on. Actually, such topics are fundamental, but they are addressed elsewhere in a more denominational way. The present text is influenced in various ways by that approach; however, this is a multidimensional, ecumenical psychology, not a specific theology. Our present terms are therefore adaptations of spiritual concepts integrated with psychological concepts that we consider valuable. The main topics of spiritual literature do emerge to a degree, however, as important aspects of our analysis of the psychospiritual themes.

Eternal Spiritual Identity Versus Mortal Overlay

Consistent with our assumption that each person has an eternal, indestructible, personal, spiritual identity that persists through time and eternity, we assert that as creations of God, eternal identities have noble, infinite potential. This conception is compatible with some humanistic and psychodynamic theories that emphasize human potential and self-actualization. The potential development of identity can go awry because of imperfect or abusive parenting, social chaos, biological deficiencies, self-destructive choices, distorted perceptions and debilitating emotional symptoms, dysfunctional coping mechanisms, and so on, so that a mortal overlay develops that obscures the person's eternal identity. Bergin (2002) described the mortal overlay as

> the unique, complex set of characteristics that covers or "overlays" our spiritual selves during earthly life. It is the combined physical body and mortal mind with all their positive and negative features acquired through biology, genetics, and life experience. It is not fixed but varies over the course of a lifetime according to biological changes, personal choices, environmental events, and spiritual influences. (p. 29)

The concept of the mortal overlay should not be confused with the dualistic perspective of the "pure spirit" and the "depraved flesh." There are many positive aspects of the mortal overlay that are a necessary and essential part of being human that can help people affirm and integrate their eternal spiritual identity into their overall sense of identity. According to our spiritual view of personality development, when people get in touch with their eternal spiritual core, with all of its dignity and power for enhancement, the negative aspects of the mortal overlay begins to dissolve, and they begin to overcome their pathologies and grow in healthy ways (Ellsworth, 1995). We say more about this process in the section below titled "View of Therapeutic Change" and in chapter 6.

The following personal experience of a student we studied at Brigham Young University (BYU) illustrates what we mean by getting in touch with and affirming one's eternal spiritual identity. It is similar to Maslow's (1968) accounts of acute identity experiences. A young man we call J. was adopted as a young child. When J. started elementary school, he heard people refer to him as "the adopted one." The pain of this was deepened by the taunting of another young child who talked of him as, "not being one of your own family." J. continued to struggle with these doubts about his identity until the age of 15. The following is his account of what happened:

> Then came what I believe to be my acute identity experience. My father was seriously hurt in a farming accident. After he had been taken to the hospital we were told by the doctors that there was a possibility he might not live. My mother and sister emotionally collapsed. It was the first time I had seen both of them in hysterics. I was in a mild state of shock. That night as I lay in the hospital corridor, I began to be afraid as I never had been in my life up to that point. I was so horribly afraid that the only thing I could think to do was to pray. Then I had one of the most spiritual experiences I have ever had. My acute identity experience was the knowledge I experienced and carried with me after that night that I was really secure in my family life as a son and a brother. I knew that I had been sealed eternally to my family and that I am secure and have strength and an understanding of my identity that I did not have before this experience.

This experience, one among hundreds reported by college students in our classes and studies, suggests an underlying reality to one's identity that, although often obscured by life experience, can be penetrated by the spirit creating a revelatory perception for the individual of the nature of the eternal self. Such spiritual identity experiences, which carry the understanding beyond the temporal or empirical world, are healing and integrative. They increase people's faith in God and promote a sense of spiritual purpose and meaning. They can promote positive self-esteem and help individuals overcome emotional problems and unhealthy lifestyle behaviors (P. S. Richards, 1999).

Poll and Smith (2003) recently proposed a model of spiritual identity development that is based, in part, on our theistic model of personality. They hypothesized that "by reflecting upon spiritual experiences from the past and by projecting such experiences into the future through faith, individuals are able to feel continuity and constancy of their spiritual selves as eternal beings" (p. 133). They theorized that individuals may go through a four-stage developmental sequence in coming to a sense of their spiritual selves:

1. *Preawareness:* The time before individuals consciously regard themselves in spiritual terms.
2. *Awakening:* A period of learning, crisis, or conflict that prompts an awareness of the self in relation to God.
3. *Recognition:* Development of a consistent spiritual identity as individuals have more spiritual experiences and reflect on similar experiences from the past.
4. *Integration:* The stage at which individuals recognize their own spiritual nature and accordingly perceive and interact with the world, God, and other human beings. (Poll & Smith, 2003, pp. 133–134)

They also hypothesized that spiritual identity development might begin in early childhood, but that it may also commence or resume in adulthood after a spiritual reawakening. Poll and Smith's spiritual identity development model has received some empirical support in a recently conducted 17-year longitudinal follow-up study (Poll, Richards, & Smith, 2004). Their model may prove useful for psychotherapists, because it provides a rationale for understanding and intervening appropriately with clients who are at different stages of spiritual identity development. Many therapies, to some degree, may help clients progress in their spiritual development even though spiritual issues are not explicitly stated in their theories of change. Theistic psychotherapy helps clients to do this with added strength by virtue of spiritual techniques, such as meta-empathy (i.e., the therapist's perceiving and communicating accurate perceptions of the person's spiritual nature), meditation, prayer, illumination, spiritual communion with the revealing spirit of God via acute identity experiences, special blessings, fasting, and other spiritual interventions discussed in chapters 9 and 10 of this book. Regardless of therapists' theoretical and technique orientations, an understanding of spiritual identity development can prove helpful to them as they work with theistic clients. We have noted in our own clinical work how the potency of professional, secular techniques is often enhanced by the unusual energy and illumination of spiritual experiences.

Our outline of eternal identity versus mortal overlay illustrates how a spiritual perspective complements and expands on the secular understanding of healthy personality development. Of course, identity is only one of many areas in which the phenomenology of religious experience shows evidence of processes that are difficult to describe in ordinary psychological terms but have as profound or more profound effects than any behavior change procedures that we know of in the ordinary professional domain. A full analysis of this and the other topics included in Exhibit 5.1 cannot be adequately explained in this chapter and are the focus of another book (Bergin, 2002). For our purposes here, brief accounts of the additional subtopics will suffice.

Agency Versus Impairment

We oppose radical determinism and assert that human beings are normally personally responsible for their choices and actions. This agentive capacity is a God-given gift. Because of it, people have the opportunity to grow, to refine themselves as eternal beings, and to serve others and transcend ordinary human existence, much as Maslow (1971) suggested was possible. However, because of one's own bad choices (as in addiction), actions by others (as in child abuse), or biological influences (as in brain disorders), agency may be impaired. Psychopathology consists largely of the loss of ability to make rational choices and to enact them. Self-regulative capacities are displaced by loss of internal control or by environmental or biological control from other sources (Bergin, 1969).

When people's sense of eternal identity is affirmed and their agency is strengthened through spiritual experiences, their feelings of responsibility and their self-regulative capacities are enhanced. As they learn to respond to the promptings of the Spirit of Truth, their commitment to healthy lifestyles increases. A major purpose of most therapies is to enhance self-regulatory function and feelings of efficacy (Bandura, 1986, 1997), as well as to strengthen feelings of responsibility for choices and actions, and for the healthiness of interpersonal relationships.

Such improvements free the person's agency from bondage and open the person to spiritual guidance in establishing a mentally healthy way of living. In many cases, standard treatment is required to enhance agency before spiritual techniques and discussion of values and lifestyle issues can be effective. In the later phase of therapy, spiritual guidance can assist in establishing a lifestyle that avoids any previous irresponsible or ineffective patterns and maintaining the improvements gained through therapy, thus avoiding relapse. This philosophy is similar to the approach in medicine, which helps patients to establish a physically healthy lifestyle in order to maintain improvement after treatment is discontinued or to prevent disease. Sometimes, however, a spiritual focus is needed at the beginning of therapy in order to arouse motivation necessary for change, such as in the 12-step programs for addiction.

Moral Responsibility Versus Relativism and Uncertainty

Our view of personality and mental health is value-laden: certain ways of being and acting are preferable to others. The value themes in Exhibit 5.2 reflect the classic notion of "good versus evil," although they are applied here to issues of personality and psychotherapy. Just as we believe that there is a spirit of good that comes from God, we also conclude that there is an opposing spirit of evil (Dickson, 1995; Peck, 1983).

When people follow the influence of the spirit from God and choose or work on behalf of the positive ends of the dichotomies in Exhibit 5.2, pathologies are more likely to be prevented and mental health promoted through therapy or other means. When people choose or are conditioned to accept the negative side, their health and human potential is constrained or undermined. The goals or values of spiritual, theistic therapy thus favor the appropriate development of the positive aspects of each dimension in Exhibit 5.2: identity, agency, morality, integrity, power, intimacy, and family kinship.

All religions, philosophies, spiritual perspectives, and cultures embody systems of values that they identify as important, preferred, acceptable, and worthy of transmission across generations and subgroups. These impose a moral order on personal behavior and social interaction, and they may generate internal feelings of worth or of shame and guilt, depending on one's conformity to them. As they mature spiritually and psychologically, people need to develop, internalize, and live in harmony with a moral value system (Bergin, Payne, & Richards, 1996; P. S. Richards et al., 1999). There is much literature on this topic in psychology (moral development), anthropology, philosophy, political science, and so on. Although cultures differ in what they value, such cultural relativism does not support ethical relativism (Kitchener, 1980a, 1980b). Cultures are unequal with respect to their capacity to engender personal growth and adjustment.

Mental health is sustained by a viable moral belief system that includes mentally healthy values (Bergin, 1985). It is clear that many mental health professionals endorse such a view and that they endorse particular values (see chap. 6, this volume) as being favorable to mental health (Bergin & Jensen, 1990; Jensen & Bergin, 1988; Peck, 1978). According to our spiritual view of personality development, as people respond to the Spirit of Truth, they recognize and internalize healthy values and learn to regulate their conduct in harmony with them.

Without an orienting system for assessing the value of one's conduct or that of others, self-effectiveness and self-regulation, which are vital to civilized and normal behaviors, are undermined (Bandura, 1986). Although the specific ways in which people apply general moral principles may vary, and although individuals often disengage their moral standards for the sake of defenses or gratification (Bandura, 1986), the importance of moral principles for a mentally healthy and socially constructive lifestyle is clear (Bergin et al., 1996; Jensen & Bergin, 1988). It is also clear that feelings of spiritual conviction give to personal value systems the added dimensions of motivation, courage, and endurance, despite the temporary pain (facing defenses or resisting impulse gratification) that this may require. The long-term, socially responsible perspective provided by a spiritual worldview encourages the sacrifice of immediate neediness (if contrary to moral commitments) on behalf of higher principles, long-range consequences, and the impact on others, both proximal and distal. Such a perspective has been noted by Fowler (1996) to be the highest level of faith development. Emmons's (1999) theorizing and research about spiritual motivation and strivings is also consistent with the idea that spiritually motivated goals and values can have a healthy, integrative influence on human personality functioning.

Relativistic morality is less likely to be enduring because (a) there is less conviction that the moral principles are a general aspect of the moral nature of humans and the universe and (b) convenience or immediacy in adapting to momentary situations may cloud judgment and lead to self-justification rather than reasoned assessment. Such a philosophy does not recognize sufficiently the enduring contribution of values derived from experience across human history and cultural development (Campbell, 1975).

Inspired Integrity Versus Deception

Extensive literature now points to the importance of honesty in relationships for the sake of individual and interpersonal health. Authenticity, congruence (Rogers, 1961), openness, and so on are woven into most theories of change. Inauthenticity and deception of self and others have been woven into many theories of psychopathology, beginning with psychoanalysis and extending to family systems theory.

The commandment "thou shalt not bear false witness" is fundamental to most religious traditions. Belief in it is a strengthening factor in the analysis of self and self-in-relationship. Deception of self and others is at the root of defense mechanisms, interpersonal conflict, and much pathology in general. This is a transparent fact to most clinicians.

Integrity, on the other hand, requires one to be sensitively attuned to the Spirit of Truth. It includes a resilient willingness to face the facts: to "be true," to be nonoffensive, to avoid blaming others, and to accept responsibility for one's defects and bad conduct, even when it hurts to do so. Integrity is "egoless" in the senses that the prideful protection or advancement of the ego is given up and one elects to absorb the painful truths that defenses and deceptions have hidden from the self and others. This may not be easy, especially in severe cases, but it is essential to real healing. Living a lie is, in the long run, harder than living truthfully (Peck, 1983; Warner, 1986, 1995, 2001; Warner & Olson, 1984), and living truthfully includes the courage to confront the lies perpetrated by others as well as those within oneself.

The therapeutic solution to deception may be direct, as in group confrontations among addicts and sex offenders, or it may be indirect, as in the sharing of narratives by those who have successfully faced themselves and life with integrity (Warner, 1995). The spiritual dimension is integral to the development of integrity, for when people have a strong sense of spiritual identity and affirm their personal responsibility, they are led by the Spirit of Truth to value honesty. As they make the choice to be true to the truth (with guidance, example, confrontation, rewards or analysis of defense), a spiritual burden of alienation from God is lifted and they are blessed by an infusion of strength and healing, an "integration" in the classical meaning of the term *integrity*. With the healing of self comes the healing of relationships as well.

Benevolent Power Versus Authoritarianism

As many conceive, power is the ability to control, to decide, to dispense consequences; however, it is also the ability to make a difference, to influence, and to collaborate in causing change or resisting it. Power must be considered in discussions of spirituality because of its potential for harm and its potential for good in human relationships. It stands next to intimacy as a factor in relationships, but it is often orthogonal to it. Power can be used to broaden the potentialities of others and to stimulate their growth, or it can narrow a person's possibilities and be used to degrade or defeat.

Negative correlations between authoritarianism, or controlling uses of power, and positive mental health have been well known since the classic post–World War II study conducted by Adorno, Frenkel-Brunswik, Levinson, and Sanford (1950). The benefits of benevolent uses of power are equally evident. This dual potential is evident in marriage relations and in relations between parent and child, employer and employee, therapist and client, and, of course, governor and the governed.

Human relations are strengthened as individuals grant to one another the freedom to grow in identity and relationships. Ideal power—benevolent relationships—set limits on intrusions by one person on another and provide stimuli and opportunity for personal growth and individual, collective, and social welfare. A good home and family life thus would provide rules that set limits, a safe and securely regulated structure, and the social–emotional processes that contribute to normal development and self-actualization. In business and industry, many modern developments in ethics, training, and governing are benevolent changes from earlier authoritarian systems (Covey, 1989; Scott & Hart, 1989).

Abuses of power are, of course, omnipresent in modern life. In the family, one-sided decision making or the misuse of authority to demean, degrade, punish, constrict, or brutalize represents this negative pole. Religious institutions and the individuals who represent them also sometimes abuse their authority. This occurs when being "authoritative" (i.e., using power benevolently) degrades into "authoritarianism" (i.e., using power abusively). Political and family abuses of power are sometimes even justified in religious terms: "It is the will of God that you (especially women) submit to me," "Destroy or kill in the name of God," "Giving me sexual gratification is ordained of God," and so on. These are dramatic abuses of theistic belief systems, and they are inconsistent with the Spirit of Truth. Institutionalized authoritarian cultures of belief and oppression have no spiritually legitimate claim to spiritual insight, authority, or power; however, helping religious clients, especially women (Rayburn, 1985) reframe perspectives on organizations they feel allegiance to can be a delicate and difficult task.

Alert therapists know that the evils of authoritarianism may lurk behind seemingly "nice" organizations, families, or religious groups with which clients are affiliated. Sometimes therapists must help their clients to resist, reform, or flee from such systematic forms of abuse of the human spirit. They also may need to confront clients who use their power in abusive ways (e.g., cases of child and spouse abuse). A spiritual approach can sometimes break down habits of anger and violence and affirm the morality and healthy consequences of benevolent power. Angry, abusive people are often hard to influence. Sometimes conversion experiences, or what W. R. Miller and C'deBaca (1994) referred to as "quantum" change, are needed, but these are hard to orchestrate.

People who hearken to the Spirit of Truth value benevolent use of power. They use their authority to serve the needs of people. Thus, instead of people existing for the sake of those in authority (e.g., religious leaders, politicians, parents, teachers, therapists), the authority system exists for the sake of people. Those in authority are thus called on by promptings of the Spirit of Truth to devote their energies and sacrifice their self-interests for the benefit of others. The preferred mode of influence is through information and persuasion in a coaching style rather than a controlling style. This makes communication, communion, and even intimacy possible, whereas authoritarianism destroys all of these.

Faithful Intimacy Versus Infidelity

Teachings of the world religions and the conclusions of behavioral science concur in the notion that intimacy, affection, and love are fundamental to human happiness and optimal functioning. They also concur that capriciousness, abuse, exploitation, and faithlessness in such relationships are harmful. A national survey of mental health professionals supports the same view (Jensen & Bergin, 1988).

Studies of marital conflict, divorce, and infidelity support the claim that faithful intimacy is beneficial, as do studies of parent–child relations and therapeutic relationships. Erikson's (1963) notion that the capacity for intimacy grows out of healthy psychosocial development and builds on adaptive identity formation is pertinent, as are the arguments by Gilligan (1982); Mahler, Pine, and Bergman (1975); Bowlby (1969); and many others that intimate attachment and love are fundamental to normal human personality development (Hetherington, Parke, & Locke, 1999).

Much of the energy of psychotherapy is devoted to instituting or restoring capacities for normal intimacy along with social skills to maintain viable loving relationships. We have said that God is truth, or the Spirit of Truth, but equally valid is the statement that "God is love," and God's love is faithful, stable, and unwavering. As people affirm their spiritual identity and respond to the Spirit of Truth, they are led to value faithful intimacy and love, a process that can be facilitated by a spiritual, theistically oriented therapy. There are many models of both faithfulness and infidelity, in the broad sense of these terms, in the scriptures and in life; therefore, it is not difficult for therapists to find examples to use in helping clients to understand this theme and its possible consequence (cf. V. L. Brown, 1981).

The religious or spiritually inclined client's thoughts can be easily opened to the conviction that there is something universal or transcendent about faithful intimacy that is built into people's nature as human beings. Such conviction can provide the needed motivation to resist temptations to be faithless, exploitative, or abusive. The feeling that the Creator is the author and supporter of faithful love can provide courage during moral crises, whether these pertain to intimacy defined broadly as interpersonal goodness or defined narrowly as sexual fidelity.

Erikson (1963) placed isolation opposite to intimacy, which is a valuable point. *Alienation* might also be used as an opposing pole, but we find *infidelity*, as we have defined it, to be the best concept to place opposite real intimacy, and we think that it has more far-reaching consequences for a value-based theory of personality and change.

Marriage, Family, and Community Versus Alienation and Isolation

Family kinship is a natural subtopic within the intimacy domain because the most powerful intimate relationships, including but not limited to sexual ones, occur throughout the world within family structures. The powerful potential of such relationships and social structures is evident in the benevolent consequences of positive family ties and the equally malignant results of disruptive and destructive family relations. Although domestic violence, rape, divorce, open marriage, serial monogamy, various forms of cohabitation, promiscuity, child physical and sexual abuse, and other forms of sex outside marriage have threatened or distorted the long-held meanings of kinship (especially in North America and Europe), the vast majority of world cultures continue to be rooted in familial kinship systems or networks. It is particularly striking that the so-called Third World cultures of Africa, Asia, and Latin America, which some consider to be inferior economically and intellectually, have held firmly to kinship traditions and have defined the family in terms of larger networks of relationships than the nuclear family. Many of these cultures derive from religions other than Judeo-Christian traditions. Some observers believe, as we do, that their broad sense of family is healthier and provides more opportunity for emotional intimacy and social support than modern Western traditions (V. L. Brown, 1981; Uzoka, 1979).

From a spiritual viewpoint, we assume that marriage is ordained of God and is good for human beings, and that procreation and the care and nurturing of offspring in the context of a moral value system are essential to a good society (Bennett, 1993) and to lasting mental health. People who sense the Spirit of Truth will be led to value marriage and family kinship and will show commitment to lifestyles and traditions that support family life. We thus assume that theistic tradition dictates a sociological definition of mental health rather than a merely clinical, individual view. In this sense, behaviors and lifestyles that undermine family kinship and society are pathological, even if the individuals engaging in them are not mentally ill in the *Diagnostic and Statistical Manual of Mental Disorders*, 4th edition (*DSM–IV*; American Psychiatric Association, 1994) sense of the term. Therapeutically, theistic, spiritual perspectives are strongly supportive of marriage and family life, particularly when therapies are aimed at resolving alienation and restoring faithful intimacy within a tradition of sanctioned kinship and benevolent social structure.

Communal structure is a logical correlate of marriage and family life, providing additional opportunities for individuals to have group and community identification and support. Erikson's (1963) notion that the case history is embedded in history or that the individual is embedded in the culture is pertinent. Religious communities are often excellent resources for support and healing, including a sense that the self and one's family are part of a larger coherent whole. Indeed, Erikson argued that identity is never completely formed without this sense of group identification. Perhaps it is this principle that makes ongoing self-help groups, such as Alcoholics Anonymous, so valuable (McCrady & Miller, 1993). The modern decline of communal structures, with their points of social identification, is an indicator of social decay and personal disarray. For example, street gangs appear to provide substitutes for the loss of family. They exemplify our notion of alienation—from parents, society, and social responsibility—that opposes that basic unit of nearly all societies: the legally or custom-sanctioned family kinship system. People who are in harmony with the Spirit of Truth value their religious and cultural community, and they make efforts to contribute to such communities' cohesion and welfare.

Progression Versus Stagnation

It is clear, therefore, that people can understand and regulate their lives through spiritual means. Such change requires both faith and initiative. People who gain a sense of their spiritual, eternal identity and follow the enticings of the Spirit of Truth will want to grow, and many do so through the steps listed in Exhibit 5.1. In the process, they will progress toward fulfilling their divine potential, developing their capacities and talents, and seeking to overcome or compensate for deficiencies and disturbances. As they grow, they will also use their abilities and energies in socially benevolent and constructive ways. They will give of themselves because they now have more to give, and they will understand that giving of self not only strengthens their interpersonal and social fabric, but also their own personhood.

In contrast, those who are less in touch with their spiritual identity and with the Spirit of Truth are more likely to stagnate and fail to grow in healthy and productive ways. Their stresses of life and disturbances are likely to direct them toward self-preoccupation, and their ability to adapt and to be an influence for good will diminish. Their motivation and ability to change will be encumbered by an absence of faith and of vision for the future. Personal pathologies and the negative influence of associates may keep them from growing. For such individuals, spiritual awakening may be crucial to curbing downward emotional cycles and self-defeating behaviors. Alliance with a spiritually motivated therapist and, in some cases, a cohesive group, can strengthen them and help them to alter their course. Then a combination of spiritual vision that is harmonious with the positive dimensions listed in Exhibit 5.1 and application of effective therapies can make the process of personal change complete.

View of Therapeutic Change

Because humans are multisystemic holistic beings, healing and therapeutic change are usually multidimensional processes. Pharmacological, behavioral, cognitive, social, emotional, and educational interventions may all be of assistance to clients. But enduring healing often requires a spiritual process.

We posit that when people are born, their eternal spiritual identity begins to be covered by a mortal overlay, which, as discussed above, includes positive and negative characteristics that are acquired through biology, genetics, life experiences, and personal choices (Bergin, 2002). Some aspects of the mortal overlay are particularly harmful to human development and functioning, such as biological predispositions for various physical and psychological disorders; emotional, physical, and sexual abuse; neglectful and shaming parenting; divorce; and substance abuse. When such disorders and life experiences become part of one's mortal overlay, healing and growth can be a difficult and lengthy process if the eternal spiritual identity is seriously obscured from the individual's awareness, as well as from that person's family and friends.

To achieve spiritually energized therapeutic change and healing, clients need to get in touch with and affirm their eternal spiritual nature. Theistic psychotherapists seek to help clients uncover or move past the obscuring layers of the mortal overlay so that they can once again recognize and feel their divine worth, lovability, goodness, and potential. Spiritual practices and interventions such as praying, contemplating, meditating, reading sacred writings, journaling spiritual matters, forgiving, repenting, worshipping, engaging in religious rituals, providing and receiving service and fellowship, seeking spiritual direction, and receiving moral clarification and instruction can often help to facilitate this spiritual healing process (P. S. Richards & Potts, 1995b). Ultimately, we believe that God's loving and healing influence helps clients to exercise the faith necessary to recognize and feel their eternal spiritual identity and worth.

To experience a spiritual assurance of God's love and of their own lovability and goodness deeply changes the way people think and feel about themselves. They find it easier to feel and accept love and validation from their therapist and from significant others. They begin to heal from the inside out. Such experiences often increase clients' faith in God and in spiritual realities, change their identity (eternal being of great worth), heal their shame or feelings of badness, and reorient their values (from a secular or materialistic value system to a more spiritual one). These inner changes in beliefs and values lead to outer changes in their lifestyles, which lead to healthier behaviors and reductions in psychological and physical symptoms and problems (P. S. Richards, 1999). Thus, when clients open their hearts to God's love and healing, then psychotherapists simply become facilitators and witnesses to a healing process that transcends ordinary psychological change.

The following case illustrates this spiritually energized change process—a powerful phenomenon that can promote enduring therapeutic change. Janet was a 36-year-old Latter-Day Saint, married homemaker, and mother of three children.[1] Janet was suffering from a number of symptoms and issues that were detracting from the quality of her life and relationships, including moderate depression and anxiety, symptoms that were most often triggered by conflicts in her family relationships. Janet also suffered from deep-seated doubts about her worth and goodness—doubts that had been sown in the abuse and neglect she had gone through as a child and adolescent. Janet also acknowledged that she and her husband had some "difficulties with physical intimacy." In regard to her spirituality, although it was clear that Janet was a devout believer and that overall her religious involvement was a positive influence in her life, she had some perfectionistic tendencies and was overly concerned about religious rules and appearances, perhaps because of her underlying feelings of deficiency and badness.

Janet's treatment lasted one year. During therapy, Janet had several spiritual experiences that affirmed and deepened her sense of spiritual identity and worth. This seemed to anchor and energize the growth she experienced in her self-esteem and self-confidence, marriage and family relationships, and relationship with God. Approximately one year after the termination of her therapy, Janet wrote a letter to her therapist indicating that she was still doing well, both personally and in her marriage, family, and spiritual life. Janet also shared the following perceptions about how she had been helped by therapy:

> The "me" that was in your office one year ago did not need changing, but emergence. Therapy freed me to be who I really am and to come to love and trust that beautiful person. I had a lot of pain and hundreds of hurtful messages stored inside of me. You replaced them with truth and love. Because of therapy, it was much easier to learn of the kind of love the Heavenly Father has for me.
>
> When I learned that God loves me, trusted me, and saw me as a worthy daughter, I was freed to enjoy my life. I used to think that I was likely to "ruin" those I loved because I was made of "bad stuff." I approached my relationships with fear. When I recognized my goodness, I did not look for my loved ones to fail as a result of my "badness," but could appreciate their goodness and enjoy loving them. Because of therapy, I have learned to love my family in more joyful and accepting ways.

---

[1] This case was reported in its entirety in P. S. Richards (2005).

I now consider my womanhood a dynamically divine bestowal that is part of the gift of me. Sexual relations with my husband have become a way of experiencing and showing love. It is a reaffirmation of my good nature, not a distortion of it.

I now believe that when I pray I am praying to a Father who loves me and is delighted to hear from and be a part of my life. He loves me because he knows me to my very core. He sees the good in me and so do I. From this sense of goodness, I find the desire and courage to share myself with others and grow in their love. (P. S. Richards, 2005, pp. 281–82)

When people assume that who they are transcends the ordinary collection of emotions, actions, and cognitions that surface visibly in therapy, then the "game" of treatment, the dance of therapeutic encounter, takes on a new dimension and becomes a spiritual encounter as well. When Rogers (1973) said that he believed in "other" realities, he had the courage to act on the assumption, as he did with so many of his other insights. He came to believe, as we do, that the spirit of the therapist can perceive, respond to, and help heal the spirit of the client (C. Rogers, personal communication, June 9, 1986). We return to this topic later when we discuss *meta-empathy*.

EMPIRICAL FOUNDATIONS OF THEISTIC PSYCHOTHERAPY

Spiritual phenomena or experiences, although difficult to describe and measure, can be inferred through observable means, often quantitative or qualitative self-reports. These reports can be reliably structured informants, such as standardized questionnaires, content analysis systems for interviews, and so on. In principle, these phenomena can be studied like other "private" events such as cognitions and feelings (e.g., attitudes, beliefs, love). In addition to standardized measures, qualitative and hermeneutic approaches are essential to understanding such phenomena.

The following review of research literature and related conceptual content provides a substantive basis for the theoretical content and clinical implications discussed earlier in this chapter. Note, however, that relatively little of this literature is based on phenomenological and qualitative studies, although we review some of these studies. We anticipate that when more qualitative studies are done, the picture of these phenomena will be even more enlightening and convincing than the present portrayal, which is mainly through traditional "objective" measures and statistics.

Spiritual and Religious Factors and Health

There is now substantial evidence that spirituality can be defined and described in consensually acceptable ways and that these descriptions bear significant and sometimes powerful relations with other phenomena, including physical and mental health. Most of the research on religion and health has examined the relationship between measures of religious commitment and various accepted indicators of physical and mental health. Several recent books provide up-to-date and comprehensive reviews of the empirical research on religion, spirituality, and health (e.g., Koenig, McCullough, & Larson, 2001; Pargament, 1997; Plante & Sherman, 2001).

The *Handbook of Religion and Health* (Koenig et al., 2001) is a particularly comprehensive resource on this topic. Table 5.1 summarizes some of the authors' findings about religion and health, based on their examination of over 1,600 empirical studies and reviews. These studies provide strong support overall for the health benefits of religious commitment and involvement, a finding that is consistent with the conclusions of numerous other literature reviews of the past two decades (e.g., Batson, Schoenrade, & Ventis, 1993; Bergin, 1983, 1991; Gartner, Larson, & Allen, 1991; Koenig et al., 2001; Larson & Larson, 1994; Payne, Bergin, Bielema, & Jenkins, 1991).

Physical Health

Religiously active people show lower rates of incidence for a vast array of diseases, including heart disease, hypertension, immune system dysfunction, cancer, and age-related disability. Religious people tend to live longer. Coping tends to be better for disease, pain, death, and other forms of stress. Recovery rates from surgery are better for religiously active individuals. Religious people are also less likely to engage in unhealthy behaviors such as cigarette smoking, alcohol and drug use, and high-risk sexual behaviors. Members of certain religious groups are also more likely to follow healthy diets (Koenig et al., 2001; Larson & Larson, 1994; Martin & Carlson, 1988; Plante & Sherman, 2001).

Mental Health

During the 1980s and 1990s, there was a significant increase in research concerning the relationship between religion and mental health. The conclusions summarized below are based on the work of Batson et al. (1993), Bergin (1983), Gartner et al. (1991), Koenig et al. (2001), and Payne et al. (1991).

Religion and Psychological Adjustment. Many studies have shown that religiously committed people tend to report greater subjective well-being and life satisfaction. Several large epidemiological studies have found negative relationships between religious participation and psychological distress. Studies have also shown that people who are religiously active tend to have lower levels of hostility and stronger feelings of hope and personal control than those who are not.

TABLE 5.1

Summary of Research Findings on Religion and Mental and Physical Health from the *Handbook of Religion and Health*

Conditions	Findings
Physical health Heart disease	Because of the strong relationship between religious beliefs and activities and the many risk factors for coronary artery disease (CAD), there is reason to hypothesize some sort of relationship between religiousness and heart disease. CAD rates vary across different religious groups. Studies show that Jews and Protestants are at higher risk than Catholics and that Mormons and Seventh-Day Adventists are at lower risk of CAD than the general population. Diet, health behaviors, and quality of social and family life probably account for much of this lowered risk.
Hypertension	There is mounting evidence that involvement in organized religion can provide individuals with greater social support, enhance self-esteem, and reduce the negative effects of stress on blood pressure. In studies that examined the relationship between religion and blood pressure, 14 of 16 found lower blood pressure among the more religious individuals. This effect was especially strong for diastolic blood pressure.
Cerebrovascular disease and the brain	As of 2001, three studies had been conducted that provide relatively weak support for the hypothesis that greater religiousness might help to prevent stroke. Some studies suggest an association between activity of the temporal lobes and mystical experiences; however, there are alternative superempirical explanations for mystical phenomena.
Immune system dysfunction	A variety of multisystemic factors influence immunity. Because many of these factors relate to religious belief and practice, it is plausible that religiousness may lead to better immune function. Indeed, there is some research evidence that religious practices such as prayer, meditation, and faith may be correlated with lower serum cortisol levels. In addition, there is some evidence that religiousness is linked to better immune functioning in elderly people and in people with AIDS.
Cancer	Some influences that are negatively related to religion, such as low levels of social support, depression, hopelessness, and pessimism might adversely affect the immune mechanisms that slow the development and spread of cancer. Certain religious groups (e.g., Mormons and Seventh-Day Adventists) have much lower cancer rates than the general population. Some studies have shown that, once cancer develops, those who use religion to help cope with the disease experience less anxiety, which leads to a better prognosis.
Mortality	Much research has revealed an association between religion and greater longevity. Frequent religious attendance is associated with a substantial reduction in the risk of dying within a 5- to 28-year follow-up period.

(continued)

TABLE 5.1 (Continued)

Conditions	Findings
Physical health	
Disability and coping	There appears to be a consistent negative correlation between community religious activity and physical disability. Religious involvement may help to prevent the onset and progression of disability in older adults. Research indicates that religious involvement may buffer disabled people and their caregivers against negative mental health consequences associated with physical disabilities.
Pain and other somatic symptoms	Some studies have shown a positive relationship between prayer and pain intensity level. This may be because of the fact that religion is used as a coping mechanism when other methods have failed. There is also evidence to suggest an inverse relationship between religiousness and pain intensity. This may be caused by factors such as better mental health and greater social support among more religious people. More research is needed on this subject.
Health behaviors	Many studies have shown that religious people are less likely to engage in unhealthy behaviors such as cigarette smoking, alcohol and drug use, premarital sex, extramarital affairs, or risk-taking behaviors. Religious people are more likely to wear seatbelts. Certain religious groups, such as Seventh-Day Adventists and Mormons, are more likely to follow healthy diets that are high in nutrients and low in fat.
Mental health	
Well-being	Approximately 80% of the 100 studies that have looked at the relationship between religious involvement and well-being report a positive correlation between Christian, Islamic, and Judaic religiousness and greater happiness, life satisfaction, moral, or other measures of well-being. Of these studies, 13% reported no association between religiousness and well-being and 7% reported mixed findings. Most of these studies were cross-sectional, thus more prospective cohort studies are needed to examine changes in well-being related to religiousness over time.
Depression	Two groups of people are at elevated risk for depression: people not affiliated with any religion, and Jews. People that are frequently involved in a religious community and who highly esteem their religious faith for intrinsic reasons may run less risk of becoming depressed, and when depressed recover more quickly. Religiousness motivated by extrinsic motive, on the other hand, is a risk factor for depression. Some forms of religious involvement lead to lower likelihood of depression during and after stressful events, whereas others actually increase the risk of depression. Experimental research indicates that religious activities may reduce depressive symptoms and that religiously accommodative psychotherapy is at least as effective at treating depression as secular therapy.
Suicide	Religious involvement is negatively correlated with suicide, suicidal behavior, and suicidal ideation across many samples from many nations. It is likely that this negative correlation is mediated by psychological factors such as reduced depression, higher self-esteem, moral objections, and social factors such as lower divorce rates and increased social support, which are all associated with religious involvement. There is little longitudinal research on the relationship between religion and suicide.

Anxiety disorders	The majority of evidence indicates that religion, especially intrinsic religiousness, tends to protect against anxiety; however, one study found that religiousness is positively correlated with the severity of obsessive–compulsive disorder. Religious involvement may be particularly important in protecting individuals with major medical illnesses from experiencing anxiety associated with dependency, loss of control, and end-of-life issues. Religious interventions appear to be helpful in treating religious patients with anxiety.
Schizophrenia and other psychoses	It is not likely that religious factors play a role in the etiology or course of schizophrenia, given the biological nature of this disease; however, there is no prospective research on religiousness as a predictor of schizophrenia, and therefore few conclusions can be drawn. Even though psychotic patients often have religious delusions, many studies show that religiousness is not correlated with schizotypal or psychotic thinking. In addition, some studies show a negative relationship between psychotic tendencies and religiousness. Religious–spiritual interventions and religious communities may facilitate healing and reduce the isolation of individuals with schizophrenia.
Alcohol and drug use	As of 2001, there were approximately 100 studies indicating that religion may be a deterrent to alcohol or drug abuse in children, adolescents, and adults. In reality, greater religious involvement is associated with less likelihood of initiating alcohol or other drug use or abuse. The exact reason for this correlation is unknown, but it may be because of the influence religion has on friend selection, moral values, and coping skills. Church-based programs, 12-step programs, and private spiritual practices have been shown to significantly improve rehabilitation of individuals with addictions to such substances.
Delinquency	There is growing evidence that religious involvement may help buffer against delinquent attitudes and behaviors involving both victimless and victim-related crimes. Thus, religiousness in youth may decrease the risk of adult criminality. It is also apparent that specific kinds of religious activity can help direct individuals that have become involved in deviant behavior back to a course of less deviant behavior.
Marital instability	Because of the serious negative consequences of marital instability on individuals, families, and society at large, many studies have been done to determine the role that religion plays in promoting marital stability. Numerous studies have found a positive relationship between religious involvement and marital stability. Studies have shown that couples that have enjoyed satisfying long-term marriages often cite religion as a key factor to their success. This relationship may be because of increased commitment, religious monogamy, proscriptions against divorce, and spiritual well-being.
Personality traits (hostility, hope, and control)	There is a robust, positive association between high levels of religious or spiritual involvement and low levels of hostility and high levels of hope. Intrinsic religiousness is not correlated with external locus of control, and some religious problem-solving styles may allow religious people to maintain an internal locus of control while believing that God is also in control. This combination may help religious people maintain health and recover more quickly from life stress. These three personality variables have been shown to predict both mental and physical health.

Note. Data from Koenig, McCullough, and Larson (2001).

People who engage in religious coping (e.g., praying, reading sacred writings, meditating, seeking support from religious leaders and community) during stressful times tend to adjust better to crises and problems. Evidence shows that people who turn to God for help in coping with stress have lower levels of anxiety, less depression, greater self-esteem, and higher psychosocial competence.

Many studies have provided evidence that people who are intrinsically religious report less anxiety, including less death anxiety, than those who are not. These persons also experience more freedom from worry and neurotic guilt (i.e., guilt in the absence of wrongdoing, resulting in depression, anxiety, or obsessions) than do less religious people.

Several studies with nonclinical samples have shown that religious commitment is usually associated with lower levels of depression. Some evidence also suggests that church attendance is strongly predictive of less depression in elderly people.

Social Conduct. Studies have consistently shown that people who attend church are less likely to divorce than those who do not. Studies have also consistently shown a positive relationship between religious participation and marital satisfaction and adjustment.

Considerable evidence indicates that those with high levels of religious involvement are less likely to use or abuse alcohol, with lower rates among members of denominations that discourage or prohibit alcohol consumption. There is also extensive evidence that religiously committed people are less likely to use or abuse drugs.

Many studies have shown that religious denominations that have clear, unambiguous prohibitions against premarital sex have lower rates of premarital sex and teenage pregnancy than others. Research has consistently shown that religious commitment, as measured by church attendance, is negatively associated with delinquency. Finally, numerous studies have found that religiously committed people report fewer suicidal impulses and more negative attitudes toward suicide, and they are less likely to commit suicide than nonreligious people.

Religion and Serious Mental Illness. Empirical evidence on the relationship of spiritual and religious variables with serious mental illness—such as major affective disorders, personality disorders, eating disorders, schizophrenia, and other psychotic disorders—is dramatically less abundant than on the other categories of human functioning, because most studies have been done on cross sections of college students. Some findings do show that people with psychosis are less likely to be involved in religion (Stark, 1971), but this could be because their disorder precludes activity in many of life's social dimensions.

In general, few comparisons have been made of truly pathological versus nonpathological groups, and insufficient assessments are available showing rates of specific clinical disturbances within random samples of particular religious and nonreligious populations. Judd's (1985) accumulation of Minnesota Multiphasic Personality Inventory data from studies of many religious groups showed normal mean profiles and no differences across mainstream denominations in the United States. Because evidence to date is ambiguous, no firm conclusions can be drawn about religion and serious mental disorders. More studies are needed.

Some Caveats

Although many studies show positive relationships between religion and a variety of health indices, there are several important reservations to be noted about these findings: (a) most of the data are correlational, partly because researchers cannot experimentally manipulate a person's spirituality; (b) most researchers do not control for additional variables that may contaminate religion and health correlations (e.g., marital status is related to both religiousness and mental health); and (c) the definition and measurement of spiritual or religious variables are not well-refined, which leads to large error variances and frequent small correlations.

Despite these difficulties and limitations, research on religious variables is not inferior to research on many other personal, social, and health variables. Numerous studies show a pattern of findings favorable to religious involvement that has not previously been consistently identified. This pattern is particularly relevant to practice, because about one third of the U.S. population identifies religion as the most important factor in their lives, and another third considers it to be among the more important influences (see Bergin et al., 1996, p. 304).

Although the accumulating evidence for mental and physical health benefits of some features of religiousness and spirituality is gaining recognition, we realize that the picture is not always positive. Clinical practitioners who are treating disturbed individuals often see some of the worst aspects of religion, and we address such issues in the clinical chapters. Another important consideration is that statistical data results do not have to be approached spiritually: many have valid naturalistic interpretations.

Possible Interpretations of the Empirical Findings

Levin (1995), a social scientist at the Eastern Virginia Medical School in Norfolk, Virginia, has suggested some possible interpretations of the empirical findings. We have rephrased his outline according to our understanding of the issues:

1. Religious belief and affiliation provide a person with a secure sense of identity, which lowers one's average anxiety level and facilitates resiliency under stress.

2. Religious conviction may provide a sense of purpose and meaning that enables rational interpretations of life's problems, including death.
3. Positive emotions of hope, faith, optimism, and catharsis emerge from beliefs and rituals, including the process of forgiveness and the hope of healing and redemption.
4. Religious affiliation links one with a network or community of believers that provides a feeling of belonging, family, and social support in times of need, as well as a steady flow of opportunities to serve other people.
5. Religion through prayer, ritual, worship, and so forth provides inner experiences of communion between the individual and the "Higher Power" that may yield insight or peace even if there is not a Higher Power.
6. Many beliefs lead to a lifestyle that includes healthy habits and a healthy inner sense of responsibility and self-control. For example, Mormons and Seventh-Day Adventists show positive health indicators because they do not smoke, drink liquor, or eat meat immoderately.

Actually, all of these "natural" explanations imply that religion can be a powerful, beneficial sociocultural factor, even without invoking the influence of God; however, we conclude that none of these influences would be enduring or powerful if the influence of God were not present. Levin (1995) offers another alternative interpretation: that there is a superempirical healing energy activated by religion that is, in effect, a divine blessing on the human bioenergetic system.

Regardless of how it is interpreted, the correlation between religion and health shows substantial statistical data in harmony with the theistic hypothesis that faith in God and religious involvement can have beneficial effects on human functioning. Despite the documented successes in finding statistical correlations between various spirituality measures and diverse indexes of physical and mental health, Slife, Hope, and Nebeker (1999) argue that this field of inquiry is laced with inconsistencies and incompatibilities in its definitions, methodologies, and theoretical concepts. Improving the coherence and efficacy of this work clearly is a prime objective for the future, and doing so could enhance the strength of the findings (Plante & Sherman, 2001; Miller & Thoresen, 2003).

THEISTICALLY BASED SPIRITUAL REALITIES

The previously described account of quantitative research supports a scholarly spiritual perspective. Compared with the dearth of academic substance that existed in the mid 20th century for such a view, the extent and quality of the current empirical findings are stunning. We consider these data to be valuable and important; however, a spiritual worldview goes far beyond such ordinary empirical findings to contribute profound implications for understanding human personality and functioning. Although quantitative results make a considerable impact, they are not the main foundation of a spiritual perspective. We emphasize that the following content departs from a quantitative empirical philosophy and method to provide a serious introduction to spiritual ways of knowing that we consider to be of great importance. This approach depends on careful study of individual cases using qualitative procedures that aspire to "subjective proof." Some of these "small-N" studies also include parallel quantitative procedures (e.g., Bergin et al., 1994). Our effort to establish "spiritual validity" thus goes beyond the merely anecdotal.[2]

The accumulated careful research in the religious and spiritual domain by behavioral scientists is now amenable to articulation with the worldwide findings from descriptive ethnographic studies by comparative religionists and cultural anthropologists (see chap. 4, this volume). The overarching conclusion we draw from all of this work is that the variegated human family has in common the belief that there is another world besides the one people perceive by biological senses and/or scientific instruments. Equal in importance and universality to the worldwide cultural acceptance of family, kinship, and economic and political structures, this belief in "something more" or "something beyond" is no longer easily trivialized by naturalistic scientific interpretations or the waning "secularization hypothesis" of sociology (Hoge, 1996). Therefore, all divisions of inquiry—behavioral, natural, and cultural—have become open to spiritual perspectives—an openness that is unique to this century.

We have already presented substantial empirical findings of mental and physical health benefits for many (but not all) kinds of religious and spiritual commitments. We have also noted the possibility of a superempirical healing energy. Not only are many competent academicians attracted to these new findings and theories (see Templeton & Herrmann's 1994 review),

---

[2] In the previous edition of this book (P. S. Richards & Bergin, 1997), we narrated a variety of parting visions and near-death experiences that M. Morse (1994a) reported and that our colleagues and friends have personally experienced and shared with us. We described these experiences in narrative form as stimuli to readers' *spiritual* understanding and way of knowing rather than as "proof" in the logical or scientific sense. This spiritual "way of knowing" is essential to a theistic strategy (James, 1902/1936), as we discuss further in chapters 6 and 11. Because of space limitations, we do not provide multiple narratives in this volume. Instead we provide brief summaries of the research findings concerning these phenomena. Nevertheless, we wish to reaffirm the importance of qualitative and spiritual ways of knowing for the understanding of spiritual realities. We refer readers to the first edition of this book and to the books cited above for more in-depth narratives. We say more about qualitative methodologies and spiritual ways of knowing in chapter 12.

these perspectives are also consonant with the existential and religious worldviews of the vast majority of human beings, including the Native American cultures of North and South America, the nations of Western civilization, and the people of Asia. All of these, both empirical and philosophical, constitute an overwhelming assemblage of witnesses for a spiritual reality. This spiritual perspective has become easier to accept now that biology and physics have unveiled so many hidden realities behind observable phenomena, such as the fluctuating particles of nuclear mystery that are now captured in poetic metaphors like "quarks," "charm," and the "dance" of electrons.

For clinicians, the important point is that most people who they will be paid to treat believe in this reality: that they have an internal spiritual existence and that their identity, spirit, or personality will persist after death. Many people also believe that they can communicate with God through prayer or other spiritual practices. Many people also believe that their personal faith and spirituality can help them cope and heal—physically and emotionally. We believe that they are right. We have had our own ineffable spiritual encounters with the eternal that undergird our personal lives and professional work. The qualitative and quantitative findings we review of death-related visions, mystical and spiritual experiences, and spiritual and faith healing incidents provide further evidence of the role of spiritual realities in human functioning. Although such findings are wrenching to traditional empirical philosophies, they continue to accumulate, often from surprisingly reliable witnesses. Although we have long-standing spiritual convictions, we have been somewhat startled by the evidence that we have reviewed, and we have had to stretch our conceptual boundaries as well.

We are aware, of course, of the various naturalistic explanations that have been offered to account for near-death experiences, parting visions, faith healings, and other spiritual experiences, such as oxygen deprivation to the brain, chemically induced hallucinations, psychological defenses, delusions, irrationalities, and so on (e.g., Blackmore, 1993; Groth-Marnet, 1989; M. Morse, 1994a; Ring, 1980; Rivas, 2003; R. K. Siegel, 1980). However, those who try to explain all spiritual experiences in naturalistic terms seem more incredulous than those who are willing to stretch their theoretical boundaries to take in evidence from the invisible, spiritual, but real world. William James, perhaps the greatest of American psychologists, was willing to do this (James, 1902/1936), but the majority of modern psychologists have forgotten his great example. We consider ourselves to be directly in the Jamesian tradition. We respect him and his work, and we wish to apply his insightful perspectives of a century ago to our modern research.

Death-Related Visions and the Human Spirit

To probe more deeply into the dynamics and importance of the spiritual perspective, we turn now to *death-related visions* of the ancient view that humans have a spirit or soul. Sacred texts attest to this notion, and theologians and scholars have wrestled with it for centuries (Elkins, 1995).

That there could be a spiritual energy source integrated with the mind and body of human beings is a challenge to mainstream, traditional theories. It is also an appealing invitation to reach beyond the visible, material world to those invisible realities that may be more powerful and lasting than phenomena that people can observe using their senses.

Death-related visions are a manifestation that clinicians can investigate. Although such inquiry can bring one close to the region of pure speculation and wishful fantasy, clinicians who are careful in their investigations and reporting may also come closer to God and learn to recognize the spiritual realities that exist in the universe. M. Morse (1994a) offered this definition for death-related visions:

> A general label for the broad category of spiritual experiences that take place in the arena of death. They are paranormal experiences that happen to normal people. Death-related visions include such events as near-death experiences, after-death visitations, and healing visions. Also included are pre-cognitive experiences, dreams, visions, and other premonitions of death that come true. (p. IX)

The International Association for Near-Death Studies and its affiliate journal have become rich resources for careful research on these unusual phenomena. Although such research tends to get pushed by mainstream scholars into the category of the scientific fringe, we believe that such stereotyping is unfair and misleading. We were skeptical, beginning with the publication of Moody's (1975) book *Life After Life,* but we have changed our view because of a large accumulation of careful research that has been done since then. Although the popular near-death literature is rife with popularized accounts of visions and transportation to other worlds, we believe that part of the scholarly literature is good. We believe that something real is happening with these experiences, and that the happenings are consistent with themes in major world religions.

Numerous books and articles have been written about death-related visions, some of which are enlightening and others far from scholarly. Some of the more scholarly books include *Life at Death: A Scientific Investigation of the Near-Death Experience* (Ring, 1980); *Parting Visions: Uses and Meanings of Pre-Death, Psychic, and Spiritual Experiences* (M. Morse, 1994a); *Recollections of Death: A Medical Investigation* (Sabom, 1982); *Mindsight: Near-Death and Out-of-Body Experiences in the Blind* (Ring & Cooper, 1999); *Light and Death: One Doctor's Fascinating Account of Near-Death Experiences* (Sabom, 1998); and *Religion, Spirituality, and the Near-Death Experience* (Fox, 2003). In addition, the American Psychological Association recently published an edited volume called *Varieties of Anomalous Experience* (Cardena, Lynn, & Krippner, 2000), which includes a chapter on near-death experiences (Greyson, 2000).

Near-Death Experiences

In his pioneering study, Moody (1975) identified a number of elements that seem to characterize many near-death experiences (NDEs):

1. feeling ineffability,
2. hearing oneself pronounced dead,
3. experiencing feelings of peace and quiet,
4. hearing unusual noises,
5. seeing or passing through a dark tunnel,
6. leaving one's body,
7. meeting spiritual beings,
8. experiencing a bright light or being of light,
9. having a panoramic life review,
10. sensing a border or limit, and
11. coming back into the body.

Ring's (1980) qualitative study of 102 near-death experiencers (NDEers) provided general confirmation of Moody's description of NDEs. Ring (1980) also concluded that NDEs tend to unfold in a stage-like or sequential manner: (a) feeling peace and a sense of well-being; (b) experiencing separation from the physical body; (c) entering a transitional realm of darkness; (d) seeing a brilliant light; and (e) entering through the light into another realm of existence. He also found that more than 50% of those he interviewed reported that they had made a decision to come back or were sent back to their physical bodies. Some people also reported a life review and encounters with a presence or being of light and/or deceased loved ones (Ring, 1980).

Many other studies during the past two decades have provided general confirmation of the nature and reality of NDEs. It is now a well-accepted fact that anywhere from 5% to 30% of those who come close to death have an NDE (Greyson, 2000). This acceptance is reflected in the inclusion of the following definition of *near-death experience* in *The Dictionary of Modern Medicine* (Segen, 1992):

> A phenomenon of unclear nature that may occur in patients who have been clinically dead and then resuscitated; the patients report a

continuity of subjective experience, remembering visitors and other hospital events despite virtually complete suppression of cortical activity; near-death experiences are considered curiosities with no valid explanation in the context of an acceptable biomedical paradigm. (p. 483)

This definition also acknowledges that the meaning of the NDE remains a subject of professional debate. Nevertheless, a number of well-documented case reports of NDEs, as well as several carefully conducted research studies, have made it increasingly difficult for skeptics to simply discount NDEs as simply physiological or psychological epiphenomena. To illustrate, we briefly describe one case report and two research studies.

Michael Sabom, a cardiologist who has interviewed many people who have had NDEs in hospital settings, described in considerable detail the NDE of a woman who had complications during brain surgery for a cerebral aneurysm (Sabom, 1998). This case provided continuous documentation of the woman's medical and physiological state during surgery and during her NDE, including her cerebral cortical brain activity and evoked potentials in the brain stem. Despite totally flat electroencephalograms of her cortex and brain stem, along with a lack of blood in her brain, this woman reported a very deep NDE, including an out-of-body experience. While out of her body, she viewed the operating room from above the neurosurgeon's shoulder and later accurately described the doctors, nurses, and technicians in the room, as well as several peculiar details of the surgery (Sabom, 1998). Such cases are extremely difficult to account for in biomedical, naturalistic terms (Greyson, 2000).

Pim van Lommel and his colleagues in the Division of Cardiology at the Hospital Rijnstate in Arnhem, the Netherlands, studied 344 successfully resuscitated cardiac arrest patients and reported their findings in *The Lancet* (van Lommel, van Wees, Meyers, & Elfferich, 2001). They found that 18% of the cardiac arrest patients reported a Moody/Ring type of NDE, and 12% reported a deep or core NDE. Some of the noteworthy features of this study were (a) it was a prospective study rather than retrospective, which enabled the researchers to interview the cardiac arrest survivors within a few days of resuscitation; (b) detailed data were available regarding the NDEers' medical and physiological conditions during and after their cardiac arrest and NDEs; (c) statistical analyses of the data enabled the researchers to examine whether NDEs were associated with certain medical and physiological states; and (d) two- and eight-year follow-up interviews of the NDEers and a control group of non-NDEers were conducted to better understand the longevity and impact of the NDEs.

Van Lommel et al. (2001) concluded that psychological, neurophysiological, or physiological factors could not account for the NDEs of the cardiac arrest patients in their study. They also concluded that the NDEs were associated with positive and long-lasting changes in attitudes and behaviors, including a more loving and empathic attitude, more involvement with family, a greater sense of life purpose and meaning, more interest in spirituality, less fear of death, a stronger belief in an afterlife, and a greater appreciation of ordinary things. Such positive life changes have also been observed in numerous other studies of NDEers (e.g., Moody, 1975; M. Morse, 1994a; Ring, 1980; Sabom, 1982). Van Lommel et al. (2001) concluded their research article by suggesting that NDEs

> might be a changing state of consciousness (transcendence), in which identity, cognition, and emotion function independently from the unconscious body, but retain the possibility of non-sensory perception. Research should be concentrated on explaining scientifically the occurrence and content of NDE, focusing on certain specific elements of NDE, such as out-of-body experiences and other verifiable aspects. Finally, the theory and background of transcendence should be included as a part of an explanatory framework for these experiences. (p. 2044)

Another study that challenges naturalistic explanations of NDEs investigated the out-of-body experiences of blind individuals (Ring & Cooper, 1997). Ring and Cooper (1997) interviewed 21 NDEers, of whom 10 were congenitally blind, 9 had lost their sight after the age of 5, and 2 were severely visually impaired. Participants reported *visual* observation of persons, places, and events that require "seeing." Although the "vision" of blind people is somewhat different from that of a person who has always had sight, evidence from these respondents suggests they were able to see via spiritual "eyes" physical objects they had known previously only through their other senses (Ring & Cooper, 1997).

Other Death-Related Experiences

Although they have attracted less research, a variety of other death-related experiences have been reported in the literature, including (a) visions or visitations of the deceased to their loved ones; (b) dreams, visions, and other premonitions of the living that a loved one has recently died or is going to die; and (c) near-death visions where someone who is about to die sees and describes loved ones who have previously passed on (M. Morse, 1994a, 1994b). Melvin Morse, a clinical professor and pediatric physician at the University of Washington Medical School, collected and described many of these spiritual phenomena. We refer interested readers to his book for numerous narrative descriptions of such experiences, as well as near-death experiences, many of which were reported by physicians, nurses, and other professionals (M. Morse, 1994a).

M. Morse (1994a) summed up his observations of an array of findings about death-related visions with the following statements, with which we concur:

> People who have visions of this type enjoy excellent mental health. . . . There is some evidence that they are actually physically changed by their encounter with the light. It may alter the subtle electromagnetic fields that surround our bodies . . . near-death experiences are not the result of brain dysfunction. Similar transformative effects are not seen after hallucinations from oxygen deprivation, narcotics, and acute psychotic events. (p. 160)
>
> There is strong scientific support for my conclusion that there are physical and spiritual patterns that interconnect all of life. Modern physicists teach us that life is light, of varying wavelengths. . . . Electromagnetic forces unify everything we consider to be real. (pp. 162–163)
>
> We have a large area of our brain devoted to spiritual visions and psychical abilities . . . the right temporal lobe and surrounding structures. . . . We have a portion of the brain that connects us with the divine. But are these experiences . . . proof of life after death? As far as I am concerned, the answer is yes. (p. 173)

Without further arguing the extensive evidence, we add our names to the growing list of traditional scholars (see chap. 1, this volume) who have concluded that there is a spirit or soul capable of perception and action, a spirit normally integrated with the physical body that constitutes the lasting or eternal identity of the individual. It is apparently through the human spirit that the spirit of God most readily has its influence on people's thoughts, feelings, actions, and well-being. We assume that the spirit interacts with other aspects of the person to produce what is normally referred to as personality and behavior.

Mystical and Spiritual Experiences

Mystical and spiritual experiences also have important implications for a theistic orientation. Mystical and spiritual experiences are not well understood by naturalistic scientists, but they are common and have been the subject of considerable scholarship (e.g., Hood, 1995).

In a June 2002 Gallup survey, 41% of Americans indicated that they had a "profound religious experience or awakening that changed the direction of [their lives]" (Gallup, 2003, p. 7). This confirms previous surveys that have consistently found that more than 30% of Americans have reported life-changing religious experiences (Gallup, 2003). Consistent with Gallup surveys, Greeley (1975) found in a national sample of 1,468 persons that approximately 35% of the respondents indicated that on one or more occasions they had felt as though they were "very close to a powerful, spiritual force" that seemed to lift them out of themselves (Greeley, 1975). Such findings have been replicated with much consistency in numerous other surveys, including one conducted in Great Britain (Hay & Morisy, 1978).

Considerable research has been done about the nature of mystical and spiritual experiences and their psychological and religious correlates (Hood, Spilka, Hunsberger, & Gorsuch, 1996; Spilka, Hood, & Gorsuch, 1985; Wulff, 2000). Mystical experiences seem to share the following common core of essential characteristics:

1. *Noetic:* They are perceived as a valid source of knowledge.
2. *Ineffable:* They cannot be adequately described.
3. *Holy:* They are perceived by those who experience them as an encounter with the sacred or divine.
4. *Pleasant:* They bring feelings of peace, bliss, and joy.
5. *Paradoxical:* They defy logic.

Some people report that they sensed inner subjectivity, unity of all things, timelessness and spacelessness, and loss of self (Spilka et al., 1985). Research has also shown both mild and extreme types of mystical experiences, with the extreme ones adding a number of distinctive elements, such as dramatic mood swings and the use of various ascetic practices (Wulff, 2000). Although more studies are needed, research to date suggests that mystical experiencing is not usually associated with psychopathology but is most often correlated with better psychological functioning (Spilka et al., 1985; Wulff, 2000). There is also some evidence that mystical experiences may promote therapeutic healing and change (Wulff, 2000).

In addition to these classic aspects of mystical experience, people throughout the ages have reported a variety of other types of spiritual manifestations, including

1. "hearing" the voice of God within their minds;
2. receiving spiritual impressions and insights;
3. having an inspirational dream or vision;
4. experiencing the presence (or spirit) of God;
5. feeling the presence of deceased loved ones;
6. feeling loved and forgiven by God;
7. receiving flashes of insight and inspiration when confronted with difficult problems;
8. experiencing feelings of awe, gratitude and oneness with God and others; and
9. receiving spiritual impressions or warnings that protect self and/or loved ones from danger (Griffin, 2000; W. R. Miller & C'DeBaca, 1994).

Such experiences sometimes come unbidden and unexpected, but at other times accompany religious practices such as praying, meditating, worshipping, participating in religious rituals, and studying scriptures.

Many types of spiritual experiences are normative in various theistic religions, and the report of such experiences is not usually associated with psychopathology (Sanderson, Vandenberg, & Paese, 1999). Furthermore, spiritual experiences often provoke major life changes and positive and enduring transformations in the values and lifestyles of those who experience them (W. R. Miller & C'DeBaca, 1994).

Spiritual and Anomalous Healing Experiences

Human history is replete with accounts of miraculous faith healings and other unexpected recoveries from serious illness and injury (Benor, 1992; McClenon, 2002). Although a proportion of these accounts are probably not genuine or may be "spontaneous" remissions, many of them have occurred in modern times, are medically well documented, and cannot be explained in the context of conventional biomedicine (Benor, 1992; Benson, 1996; Krippner & Achterberg, 2000; Levin, 2001).

Studies and case reports that examine the phenomenology of spiritual and anomalous healing experiences[3] have found that, during the time such healing takes place, it is not uncommon for people to "see religious figures or balls of great white light, to have special dreams or visions, and to feel heat and tingling in the location of the problem" (Krippner & Achterberg, 2000, p. 363). Positive emotions and long-term improvements in mental, spiritual, and physical well-being have also been reported by those having these experiences (Benson, 1996; Krippner & Achterberg, 2000; Levin, 2001). Many people attribute their healing and recovery to spiritual beliefs, practices, and influences, such as prayer, meditation, guided imagery, sense of purpose, and faith rather than to medical treatment (e.g., Benson, 1996; Hirshberg & Barasch, 1995; Krippner & Achterberg, 2000).

A variety of alternative, complementary, and spiritual healing practices have been described, including intercessory prayer, faith healing, distant or nonlocal healing, laying on of hands, shamanic healing, and psychic healing (Krippner & Achterberg, 2000; Krippner & Welch, 1992). These healing practices attract many practitioners and patients, and they are considered normative in many religious traditions in the world. Such healing practices are sufficiently widespread and influential throughout the world that in 1995 the Office of Alternative Medicine of the U.S. National Institutes of Health convened a panel to study them (Krippner & Achterberg, 2000). Such

---

[3] Cardena, Lynn, and Krippner (2000) defined anomalous experience as "an uncommon experience" or one that deviates "from ordinary experience or from the usually accepted explanations of reality" (p. 4).

increased interest among medical and psychological researchers in spiritual and anomalous healing may lead to better understanding and clearer differentiation between the roles of spiritual and other factors in health and healing.

Caveats and Countercritique

The foregoing material is only a small sample of the qualitative and quantitative research that indicates the existence of spiritual realities. Many of the reports have no specific reference to God, whereas others do. In either case, the experiences often have positive transforming effects, causing many to report an increase in spirituality and in faith but a decrease in denominational adherence (W. R. Miller & C'DeBaca, 1994; Ring, 1980; Ring & Valarino, 1998; Sabom, 1982; Sutherland, 1992). The related epistemology of religious experience has a long history in philosophical scholarship, which we cannot review here, but we call attention to Alston's (1991) excellent review and modern rationale for the perceptual knowledge of God.

We recognize that many mainstream scientists have a deep-seated skepticism and resistance to our suggestion that the types of experiences we have described are grounded in spiritual realities. As we have acknowledged, we agree that healthy skepticism is needed when evaluating such reports. Nevertheless, there is a difference between healthy skepticism and closed-minded dogmatism, and we fear that an unexamined acceptance of scientific naturalism constrains many scientists from openly examining the evidence for spiritual realities.

Skeptics of research on spiritual experiences such as death-related visions, mystical experiences, and anomalous healing experiences have discounted the reality of such phenomena on several grounds (Griffin, 2000): (a) most researchers who study spiritual experiences believe in their reality and are thus biased; (b) spiritual experiences conflict with the naturalistic scientific worldview; (c) studies of spiritual experiences are difficult to replicate, which calls into question their reality; and (d) studies of spiritual experiences may be discounted because of methodological flaws.

It is beyond the scope of this chapter to respond to each of these criticisms in detail, but we will briefly comment on each of them. First, although it is probably true that most who research spiritual realities believe in them and thus have biases that influence their interpretations of the evidence, this is also true of skeptics. All researchers, including those committed to the dominant scientific naturalistic worldview, have theological and philosophical beliefs that influence and bias their scholarship and interpretations of data (Slife & Williams, 1995). The assumptions of the scientific naturalistic worldview (see chap. 2, this volume) have gone unquestioned for so long that many scientists are not even aware of the implicit biases that shape their work and constrain their understandings and interpretations (Griffin, 2000; Slife & Williams, 1995; Slife et al., 1999). The fact that researchers may have positive views of spirituality does not automatically invalidate all of the findings they report regarding spiritual experiences. Such an argument would invalidate most if not all scientific findings, for the notion of an unbiased, value- and assumption-free scientist is a myth.

Second, although it is true that theistic interpretations of spiritual experiences conflict with the scientific naturalistic worldview and a materialistic understanding of the nature of matter, to rule out spiritual realities on such grounds is tautological (Griffin, 2000). The most compelling reason many skeptics have proffered for rejecting all of the evidence for spiritual realities and other anomalous experiences is "that the 'accepted [scientific naturalistic] framework' is correct" and that data that do not fit this framework are therefore incorrect (Griffin, 2000, p. 218). To say that interpretations of empirical data that do not fit naturalistic and materialistic assumptions are spurious is to assume *a priori* that the materialistic naturalistic worldview is true. Ruling out any and all data that do not conform to the naturalistic materialistic worldview by such circular reasoning does not make this worldview true. As we discuss in chapter 4, there are many reasons to question the empirical and philosophical adequacy of the scientific naturalistic worldview (Griffin, 2000). Naturalistic interpretations, therefore, should not be privileged over theistic interpretations of spiritual and other anomalous experiences simply because they better fit the prevailing scientific naturalistic framework.

Third, although much of the research about spiritual and anomalous experiences does not meet rigorous scientific standards of experimental control and replicability, these weaknesses do not render these experiences unreal or unimportant. Critics of research on spiritual and anomalous experiences often insist on rigorous standards of replicability and experimenter control for such studies but fail to acknowledge that similar rigorous standards are not applied in other sciences, including astronomy, psychology, and sociology (Griffin, 2000). McClenon (1984) argued that there "should be no need for a completely repeatable experiment to make any field legitimate. If psychology and sociology were stripped of all their 'nonrepeatable' experiments, they would be restricted to only their most simplistic and absurdly commonsensical formulations" (p. 12).

Additionally, critics who insist on strict experimental control and replicability as criteria for valid studies of spiritual phenomena often fail to recognize that such criteria are value preferences based on particular philosophical assumptions—they are not absolute truths about how research must be conducted (Slife, 2004). As we discuss in chapters 2 and 4, the philosophies of empiricism and universalism assume that what is real must be observable, measurable, and subject to replication and experimenter control. But if spiritual or anomalous phenomena are not easily observed or measured, and if the contexts and conditions within which spiritual or anomalous realities can be experienced are difficult to create and control by researchers, then it may be difficult or impossible to study these phenomena using traditional experimental methods (Griffin, 2000; Slife et al., 1999).

In contrast, the philosophies of epistemological pluralism and contextuality assume that many real phenomena, including spiritual and anomalous ones, are not subject to experimenter control or replication. These philosophies question whether experimental control and replication are always the best criteria for deciding whether a phenomenon is real. Epistemological pluralism and contextuality suggest that other methodologies, such as qualitative investigations, case studies, and methods yet to be invented are needed for scientists to gain insight into spiritual and anomalous phenomena.

Fourth, some critics of research on spiritual and anomalous experiences argue that such studies can be discounted as evidence because they are methodologically flawed. It is true that many studies on spiritual phenomena do have flaws—some of them serious—but this is also true of most studies in all of the sciences, particularly psychology and other human and health sciences. Many critics insist that studies that make extraordinary claims, such as those on spiritual and anomalous experiences, must provide extraordinary evidence (Griffin, 2000). The problem is that virtually no research study is without flaws, and so skeptics who wish to discount findings can always find reasons to do so. As described by McClenon (1984),

> Sooner or later, the critic will ask for information that is no longer available or for a degree of experimental control and exactitude that is desirable in principle but impossible in practice. One rhetorical ploy is to demand total perfection. It is always possible for critics to think of more rigid methodological procedures after an experiment has been conducted. (p. 89)

As with the issues of experimenter control and replicability, skeptics who are committed ideologically to the scientific naturalistic worldview often apply the standards of methodological rigor selectively. They tolerate methodological flaws in studies that are in harmony with naturalistic understanding of the world but insist on strict standards of rigor for studies that might conflict with their preconceptions (Griffin, 2000). In ruling out theistic interpretations of research findings, they often propose alternative explanations for the findings about spiritual and anomalous experiences to be consistent with the scientific naturalistic worldview (e.g., Blackmore, 1993). Often these alternative explanations are even less consistent with the data than spiritual explanations, but they are preferred by the critics simply to harmonize with naturalistic views of reality (Griffin, 2000). However, as Truzzi (1980) pointed out,

> The burden of proof for such alternatives must rest with the proponents for such alternatives (many of which have been shown to be quite inadequate to fit the facts). . . . Science primarily grows through continued research and not mainly through criticism based upon what might have gone wrong in experiments that we might wish to see invalidated. One can *hypothetically* explain away *any* result in science. Criticisms, just like the claims of the proponents, must also be falsifiable if we are to consider them scientific statements! (pp. 39, 46)

In closing, the "methodological imperialism" of some naturalists constrains the creativity needed to address the surprisingly and increasingly robust indicators of "other" realities. We hope that scientists will approach the study of spiritual and other anomalous experiences with open minds. We hope that they will not rule out theistic understandings of these experiences *a priori* simply because such understandings call into question the prevailing assumptions of the materialistic and naturalistic scientific worldview. We believe that a better understanding of such spiritual experiences could have important implications for science and humanity. In particular, we are hopeful that a better understanding of spiritual realities could increase health professionals' ability to assist members of the human family in coping with and healing from life's challenges and vicissitudes.

CONCLUSION

In this chapter we discuss a complex spectrum of topics that are fundamental to a spiritual strategy in personality theory and psychotherapy. A single chapter does not do justice to the extensive literature, the concepts, or the practical implications that flow from them. The strong trends that are altering the flow of professional work in mental health are difficult to condense and articulate. We expect that we, along with many colleagues, will be working on this new frame of reference for a long time.

In the meantime, we want to be as clear as possible. We are saying that there is a spiritual reality that is linked with divine intelligence, or the Spirit of Truth. This is not "pop psychology." We intend it to be serious—philosophically, empirically, and clinically. It finds support in the history of world cultures, a century of behavioral science, and the intense and inspired work of many sophisticated professionals over the past 30 years. It is not new, but its format and style as an approach to psychotherapy are new.

The assumptions and the bipolar constructs we have presented emerge from a context of multiple influences and authors. We have stated them boldly so that this unique perspective will stand out and will give direction to the next steps in research, theory, and practice. We cannot state too emphatically that people are eternal spiritual beings who have the capacity to communicate with and be influenced by their Creator through spiritual means.

By asserting this theistic strategy, we do not intend to denigrate the positive contributions of naturalistic, secular, and humanistic approaches. When possible, these approaches need to be integrated or built together into a more compelling picture of human functioning. Openness to new and different ideas is essential. Similarly, our emphasis on qualitative and narrative inquiries does not mean that standard research and statistical methods should be abandoned. Fortunately, our review of such research has provided substantial hope that there is something to the spiritual phenomena we posit but can only infer from quantitative studies. We hope that new methodologies will be developed that can match the elusive but powerful energies that manifest themselves in the human spirit.

Finally, we need to reaffirm that human personality is inherently relational. In this, the social constructionists and postmodernists are correct. The great commandments of the major religions concur as they emphasize people's relationships to God and to each other. The human race is a family, and people's kinship flows from a common creation. When identity and agency are optimally functional, their nature and influence shape and are shaped by the basic sociality of humanness as expressed in integrity, intimacy, fidelity, kinship, benevolent power, and communal structure, with a commitment to human welfare through personal responsibility.

IV

THEISTIC PSYCHOTHERAPY: PROCESS AND METHODS

6

A THEISTIC VIEW
OF PSYCHOTHERAPY

I am astonished that my scientific studies have so conclusively shown that our bodies are wired to believe, that our bodies are nourished and healed by prayer and other exercises of belief. . . . My reasoning and personal experience lead me to believe that there is a God. And yes, a thoughtful design must have been at work in the universe in which such definite patterns emerge, in which such incredible coincidences produced our world, and in which humans are wired to bear a physiologically healing faith.

—Herbert Benson, MD

Each of the major mainstream psychotherapy traditions offers a somewhat unique perspective about the nature of treatment. None of them, however, adequately incorporates a theistic, spiritual view of the world and of human personality. Given that in North America and Europe more than 80% of the population professes belief in, or is affiliated with, one of the theistic world religions (D. B. Barrett & Johnson, 2002), we think the need for a theistic psychotherapy orientation—an orientation that is more culturally compatible with the worldviews and values of theistic clients—is obvious. Although theistic psychotherapy has not yet taken a place of equality with mainstream secular therapy traditions with regard to the attention it is given in textbooks, journals, and graduate training programs, we anticipate that theistic clients from many cultures will readily accept it.

In this chapter we describe some of the distinctive features of a theistic psychotherapy orientation. Our view is grounded in the theistic conceptual framework we describe in previous chapters, which includes our theological premises (chap. 4), philosophical assumptions (chap. 4), and model of personality (chap. 5). This conceptual framework influences our understanding of (a) the purpose and goals of therapy, (b) the therapist's role in therapy, (c) the client's role in therapy, and (d) the nature of the therapy relationship.

PURPOSE AND GOALS OF THERAPY

The most distinctive thing about our orientation that differentiates it from the major secular therapeutic systems is the idea that God can intervene in the lives of human beings to help them cope, heal, and change. Theistic psychotherapists, therefore, may encourage their clients to explore how their faith in God and personal spirituality may assist them during treatment and recovery. They may also implement spiritual interventions designed to help clients heal and grow spiritually. We think that therapeutic change is facilitated and is often more profound and lasting, when people heal and grow spiritually through God's inspiration and love (P. S. Richards, 1999). No mainstream secular psychotherapy orientation acknowledges the possible existence of God and spiritual realities, let alone makes faith in God's loving and healing influence the foundation of its theory and approach (Bergin, 1980a; Jones, 1994).

In addition to theistic axioms, we endorse a multidimensional view of human nature, personality, and therapeutic change. Biological, emotional, social and systemic, cognitive, behavioral, and spiritual processes affect human functioning. Because of this, no strategy, including a spiritual one, should be used exclusively but rather as part of a multidimensional, integrative approach. During the assessment phase of treatment, psychotherapists should attempt to understand their clients in a multidimensional way. Therapy goals should be pragmatically tailored to best meet the unique needs, concerns, symptoms, and preferences of individual clients, and this may or may not include religious and spiritual goals. However, with many clients, such goals are crucial for success.

We assume that the overall purpose of psychotherapy is to help clients cope with and resolve their presenting symptoms and concerns and also to promote their long-term healing, growth, and well-being. We assume that the latter goal can be enhanced through spiritual beliefs, influences, behaviors, and communities, because they are especially helpful in establishing value-based lifestyles that maintain lasting change and continuing growth (Larson & Larson, 1994).

THE THERAPIST'S ROLE

Professional and spiritual preparation is essential for those who wish to be effective theistic integrative psychotherapists. Theistic psychotherapists must be well trained in mainstream secular psychotherapy traditions so that they can thoughtfully and effectively integrate concepts and interventions from these traditions into their theistic framework. They must also obtain training in multicultural counseling and religious aspects of diversity. They should also seek to develop a number of other skills, including the capacity to adopt a denominational therapeutic stance when appropriate, establish a spiritually open and safe therapeutic alliance, assess the religious and spiritual dimensions of their clients' lives, appropriately handle values issues in therapy, implement spiritual interventions in an ethical and effective manner, and help clients to tap into the resources of their spiritual beliefs, practices, and community to assist in the treatment and healing process. Theistic psychotherapists must also take care of their psychological well-being so that they can model healthy psychological and interpersonal behavior for their clients. They also need to take care of their own spiritual well-being, so that they are spiritually prepared as they work with their clients. We discuss each of the skills and attributes in more detail below. In Exhibit 6.1 we provide a list of proposed competency aspirations for theistic psychotherapists. This list is not intended to define the minimum competencies required in order to ethically and effectively practice theistic psychotherapy. Rather, it represents our first attempt to articulate an ideal list of competencies to which theistic psychotherapists may wish to aspire.

Adopting an Ecumenical Stance

The capacity to adopt an ecumenical therapeutic stance is essential for therapists who work with religious and spiritual clients. The word *ecumenical* means "of worldwide scope or applicability" (American Heritage Dictionaries, 1992, p. 584), interdenominational, or open to diverse perspectives. We define an *ecumenical therapeutic stance* as an attitude and approach to therapy that is suitable for clients of diverse religious affiliations and backgrounds. Therapists should use an ecumenical therapeutic approach during the early stages of therapy with all clients and over the entire course of therapy with clients whose religious affiliation or beliefs differ significantly from their own. This multicultural approach to therapy goes beyond contemporary multicultural approaches by emphasizing the specific attitudes and skills that therapists need in order to understand and sensitively intervene in the spiritual dimensions of their clients' lives. The foundations of this stance are the attitudes and skills developed as an effective multicultural therapist.

Multicultural therapeutic attitudes and skills have been described in detail elsewhere (e.g., Ponterotto, Casas, Suzuki, & Alexander, 1995; Ponterotto, Suzuki, & Meller, 1996; D. W. Sue & Sue, 1977, 1990; D. W. Sue, Bergnier, Duran, Feinberg, Pedersen, et al., 1982; S. Sue, Zane, & Young, 1994). Unfortunately, therapists who have developed multicultural attitudes and skills, which enable them to deal sensitively with many human differences, are not always able to apply these attitudes and skills in their work with religious and spiritual clients. Although multicultural sensitivity has increased remarkably within the psychotherapy profession during the past

EXHIBIT 6.1
Competency Aspirations for Theistic Psychotherapists

1. Theistic psychotherapists ground their therapeutic orientation in their theistic worldview and seek to coherently integrate secular interventions into their theistic framework.
2. Theistic psychotherapists seek ecumenical expertise in religious and spiritual aspects of diversity.
3. Theistic psychotherapists seek denominational expertise in order to better assist clients from specific religious denominations.
4. Theistic psychotherapists understand and follow professional ethical guidelines and standards and are aware of special ethical concerns that may arise when religious and spiritual issues are part of treatment.
5. Theistic psychotherapists seek to create a spiritually open therapeutic environment so that their clients understand that it is safe and appropriate to discuss their religious and spiritual beliefs and concerns.
6. Theistic psychotherapists capably and routinely assess the religious and spiritual dimensions of their clients' lives as part of a multidimensional assessment strategy.
7. Theistic psychotherapists help clients to formulate religious and spiritual goals for treatment when appropriate.
8. Theistic psychotherapists effectively implement religious and spiritual interventions during therapy, when appropriate, in order to help clients tap into the resources of their faith and spirituality.
9. Theistic psychotherapists understand when religious and spiritual interventions are contraindicated and avoid using them in such situations.
10. Theistic psychotherapists establish respectful relationships with leaders and professionals in their clients' religious communities and consult with or refer to them when appropriate.
11. Theistic psychotherapists understand how to handle value conflicts that may arise during therapy in an ethical and effective manner with respect for their clients' agency and well-being.
12. Theistic psychotherapists understand how to model and teach health and human welfare values when it is relevant to their clients' growth and well-being.
13. Theistic psychotherapists take care of their own spiritual well-being so that they are spiritually as well as professionally prepared to work with clients.
14. Theistic psychotherapists seek to create a spiritual "space" during therapy so that spiritual insights, feelings, and influences can potentially be experienced and explored.
15. Theistic psychotherapists seek to have brotherly or sisterly love for clients—and a desire to promote their emotional and spiritual welfare, growth, and autonomy.

two decades, religious and spiritual issues have been neglected in training programs and the multicultural literature (Bergin, 1980a, 1983; Henning & Tirrell, 1982; Tan, 1993). Because of personal biases, lack of knowledge and empathy, and fears about religious and spiritual matters, many therapists remain unprepared to work sensitively with religious and spiritual clients and issues (Bergin, 1991; Henning & Tirrell, 1982).

Effective ecumenical therapists must be able to generalize multicultural attitudes and skills to the religious and spiritual domains. Therapists with good ecumenical skills

1. are aware of their own religious heritage and values and are sensitive to how they could affect their work with clients from different spiritual traditions;
2. are capable of communicating understanding and respect to clients who have spiritual beliefs that are different from their own;
3. understand how their own spiritual beliefs could bias their clinical judgment;
4. are sensitive to circumstances (e.g., value conflicts) that could dictate referral of a religious client to a therapist with more religious expertise;
5. seek knowledge about their clients' religious beliefs and traditions;
6. avoid making assumptions about clients based on religious affiliation alone but seek to understand each client's unique spiritual worldview and beliefs;
7. understand how to sensitively handle value and belief conflicts that arise during therapy;
8. make efforts to establish respectful and trusting relationships with professionals and leaders in their clients' religious communities;
9. seek to understand the spiritual resources in their clients lives and encourage their clients to draw on these resources in their efforts to cope, heal, and change; and
10. use religious and spiritual interventions that are in harmony with their clients spiritual beliefs when it appears such interventions could be helpful to their clients.

All therapists, regardless of whether they wish to use spiritual interventions in therapy, are ethically obligated to increase their sensitivity to religious and spiritual clients and issues (American Psychological Association [APA], 2002a). Some of the suggestions that have made therapists more aware of the general issues of diversity may be applied in the religious and spiritual domains. For example, psychotherapists should explore and examine their own religious and spiritual heritage, assumptions, biases, and values (cf. Kelly, 1995; Lovinger, 1984), and seek to increase their knowledge, understanding, and empathy for other religious and spiritual traditions, cultures, and beliefs. Studying books on world religions (e.g., Carmody & Carmody, 1989; Farah, 1994; Jacobs, 1984; Nielsen, Hein, Reynolds, Miller,

Karff, et al., 1988; Smart, 1994), taking classes on different world religions, and attending religious services of other faiths contribute to this understanding. Some universities and professional conventions offer courses and seminars in psychology and sociology of religion, and professional literature today includes materials on spiritual issues as well.

Adopting a Denominational Therapeutic Stance

The capacity to adopt a denominational therapeutic stance, when appropriate, also can enhance therapists' effectiveness with some clients. The word *denomination* means "a large group of religious congregations united under a common faith and name and organized under a single administrative and legal hierarchy" (American Heritage Dictionaries, 1992, p. 499). We define a *denominational therapeutic stance* as an approach to therapy that is tailored to clients who are members of a specific religious denomination.

A denominational therapeutic stance builds on the foundation laid earlier in therapy by the therapist's ecumenical stance, but it differs in that the therapist tailors assessment methods and interventions more specifically to the client's particular denominational beliefs and practices. Thus therapists may become more directive, challenging, and educational in their style. However, if nonreligious or atheistic therapists feel that adopting such a stance would require them to be incongruent with clients or compromise their own beliefs and values, we do not advocate that they adopt a denominational stance. Many therapists will be most helpful to clients if they function only within an ecumenical stance.

Therapists who use a denominational approach should do so only with clients who view them as being able to deeply understand, accept, and respect the client's religious and spiritual culture and beliefs, a condition that is most likely to occur if the therapist shares the client's religious denomination or has acquired an in-depth understanding of it (P. S. Richards & Bergin, 2000). Even with such trust and credibility, therapists should use a denominational approach only after careful assessment of the religious and spiritual beliefs of the client has confirmed that (a) the therapist adequately understands the client's unique beliefs; (b) the client has a positive attitude toward religion and spirituality and can address issues of anger, fear, or unhealthy dependency toward religious authorities or God; and (c) the client has explicitly indicated a willingness to participate in denominational assessments and interventions.

When appropriate, a denominational therapeutic stance can give therapists leverage to help clients. Therapists with a deep understanding and experiential familiarity with a religious denomination and culture are more capable of responding to the fine nuances of a client's religious and spiritual issues. They can more fully appreciate, honor, and use the unique religious beliefs and spiritual resources of the client's religious tradition. In addition, they are in a position to critique the tradition and offer credible alternatives to mentally unhealthy themes that may arise therein.

Clinical descriptions of denominational approaches with clients from a variety of specific religious denominations have been published (e.g., Kelly, 1995; Koltko, 1990; Lovinger, 1984; P. S. Richards & Bergin, 2000; Worthington, 1990), providing valuable insight into the complexities and potential benefits of a denominational stance. Throughout the remainder of this book, we discuss various clinical issues (e.g., assessment, ethics, and interventions) from both the ecumenical and denominational perspectives. The ecumenical therapeutic approach tends to be more implicit and the denominational more explicit in its use of spiritual resources in therapy. Tan's (1996) discussion of implicit and explicit integration of religion in clinical practice is helpful for understanding this distinction.

Building a Spiritually Open and Safe Therapeutic Alliance

Research has consistently shown that regardless of a therapist's theoretical orientation, psychotherapy tends to be most effective in the context of a therapeutic relationship, alliance, or bond. Conditions such as rapport, trust, empathy, warmth, respect, acceptance, and credibility have been consistently associated with positive therapy outcomes (Lambert & Bergin, 1994). In fact, for many clients these relationship factors seem to contribute more powerfully to positive therapy outcomes than do therapy techniques or interventions (Orlinsky, Grawe, & Parks, 1994).

Establishing a trusting therapeutic relationship and a mutual working alliance is crucial in exploring religious and spiritual issues. Spiritual beliefs and feelings are usually private, even sacred, experiences for which clients who do not feel a great deal of trust for their therapists are unlikely to freely discuss and work through. Building a trusting therapeutic alliance with religious and spiritual clients is not always easy, as the professions of psychology and psychotherapy have historically been biased against religion and religious believers (Bergin, 1980a). Being aware of this bias, many religious and spiritual clients have fears and suspicions about "secular" psychotherapists and the process of psychotherapy itself (Bergin, 1983; P. S. Richards & Bergin, 2000; Worthington, 1986).

A letter to the editor from a self-identified "born-again" Christian psychologist published in the *Minnesota Psychology Association Newsletter* (M. W. H., 1986) illustrates how deeply some religious people distrust psychotherapists and the process of psychotherapy:

> Psychotherapy is one of the most hellish and devastating practices that mankind has contrived. Psychotherapy manipulates, abuses, and destroys those persons who seek help for their problems through it.

Psychotherapy makes the "patient" dependent upon the psychotherapist, and I have found psychotherapists to be, for the most part, unspiritual, anti-God, egotistical, and WRONG. Many psychotherapists suffer from the same, or worse, life and personality problems as the persons they pretend to help. (p. 10)

Another more recent example of such distrust can be found in *Creating Evil: Psychiatry Destroying Religion* (Citizens Commission on Human Rights International [CCHR], 1997), a booklet that attacks psychiatry and psychology and portrays them as enemies of religion. CCHR is an organization established in 1969 by the Church of Scientology, which has more than 125 chapters in 28 countries. CCHR states that its purpose is to "investigate and expose psychiatric violations of human rights and to clean up the field of mental healing. . . . [It objects] to the materialistic view advanced by psychiatry and psychology alike, that man is a soulless animal, the antithesis of a Scientologist's belief that man is a spiritual being" (CCHR, 1997, p. 67).

Although such intense suspicions and distrust are undoubtedly extreme views, their existence demonstrates the "religiosity gap" that exists between the mental health professions and the general public (Bergin, 1991). Psychotherapists tend to be less religious than their clients (Bergin & Jensen, 1990), and many people with emotional problems prefer to seek assistance from clergy rather than professional therapists (Chalfant et al., 1990). Clearly, the mental health professions have a serious credibility problem among leaders and members of many religious communities. Worthington and colleagues (Worthington, 1986; Worthington & Scott, 1983) have identified several possible concerns that conservative Christian clients may have about therapists:

Conservative Christians fear that a secular counselor will (a) ignore spiritual concerns, (b) treat spiritual beliefs and experiences as pathological or merely psychological, (c) fail to comprehend spiritual language and concepts, (d) assume that religious clients share nonreligious cultural norms (e.g., premarital cohabitation, premarital intercourse, divorce), (e) recommend "therapeutic" behaviors that clients consider immoral (e.g., experimentation with homosexuality), or (f) make assumptions, interpretations, and recommendations that discredit revelation as a valid epistemology. (Worthington, 1986, p. 425)

Such concerns are not uncommon among adherents to other religious faith, and such fears are not completely unfounded (Bergin, 1980a, 1983; P. S. Richards & Bergin, 2000; Worthington, 1986). Thus therapists may need stronger efforts to build trust and establish a therapeutic alliance. In addition, because religious beliefs and spirituality have not traditionally been addressed by psychotherapists (Ganje-Fling & McCarthy, 1991; Henning & Tirrell, 1982), clients may not consider it desirable or appropriate to discuss such issues in therapy. Thus, therapists may need to communicate explicitly to clients that sharing and exploring their religious and spiritual beliefs and concerns during therapy is appropriate if they desire to do so.

What can psychotherapists do to create a trusting, spiritually safe, and open therapeutic climate? Assuming that they have developed the necessary multicultural attitudes and skills and have successfully generalized these to the religious and spiritual domains, there are several other specific things they can do. For example, therapists can assess clients' interest in pursuing spiritual issues by an appropriate intake questionnaire (see chap. 8, this volume). They should inform clients in their informed consent document that they are willing to discuss and explore religious and spiritual issues in an open, respectful, and sensitive way. Fears that clients have that a secular psychotherapist may view the client's spiritual beliefs as pathological also could be anticipated and addressed briefly in the informed consent document. Therapists also should inform clients that they may use spiritual interventions that seem appropriate, but only after obtaining the client's explicit permission. An example of portions of such an informed consent document is provided in Exhibit 6.2. During therapy sessions, therapists can appropriately reinforce their openness to exploring religious and spiritual issues and respond respectfully to fears their clients may express.

Therapists should generally avoid religious symbols, pictures, or dress that "advertises" religious affiliation or beliefs. With an ecumenical therapeutic stance, therapists avoid verbally disclosing details about their own religious affiliations or beliefs unless clients ask directly, and even the request may require careful exploration of why the question arises. Prematurely discussing details of one's affiliation or beliefs may "turn off" clients whose affiliation and beliefs differ. For example, prominently displaying Christian pictures or symbols in a therapist's office may attract Christian clients but make it more difficult to establish rapport and credibility with non-Christian clients. By communicating openness to exploring the client's religious and spiritual issues without prematurely disclosing specific details about their own, therapists will increase the likelihood of establishing trust and rapport with a wider range of clients.

Psychotherapists should deal with religious differences and value conflicts that they feel with their clients in an open, respectful, and tolerant manner. Inevitably therapists and clients will occasionally become aware of major differences of opinion toward certain beliefs or social values (Corey, Corey, & Callanan, 2003). Differences in religious affiliation and disagreements about specific religious doctrines or moral behaviors (e.g., abortion, premarital and extramarital sex, and homosexuality) can undermine trust

Information Regarding Counseling Services

Training and Experience

Welcome to the Center for Change. I received my doctorate in counseling psychology in 1988 from the University of Minnesota. Both my doctoral training program and internship training were accredited by the American Psychological Association. I qualified for licensing as a psychologist in the state of Utah by completing additional postdoctoral training and by passing the national psychologist licensing examination. I remain current by attending continuing education workshops and psychological conventions. I also have obtained specialized education and training in working with religious and spiritual issues in counseling by attending professional presentations at conventions, reading professional literature, and consulting with colleagues who have an expertise in spiritual counseling approaches.

My Approach To Counseling

My orientation as a counselor is "eclectic." In selecting treatment methods, therefore, I tend to draw ideas and techniques from a number of the major counseling approaches whose utility has been supported through research (e.g., cognitive therapy, behavioral therapy, client-centered therapy, family systems therapy, and psychodynamic therapy). I also believe that a spiritual perspective is important in counseling, and I am open to exploring any religious or spiritual concerns or issues you might have. I may also suggest that you participate in spiritual practices or interventions that are compatible with your beliefs if I believe they may help in your growth and progress. Of course, you will never be compelled to participate in psychological or spiritual interventions that you do not wish to engage in.

During the early phase of counseling (the first few sessions, generally), I will encourage you to share information with me that will help me understand you and that will help me know more about the nature and history of the concerns that brought you to counseling. As such, I may inquire about a number of aspects of your life (e.g., work, family, church, social relationships, health, spirituality). I also may ask you to take one or more psychological and spiritual assessment tests to help me gain more insight into your concerns.

and seriously threaten the therapeutic alliance if prematurely or inappropriately disclosed or addressed (Corey et al., 2003; P. S. Richards & Bergin, 2000; P. S. Richards & Davison, 1989). When such value conflicts become salient during therapy, it is important for therapists to acknowledge their values openly while explicitly affirming clients' rights to differ without having their intelligence or morality questioned. Therapists should also discuss openly with clients whether the conflict threatens the therapeutic alliance in a way that makes referral advisable. Handling value conflicts in therapy can be difficult; further discussion and more specific guidelines are presented later in this chapter in the section on therapeutic valuing and in chapter 7 in the section on ethical issues.

Psychotherapists should listen carefully and communicate empathy and respect for their clients' belief tradition when clients risk such self-disclosure. Therapists do not have to agree with their clients' views, but they should remember that disclosing sacred religious and spiritual beliefs is anxiety-provoking, because beliefs may have been previously discounted, ridiculed, or pathologized (Bergin, 1980a; P. S. Richards & Bergin, 2000; Worthington, 1986).

The following letter to the editor by a college student, which was published in 1989 in the Central Washington University campus newspaper, illustrates an attitude that devoutly religious people often encounter, particularly in professional and academic settings:

> Like most of my contemporaries, religion was force-fed me before I even learned to walk and talk. When I reached age 18, I rebelled by visiting the pastor of my church and telling him that I would discontinue my membership. I stated my reasons: Religion was not derived from common sense, but from superstition resulting from ignorance, fear of the unknown, fear of death. It is based on emotions!
>
> So who do we pray to? Some spirit we invented to help us make it through the day? Sure life is tough. Taking some sort of drug makes it easier. Some turn to alcohol, some to narcotics, some to religion to numb the senses, to soothe, to lull.
>
> Religion has never solved anything. Hitler's SS had "God with us" engraved on their belt buckles. The Jews are convinced of the superiority of their beliefs. So what makes Christians, who claim to be the one and only, so special?
>
> Ah yes, and the Bible! Every religious cult has its own sacred scriptures. Ours is a historical account of ancient Hebrew tribes, with lots of stone-age level thinking and misinterpretation of natural phenomena mixed in. Also lots of ghost stories and other tales based on imagination rather than fact. As a child I thought it was fascinating. Now I am an adult, and I no longer believe in fairy tales. (E. Pope, 1989, p. 2)

Such attitudes are widespread and are often publicly expressed, even in professional and academic settings and publications (e.g., Ellis, 1980). Fearing ridicule, religious people may be apprehensive about sharing spiritual beliefs and experiences. Thus, what they do disclose, from whatever cultural and family history, should be treated with empathy and respect. Therapists may want to explicitly acknowledge to a client who has disclosed such information that this disclosure is not easy and they respect the client for having the trust and courage to do it. It might be appropriate and even necessary to assure clients that they are not viewed as childish, stupid, or deranged for having such beliefs (although the therapist may consider the beliefs dysfunctional from a clinical perspective).

Assessing the Religious and Spiritual Dimensions

We endorse a multidimensional, holistic assessment and client conceptualization strategy. Therapists should globally assess their client's functioning—physically, emotionally, socially, cognitively, behaviorally, and spiritually. We are not the first to advocate such an approach, of course. For example, Lazarus (1973, 1976) proposed this in the early 1970s when he described his multimodal behavior therapy. His multimodal assessment approach advocated examining each area of a person's BASIC ID: behavior (B), affect (A), sensation (S), imagery (I), cognition (C), interpersonal relationships (I), and drugs or biology (D) (Lazarus, 1989). If spiritual (S) were added to this schema, it could become BASIC IDS. With the rise in prominence of the eclectic or integrative psychotherapy tradition, many psychotherapists now, to one degree or another, assess and conceptualize their clients in such a multidimensional manner.

A unique contribution of a theistic strategy to a multidimensional approach is to provide therapists with a rationale for assessing and conceptualizing the religious and spiritual dimensions of their clients' lives. As part of an ecumenical therapeutic stance, during their regular assessment, therapists should globally assess their clients' worldview; the extent to which a client views the world through a Western (monotheistic), Eastern (polytheistic or pantheistic), or naturalistic (scientific) lens. They should gather information about clients' religious and spiritual upbringing, current religious affiliation, and beliefs and practices, along with information about their clients' problems and symptoms, seeking to understand whether their clients' religiosity or spirituality is in some way intertwined with or contributes to the problems and disturbance. They should also attempt to determine whether their clients have religious and spiritual resources that could be used in therapy to help promote coping, healing, and change.

Most psychotherapists are not used to routinely gathering information about the religious and spiritual dimensions of their clients' lives, and doing so effectively and sensitively is not necessarily easy. Some of this assessment information probably can be obtained fairly quickly through global ecumenical questions on client intake questionnaires or during clinical interviews early in therapy. More specific religious and spiritual assessment information may need to be obtained by using denominationally specific questions and assessment measures or by consulting with religious leaders or other experts in their clients' religious tradition. Despite the potential difficulties, we believe that some attention to religious and spiritual issues during assessment is crucial if therapists are to more adequately conceptualize their clients' presenting symptoms and concerns and to better understand how to assist them. In chapter 8 we discuss assessment issues in more depth and offer more detailed rationales and approaches.

Implementing Religious and Spiritual Interventions

Therapists should, after carefully assessing and conceptualizing their clients, tailor treatment interventions to fit individual clients' unique symptoms and problems. In doing so, most therapists now consider a variety of behavioral, cognitive, affective, psychodynamic, and systemic interventions (Jensen & Bergin, 1988). A theistic strategy provides a wide range of explicitly religious and spiritual interventions that most mainstream psychotherapists have not known of or systematically used, including praying for clients, encouraging clients to pray, discussing theological concepts, making reference to scriptures, using spiritual relaxation and imagery techniques, encouraging repentance and forgiveness, helping clients live congruently with their spiritual values, self-disclosing spiritual beliefs or experiences, consulting with religious leaders, and using religious bibliotherapy (Ball & Goodyear, 1991; Kelly, 1995; P. S. Richards & Potts, 1995b; Worthington, Dupont, Berry, & Duncan, 1988). Most of these spiritual interventions are actually practices that have been engaged in for centuries by religious believers. They have endured because they express and respond to the deepest needs, concerns, and problems of human beings (Benson, 1996; W. R. Miller, 1999; P. S. Richards & Bergin, 1997, 2000). These interventions and others are discussed in detail in chapters 9 and 10.

The general purposes of such interventions are to help clients affirm their eternal spiritual identity, follow the influence of the Spirit of Truth, seek to live in harmony with moral universals, and use their spiritual resources and influences to better cope, heal, and change. Therapeutic change and healing can be facilitated through a variety of means, including physiological, psychological, social, educational, and spiritual interventions. But in our view, complete healing and change requires a spiritual process. Therapeutic change is facilitated, and is often more profound and lasting, when people heal and grow spiritually through God's inspiration and love. Religious and spiritual interventions are especially suited for helping clients feel God's love and inspiration during their journeys of therapeutic healing and growth.

Some spiritual interventions require that the therapist believe in God and in spiritual realities (e.g., praying for or with clients, self-disclosing or modeling spiritual experiences or behaviors, sharing one's belief and faith in spiritual realities). However, other interventions can be used by nonreligious therapists, because they require only a willingness to respect and affirm the client's spiritual beliefs. For example, assessing clients' spiritual worldviews and religious histories, consulting with clients' religious leaders, encouraging clients to use the religious resources in their lives (e.g., prayer, meditation, scripture study, social support from members of their religious community), and analyzing the personality implications of religious doctrine and spiritual concepts are interventions that any therapist could use.

Many other considerations may influence therapists' decisions about which spiritual interventions, if any, to use with a given client, including the severity of the client's disorder, the nature of the intervention, the nature of the client's presenting concerns, the client's spiritual status and readiness, and the therapist's theoretical orientation. We explore these complexities in later chapters, particularly chapter 7.

Communicating Moral and Ethical Values

Another contribution of the theistic, spiritual strategy to the therapist's role is to provide important insight into how therapists should deal with values in therapy. The theistic world religions make three important assumptions about the nature of morality and values: (a) that there are moral absolutes or universals that God has revealed to guide and benefit human beings (Smart, 1983); (b) living one's life in harmony with these moral absolutes or universals is desirable because such principles and commandments promote spiritual growth and harmonious relationships with God and with other human beings; and (c) that these values should be taught and transmitted to others (Smart, 1983, 1993).

These three theistic assumptions about morality and values have several important implications for psychotherapists and clients. First, therapists should not adopt an ethically relativistic therapeutic stance. Ethical relativism is questionable (see Bergin, 1980c; R. F. Kitchener, 1980a); all values are not of equal worth and validity. Some do more to promote spirituality, mental health, and harmonious interpersonal and social relations (see chap. 5, this volume; see also Jensen & Bergin, 1988). Second, as discussed in chapters 4 and 5, metaphysical beliefs and values do affect people's goals, lifestyle, and physical and mental health. Therapists should let clients know that their value choices do have consequences, and they should help clients examine these. Third, teaching, endorsing, and modeling healthy moral values is a desirable, ethical, and honorable activity. Therapists should accept that they are value agents and deliberately attempt to model and communicate healthy moral and ethical values to their clients (London, 1986; Lowe, 1976). By doing so, they can help clients learn to listen to their conscience, follow the Spirit of Truth, and internalize healthy values to optimize their development and growth.

This view of values and therapeutic valuing provides an alternative that may be more appropriate for religious clients compared to secular ways of handling value issues in psychotherapy. Despite the current recognition that therapy is a value-laden process (e.g., Bergin, 1980a, 1980b, 1980c; Beutler, 1972; Kessell & McBrearty, 1967; R. F. Kitchener, 1980a; London, 1986; Lowe, 1976; Patterson, 1958), uncertainty and ambiguity are widespread in the profession about how therapists should handle values issues

(Bergin, Payne, & Richards, 1996). Mixed messages and double standards are sometimes adopted by professional organizations. In addition, there are few training opportunities or specific guidelines about how to work ethically with values in therapy. As a result, many therapists give lip service to the notion of not imposing their values on clients, but implicitly advance their value agendas during treatment. The social and cultural "war of values" occurring in the political and public arenas may be carried out implicitly in therapy offices with vulnerable, unsuspecting clients.

At least four common problematic value styles or approaches can be found among therapists: deniers, implicit minimizers, explicit imposers, and implicit imposers. *Deniers* are outwardly accepting: "Maybe some therapists impose their values on clients, but I don't. I am more open-minded and liberal in my views than such therapists. I believe that if a client values something, then it must be valuable and okay." Deniers believe that the values of all cultures and clients are equally acceptable (ethical relativism). They believe there is no "right way" to believe; unfortunately, this is a statement of a belief about the right way to believe. Deniers fail to recognize that even their ethically relativistic worldview is value-laden and that they influence their clients with their relativistic values. *Implicit minimizers* say: "Maybe I can't totally keep my values out of therapy, but I can minimize their impact by not sharing them or revealing them to clients." Implicit minimizers do not recognize that failing to be explicit about their values can often be more coercive than being explicit.

Explicit imposers openly proselytize their value agendas: "My beliefs and values about various issues (e.g., gender roles, sexual orientation, religion) are correct, and the world will be a better place if I get my clients and society to accept these values. I will be clear and up front with my clients about my values and if they have a problem with this they can look elsewhere for therapy." Explicit imposers zealously declare their values to all clients who will listen and, to one degree or another, punish those who do not agree with them. *Implicit imposers* are more subtle: "My beliefs and values are correct, and the world will be a better place if I get my clients and society to accept these values. I will find subtle ways to work them into my therapy sessions." Implicit imposers deliberately, subtly, and covertly attempt to convert clients to their worldview and value agenda. All of these approaches are problematic because they tend to reduce clients' freedom to grow in their ability to make choices about the direction of their lives.

According to our theistic, spiritual strategy, a moral framework for psychotherapy is possible. By *moral framework*, we do not mean a detailed list of moral instructions; this would deny the diversity of clients' orientations and interfere with the need for clients to grow by learning to make value choices and accept the consequences. A moral framework to guide psychotherapy can be formed of general moral values or principles common to most world religions. Jensen and Bergin (1988) found that psychotherapists show high agreement about general values or principles that are important for a mentally healthy lifestyle (see Table 6.1). Clearly, these value survey results substantially overlap spiritually based values. Thus the psychotherapy profession and the world's great religious traditions both contribute insight into general healthy values or principles that can be used to guide and evaluate therapy. There is no need to lapse into ethical relativism and the belief that "anything goes."

Therapists can both respect client diversity and adopt a therapeutic strategy that endorses moral values that facilitate human growth, functioning, and interpersonal relationships. We have called these *health and human welfare values* (see chap. 5, this volume). How can therapists implement this strategy? We consider that the most ethical and effective way is to adopt an explicit minimizing value stance. *Explicit minimizers* admit: "I can't keep my values out of therapy, nor is it desirable to totally do so." They believe that it is important for therapists to be open about the values that influence their therapeutic decisions and recommendations throughout the course of therapy. They also believe that therapists should openly discuss and help clients to examine the values that may be affecting the client's mental health and interpersonal relations. Explicit minimizers believe that by being explicit about their own and their clients' values and actively endorsing consensus values that promote healthy functioning, while communicating to clients that disagreement will not result in condemnation, they maximize clients' freedom of choice.

As they seek to model and teach health and human welfare values, therapists need to remember that there are many potential "value agents" in their clients' lives. Mainstream society, religious organizations, ethnic–cultural groups, families, and professional organizations (including the psychotherapy profession) potentially influence the values of clients. Although they should not seek to undermine or supplant the other value agents in clients' lives, therapists should help clients become aware of whether these values are influencing them in healthy or unhealthy ways.

When therapists help clients examine and understand the value influences in their lives, clients are able to make thoughtful, reasoned choices about which values they wish to internalize and apply. Therapists may appropriately share, openly but nondogmatically, their own values, along with those of the psychotherapy profession (see Bergin, 1985; Jensen & Bergin, 1988) and the client's religious tradition. However, therapists' primary goal should be to promote clients' self-determination, not to be a "missionary" for a particular value (Bergin, 1985, 1991). In this sense, we disagree with London's (1986) notion that therapists are or should be "secular priests," but we agree with him that moral and values issues must be discussed. Although the "missionary" or "religious authority" roles have appropriate

TABLE 6.1
Responses by Mental Health Professionals to 10 Value Themes

Theme and sample items	Important for a positive, mentally healthy lifestyle		Important in guiding and evaluating psychotherapy in all or many clients
	Total percent agree[a]	Percent agree[b]	Percent agree
Theme 1 (5 items): Competent perception and expression of feelings	97	87	87
29. Increase sensitivity to others' feelings	98	93	92
30. Be open, genuine, and honest with others	96	86	87
Theme 2 (10 items): Freedom, autonomy, and responsibility	96	88	85
7. Assume responsibility for one's actions	99	98	98
5. Increase one's alternatives at a choice point	100	96	96
11. Increase one's capacity for self-control	99	86	89
10. Experience appropriate feelings of guilt	88	70	65
Theme 3 (9 items): Integration, coping, and work	95	81	81
50. Develop effective strategies to cope with stress	99	97	97
49. Develop appropriate methods to satisfy needs	99	95	94
53. Find fulfillment and satisfaction in work	97	86	82
54. Strive for achievement	83	52	58
Theme 4 (5 items): Self-awareness and growth	92	74	77
37. Become aware of inner potential and ability to grow	96	89	90
42. Discipline oneself for the sake of growth	82	54	59
Theme 5 (12 items): Human relatedness and interpersonal and family commitment	91	77	73
12. Develop ability to give and receive affection	97	94	95
35. Increase respect for human value and worth	98	88	79
17. Be faithful to one's marriage partner[c]	91	78	70
19. Be committed to family needs and child rearing	90	80	76
41. Become self-sacrificing and unselfish	52	26	30

(continued)

TABLE 6.1   (Continued)

Theme and sample items	Important for a positive, mentally healthy lifestyle		Important in guiding and evaluating psychotherapy in all or many clients
	Total percent agree[a]	Percent agree[b]	Percent agree
Theme 6 (3 items): Self-maintenance and physical fitness	91	78	71
45. Practice habits of physical health	94	77	69
46. Apply self-discipline in use of alcohol, tobacco, and drugs	95	83	75
Theme 7 (6 items): Mature values	84	66	68
56. Have a sense of purpose for living	97	87	85
14. Regulate behavior by applying principles and ideals	96	81	78
55. Adhere to universal principles governing mental health	67	47	55
Theme 8 (4 items): Forgiveness	85	64	62
60. Forgive others who have inflicted disturbance in oneself	93	77	78
62. Make restitution for one's negative influence	79	54	51
Theme 9 (9 items): Regulated sexual fulfillment	63	51	49
27. Understand that sexual impulses are a natural part of oneself	97	94	85
24. Have sexual relations exclusively within marriage	63	49	49
25. Prefer a heterosexual sexual relationship	57	43	39
17. Be faithful to one's marriage partner	91	78	70
Theme 10 (6 items): Spirituality and religiosity	49	34	29
69. Seek spiritual understanding of one's place in the universe	68	53	41
68. Seek strength through communion with a Higher Power	50	34	31
67. Actively participate in a religious affiliation	44	28	25

Note. N = 425. The Mentally Healthy Lifestyle scale provided for seven possible ratings: hi, med, and lo agree; uncertain; and lo, med, and hi disagree. The Guiding and Evaluating Psychotherapy Scale (Jensen & Bergin, 1988) provided for four categories: applicable to all, many, few, or no clients.
[a] Hi, med, and lo.
[b] Hi and med only.
[c] This item appears under two themes (5 and 9). The full scale included 69 items.
From "Mental Health Values of Professional Therapists: A National Interdisciplinary Survey," by J. P. Jensen and A. E. Bergin, 1988, *Professional Psychology: Research and Practice, 19,* 290. Copyright 1988 by the American Psychological Association.

places, they should be distinguished from the role of professional psychotherapist. In chapters 7 and 9 we discuss further our views about how psychotherapists should handle value issues in therapy.

Creating a Spiritual Space for Therapy

Another contribution our theistic strategy makes to the understanding of the therapist's role is that therapists may seek, and on occasion experience, spiritual companionship, guidance, and enlightenment as they assess, relate with, and intervene in their clients' lives. To do this therapists enter into meditative, reflective, or prayerful moments before, during, or after sessions, seeking, we believe, to prepare themselves spiritually so that if God is willing they can receive spiritual assistance. We believe that some of the most powerful healing moments in therapy come with this assistance.

We recognize that this assertion may seem radical, unscientific, and even irrational to nonreligious or atheistic therapists. But many, including the most "scientific," agree that psychotherapy is both a rational–empirical *and* a creative–intuitive process. Many who do not give a spiritual interpretation still experience "gut-level" hunches or intuitive insights about assessment questions to ask or interventions to make, or that their therapeutic relationship at times takes on a type of spiritual connection, quality, or presence (e.g., Buber, 1996/1923; Rogers, in Kirschenbaum & Henderson, 1990).

We recognize that not all intuitive connections with clients indicate spiritual influences in the relationship. Not all hunches are transcendent spiritual insights or enlightenment; some may occur when the complete gestalt of one's clinical experience and impressions come together in a nonrational, holistic manner. Although such experiences are difficult to explain in strictly cognitive or intellectual terms, spiritual explanations need not necessarily be invoked to account for them.

Nevertheless, orthodox and devout believers in all the theistic world religious traditions embrace the belief that God can spiritually guide and enlighten human beings. We and many other psychotherapists believe that transcendent spiritual guidance and enlightenment are possible during therapy (e.g., Chamberlain, Richards, & Scharman, 1996; P. S. Richards & Potts, 1995a, 1995b; West, 2000). We encourage theistic psychotherapists to take care of their own spiritual well-being so that they are spiritually prepared as they work with their clients. One important aspect of therapists' spiritual preparation is to seek to live in congruence with their personal value system. We also encourage psychotherapists to pray and meditate, or to engage in other spiritual practices that they find help them to be more attuned spiritually during their therapy sessions.

Research to date suggests that many therapists do engage in prayer and other spiritual practices in an effort to spiritually prepare for their work (e.g., Chamberlain et al., 1996; West, 2000). Research also suggests that therapists believe that spiritual influences can assist them during psychotherapy (e.g. Chamberlain et al., 1996; O'Grady & Richards, 2004; P. S. Richards & Potts, 1995a, 1995b; West, 2000; White, 2002). Below we discuss several but not all of the ways that spirituality may become a part of the therapy process.

Spiritual Space and Connection

Consistent with our recommendation earlier in this chapter that therapists seek to create a spiritually safe and open environment for clients, West (2000) encouraged therapists to create *spiritual space* for their clients:

> Firstly, . . . [spiritual spaces] could be seen as gaps or openings in the interaction with the client in which the psychic and/or spiritual is latent or tacitly present, and could be made explicit by some spiritual intervention. Secondly, they could refer to openings or spaces between ordinary and extraordinary reality that could be created by appropriate rituals or ceremonies, or merely noticed when they occurred spontaneously. (p. 71)

West (2000) suggested several features that help create a space for spiritual influences and experiences in psychotherapy, including (a) accepting that therapy can be a spiritual space, (b) tolerating silence and not using techniques so that the spiritual space can unfold, (c) "listening" in a deep and holistic manner to words, feelings, and spiritual impressions, (d) speaking authentically by appropriately sharing feelings of the heart, and (e) accepting the spiritual experiences that occur. We agree that the concept of spiritual space has important implications for the training, practice, and supervision of psychotherapists. We ask if therapists and supervisors are willing to create a space, an environment, where spiritual influences can be experienced.

Some therapists have reported experiencing deep spiritual connection or spiritual communion with their clients (Chamberlain et al., 1996; West, 2000; White, 2002; O'Grady & Richards, 2004). This spiritual connection or communion, reminiscent of the *I—Thou* relationship described by Buber (1996), enhances therapists' empathy for their clients and helps both the client and the therapist to grow. Therapists have described this experience in different ways, including (a) feeling part of something bigger than themselves or their client, (b) feeling that grace is present, (c) feeling that God is present, (d) feeling the presence of healing energies or spiritual beings, and (e) feeling that something special has happened with the therapist, client, and God (Chamberlain et al., 1996; West, 2000; White, 2002). One therapist said,

When two people are in resonance, when there is a common purpose and there is something of a common field, and there is harmony there— I do think that there is often at that moment something else, something of the 'other' comes in at that point. That is my experience, that suddenly there is more than just two people in the room. Now whether that's grace, whether that's insight, whether that's healing, it depends on your language. (West, 2000, p. 67)

Another therapist experienced a sense of unity:

I've had those occasions where it's like you say something in a metaphorical sense and they'll respond with a sense, and I don't know exactly how to explain it except sometimes there's an intuitive sense that you both have about what's going on and it's almost like knowing what they're feeling or thinking about without knowing. (Chamberlain et al., 1996, p. 41)

Inspired Assessment and Intervention Insights

Some therapists have reported receiving inspiration and enlightenment that has helped them (a) more clearly assess and understand their clients' problems and (b) implement appropriate therapy interventions (Chamberlain et al., 1996; West, 2000; White, 2002). These feelings of inspiration are sometimes described as "promptings," "whisperings of the spirit," "hunches," "revelation," "sixth sense," and "gut feelings." Therapists often perceive that following such spiritual promptings leads to more accurate assessments and more successful interventions, which strengthens their belief that God has inspired and guided them (Chamberlain et al., 1996; West, 2000; White, 2002).

We refer to spiritually inspired assessment as *meta-empathy*. Meta-empathy goes beyond the ability to synthesize ordinary clinical observations in the creative way that all good clinicians do to include an openness to impressions that convey spiritual insights or convictions about the individual that differ from ordinary diagnostic categories or treatment "hunches." Steady practice, based on a degree of faith that "something more" can happen, will result in the ability to discern inspired insights as different from ordinary clinical hypothesizing or speculating. An illustration of a meta-empathy experience is provided in the following case:

A young man who had recently returned from military service sought help from his therapist with a problem of compulsive masturbation and related sexual problems. He had a Beck Depression Inventory score of 11 and was diagnosed as dysthymic with identity confusion. As the therapist, a clinical psychologist, first analyzed the problem, he decided to use a cognitive–behavioral approach, including rational–emotive therapy and self-regulation techniques. However, during the fourth session, while reflecting meditatively on the client's lack of progress, the meta-empathic intuition came to the therapist that "sex is not the problem."

The therapist discussed the meaning of this thought with the client for some time, and they concluded that the real issues concerned the client's sense of self, his purpose in life, his relationships, and his plans for the future. This was a deeply spiritual and moving experience for both the therapist and the client. This resulted in a remarkable change in the client's demeanor and motivation to take responsibility for the next steps, which he did. It also took the focus away from sexual problems as a target symptom. Two outside reviewers of the videotape of this session concluded that a tremendous transformation occurred in him during this hour, from a dysthymic state to an integrated sense of focus about self and life that was very hopeful. In a follow-up session several months later, the client explained that his sense of self and his life focus had become better integrated and that he had chosen to do humanitarian service as a missionary in another country. His posttreatment depression score was a 1!

Consider another meta-empathy experience related by a psychiatrist interviewed in Chamberlain et al.'s (1996) qualitative study of experienced Latter-Day Saint therapists:

> I have a certain intake format that I use for clients. But I was impressed to ask this woman something about somebody, a grandfather. I said, "Was there anything with your grandpa?" Well, that's not in my history, I don't ask that kind of thing. I ask generally if there was any abuse of any kind, but this was a 65 or 68-year-old [woman], who just broke down and cried about how her grandfather had sexually abused her and she'd never told anyone her entire life. . . . I mean, ordinarily, I would never have pursued that. Instead, I would have taken just the general history. (p. 63)

Some therapists have also reported feeling inspired in the interventions they use during therapy (Chamberlain et al., 1996; West, 2000; White, 2002). Spiritual guidance can enhance therapists' ability to appropriately select and effectively implement standard secular interventions, as well as commonly used spiritual interventions such as discussing the client's religious beliefs, encouraging clients to seek support from religious leaders and community, encouraging clients to pray, recommending spiritual bibliotherapy, and so on (P. S. Richards & Potts, 1995a). At other times, inspiration leads therapists to say or do something in therapy that was not planned and that is not typically used by the therapist, such as inviting a client to engage in religious visualization, praying at the beginning of a marital therapy session, playing a religious song during therapy, asking a client an unusual question, sharing an unusual insight or perception about a client, encouraging a client to engage in service to others, and encouraging a client to seek forgiveness from God (Chamberlain et al., 1996).

In speaking of such inspiration, one therapist said: "I have a feeling in a session of sometimes being taken beyond just what I can do. It's a feeling almost of words coming out of my mouth that I didn't know were going to be spoken, that sense of almost being taken beyond my knowing." (West, 2000, p. 107)

Another therapist explained the feeling further:

> Sometimes . . . an idea comes into your mind, "This is the right thing to do." "This is the right thing to say." Or ideas, a number of times, just come into my mind. Some of them I maybe have never thought of before, to be right truthful with you. It's like . . . pure intelligence flowing into your mind, you know the source of it. And so it ranges anywhere from ideas coming into your mind, to a very warm, comfortable feeling . . . I'll utter a silent prayer for help and direction and can know which way to move. (Chamberlain et al., 1996, p. 40)

These spiritually guided assessment and intervention cases illustrate our view that spiritual resources for change exist beyond the ordinary clinical procedures that are used, and that some intuitive insights and hunches that occur in therapy come from the divine source. We believe that most often such experiences are not dramatic but come as quiet, gentle impressions to the mind and heart of the therapist. These impressions, if genuinely spiritual, will give the therapist important insight into the client and his or her problems and interventions that may be effective. If heeded, such impressions should facilitate clients' therapeutic growth, and client's reactions will often confirm their validity.

When therapists receive such impressions, they should not, of course, announce to clients that they have received a revelation from God on the client's behalf. Rather, such impressions should be received quietly, humbly, and privately. Therapists should act on their intuitive impressions cautiously and nondogmatically, remaining open to the possibility that they could be wrong. We hope that therapists who believe in the reality and possibility of spiritual guidance and enlightenment will more often seek it as they assess and treat their clients. Doing so should increase therapists' capacity to understand accurately the nature of their clients' issues and intervene more effectively.

Recognizing and Exploring Spiritual Experiences

Therapists can also bring spirituality into therapy by helping clients to recognize and explore spiritual feelings and experiences that may occur both within and outside of therapy. Doing this can help clients to experience and recognize the healing blessing of divine providence in their lives, which may strengthen their spiritual identity, sense of life purpose, and feelings of gratitude (P. S. Richards, 2005). As clients see God's active participation and partnership in their lives, they often grow in their belief that God loves them. A natural extension of experiencing God's providence and love is that clients often have increased motivation to alter negative attitudes and behaviors, a psychological and spiritual turning about that constitutes genuine repentance. In addition, it is common for them, having received divine love, to offer similar love to those around them, especially to their family and loved ones.

Griffith and Griffith (2002) have provided much insight into why it is important for therapists to listen for and to clients' sacred stories, metaphors, spiritual experiences, and conversations with God. They also discussed a number of attitudes and skills that may help therapists succeed at including the spiritual in their therapeutic conversations: (a) foster within ourselves curiosity, wonder, and openness to the being of the other; (b) seek to attenuate our cynicism and certainty; (c) promote a climate of openness and respect by democratizing the structure of therapy; (d) communicate respect for the personhood of clients; (e) sustain embodied states (pay attention to feelings and bodily sensations) that permit spiritual or religious experiences to be recognized, understood, and expressed; and (f) carefully listen to what clients spontaneously speak about when they feel safe and respected.

THE CLIENT'S ROLE

The major psychotherapy traditions and the theistic spiritual strategy have certain common expectations about what clients are supposed to do during therapy. First, they need to show up for therapy and disclose to their therapists their concerns, problems, and symptoms. They are also expected to provide background history and assessment information to help their therapists understand them, including their perceptions of self, others, and the world. Clients also are expected to try out or participate in interventions designed both to assist them in coping with and resolving their presenting problems and concerns and to promote their long-term healing and growth.

The theistic strategy makes three unique additional contributions to the client's role in psychotherapy. First, for complete healing and growth, it is important for clients to examine and understand how their religious and spiritual background and beliefs affect their emotional and interpersonal functioning. Clients are not forced to do this, of course, but are invited to explore how their beliefs may affect their lives. Second, it is important for clients to attend to their spiritual needs and growth, along with their emotional or interpersonal issues and seek to understand how these may be intertwined. This may involve examining doubts and concerns or exploring spiritual goals and aspirations. Third, it is important for clients to draw on the spiritual resources in their lives to assist them in their efforts to change. Clients who believe in God are encouraged to seek God's guidance, enlightenment, and healing power to help them cope, heal, and grow better. They also may need to seek and obtain social, emotional, or spiritual support and guidance from members of their spiritual community.

NATURE OF THE THERAPY RELATIONSHIP

We agree with Rogers (1951, 1961) that unconditional positive regard, warmth, genuineness, and empathy are essential conditions of a professional therapeutic relationship. In addition to these foundational conditions, as discussed earlier, we consider it essential that the therapeutic relationship is spiritually open and safe. Clients need to know that it is acceptable to talk about their religious and spiritual beliefs and concerns and that when they do, their therapist seeks to understand and empathize with them. Clients must also know that they have the right to have different religious and spiritual beliefs than those of their therapist and that their therapist will not attempt to proselyte or convert them.

The therapeutic relationship must be characterized by honesty and by respect for clients' autonomy and freedom of choice. Therapists should encourage clients to honestly and openly explore their values and lifestyle choices, particularly if these values and lifestyle choices seem to be contributing to their presenting problems and symptoms. However, therapists must guide this exploration respectfully, with utmost regard for their clients' autonomy and freedom of choice. Therapists may need on occasion to tell clients that their values or lifestyle choices seem physically or psychologically unhealthy, but this should be done in a noncondemning, nonshaming manner. Therapists should make it clear that their clients have the right to disagree with them regarding values, beliefs, and lifestyle choices without fear of punishment or arbitrary withdrawal of services.

An optimally healing therapeutic relationship must also include the quality of charity or brotherly and sisterly love (Fromm, 1956). According to Fromm,

> The most fundamental kind of love, which underlies all types of love, is *brotherly love*. By this I mean the sense of responsibility, care, respect, knowledge of any other human being, the wish to further his life. This is the kind of love the Bible speaks of when it says: love thy neighbor as thyself. Brotherly love is love for all human beings. (p. 39)

There is a spiritual quality to the therapeutic relationship at its best that is characterized by brotherly and sisterly love with a deep spiritual connection. Therapists should seek to care about and love their clients in an ethically appropriate manner. By caring deeply about their clients' emotional and spiritual welfare, growth, and autonomy, therapists can create a therapeutic climate and relationship that are emotionally and spiritually healing.

The healing power of love is illustrated in the following excerpt from a letter that one of our clients wrote several months after she terminated therapy:

> I was completely unprepared for what I found in your office that first visit. You were caring and you connected to what I was sharing with you. You were compassionate about my fears. The thing I remember most is that the room felt like a safe haven. There was a very special spirit in your office. It was peaceful and you were accepting. I left feeling as though my spirit had been soothed and that for the first time in my life I could let my guard down at least a little. I recognized on that very first visit that I could be real in your office. I was glad that you were kind, but I did not expect you to care about me. Soon I learned that I mattered to you in a real way. Little did I know then just how important that caring would be for my healing. (P. S. Richards, 2005, p. 21)

Another important characteristic of the therapeutic relationship is that it should be spiritually affirming. Therapists should seek to affirm in culturally sensitive and appropriate ways that their clients are creations or children of God who have eternal, divine potential and worth. To experience a deep affirmation of one's eternal, spiritual identity and worth can be a life-transforming event.

To care deeply about their clients' emotional and spiritual welfare and growth enables therapists to provide the kind of relationship that invites the Spirit of Truth and love of God to be present during therapy. Feeling the love and concern of their therapist opens clients' heart and minds to experience God's love. Feeling the love of God and the love of others (including their therapist) often connects clients with their sense of spiritual identity and worth. Thus charity, or love, has great healing power.

Of course, many clients may not be easy to care about. In addition, many clients and some therapists have problems maintaining appropriate interpersonal boundaries. Thus, in saying that therapists should seek to have brotherly or sisterly love for their clients, we wish to add some caveats. First, with some clients, perhaps the best that therapists can do is to tolerate them. If toleration cannot be achieved, then making an appropriate referral is the best option. Second, by "loving clients" we of course do not mean that therapists may get sexually involved with them. Sexual intimacies between therapists and clients are clearly unethical (American Psychological

Association, 2002a) and harmful. When therapists become sexually involved with clients, their caring and love becomes destructive and pathologizing instead of healing. Therapists must keep their boundaries clear and maintain appropriate professional relationships with all of their clients.

INTEGRATING THEISTIC PSYCHOTHERAPY WITH SECULAR TRADITIONS

We recommend that psychotherapists integrate the theistic perspectives and interventions described in this chapter with mainstream therapy traditions. However, as discussed earlier, we recognize that the mainstream secular traditions are grounded in the naturalistic–atheistic worldview and in philosophies and theories that conflict with theistic perspectives. How then can theistic psychotherapists resolve these conflicting theological, philosophical, and theoretical notions so that their conceptual frameworks and therapeutic approaches are not riddled with inconsistencies? Consider the following true case example that illustrates this potential problem:

> Jeff was a Ph.D. student who was doing his internship at a university counseling center. He believed in God and was trying to develop a therapeutic approach that was in harmony with his religious beliefs and values. During his counseling theories course earlier in his program, Jeff had found Rogers' (1961) person-centered therapy approach appealing. He believed that many of the tenets of this approach were consistent with his religious values, particularly Rogers' emphasis on the importance of unconditional positive regard, congruence, and the organismic valuing process. Jeff failed to recognize that the person-centered approach is based on at least two assumptions that conflicted with his religious beliefs: namely, (1) humans are supreme, not God, and (2) values are relativistic—whatever values clients decide are right or moral for them are okay.
>
> While working with a female client, Susan, who was experiencing conflicts between her religious values about the importance of sexual chastity before marriage and opportunities to engage in promiscuous sex, Jeff adopted a non-directive person-centered approach, even though he and Susan both belonged to a religion that condemned unchastity. He encouraged Susan to explore her conflicted feelings and to make the choice that would feel congruent and healthy to her, assuming that Susan's organismic valuing process would lead her to make a choice that would be both healthy and in harmony with her religious beliefs. Jeff was surprised and dismayed when Susan announced at the beginning of a subsequent therapy session that she had decided she "felt good" about relaxing her sexual standards and engaging in a sexually active lifestyle. When Jeff expressed his disappointment to Susan about her

choice, she felt hurt and upset with him, saying "You said you trusted in my ability to make a choice that is right for me! Why are you disagreeing with me now?"

Jeff had failed to recognize that the assumption that clients' organismic valuing process leads to healthy and moral choices is based on relativistic and humanistic assumptions about values and human beings. From this perspective, Susan is her own ultimate moral authority. Thus Susan cannot make a poor value choice as long she makes choices consistent with her own inner feelings and preferences about what is right for her. If Jeff had been clearer about these assumptions and their possible influence on the therapeutic process, he could have modified his approach so that it was more in harmony with his theistic beliefs as well as Susan's theistic beliefs.

Consistent with the Roger's person-centered tradition, our theistic approach endorses the importance of positive regard for and congruence with one's beliefs and values. However, theistic assumptions concerning the existence of a Supreme Being, the existence of moral universals, and the reality of evil and sin lead to alternative perspectives concerning how therapists might wish to handle value conflicts such as Susan's. For example, appealing to sources "outside of one's self," such as to God and to other religious authorities, can be viewed as a mature way to approach moral and ethical decisions and may be encouraged in therapy (P. S. Richards & Davison, 1992; P. S. Richards, Rector, & Tjeltveit, 1999).

Instead of simply affirming his belief that Susan could arrive at the correct value choice simply by listening to her "inner feelings" about what felt best or most congruent regarding her sexual lifestyle, Jeff might have encouraged Susan to consider what insight and guidance her religious tradition might offer her. He might also have encouraged her to seek God's guidance and inspiration through prayer and contemplation or to consult further with the leader of her congregation. Discussions with Susan about the reality of good and evil in the world, the nature of temptation and sin, and the consequences of sexual promiscuity might also have been appropriate, assuming that Susan wished to explore this aspect of her value conflict. Of course, therapists must take care not to shame clients about values and lifestyle choices while still reserving the right to share their spiritually informed clinical wisdom about moral issues (Bergin, 1991; P. S. Richards et al., 1999). A theistic conceptual framework, therefore, if consistently and explicitly held, can lead to entirely different goals and interventions than secular therapy approaches.

As illustrated in this case example, as well as in Figure 1.1 (see chap. 1, this volume), we affirm the need for consistency between therapists' theological views, philosophical assumptions, theoretical ideas, and therapeutic practices. It is problematic for psychotherapists who believe in God to endorse philosophies, theories, or techniques that conflict with the theistic worldview (e.g., determinism, materialism, relativism, and hedonism). We agree with those who have argued that integrative approaches require "a single set of assumptions and thus a single theory" to bring coherence and organization to the therapeutic situation (Slife & Reber, 2001, p. 216).

The first step for therapists in developing a sound theistic approach consists of carefully examining the theological, philosophical, and theoretical assumptions that underlie it (Slife & Williams, 1995; Slife, 2004). Therapists will undoubtedly find that to be conceptually consistent they have to abandon, revise, or reframe some of the secular perspectives and interventions they accepted earlier in their careers (Jones & Butman, 1991; Slife & Reber, 2001). Unfortunately, graduate training programs often do not help students examine and understand the worldview and philosophical assumptions that underlie different therapeutic approaches. Psychotherapists may need to do their own reading or seek continuing education opportunities in order to become familiar with the conceptual foundations of the various psychotherapy traditions they wish to combine with their theistic framework.

CONCLUSION

The unique and important contributions that a theistic, spiritual strategy makes to the understanding of psychotherapy are summarized in Exhibit 6.3. We believe that psychotherapists who incorporate this strategy will be more likely to (a) fully understand and empathize with their theistic clients; (b) recognize cultural blind spots that cause them to unknowingly show disrespect or insensitivity to their clients' religious and spiritual values; (c) successfully contextualize their interventions so that they are in harmony with their clients' religious and spiritual beliefs; and (d) competently use religious and spiritual resources in their clients' lives that can powerfully assist their clients' efforts to cope, heal, and grow. We hope that theistic psychotherapists from diverse traditions will find the view of psychotherapy we have described in this chapter helpful.

EXHIBIT 6.3
Distinguishing Characteristics of Theistic Psychotherapy

Goals of therapy	Therapist's role in therapy	Role of spiritual techniques	Client's role in therapy	Nature of relationship
Spiritual view is part of an eclectic, multisystemic view of humans and so therapy goals depend on the client's issues. Goals directly relevant to the spiritual dimension include the following: (a) help clients affirm their eternal spiritual identity and live in harmony with the Spirit of Truth; (b) assess what impact religious and spiritual beliefs have in clients' lives and whether they have unmet spiritual needs; (c) help clients use religious and spiritual resources to help them in their efforts to cope, change, and grow; (d) help clients resolve spiritual concerns and doubts and make choices about role of spirituality in their lives; and (e) help clients examine their spirituality and continue their quest for spiritual growth.	Adopt an ecumenical therapeutic stance and, when appropriate, a denominational stance. Establish a warm, supportive environment in which the client knows it is safe and acceptable to explore his or her religious and spiritual concerns. Assess whether clients' religious and spiritual beliefs and activities are affecting their mental health and interpersonal relationships. Implement religious and spiritual interventions to help clients more effectively use their religious and spiritual resources in their coping and growth process. Model and endorse healthy values. Seek spiritual guidance and enlightenment on how best to help clients.	Interventions are viewed as very important for helping clients understand and work through religious and spiritual issues and concerns and for helping clients draw on religious and spiritual resources in their lives to assist them in better coping, growing, and changing. Examples of major interventions include cognitive restructuring of irrational religious beliefs, transitional figure technique, forgiveness, meditation and prayer, scripture study, blessings, participating in religious services, spiritual imagery, journaling about spiritual feelings, repentance, and using the client's religious support system.	Examine how their religious and spiritual beliefs and activities affect their behavior, emotions, and relationships. Make choices about what role religion and spirituality will play in their lives. Set goals and carry out spiritual interventions designed to facilitate their spiritual and emotional growth. Seek to use the religious and spiritual resources in their lives to assist them in their efforts to heal and change. Seek God's guidance and enlightenment about how to better cope, heal, and change.	Unconditional positive regard, warmth, genuineness, and empathy are regarded as an essential foundation for therapy. Therapists also seek to have charity or brotherly and sisterly love for clients and to affirm their eternal spiritual identity and worth. Clients are expected to form a working alliance and share in the work of change. Clients must trust the therapist and believe that it is safe to share their religious and spiritual beliefs and heritage with the therapist. Clients must know that the therapist highly values and respects their autonomy and freedom of choice and that it is safe for them to differ from the therapist in their beliefs and values, even though the therapist may at times disagree with their values and confront them about unhealthy values and lifestyle choices.

7

ETHICAL AND PROCESS ISSUES AND GUIDELINES

Psychotherapists have . . . two functions, one scientific and one moralistic . . . the scientific function . . . is that of manipulators of behavior . . . their moralistic function is that of a secular priesthood.

—Perry London

Psychotherapists who use a theistic, spiritual strategy face a number of potentially difficult ethical questions and challenges. Engaging in dual relationships (religious and professional), displacing or usurping religious authority, imposing religious values on clients, violating work setting (church–state) boundaries, and practicing outside the boundaries of professional competence have been cited as potential ethical pitfalls for such therapists (Bergin, Payne, & Richards, 1996; Lomax, Karff, & McKenny, 2002; P. S. Richards & Potts, 1995b; Tan, 1994, 2003; Tjelveit, 1986, 1999; Yarhouse & VanOrman, 1999; Younggren, 1993).

We recognize that such dangers exist, but maintain that therapists can take steps to minimize and avoid them. In this chapter we discuss each of these ethical dilemmas and provide a checklist of recommendations for avoiding problems in each area. Throughout this chapter we also present a number of ethical dilemma cases to illustrate the principles and to stimulate reflection and critical analysis.

We also offer process guidelines concerning when and how it may be appropriate to implement spiritual interventions in psychological treatment, along with when they may be contraindicated. The guidelines and suggestions offered in this chapter are for psychologists and other mental health professionals, not for pastoral counselors or clergy. Although clergy members may find some of these perspectives useful, we acknowledge their right to define their own ethical and process guidelines.

ENGAGING IN DUAL (RELIGIOUS AND PROFESSIONAL) RELATIONSHIPS

The ethical guidelines and codes of all of the major mental health professions include cautions and prohibitions against engaging in dual or multiple relationships with clients (e.g., American Association for Marriage and Family Therapy [AAMFT], 2001; American Counseling Association [ACA], 1995; American Psychiatric Association, 2001; American Psychological Association [APA], 2002a; National Association of Social Workers [NASW], 1999). Such relationships are discouraged and sometimes prohibited because it is recognized that they may place clients at risk of being exploited or otherwise harmed by therapists (Corey, Corey, & Callanan, 2003; Herlihy & Golden, 1990; Pope, 1985). There are a variety of dual relationships that psychotherapists should avoid: (a) therapist and lover, (b) therapist and personal friend, (c) therapist and business partner, (d) therapist and professor, or (e) therapist and supervisor (Corey et al., 2003; Keith-Spiegel & Koocher, 1985).

Religious psychotherapists should seek also to avoid the dual relationships of therapist–religious leader and therapist–religious associate, except when well-defined pastoral counseling with clear boundary conditions has been set up as a congregational service. Therapist–religious leader dual relationships occur when therapists who hold ecclesiastical positions in their religious denomination (e.g., priest, minister, rabbi, or bishop) provide therapy in a mental health setting or charge a fee for therapy to members of their faith over whom they have ecclesiastical responsibility or authority. Although such relationships are not common, because only a minority of psychotherapists hold ecclesiastical positions, when they occur they are problematic for several reasons.

First, in such situations, the boundaries between the roles of mental health and ecclesiastical professionals are easily violated. For example, therapists might perform ecclesiastical functions in the professional setting that they should perform only in the religious setting and in their ecclesiastical role (e.g., absolving or pardoning their clients' sins on behalf of a church). Second, clients may feel unsafe freely disclosing and exploring all of their concerns when the therapist has religious authority over them. For example, clients may feel less willing to discuss sexual problems, violent episodes, or financial misdeeds if the therapist has authority to take ecclesiastical action against them (e.g., excommunication). Third, the potential for a conflict of interest is greater in such dual relationships. For example, therapists could refer large numbers of people over whom they have ecclesiastical authority to their private practice psychotherapy office in order to benefit financially. Fourth, normal friendships or close working relationships within the congregation could be compromised by the ecclesiastical leader knowing too much private information about too many of the members. Counseling efficacy might also be compromised by outside associations. Fifth, in the case of confessed child abuse, clergy may not be legally required to report, but therapists are. If religious leaders provide professional therapy to members of their congregation, they would have to violate the "clergy–penitent" privilege and report the abuse, thereby undermining the confidence and trust they enjoy as a religious leader.

Because of such potential problems, therapist–religious leader dual relationships should be avoided. This does not mean that ecclesiastical leaders, even those who are licensed therapists, cannot ever provide counseling to members of their own congregations. Ecclesiastical leaders may have this right by virtue of their religious calling, but we believe they should only provide such services (a) free of charge, (b) in an appropriate religious setting, (c) after making it clear that they are providing the counseling or therapy in their role as the member's ecclesiastical leader, and (d) with the understanding that the content addressed will be specific to pastoral issues and not range indiscriminately into emotional problems, which generally would be best referred to a mental health professional.

Therapist–religious associate dual relationships occur when psychotherapists who are active in their religious community but are not in positions of ecclesiastical authority provide therapy to members who belong to the same religious congregation (see Exhibit 7.1 for a case example). Such relationships are more common than therapist–religious leader dual relationships and are problematic for several reasons. First, if therapists provide psychotherapy to members of their own congregation, they may find it difficult to avoid outside social contacts with such clients, because they are likely to see these clients in the religious setting. Frequent social contacts outside the therapy session increase the risk that a therapist–personal friend, therapist–lover, or therapist–business partner dual relationship will develop. Second, clients who are working with a therapist from their own congregation may feel awkward and uncomfortable seeing the therapist at religious meetings and social gatherings, because they know the therapist has heard their whole life story with all of its embarrassing details. Some clients may actually avoid attending religious meetings and activities out of embarrassment or fear that they will see the therapist. Third, therapists are at greater risk of inadvertently violating their clients' privacy and confidentiality when they have contact with their clients in a religious setting. For example, a therapist who has difficulty remembering in which setting he or she has learned something about the client may inadvertently disclose something

EXHIBIT 7.1
Ethical Dilemma Case Vignette 1:
Therapist–Religious Associate Dual Relationships

Case description

While living in a small rural community in the midwestern United States during the last year of his doctoral program, Bill was contacted by the religious leader of his congregation and asked whether he would provide marital counseling to a couple who also attended this congregation, with whom Bill and his wife had socialized on occasion. Bill explained to the religious leader that it would be inappropriate for him to provide counseling to the couple because of dual relationship concerns. The religious leader told Bill that the couple had specifically requested to meet with him because he was a member of their faith (Seventh-Day Adventist) and that they would not go to a non-Adventist therapist. The religious leader pointed out that there were no other Seventh-Day Adventist therapists available within 150 miles of their community and again petitioned Bill to see the couple.

Questions

1. Do you believe Bill should consider seeing the couple? If so, why? If not, why?
2. Bill tells the religious leader that he must consult with his supervisor to determine whether he can see the couple. If you were Bill's supervisor or colleague, what would you advise him?
3. If Bill decides to talk to the couple, what conditions or boundaries might he establish in this situation to minimize the risks?
4. What ethical principles should guide Bill's decision making in this case?

Discussion

In our view, two ethical principles must be considered in this case: (a) avoiding dual relationships, and (b) promoting the couple's welfare. We believe that Bill should not engage in a dual relationship with the couple. Although it might seem that Bill is failing to promote the clients' welfare by not providing therapy to them, he might actually harm them more by doing so than by choosing not to counsel them. We would advise Bill to talk to the couple and express his wish that he could help them, but also help the couple understand the problems associated with dual relationships and that, ultimately, his efforts to help them could harm them more than benefit them. Bill could discuss with the couple their concerns about seeing a non-Adventist therapist and recommend one who he felt confident would understand and respect their religious beliefs and values. He could invite them to call him if they had any questions or concerns about their non-Adventist therapist, although again making it clear that he could not become their therapist. If the couple refused to see the therapist Bill recommended, Bill could recommend some marital self-help literature for the couple. He could also recommend that they consult with their religious leader further about their problems. Bill could also offer to provide some information and training about marriage counseling to the religious leader. Bill could also consider offering an educationally oriented (nontherapeutic) marriage enrichment seminar for couples in the community and invite the couple to attend.

discussed during therapy that should have been kept confidential. Even asking a client to reschedule an appointment could represent a major breach of confidentiality if it is done in the religious setting and is overheard. Fourth, clients may broach therapy concerns in the religious setting (e.g., about their issues or concerns about treatment) that can be awkward and even destructive for the religious associate relationship.

Because of these and other potential concerns, therapist–religious associate dual relationships should be avoided. We recognize that it is not always easy to avoid requests to provide professional services to members of one's own religious congregation. Many religious people do prefer to seek psychological help from professionals who share their religious faith (Worthington, 1986), and so they are likely to request assistance from a professional in their own congregation who they already know and trust, particularly in rural communities where there are few mental health professionals and even fewer who share the client's religious beliefs. Nevertheless, great care needs to be exercised before entering into such relationships, even in such situations. Both client and therapist can protect themselves by having such therapeutic arrangements approved and monitored by a mutually chosen third party or board of review.

Checklist of Ethical Recommendations: Avoiding Dual Relationships

We recommend the following "dos and don'ts" for therapists in avoiding dual relationships:

1. Therapists should avoid therapist–religious leader and therapist–religious associate dual relationships.
2. After carefully considering the circumstances, if a therapist believes that a dual relationship may be in a person's best interest, the therapist should, before entering into such a relationship, consult with his or her supervisor and professional colleagues to see whether they agree.
3. If the therapist and professional colleagues agree that the risk of a professional–religious dual relationship is warranted, the therapist should carefully define and limit the extent of the dual relationship and explain the risks and boundaries to the client.
4. The therapist should consult frequently with professional colleagues about the case as the dual relationship proceeds. If at any time the client, the therapist, or the therapist's professional colleagues believe the client is being harmed by the dual relationship, the therapist should terminate the relationship and refer the client to another therapist.

5. The therapist should continue to consult with and inform professional colleagues about the case until the dual relationship has ended and the case has been carefully documented.

DISPLACING OR USURPING RELIGIOUS AUTHORITY

Another ethical danger that all psychotherapists need to be aware of and avoid is that of displacing, usurping, or undermining the authority and credibility of their clients' religious leaders. We recognize, as discussed in chapter 2, that some early leaders in psychiatry and psychology (along with other scientists) deliberately sought to challenge and undermine religious tradition and authority. As the authority of religious leaders declined, some psychotherapists moved toward the role of "secular priests," thus assuming some important functions traditionally fulfilled by religious leaders (London, 1964, 1986; Lowe, 1976). In discussing this phenomenon, Lowe (1976) observed that "many therapists would happily preempt the theologian's traditional role completely" (p. 233). Lowe's observation is probably still correct. We believe that it is time for this to change.

There are several ways in which psychotherapists may undermine the authority and credibility of their clients' religious leaders. Perhaps the most benign way this occurs is for therapists' to neglect to consult, cooperate with, or refer to the religious leader or pastoral counselor. Ethical guidelines of the mental health professions state that their members should treat helpers from other professional specialties with respect and collaborate with or refer to these professionals if doing so would appear to be in the best interest of their clients (ACA, 1995; American Psychiatric Association, 2001; APA, 2002a). Most psychotherapists routinely consult and collaborate with allied mental health professionals (e.g., marriage and family therapists, psychiatrists, psychologists, school counselors, and social workers), and they also occasionally consult with other professionals (e.g., physicians, educators, and lawyers). However, most mainstream psychotherapists rarely consult, collaborate with, or refer to their clients' ecclesiastical or religious leaders.

Neglecting to consult with clients' religious leaders is unfortunate, because clients' religious leaders and community can be an important resource. For example, when clients are suicidal, isolated, grieving, or lonely, the social support of members of the religious community can be of great coping assistance. Some religious communities can provide financial or employment assistance if needed. For those who feel a lack of meaning and life purpose, religious communities can provide opportunities for fulfilling altruistic service. Psychotherapists have an ethical obligation to tap into these resources, when appropriate, on behalf of their clients (see Exhibit 7.2).

Ethical Dilemma Case Vignette 2: Consulting With Religious Leaders

Case description

Debbie was a licensed psychologist in Texas who worked in a private practice outpatient setting. George, a devout Christian (Baptist), presented for treatment because of severe depression that began after his wife divorced him approximately six months after they had moved to Texas. During the first session, Debbie's assessment revealed that George was highly suicidal. Debbie also ascertained that George had no family members or close friends in the area because he had only recently arrived in Texas and he had depended almost exclusively on his ex-wife to fulfill his emotional and social needs.

Question

1. In addition to typical psychological interventions (e.g., getting a contract, removing weapons and toxic drugs from George's home, instilling hope), how might Debbie consulting with George's religious leader help him?

Discussion

As part of the treatment of suicidality, therapists should help clients build support systems to avoid isolation. Because George is a devout Baptist, it is possible that he has established some contact with a Baptist congregation in the community. Even if he has not yet established this connection, Debbie should encourage him to reach out to members in his religious community during his time of isolation and need. She should also ask George for permission to contact his religious leader. Once permission is granted, Debbie should contact George's leader and help him or her to understand George's circumstances and needs and ask if there are any support and resources available in the religious community to assist George. George's religious leader hopefully will mobilize some fellowshipping and social support from within the religious community to assist George and perhaps suggest some meaningful activities and service that George can become involved in to help him overcome his isolation and hopelessness.

Another way therapists may displace the authority of their clients' religious leaders is to confuse the boundaries of their respective roles. This occurs when the therapist takes on tasks and functions that are appropriately performed only by the client's ecclesiastical or spiritual leaders or when the client perceives that the therapist is performing such tasks and functions. Therapists who use spiritual interventions may be vulnerable to such boundary violations and need to give careful thought about how they can keep their role separate from that of their clients' religious leaders (see Exhibit 7.3).

Unfortunately, it is not easy to keep these role boundaries clear because there is considerable overlap between the roles and functions of counseling and ecclesiastical professions (Ganje-Fling & McCarthy, 1991; Tan, 2003). For instance, both psychotherapists and spiritual leaders provide counseling and direction to their clientele. They may explore similar issues with clients: for example, personal–emotional problems, relationships, and religious and

EXHIBIT 7.3
Ethical Dilemma Case Vignette 3: Displacing Religious Authority

Case description

Steve was a licensed psychologist who provided therapy for an outpatient mental health clinic in Utah. Steve was an active member of the Church of Jesus Christ of Latter-Day Saints (LDS). The LDS church has a lay priesthood and, in addition to his professional work, Steve was an "elder" in the church and served in a leadership position in his congregation. As part of his work at the mental health clinic, Steve led a therapy group for LDS men and women who struggled with depression. One evening, during an emotional group session, a participant named Janet (who was LDS but not a member of Steve's congregation) shared spiritual concerns and doubts she was struggling with. Toward the end of the session another group member suggested that Steve give Janet a priesthood blessing (a religious and spiritual ordinance normally provided by religious leaders or close family members). Janet immediately expressed her desire for Steve to do this, and one of the male group members offered to assist Steve in giving the blessing.

Questions

1. Should Steve give Janet a priesthood blessing? Why or why not?
2. What ethical principles should guide Steve's decision?
3. What would be the best way for Steve to handle this dilemma?

Discussion

In our view, Steve should not give Janet a blessing. If Steve were to do so, he would be performing a function that, in the LDS tradition, should be fulfilled by Janet's religious leaders or authorized family members. If Steve gave the blessing, he would be displacing or taking over a role that was not rightfully his. He would also be engaging in a dual relationship (therapist–religious leader or therapist–friend). Steve should remind Janet and the other group members that priesthood blessings should be given through appropriate priesthood channels and that he is not in such a position; he is her professional psychotherapist, and it is inappropriate for him to step out of that role into some other role. Steve should validate Janet's desire to receive a blessing and encourage her to seek it from her religious leaders or authorized family members.

---

spiritual matters (Ganje-Fling & McCarthy, 1991). Nevertheless, in most religions there are some official functions that ecclesiastical leaders perform that lay members or nonmembers are not allowed to perform: for example, absolving or pardoning sins, making authoritative pronouncements about doctrine, performing religious ordinances or rituals, and giving blessings or ordinations. Psychotherapists should not perform such functions unless they have ecclesiastical authority themselves and are clearly and appropriately functioning in an ecclesiastical role.

The most blatant way therapists undermine the credibility of religious leaders is to say or do things that denigrate or otherwise communicate a lack of respect for them (e.g., ridicule advice that clients receive from their religious leaders; suggest that clients' religious leaders are superstitious, incompetent, or deluded; or make derogatory comments about religion or religious leaders in general). Such behavior is not only unethical, but it is often harmful to the client and may even backfire and undermine the credibility of the therapist. Many devoutly religious clients hold their religious leaders in high regard, even if the leaders have done something to hurt or offend them. Clients could feel offended and lose trust in their therapists if therapists ridicule or criticize the leaders that clients respect and admire.

This does not mean that clients should not be able to express their own feelings of anger, distrust, or ridicule toward religious leaders. Listening and seeking to understand and empathize with clients who express such feelings can be appropriate and helpful, but therapists should not use such situations to air their own issues and biases toward religious authorities. It would benefit many clients if therapists would move beyond historical and personal biases and rifts to cooperate and collaborate with their clients' religious or spiritual leaders.

Checklist of Ethical Recommendations: Collaborating With Religious Authorities

We suggest the following "dos and don'ts" for therapists in collaborating with their clients' religious leaders:

1. In initial assessment interviews with clients, therapists should find out whether their clients (a) are affiliated with any particular religious tradition or denomination and (b) view their religious leaders as a possible source of support and assistance.
2. When clients view their religious leaders and community as a source of support, therapists should ask whether their client is willing to allow the therapist to consult and cooperate with the religious leaders if it seems appropriate.
3. Therapists should obtain a written release from a client before consulting or talking with his or her religious leaders. When obtaining the written release, therapists should clearly explain the purpose of the consultation and the general information they plan to share with the religious leader. Therapists should also ask the client to give the religious leader a release of information.
4. When consulting with a religious leader, therapists should (a) briefly introduce themselves, (b) mention they are seeing the particular client in therapy and that the client has given them permission for this contact with the religious leader,

(c) clearly explain that the purpose of the contact is to provide and/or seek information about the client for the purpose of helping the person better cope with and resolve his or her problems; and (d) confirm that the client has also given the leader permission to talk about his or her case.

5. If the religious leader is willing to talk, the therapist and leader should share only information that they believe is needed for both of them to be of optimal assistance to the client.

6. Therapists should respectfully thank the religious leader for assistance, ask for permission to contact the leader again if needed, and invite him or her to contact the therapist for assistance with the client if needed.

7. Before using spiritual interventions, therapists should explicitly explain to their clients that "they have no religious or ecclesiastical authority over the client and that they cannot speak for or act on behalf of the church or its leaders" (P. S. Richards & Potts, 1995b, p. 169). Therapists may wish to put this in writing in their informed consent document, or they can explain this verbally.

8. Therapists should attempt to find out what functions their clients' religious leaders might perform on behalf of their members that require official ecclesiastical authority (e.g., hearing confessions, absolving or pardoning sins, or giving blessings). Therapists should not perform such functions themselves.

9. Therapists should clarify where their therapeutic role overlaps with the role of their clients' religious leaders. For example, therapists and religious leaders often both provide individual, marital, and family counseling, and both may explore career, emotional, sexual, relationship, and spiritual issues. Therapists should be sensitive to these areas of overlap and ensure that clients understand that they may seek assistance from whoever they choose. If it is appropriate for a client to seek assistance from both a professional therapist and his or her religious leader, therapists should encourage this.

10. When using a particular spiritual intervention (e.g., prayer or religious imagery), therapists should make sure that their clients understand that it is appropriate for them to participate in that intervention during therapy. Clients may believe that some spiritual interventions or activities should be done only in private or in cooperation with their religious leader,

something that therapists should ascertain before proceeding with a spiritual intervention.

11. Therapists should not demean, criticize, or ridicule their clients' religious leaders.
12. When clients criticize or express anger toward God or their religious leaders, it is appropriate for therapists to listen empathically and to seek to understand and sensitively explore their clients' feelings and experiences. However, therapists should not add their own criticisms or tell their own "horror stories" about religion.
13. Therapists should let their clients know that, in general, they view religious leaders and communities as potential resources for support.
14. In their relationships with clients and religious leaders, therapists should attempt to communicate and demonstrate courtesy and respect.

IMPOSING RELIGIOUS VALUES

The ethical guidelines of the mental health professions encourage their members to respect individual differences (AAMFT, 2001; ACA, 1995; American Psychiatric Association, 2001; NASW, 1999). For example, the APA's (2002a) ethical guidelines state

> Psychologists respect the dignity and worth of all people, and the rights of individuals to privacy, confidentiality, and self-determination. ... Psychologists are aware of and respect cultural, individual, and role differences, including those based on age, gender, gender identity, race, ethnicity, culture, national origin, religion, sexual orientation, disability, language, and socioeconomic status, and consider these factors when working with members of such groups. Psychologists try to eliminate the effect on their work of biases based on those factors, and they do not knowingly participate in or condone activities of others based upon such prejudices. (Principle E, p. 1063)

As widely recognized, psychotherapy is a value-laden process, and all psychotherapists, to one degree or another, communicate their values (e.g., health, political, social, philosophical, religious) to their clients (Bergin, 1980a; Tjeltveit, 1986, 1999). Thus, Christian, Jewish, Muslim, atheist, agnostic, feminist, gay activist, Democrat, Republican, or Marxist therapists could be susceptible to imposing their values on clients, and they need to make conscious efforts to avoid doing this. By *imposing*, we mean using coercive methods to indoctrinate or influence clients, especially with content that is not relevant to the disorder or problem being treated. As we discuss in chapter 6, this does not preclude sharing ideas about value issues pertinent to clients' problems in an open and nonthreatening manner.

Critics of and some participants in the theistic therapy movement have expressed concern that therapists who use a theistic spiritual strategy may be especially likely to violate ethical guidelines by imposing their religious values on clients (P. S. Richards & Potts, 1995b; L. Seligman, 1988). We do not believe that therapists who use a theistic, spiritual strategy are any more likely to violate their clients' value autonomy than are other therapists. In fact, with the emphasis theistic strategies place on therapists making their values explicit at appropriate times during therapy (see chap. 6, this volume), we feel that value imposition is less likely to occur. Nevertheless, this is still a prospective problem. There are several ways that this could occur.

One form of religious value imposition occurs when therapists attempt to preach, teach, or otherwise persuade clients that their own religious or spiritual ideology, denomination, cause, or worldview is the most correct, worthwhile, moral, or healthy. Examples of religious proselytizing include but are not limited to (a) giving clients literature about the therapist's religious denomination or spiritual tradition, (b) inviting clients to attend services at the therapist's place of worship, and (c) teaching clients about the therapist's religious beliefs when such information is irrelevant to the client's issues and goals. Such religious proselytizing is clearly unethical. Therapists should not use therapy as a vehicle for promoting their particular religious or spiritual ideology or cause. This does not mean therapists cannot tell clients about their religious and spiritual beliefs at appropriate times. However, therapists should share such information only if clients ask them to, if it is clear that the therapist's beliefs may be pertinent and useful in helping clients with their issues and problems, and if the risks to the relationship caused by self-disclosure are minimal. Therapists should not disclose such information with the intent of converting clients to their own ideology or denomination.

Another form of value imposition occurs when therapists explicitly or implicitly tell clients that they are spiritually bad or deficient because of their behavior or lifestyle choices (e.g., regarding abortion, sexual orientation, gender roles, marital fidelity). It may be appropriate for ecclesiastical and spiritual leaders to tell people they behaved wickedly, but it is not appropriate for psychotherapists. Although therapists need to help clients examine their lifestyle choices and consequences, therapists should not attempt to influence clients to change their values or lifestyle by condemning or shaming them. This suggestion does not, however, preclude using the therapeutic technique of moral confrontation, which has proved useful in work with abusers and addicts, and many others.

This also does not mean that therapists should not make judgments about the possible consequences of their clients' lifestyle choices and warn clients about them. Nor does it mean that therapists cannot tell clients that they disagree with their clients' values or lifestyle choices. For example, therapists should inform clients that certain behaviors may put their physical, mental, and spiritual health at risk (e.g., drug abuse and promiscuous sex could increase the risk of AIDS, marital conflict and divorce, addiction, legal charges, and excommunication from a church); thus the therapist may explicitly disagree with such behaviors (see Exhibit 7.4). However, this information should be given to clients respectfully, with an explicit message that clients have the right to disagree with the therapist about value and lifestyle choices. An exception to this is when clients inform therapists that they have made (or plan) lifestyle choices that the therapist is legally required to report or take action to prevent (e.g., abusing children or planning to physically harm others or self). In such situations, therapists need to clearly inform clients that they disagree with such behaviors and that they are required to take action to report or prevent them.

Another form of religious value imposition occurs when therapists implicitly or subtly pursue moral, religious, or spiritual goals that are contrary to their clients' values and lifestyle choices. Examples of this would be a therapist who may agree to help a gay client work on improving his homosexual relationship but covertly attempts to undermine the relationship and convince the client that a heterosexual lifestyle is best, or a therapist who may agree to help a female business executive overcome her depression but while doing so implies that her career is the source of her depression and she should do "God's will" by giving up her career, getting married, and becoming a full-time mother and homemaker. These examples show therapists attempting to coerce clients to adopt their conservative values.

Similarly, therapists who are religiously and politically liberal may attempt to get clients to adopt their liberal values. This also is unethical. Examples of this would be a therapist who may attempt to coerce a religiously conservative client to give up his or her religious beliefs against homosexuality and to accept the gay lifestyle or a therapist who may try to influence a religiously conservative woman to give up her full-time homemaker role to pursue a career. Regardless of their personal views, therapists should not attempt to coerce clients into decisions or lifestyles that are contrary to the clients' values, wishes, and cultural context (see Exhibit 7.5).

Another form of religious value imposition occurs when therapists use religious and spiritual interventions without their clients' consent. An example of this is a therapist who prays aloud with clients at the beginning of therapy sessions without asking the clients if they would like to do so. Another instance is a therapist who, during a relaxation or self-hypnosis training session, introduces religious or spiritual images into the script

EXHIBIT 7.4

Case description

Fran was a psychotherapist and a devout Lutheran who worked in a community mental health center in a midsize city in the eastern United States. For six weeks, Fran had been providing therapy to Robert, a 27-year-old, nonreligious, married man. Robert's presenting concerns were marital problems and depression. During the past two sessions, Robert had disclosed to Fran that on two occasions recently while his wife was out of town on business trips, he had arranged for sexual liaisons with prostitutes. Robert had also admitted to a long history of sexual promiscuity beginning in his teenage years and continuing to the present. He said he believed his wife was not aware of his marital infidelity because of her heavy involvement in her career. Robert expressed little concern about his behavior; in fact, he discounted it by saying, "For all I know, when she's on her business trips, she's doing the same thing." Fran was concerned about Robert's dishonesty and sexual promiscuity for two reasons: (a) because of her religious belief that such behavior is morally and spiritually wrong, and (b) because, as a mental health professional, she believed that such behavior is destructive to mental health and relationships.

Questions

1. Should Fran confront Robert in any way about his dishonesty to his wife and about the potential damaging effects of his risky sexual behavior? Why or why not?
2. If Fran decides to confront Robert, how can she do so without shaming or condemning him?

Discussion

In our view, Fran should confront Robert about his unhealthy, sexually promiscuous behavior. She needs to do this carefully, however, to minimize the possibility that Robert will feel condemned or shamed. One way for Fran to approach this would be to tell Robert that she is concerned about his sexually promiscuous behavior because she is afraid that it may be harming him and his marriage. She should tell Robert that she has a belief, a value, that honesty and sexual fidelity are necessary for a successful marriage and for good mental health. She could say that this belief or value comes partly from her religious beliefs and partly from her training and experience as a mental health professional. She could tell Robert that most mental health professionals do believe that honesty and marital fidelity are important for mental health (see Jensen & Bergin, 1988). She should affirm Robert's right to disagree about this and reassure Robert that she is not going to condemn him or terminate her work with him if he continues his sexually promiscuous lifestyle. She could then express that she feels an obligation nevertheless to point out some of the potential consequences for Robert of such behavior: (a) he is putting himself and his wife at risk for AIDS and other sexually transmitted diseases; (b) his infidelity and dishonesty are damaging and are impairing his relationship with his wife; and (c) his sexually promiscuous behavior is a symptom of his own self-hate and emotional problems and the behavior actually maintains and contributes to the problem. After sharing these concerns, Fran should give Robert the opportunity to express and explore his thoughts and feelings about what she has said and about his sexual promiscuity and how he feels about it.

EXHIBIT 7.5
Ethical Dilemma Case Vignette 5: Core Value Conflicts

Case description

Lee was an orthodox Jewish man who was in training to become a clinical psychologist. During his internship year, a couple having serious marital difficulties presented for treatment. They had an interfaith marriage: the woman was Jewish and the man was Roman Catholic. As Lee worked with the couple, he realized that the couple's problems seemed to be caused primarily by a lack of communication and conflict resolution skills, along with sexual difficulties. The couple did not seem to have any concerns or misgivings about their interfaith marriage. However, because of his orthodox belief that interfaith marriages are not acceptable to God, Lee found himself struggling with feelings of guilt, both for trying to help the couple stay together and for hoping that they would get divorced.

Questions

1. Do you believe Lee should share his belief with the couple that interfaith marriages are unacceptable to God and that they might do better to get a divorce?
2. If you were Lee's supervisor and he disclosed his conflict to you, what would you advise him?
3. Does Lee have the right to refer this couple to a therapist who does not have a value conflict with interfaith marriages?

Discussion

Obviously, it would be unethical for Lee to "hold back" in his efforts to help the couple or to covertly attempt to influence them into getting a divorce. In our view, it would be best if Lee, with the support of his supervisor, referred this couple to a therapist who is comfortable with interfaith marriages. A supervisor who insisted that Lee should disregard his deeply held religious beliefs against interfaith marriages and continue to work with this couple would be guilty of cultural–religious insensitivity toward Lee. Although it is crucial for therapists to be open-minded and to seek to increase their multicultural sensitivity and unconditional acceptance for diverse clients, they should not be forced to help clients pursue goals that conflict with their core values. Lee should let the couple know that he does not feel he can be as helpful to them as another therapist he knows and that, to ensure that they get the best possible services, he would like to refer them to this therapist. If the couple asks Lee to tell them specifically why he feels this way, Lee should be honest and let them know that because of his religious beliefs against interfaith marriages, he finds himself conflicted—that is, wanting to help them but feeling guilty for doing so. He should reassure the couple that this is his issue, not theirs, and he should point out that many therapists do not share his views about interfaith marriages.

without first obtaining the client's permission. Of course, clients should be given the opportunity to consent to all interventions, not just spiritual ones.

Whenever therapists use an intervention (psychological or spiritual), they have made a value judgment about (a) what interventions are acceptable, good, or efficacious and (b) what goals or outcomes are good for their clients. For example, when therapists use a cognitive therapy intervention, they are assuming that cognitive therapy is a valid and useful perspective and approach and that it is desirable for clients to modify their dysfunctional or irrational thinking. When therapists ask their clients to read scriptures in the Bible, they are assuming that the Bible is a valuable source of spiritual enlightenment and that it is desirable for their clients to seek guidance from this source. Clients may or may not agree with such beliefs, and they should have the right to make an informed decision about whether they wish to participate in the particular interventions. Permission to use general types of interventions (e.g., cognitive, behavioral, spiritual) can be obtained during informed consent procedures at the beginning of therapy. Before using a specific intervention, therapists should also briefly describe it and make certain that the client is willing to participate in it.

Checklist of Ethical Recommendations: Respecting Clients' Values

We propose the following list of "do's and don'ts" for therapists in respecting their clients' values:

1. Therapists should respect the right of clients to hold religious beliefs that differ from their own, regardless of whether the client is a member of the therapist's religious denomination or tradition.
2. Therapists should not proselytize or attempt to convert clients to their own religious ideology or denomination. Passing out religious literature, inviting clients to attend religious services, and teaching clients religious doctrines or traditions with the intent of converting clients to the therapist's faith are inappropriate.
3. Therapists should not arrogantly condemn their clients for engaging in value and lifestyle choices that therapists disagree with or believe to be destructive. However, therapists are obligated to help clients examine the legal, physical, social, and mental health consequences of their lifestyle choices. If clients wish, therapists can also help clients to examine the moral and spiritual consequences and implications of their values and choices. Therapists should assist clients with such explorations in a morally and religiously open manner that is oriented toward resolving clinical problems rather than indoctrinating them ideologically.
4. When value conflicts arise between therapists and clients during therapy, therapists should respectfully and explicitly (a) express their own values, (b) acknowledge the client's

right to hold different values, (c) explore whether the value disagreement could undermine the success of therapy, and (d) decide whether referral to another therapist is indicated. Therapists should do their best in such situations to safeguard their clients' autonomy and welfare and avoid abusing their relatively more powerful position in the therapeutic relationship.

5. Therapists should pursue religious and spiritual goals in therapy only when clients have explicitly expressed their desire to do so.

6. Before implementing a religious or theistic spiritual intervention, therapists should briefly but clearly describe the intervention to the client and explain why they believe it could help. Therapists should ascertain whether their client feels comfortable with an intervention and obtain consent from the client to use it.

VIOLATING WORK SETTING (CHURCH–STATE) BOUNDARIES

Another ethical pitfall for therapists who use a spiritual strategy in civically funded settings is the danger of possibly violating laws or policies regarding the separation of church and state. A therapist surveyed by P. S. Richards and Potts (1995b) said, "I personally believe that the use of spiritual and religious techniques in therapy depends on the nature of the work place. I work for the state . . . and am not at liberty to use the spiritual or religious techniques I would like" (p. 167).

There are no professional ethical guidelines that prohibit therapists in civic settings from discussing religious issues or using spiritual interventions with clients. However, therapists are ethically obligated to obey the law (AAMFT, 2001; ACA, 1995; American Psychiatric Association, 2001; APA, 2002a; NASW, 1999), and there are some legal regulations that could affect therapists' freedom to use certain spiritual interventions in these settings (Bullis, 2001).

The First Amendment of the U.S. Constitution states that "Congress shall make no law respecting an establishment of religion, or prohibiting the free exercise thereof" (U.S. Government Printing Office, 1997). Hudgins and Vacca (1995) explained that these are referred to as the Free Exercise and Establishment of Religion Clauses of the Constitution:

The free exercise clause means that a person may believe what he wishes. He may believe in his God or no God, and government will not interfere with that belief. Government may, however, restrict the practice of one's belief if it harms or abuses the rights of others.

The establishment clause means that government is neutral in matters of religion. It does not favor one religion over another, many religions over some, or all religions over none. It does not promote one religious activity over another nor does it compel participation in a religious activity. (p. 419)

Fischer and Sorenson (1985) pointed out that "although the [First] [A]mendment seems to restrict only Congress, the same restrictions apply to all government action . . . because the Fourteenth Amendment has incorporated the [F]irst and thus applies it to any and all 'state action'" (pp. 219–220).

The proper interpretation and application of the religious clauses of the First Amendment have been issues of continual controversy in the United States (Drakeman, 1991; Flowers, 1994; Hudgins & Vacca, 1995; Weber, 1990). Despite controversy in the profession, we are not aware of any legal cases and rulings that specifically discuss how these clauses apply to psychotherapists in their work with clients. Most court cases and legal rulings regarding the separation of church and state that define appropriate behavior for government employees have involved public school teachers and administrators. Although therapists are different from officials and teachers in some important ways, they also wield considerable power to influence others, and so legal rulings that have affected school teachers and administrators may also apply, in some ways, to them.

The Establishment Clause has been the guiding principle for setting limits on what is considered appropriate behavior in government settings. Public school teachers and administrators are not allowed to do anything in the work setting that gives the impression that the government or its employees seek to promote, endorse, or establish religion (Fischer & Sorenson, 1985; Flowers, 1994; Hudgins & Vacca, 1995; Staver, 1995). Requiring or permitting public prayers (e.g., in the classroom or at commencement exercises), requiring or permitting public readings of the Bible or other scriptures for devotional purposes, sponsoring religious meetings, and proselytizing or otherwise endorsing religious doctrines are prohibited for public school teachers and administrators (Drakeman, 1991; Fischer & Sorenson, 1985; Flowers, 1994; Hudgins & Vacca, 1995; Staver, 1995).

Both students and teachers do "enjoy constitutional protection of free speech and free exercise of religion" (Staver, 1995, p. 37). Students and teachers have the right to pray, meditate, or read scriptures individually and privately in the school setting. Teachers should not, however, invite or allow students to participate in such activities with them. Students may participate in student-initiated and student-led Bible (religious) clubs on public school property, and a teacher sponsor may attend these meetings, but the teacher may not actively lead or direct the club (Staver, 1995). Students have the right to express belief or disbelief in God and religion verbally or in written papers as long as their speech does not substantially disrupt school activities (Staver, 1995). Teachers may also express their beliefs "with other teachers in the school lounge or between classes" (Staver, 1995, pp. 75–76), but they must be cautious about expressing their religious beliefs to students because of the danger of being accused of proselytizing. According to Staver (1995),

> While on school campus but before or after school hours, teachers may have certain restrictions imposed by the First Amendment Establishment Clause. . . . The younger the student, the more careful the teacher must be in matters of religion. The courts have reasoned that younger students are not able to easily separate the acts of the teacher from the acts of the school . . . . Unfortunately, no clear line has been decided as to when this age differential changes. No matter the age, however, teachers may not proselytize students in a captive setting . . . . However, "a teacher does not have to be so paranoid as to avoid a student's religious inquiry." (p. 76)

Given all of this, what can we conclude about therapists who wish to use a theistic spiritual strategy in civic settings? Which spiritual interventions are appropriate for therapists to use, and which are not? First, therapists do have the right to explore clients' spiritual issues and concerns when their clients initiate the discussions or when therapists believe that such issues are pertinent to their clients' presenting problems and the clients agree. Therapists also have the right to disclose their religious beliefs to their clients if their clients ask about the therapist's views. However, it is illegal (and unethical) for therapists in civic settings to promote, proselytize, or attempt to persuade clients, covertly or overtly, to their religious viewpoint or tradition. Of course, as discussed earlier in this chapter, ethical therapists should not do this regardless of the setting in which they practice.

Second, some spiritual interventions are risky to use in civic settings, even with adult clients. We advise therapists who work with adults in civic settings to be cautious about praying with clients, reading or quoting scriptures during therapy sessions, or giving clients religious bibliotherapy literature. Before doing any of these things, it would be wise for therapists to give clients and supervisors a document that clearly explains the purpose of such interventions and to obtain written permission to use them. Other spiritual interventions that are initiated by the therapist and carried out during therapy sessions, such as discussing religious or theological concepts, using religious relaxation or imagery, and practicing religious confrontation may also be somewhat risky. Such interventions may cause therapists to be perceived as seeking to endorse, promote, or establish religion in a government setting. Again, obtaining written permission from clients and supervisors to use these interventions would probably reduce the therapist's legal risk.

Less explicit interventions, including those that clients or therapists do on their own outside of therapy sessions, such as praying silently for clients, modeling mature values and healthy spirituality, suggesting that religious clients pray on their own outside of therapy sessions, encouraging clients to forgive others, and consulting with clients' religious leaders are less risky. In general, therapists who work with adult clients in civic settings should not be at significant risk of being accused of violating church–state regulations as long as they work within their clients' value systems and obtain explicit written client consent before using spiritual interventions. Generally, it will prove safest to be open with colleagues and supervisors about the spiritual aspects of one's approach and to have their support in advance. Gaining this prior support has worked successfully in many public agencies, especially when applying 12-step programs for dealing with addictive behaviors. Many government agencies also allow and even encourage spiritual counsel and the presence of chaplains (e.g., in state hospitals, prisons, the military, and legislative bodies).

Another consideration for therapists who work in public, tax-supported settings and are deciding whether it would be safe and appropriate to use a given spiritual intervention is the age of the client (Staver, 1995). When working with children and adolescents, therapists should be particularly cautious about using spiritual interventions, because actual or perceived abuses of governmental influence are more likely to occur (see Exhibit 7.6). In light of legal rulings about school prayer, devotional scripture reading, and proselytizing (Staver, 1995), we advise school counselors, school psychologists, and other therapists who work with minors in civic settings not to pray with clients, read scriptures to them, or pass out religious literature. Other religiously explicit interventions such as discussing religious or theological concepts, practicing religious relaxation or imagery, referral to religious leaders, and confrontation about discrepancies between religious values and behavior also may be risky and should not be used without written client, parent, and supervisor consent.

Ecumenical interventions that are not religiously or spiritually explicit or that therapists do privately, such as modeling healthy values, encouraging clients to forgive others, and praying privately for clients are less risky and should not require parental permission.

Checklist of Ethical Recommendations: Respecting Church–State Boundaries

The following represents our attempt to outline some central "dos and don'ts" for therapists in respecting church–state boundaries:

1. Therapists in civic settings should make sure that they understand and adhere to laws and workplace policies regarding the separation of church and state. Therapists should work to

EXHIBIT 7.6
Ethical Dilemma Case Vignette 6: Church–State Boundaries

Case description

Mary was a school counselor and a devout Roman Catholic who worked in a public school in a large city in the western United States. Recently, with the knowledge and permission of the client's father, Mary began to provide counseling to Sandra, a 15-year-old Presbyterian girl who was struggling with grief over the recent death of her mother. During the second session, Sandra shared her religious beliefs about death and the afterlife, and, during this discussion, Mary disclosed to Sandra that she also believes in an afterlife. During the next session, Sandra talked about her mother's funeral and shared her feelings about how helpful and kind the members of the church have been since her mother's death. Sandra also opened a Bible and read a passage from the New Testament that had special meaning and comfort to her. At the beginning of the next counseling session, Sandra told Mary that she greatly appreciated how Mary had listened to her and understood her as she talked about her mother's death and her religious beliefs about the afterlife. Sandra then said, "I feel close to you and would like to pray with you at the start of our sessions."

Questions

1. Do you think Mary should pray with Sandra? Why or why not?
2. Would it make a difference, in your opinion, who offered the prayer?
3. Do you think it was appropriate for Mary to discuss Sandra's religious beliefs with her?
4. Do you think Mary should have disclosed that she also believes in an afterlife?
5. If you were Mary's colleague and she consulted with you about how to handle this case, what would you advise her?

Discussion

In our view, Mary herself should not pray because of the danger that by doing so she could be violating church–state boundaries. There also is a danger that Mary may be perceived as attempting to convert Sandra to her faith. Perhaps it could be appropriate for Mary to permit Sandra to offer a prayer, but even this may be risky. We believe that Mary has acted appropriately in her decisions to discuss Sandra's religious beliefs and spiritual concerns with her and to listen as Sandra read the biblical scripture to her. Therapists have a right, even in civic settings with minors, to discuss whatever issues their clients wish to discuss. We think it can also be appropriate for therapists to disclose their own spiritual beliefs in some situations if it seems it will be helpful to clients. In this case, Mary's disclosure regarding her beliefs about an afterlife was done to affirm and support Sandra's beliefs, and so we believe it was an appropriate disclosure. We do think that Mary should not initiate scriptural readings with Sandra, nor should she give her other religious literature to read. If Mary wishes to use explicitly spiritual interventions, such as religious imagery or encouraging Sandra to pray and meditate outside of sessions, she should not do so without written consent from Sandra and her father.

protect both their clients' and their own free exercise of religion rights within such settings. Open discussion, negotiation, and mutual agreement among staff in the work setting are preferable to hidden agendas or power struggles over policies in this realm.

2. Therapists in civic (and other) settings should always work within a client's value framework; they should not use spiritual interventions to promote or impose a particular religious viewpoint. In their informed consent document, therapists should inform clients that this is their policy.

3. Therapists in civic settings should obtain written client and supervisor consent before using spiritual interventions. When working with children and adolescents, therapists should also obtain written consent from parents before using spiritual interventions.

4. Therapists in school or other civic settings who work with children and adolescents are advised not to pray with clients, quote or read scriptures, or pass out religious bibliotherapy literature.

PRACTICING OUTSIDE THE BOUNDARIES OF COMPETENCE

The ethical guidelines of most mental health professions prohibit their members from practicing outside the boundaries of their professional competence (e.g., AAMFT, 2001; ACA, 1995; American Psychiatric Association, 2001); for example, the APA (2002a) ethical guidelines make the following provisions:

(a) Psychologists provide services, teach, and conduct research with populations and in areas only within the boundaries of their competence, based on their education, training, supervised experience, consultation, study, or professional experience.
(b) Where scientific or professional knowledge in the discipline of psychology establishes that an understanding of factors associated with age, gender, gender identity, race, ethnicity, culture, national origin, religion, sexual orientation, disability, language, or socioeconomic status is essential for effective implementation of their services or research, psychologists must have or obtain the training, experience, consultation, or supervision necessary to ensure the competence of their services, or they make appropriate referrals, except as provided in Standard 2.02, Providing Services in Emergencies. (Standard 2.01, pp. 1063–1064)

To conform to such ethical guidelines, therapists need to make sure that they receive adequate training before incorporating a spiritual strategy

EXHIBIT 7.7
EXHIBIT 7.7
Ethical Dilemma Case Vignette 7: Respecting Boundaries of Competence

Case description

Richard was a licensed psychologist who had been trained in a respected American Psychological Association (APA)-accredited program in counseling psychology. Richard had received no training during his program about working with religious and spiritual clients and issues in therapy, nor had he received any since his graduation four years before. Richard's own worldview could be characterized as agnostic: He believed that the Christian beliefs "shoved down his throat" by his orthodox parents were "foolishness." He had not set foot in a church since he left home at the age of 18. Recently, Nagib, a devout Muslim client originally from Egypt, and his American wife, Julie, a recently converted Muslim, presented for treatment at Richard's private practice office. Nagib and Julie were experiencing severe marital conflict that seemed largely caused by differences in their cultural and religious beliefs, particularly concerning gender roles and sexuality.

Questions

1. Should Richard attempt to work with this couple? Why or why not?
2. What type of therapist would be qualified to work with this couple?

Discussion

In our view, Richard should immediately refer this couple to a therapist who has a strong background and expertise in working with religious clients and issues, preferably one with an in-depth knowledge of the Islamic faith and culture. Richard is not prepared to work with this couple for two reasons. First, he is antireligious himself and has clearly not examined or worked through his own issues (that originated in his childhood) about religion. Second, he has made no effort to study or seek training about working sensitively with religious and spiritual issues and clients in therapy. It would be unethical for him to attempt to help this couple or other clients whose religious and spiritual background and beliefs are clearly intertwined with their presenting problems. Richard has an ethical obligation to seek training and supervision so that he will be better prepared to assist religious clients in the future (American Psychological Association, 2002a).

into their therapeutic approach (see Exhibit 7.7). Unfortunately, most professional mental health training programs do not give adequate preparation for therapists to intervene in the spiritual dimensions of their clients' lives (Bergin, 1980a, 1983; P. S. Richards & Bergin, 2000; Young, Cashwell, Wiggins-Frame, & Belaire, 2002). Despite the fact that they give considerable attention to other types of diversity, few mainstream mental health programs provide course work or supervision on religious and spiritual issues in mental health and psychotherapy (Kelly, 1993; P. S. Richards & Bergin, 2000; Shafranske & Malony, 1990; Schulte, Skinner, & Claiborn, 2002; Tan, 1993). Most psychotherapists therefore will need to acquire education and training beyond that provided by their graduate programs before they will be adequately prepared to use a spiritual strategy. Because "generally recognized standards for preparatory training do not yet exist" in this domain of psychotherapy (APA, 2002a, p. 1064), it is not necessarily easy for therapists to decide what training or education they need or how they can obtain such training.

Fortunately, many resources are now available to help therapists acquire training and competency in the religious and spiritual domains. For example, there now exists a large body of professional literature that provides insight into the relations among religion, spirituality, mental health, and psychotherapy (e.g., Emmons, 1999; Kelly, 1995; Koenig, McCullough, & Larson, 2001; Lovinger, 1990; Pargament, 1997; P. S. Richards & Bergin, 2000, 2004; Shafranske, 1996; Spilka, Hood, Hunsberger, & Gorsuch, 2003; West, 2000; Worthington, Kurusu, McCullough, & Sandage, 1996; Wulff, 1997). Some universities now offer specialized courses on the psychology and sociology of religion and on religious and spiritual issues in counseling and psychotherapy. For several years, the APA's Division 36 (Psychology of Religion) has offered a continuing education workshop on these topics (Jones, 1994). In addition, many universities offer courses on different world religions and cultures.

Because such resources are now available and are continuing to increase in availability, we believe that guidelines and recommendations for education, clinical training, and therapist competency in this domain are warranted, and we provide some below. In regard to therapist competency, the Association for Spiritual, Ethical, Religious, and Value Issues in Counseling (ASERVIC, n.d.) of the ACA has developed a checklist of nine competencies for integrating spirituality into counseling and psychotherapy. Division 36 (Psychology of Religion) of the APA has also appointed a task force to develop such guidelines for psychologists. We welcome such guidelines and recommendations but are against the idea of requiring specialized certification in religious and spiritual counseling and psychotherapy for mainstream mental health professionals. We think this would be unnecessarily restrictive and could discourage competent mental health professionals from addressing clients' spiritual concerns when they wish to discuss them.

Checklist of Ethical Recommendations: Education and Training Standards

The following represents our attempt to outline some important educational and training recommendations for professional psychotherapists:

1. The foundation of effective religious and spiritual counseling is multicultural attitudes and skills (see chap. 6, this volume). Therapists should therefore study and be trained in multicultural counseling.

2. Therapists should read several good books on the psychology and sociology of religion (e.g., Spilka et al., 2003; Wulff, 1997) and on religious and spiritual issues in counseling and psychotherapy (e.g., Kelly, 1995; Lovinger, 1984; P. S. Richards & Bergin, 2000; Shafranske, 1996; Sperry & Shafranske, 2005).

3. Therapists should read current scholarly literature about religion and spirituality in mainstream mental health journals and in specialty journals devoted to these topics (e.g., *Counseling and Values; Journal for the Scientific Study of Religion, Journal of Psychology and Theology*).

4. Therapists should take at least one workshop or class on religion and mental health and spiritual issues in psychotherapy.

5. Therapists should read one or two good books on world religions (e.g., Ludwig, 1996; Nigosian, 1994; Smart, 1994) or, if possible, take a class on world religions.

6. Therapists should acquire specialized knowledge about religious traditions that they frequently encounter in therapy (e.g., by inviting clients to share information about their faith, reading literature published by and about the religious tradition, and immersing themselves in the religious culture when appropriate, such as attending worship services).

7. Therapists should seek supervision, consultation, or both from colleagues when they first work with clients from a particular religious or spiritual tradition or when clients present challenging religious or spiritual issues that the therapist has not encountered before.

8. Therapists should seek supervision, consultation, or both from colleagues when they begin to use religious and spiritual interventions in their work or whenever they use new, untested spiritual interventions.

OTHER CONCERNS ABOUT SPIRITUAL INTERVENTIONS

We are aware of two other major concerns that have been raised about the use of spiritual interventions in psychotherapy: becoming enmeshed in superstition and trivializing the numinous or sacred. We do not view these issues as ethical dilemmas; they really are just fears that scientists and religionists each have that their respective profession or domain will be contaminated by the other one. Nevertheless, we discuss these concerns here because they are often mentioned along with the ethical dilemmas discussed earlier by those who object to the idea of a spiritual strategy for psychotherapy.

Some therapists and researchers have objected to the use of spiritual perspectives and interventions on the grounds that they are unscientific and could return clinicians to the religious superstitions and irrational dogmas of past centuries (e.g., Ellis, 1971, 1980; Sagan, 1995). Such a danger could exist; however, as we discuss in chapters 3 and 5, the gap that once existed between science and religion is no longer as wide as was once perceived (Appleyard, 1992; Barbour, 1990; Jones, 1994). Explicitly theistic perspectives are no longer viewed as necessarily being antithetical to the progress of science (Appleyard, 1992; Barbour, 1990; Griffin, 2000; Jones, 1994). In addition, the movement toward methodological pluralism has enabled the study of phenomena such as spiritual beliefs and practices that were once excluded from scientific investigation. Religious and spiritual perspectives and interventions can and should be studied empirically. Thus a theistic, spiritual strategy need not be considered less rational, scientific, or empirical than any other therapeutic approach.

Some therapists have objected to the use of spiritual "techniques" on the grounds that the use of such interventions trivializes sacred things. A therapist surveyed by P. S. Richards and Potts (1995b) vocalized this concern:

> My understanding of the divine and my experience both persuade me to avoid consciously-planned use of explicit religious or spiritual matters in my work in therapy. I even cringe of thinking of these as "techniques," just as I am troubled by having such matters as "love" and "faith" spoken of as "techniques." . . . My primary concern is not our corrupting our therapy. . . . My concern is our trivializing the numinous, our losing our awe of the divine, our forgetting the fear of the LORD. (p. 167)

In light of such concerns, it is appropriate for therapists to remember that the majority of spiritual interventions that therapists have used have been practiced for centuries, in one form or another, by spiritual believers. For example, prayer, meditation, scripture study, blessings (laying on of hands), church or synagogue attendance, worship, repentance, and confession are all religious and spiritual practices that are taught and advocated by one or more of the major world religions (Carmody & Carmody, 1989; Farah, 1994; Nigosian, 1994; Palmer, Keller, Choi, & Toronto, 1997; Smart, 1994). Perhaps there is a danger that therapists could trivialize these sacred practices when using them as interventions in therapy; however, the likelihood of trivialization depends on the therapist's attitude and approach.

If therapists routinely and irreverently use spiritual interventions not because they believe in their healing power but because they view them as helpful in manipulating their clients, this behavior would trivialize or degrade sacred religious practices. We do not think therapists should do this. On the other hand, if therapists respectfully and reverently encourage clients to participate in selected religious practices that they believe will help their clients cope, heal, and grow spiritually and emotionally, this application would actually be a way of honoring and validating these practices and traditions, a way of expressing respect for and faith in their healing power. Therapists who are unwilling to help clients gain access to the healing powers available to them through their religious beliefs, practices, and community may be the ones guilty of trivializing or degrading sacred religious practices and traditions. Simply ignoring or failing to use the potential healing power of these practices is itself a form of trivialization and disrespect.

INDICATIONS AND CONTRAINDICATIONS FOR SPIRITUAL INTERVENTIONS

Theistic psychotherapy is most clearly indicated for theistic clients, particularly for those who feel that religion and faith in God are important in their lives. It is also indicated for clients, devout or not, who wish to discuss religious and spiritual issues during treatment or who view their spiritual beliefs as relevant to their presenting problems. With such clients, theistic psychotherapists can appropriately implement a variety of religious and spiritual interventions.

There are at least five situations in which religious and spiritual interventions are clearly contraindicated: (a) clients who have made it clear that they do not want to participate in such interventions, (b) clients who are delusional or psychotic, (c) clients for whom spiritual issues are clearly not relevant to presenting problems, (d) clients who are minors whose parents have not given the therapist permission to discuss religious issues or use spiritual interventions, and (e) where treatment occurs in government-supported facilities that prohibit religious interventions.

Many other considerations may influence therapists' decisions about which spiritual interventions, if any, to use with a given client. One major consideration is the nature and severity of the client's disorder. As illustrated in Figure 7.1, we believe that theistic interventions and associated social and personal resources are more effective and can be used with more concentration with less disturbed clients (e.g., clients with moderate anxiety and depression, self-esteem problems, interpersonal problems, marriage and family problems, and adjustment disorders). As the severity of the client's disorder increases, therapists must rely more on technical resources and interventions such as intensive psychotherapy, medication, and hospitalization, with theistic interventions as a more minor component of the treatment.

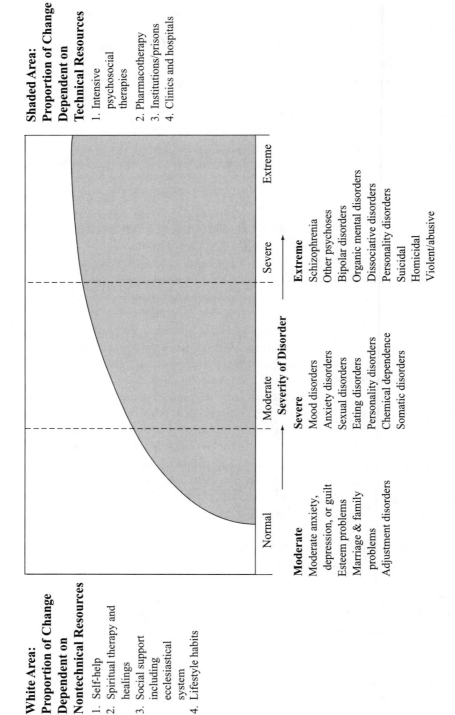

Figure 7.1. Hypothesized role of personal, social, and spiritual resources versus technical resources in treating mental disorders, as a function of severity of disorder.

For severe and extreme cases, this is especially true in the early phases of treatment. As the client gets better control of symptoms and as cognitive and self-regulatory (ego) processes become more functional, then spiritual, social, and lifestyle factors can be addressed more effectively. For a person whose mood disorder is disabling or a person who is out of control, discussion of values and spiritual issues could be irrelevant, distracting, or disturbing. After a period of treatment, such interventions may prove very useful, and near the end of therapy they can help individuals to stabilize their lifestyle, to be more resilient, and to maintain the gains that have been made.

In Table 7.1 we summarize some of the major client, process, and therapist variables that could influence whether a religious or spiritual intervention would be appropriate and effective. Generally speaking, such interventions are probably more risky or less likely to be effective when clients are young (children and adolescents), severely psychologically disturbed, anti-religious or nonreligious, or spiritually immature; view their spirituality or religion as irrelevant to their presenting problems; perceive God as distant and condemning; and have a deferring (passive) religious problem-solving style. Therapist-initiated, denominationally specific, religiously explicit, and in-session spiritual interventions are probably more risky than client-initiated, ecumenical, religiously implicit, and out-of-session interventions. It also is probably more risky to use spiritual interventions in civic- and government-supported settings than in private and religious settings. Spiritual interventions also are probably more risky and less likely to be effective if the therapeutic alliance is weak and there is low therapist–client religious value similarity. Of course, spiritual interventions are less likely to be used effectively and ethically by therapists who lack multicultural and religious sensitivity and awareness, have limited denominational expertise, and are spiritually immature. Empirical investigation of these hypotheses are needed; however, until investigations can be accomplished, therapists should at least keep these possibilities in mind as they seek to evaluate whether it would be appropriate to use such interventions with a given client.

GENERAL PROCESS SUGGESTIONS

Assuming that theistic spiritual interventions are not contraindicated, how should therapists go about implementing them during the therapeutic hour? We do not believe that a cookbook description of how to implement a theistic approach is warranted or helpful. We advocate a treatment tailoring approach in which therapists do their best to select and apply interventions that fit the unique needs, beliefs, and circumstances of each client. Therapists must thoughtfully, sensitively, and carefully select and implement the interventions that they believe will be helpful.

TABLE 7.1
Client, Therapist, and Process Variables That May Influence the Appropriateness and Effectiveness of Religious and Spiritual Interventions

Variable	Hypothesized influence
Client	
Amount of psychological disturbance	More disturbed clients may be less likely to benefit from spiritual interventions, particularly delusional, psychotic, and obsessive–compulsive clients, but when any disorder is in an intense or traumatic phase, treatment may have to begin with standard ways of reducing levels of stress.
Degree of religious orthodoxy	Clients who are more religiously orthodox may be more open to discussing religious issues and participating in spiritual interventions, but perhaps only with therapists of their own faith and in a denominationally specific manner.
Degree of religious and spiritual health and maturity (intrinsic, devout)	More religiously and spiritually healthy and mature clients may be more open to discussing spiritual issues and effectively using spiritual interventions regardless of the therapist's religious affiliation.
Type of problems or symptoms	The more clearly clients' religious and spiritual backgrounds and beliefs are connected or relevant to their presenting problems and symptoms, the more likely it is that spiritual interventions may be appropriate and effective.
Religious affiliation	Clients' religious affiliation may influence their willingness to discuss spiritual issues and the kinds of spiritual interventions they are willing to participate in (i.e., they may wish to discuss issues and participate in interventions that are compatible with their religion).
Age	Younger clients (children and adolescents) may be more willing to discuss religious and spiritual issues and participate in spiritual interventions, but the risk of ethical and legal violations may be greater depending on the setting and situation.
God image	Clients who have had positive religious experiences and perceive God as being forgiving, active, and supportive are more likely to believe that God will help them and to participate in spiritual interventions.
Religious problem-solving style	Clients who have a collaborative religious problem-solving style are more likely to participate in and benefit from spiritual interventions. Clients who have an extreme deferring (passive) or self-directing style are less likely to participate in and benefit from such interventions.

Therapist	
Multicultural and ecumenical sensitivity and awareness	Therapists who are sensitive and aware of their own religious values and biases and who have developed multicultural and ecumenical attitudes and skills should be more capable of using spiritual interventions appropriately and effectively.
Denominational expertise	Therapists who have in-depth knowledge and experience with one or more specific religious denominations should be more capable of using spiritual interventions with clients from those denominations.
Religious and spiritual maturity	Therapists who are more religiously and spiritually healthy and mature themselves should be more capable of modeling and facilitating their clients' spiritual exploration, healing, and growth.
Therapist–client religious value similarity	Greater client–therapist religious belief and value similarity may increase clients' willingness to discuss specific issues and participate in spiritual interventions.
Process	
Client-initiated discussions	When clients initiate the discussion of religious and spiritual issues, it generally should be safer and more appropriate to explore spiritual issues and use spiritual interventions because this suggests that clients are willing and ready to participate in this manner.
Ecumenical versus denominational approach	Generally, implementing spiritual interventions in an ecumenical manner should reduce the risk of offending clients, particularly early in therapy with clients whose religious affiliation or beliefs differ from those of the therapist. When high client–therapist religious value similarity exists, implementing spiritual interventions in a denominational manner may enhance their effectiveness.
In- versus out-of-session interventions	Out-of-session spiritual interventions generally should reduce the risk of dual relationships and coercing or offending clients, although there is no reason to believe that out-of-session interventions are more effective than in-session ones.
Setting	Generally, it is probably safer for therapists to use spiritual interventions in religious and private settings than in public and state settings. Clients are more likely to expect and welcome spiritual interventions in religious and private settings, and legal complications are less likely to arise.
Spiritually open and safe therapeutic alliance	When a spiritually open and safe therapeutic alliance has been established, spiritual interventions will be more appropriate, safer to use, and more effective in their outcomes.

EXHIBIT 7.8
General Process Suggestions for Therapists
Who Are Using Religious and Spiritual Interventions

1. Tell clients during informed consent procedures that they approach therapy with a theistic spiritual perspective. When appropriate, use religious and spiritual interventions.
2. Assess clients' religious and spiritual background and current status before using religious and spiritual interventions.
3. Establish a relationship of trust and rapport with clients.
4. Consider carefully whether religious and spiritual interventions are indicated (or contraindicated) before using them.
5. Describe the interventions they wish to use and obtain clients' permission to do so before implementing them.
6. Use interventions in a respectful manner, remembering that many of the interventions are regarded as sacred religious practices by believers.
7. Work within clients' value framework and be careful not to push spiritual beliefs and values on clients; it is appropriate, however, to challenge and help clients to examine beliefs that are irrational, self-defeating, and linked to the presenting problem.
8. Do not apply interventions rigidly or uniformly with all clients but use them in a flexible, treatment-tailoring manner.
9. Seek spiritual enlightenment and inspiration concerning what interventions to use and when to use them.

We offered a number of general suggestions earlier in this book to guide therapists in this process. These process suggestions are summarized in Exhibit 7.8. The guiding principles behind them are (a) deep respect for clients' autonomy and freedom, (b) sensitivity to and empathy for clients' religious and spiritual beliefs, and (c) flexibility and responsiveness to clients' values and needs. It is essential for therapists to be committed to these principles and values if they are to integrate religious and spiritual interventions into their therapeutic approach ethically and effectively.

We also wish to emphasize some special considerations that are important in child and adolescent therapy; group therapy; marriage and family therapy; and school, inpatient, or residential treatment settings. As mentioned earlier, therapists who work with children and adolescents must obtain explicit parental consent before using religious and spiritual interventions. Even with such consent, given the power differential that exists between adults and minors, therapists must be especially cautious not to impose their religious beliefs and values on children and adolescents. Therapists also must make sure that they adapt interventions to fit the language, cognitive abilities, and developmental needs of children and adolescents (Lonborg & Bowen, 2004; Vernon, 1993; Wells, 1999).

When working with groups, couples, or families, it is crucial for therapists to be sensitive to individual differences in the degree of comfort with theistic therapy. Not all group and family members or partners will be receptive to such approaches. In groups, couples, and families, religion could be an emotion-laden issue. Deep differences in religious belief and practice may exist. In addition, some partners or family members may use religion as a weapon or source of control during conflicts (P. S. Richards & Potts, 1995a). Theistic spiritual interventions may be appropriate for some group or family members or partners, but not all. Certainly there are some approaches that can be tailored to fit the unique needs of individual clients without compromising treatment efforts with other members of the group, family, or couple. We refer readers who would like more insight into the use of religious and spiritual interventions with children and adolescents, groups, couples, and families to Little and Robinson (1988); Lonborg & Bowen (2004); Lovinger and Lovinger (2004); L. Miller (2004); Propst (1988); L. Sperry and Giblin (1996); Wells (1999); Slife, Mitchell, & Whoolery (2004); and Worthington (1989a, 1990).

Theistic spiritual strategies are also being integrated into structured, multicomponent inpatient and residential treatment settings (e.g., P. S. Richards, Hardman, & Berrett, 2001; Slife et al., 2004). In such settings, therapists often implement selected theistic methods along with secular approaches with all clients at specific times or phases of the treatment process. There are at least two advantages of such techniques in multicomponent treatment settings. First, well-designed, integrated treatment approaches may be more therapeutically potent than individual interventions. Systematically combining promising theistic approaches with empirically proved secular interventions could maximize therapists' ability to help clients with specific problems and disorders. Second, because inpatient and residential settings often tend to follow structured treatment plans, it is more feasible to write detailed treatment manuals for them than it is for eclectic, flexible treatment approaches. Treatment manuals are valuable because they make it easier to train therapists in an approach, and they make controlled psychotherapy outcome research more feasible (Kazdin, 1994; Lambert & Bergin, 1994). Thus, professionals could find spiritual–secular treatment approaches easier to learn and to empirically evaluate than less structured, individualized approaches.

One major concern we have about manualized treatment programs is that they could lead to the rigid application of religious and spiritual interventions without adapting them to specific clients' values and needs (cf. Kazdin, 1994). When using such approaches, all clients may be expected to receive the same interventions; thus, there is perhaps a greater risk that therapists could impose their values on clients and coerce them into participating in interventions that are alien to their beliefs. However, therapists can apply interventions flexibly, even when using manualized treatment approaches. Spiritual interventions could potentially be dropped from the treatment package for individual clients if they conflict with the client's religious and spiritual beliefs. Perhaps the best way therapists can avoid value imposition when using treatment package approaches in inpatient and residential settings is to carefully select for treatment only those clients whose beliefs are compatible with the theistic approach used in the treatment program. To accomplish this, advertising materials and informed consent documents should describe all spiritual interventions that may be included in the treatment program, and therapists should explicitly ascertain whether clients are willing to participate in these interventions.

Another concern we have about manualized treatment approaches is that they could lead to the misapplication and trivialization of sacred religious and spiritual practices (P. S. Richards & Potts, 1995b). Some practices should perhaps be engaged in only spontaneously or when prompted by spiritual impressions. For example, is it appropriate for therapists to prescribe precisely when during treatment that clients should pray, meditate, ask for blessings from religious leaders, or seek transcendent spiritual guidance? Perhaps some spiritual practices and experience should not, or cannot, be rigidly orchestrated to fit into therapists' structured treatment plans (P. S. Richards & Potts, 1995b). The most therapists should do in the case of many religious and spiritual interventions is to encourage clients to engage in these practices *if and when* they feel ready.

CONCLUSION

Readers may have noticed that some of the ethical dangers we have discussed are more likely to be of concern when therapists work with clients from religious traditions other than their own (e.g., failing to consult or collaborate with a client's religious leaders, religious proselytizing, or practicing outside the boundaries of one's competence). Generally speaking, we believe it is safer for therapists to use a spiritual strategy with clients from their own religious tradition because misunderstandings and doctrinal disagreements are less likely (P. S. Richards & Potts, 1995b). However, some ethical violations may actually be more likely to occur when therapists work with clients of their own religious faith (e.g., dual relationships, usurping religious authority by confusing role boundaries, and imposing values by assuming that the client believes as the therapist does). Thus, regardless of the match between their own and their client's religious beliefs, therapists need to be alert to the ethical dangers we have discussed and seek to follow the recommendations we have offered.

We believe that the ethical and process recommendations we have made will help therapists to function more ethically and effectively in both ecumenical and denominational therapeutic situations. However, more denominationally specific ethical and process guidelines may be needed to supplement the general guidelines we have offered. For example, because the role distinctions between religious leaders and therapists may differ somewhat from one religious tradition to another, guidelines about which spiritual interventions therapists should refrain from using in order to avoid usurping religious authority may need to be denominationally tailored. We therefore hope that psychotherapists within each religious tradition, perhaps in consultation with their religious leaders, will articulate additional ethical and process recommendations that may be needed for their particular religious tradition. Finally, we are pleased that, since publication of the first edition of this book, a sizable number of articles and books have been published that discuss ethical and process issues and guidelines in this domain (e.g., Lomax et al., 2002; G. Miller, 2003; W. R. Miller, 1999; P. S. Richards & Bergin, 2000; Tan, 2003; Tjelveit, 1999; Yarhouse & VanOrman, 1999). More discussion, debate, and research is needed as theistic psychotherapy approaches evolve to ensure that therapists continue to progress in their capacity to use a spiritual strategy ethically and effectively.

8

RELIGIOUS AND
SPIRITUAL ASSESSMENT

We must distinguish between two kinds of religious orientation, the extrinsic value and the intrinsic value . . . the extrinsic uses his religion . . . [intrinsics] serve it . . . then live by it.

—Gordon W. Allport

Because of the eclectic movement, which recognizes human beings as multisystemic organisms (Bergin, 1988; Beutler & Clarkin, 1990; Garfield & Bergin, 1986; Norcross & Goldfried, 1992), comprehensive assessment approaches have frequently been advocated in the psychotherapy profession during the past 30 years (e.g., Beutler & Clarkin, 1990; Lazarus, 1973, 1976). Many therapists now routinely seek information about multiple aspects of each client's background and functioning when doing assessments (e.g., physical, psychological, behavioral, cognitive, educational, racial–ethnic, and familial). Unfortunately, most therapists rarely include information about their clients' religiosity and spirituality.

In this chapter, we discuss a number of reasons why it is important for all psychotherapists to assess clients' religious and spiritual backgrounds and status along with the other aspects of their lives. We identify and describe dimensions of religiosity and spirituality that are clinically relevant. We then describe a multilevel, multisystemic assessment strategy and discuss how a religious–spiritual assessment fits into such a strategy. We also discuss how intake questionnaires, clinical interviews, and standardized tests can be used to facilitate a religious–spiritual assessment.

REASONS FOR CONDUCTING
A RELIGIOUS–SPIRITUAL ASSESSMENT

There are at least five major reasons why therapists should assess their clients' religious and spiritual backgrounds, beliefs, and lifestyles; these are discussed in more detail below.

Understanding Clients' Worldviews and Thus Increasing the Capacity to Empathically Understand and Sensitively Work With Each Client

During the past 50 years, many helping professionals have asserted the importance of therapists gaining an empathic understanding of each client's subjective world or internal frame of reference (e.g., May, 1961; Rogers, 1951, 1957, 1961; Yalom, 1980). Psychotherapy outcome research has supported this assertion by documenting that therapists' empathic understanding is consistently associated with positive therapy outcomes (Lambert & Bergin, 1994; Orlinsky, Grawe, & Parks, 1994). In recent years, multicultural writers have helped clinicians realize that it is difficult for White therapists to fully understand and empathize with racial minority clients because of differences in worldviews and life experiences (Ibrahim, 1985; Ponterotto, Suzuki, & Meller, 1996; D. W. Sue & Sue, 1990). These writers have argued that therapists must seek to understand racial minority clients' worldviews if they are to avoid cultural insensitivity and bias (Ibrahim, 1985; D. W. Sue & Sue, 1990). Therapists should also follow this advice with their religious and spiritual clients. The worldviews and values of mainstream psychotherapists often conflict with those of their religious clients (Bergin, 1980a; Bergin & Jensen, 1990; Jones, 1994). Thus therapists must assess the spiritual worldview and values of their religious clients if they are to empathically understand them and avoid religious insensitivity and bias.

Determining Whether a Client's Religious–Spiritual Orientation Is Healthy or Unhealthy and What Impact It Has on Presenting Problems

Current theory and research suggest that religion is a complex, multidimensional phenomenon that has diverse effects on mental health (Bergin, 1983). For example, religious intrinsicness or devoutness has usually been found to be associated with better physical health, social adjustment, and emotional well-being (Batson, Schoenrade, & Ventis, 1993; Bergin, Masters, & Richards, 1987; Gartner, Larson, & Allen, 1991; Payne, Bergin, Bielema, & Jenkins, 1991; P. S. Richards, 1991; see also chap. 5, this volume). In contrast, extrinsic religiousness has usually been associated with poorer emotional well-being and social adjustment (Batson et al., 1993; Bergin, 1983; Bergin et al., 1987; P. S. Richards, 1991). Therefore, the empirical associations between religiousness and mental health vary depending on the definitions and measures of religiousness and mental health that are used (Batson et al., 1993; Gartner et al., 1991; Payne et al., 1991; see also chap. 5, this volume).

In the clinical situation, therapists are likely to encounter all of this complexity. The religious background and beliefs may be causing the emotional disturbance of some clients (Ellis, 1980); the religious beliefs of others may be intertwined or interacting with existing emotional problems (Bergin, Stinchfield, Gaskin, Masters, & Sullivan, 1988; P. S. Richards, Smith, & Davis, 1989); or the religious beliefs and lifestyle of others may be acting as a therapeutic influence that is helping to prevent or alleviate emotional problems (Bergin et al., 1987, 1988; P. S. Richards et al., 1989). There are some clients whose religious background, beliefs, and lifestyle could be operating in all of these ways simultaneously (P. S. Richards et al., 1989). To best assist clients, therapists need to understand the kind of impact clients' religiousness is having on their lives. Thus an assessment of clients' religious and spiritual background, beliefs, and lifestyle is essential if therapists are to succeed at this challenging task.

Determining Whether Clients' Religious–Spiritual Beliefs and Community Could Be Used as a Resource to Help Them Better Cope, Heal, and Grow

An important part of any psychological assessment is to ascertain what strengths and resources clients have that could assist them in their efforts to cope, heal, and change. For example, when assessing a severely depressed, suicidal client, it is important for therapists to determine (a) what beliefs or values the client has that could reinforce his or her desire to live and (b) whether there are family members or friends available to provide support and companionship in times of crisis. Client strengths and resources may include personal characteristics, such as their beliefs, values, abilities, and financial and employment status, as well as the client's significant others, such as family members, friends, and social community.

Religious and spiritual theologies and communities are potentially rich sources of support for clients and therapists (Duncan, Eddy, & Haney, 1981; Koltko, 1990; Pargament et al., 1987; Pargament, Silverman, Johnson, Echemendia, & Snyder, 1983). For example, religious beliefs such as "There is a God who loves me," "There is a divine purpose to my life," "I have an eternal spiritual identity," "God wants me to love and forgive others," "Suffering and trials are a necessary part of God's plan for me," and "God will give me strength and guidance to help me with my problems" can assist clients in times of crisis or at other times in therapy (Duncan et al., 1981; Koltko, 1990). In addition, religious communities can provide people with a sense of belonging and support, feelings of stability, a sense of order and purpose, opportunities to provide and receive charitable service, and even financial and employment support (Pargament et al., 1983, 1987). A religious–spiritual assessment can help therapists determine whether such resources are available in their clients' lives.

Determining Which Spiritual Interventions Could Be Used in Therapy to Help Clients

There is now widespread agreement within the psychotherapy profession that therapists should tailor their treatment interventions for each client individually on the basis of a careful assessment of the client's unique symptoms, problems, goals, and resources (Bergin & Garfield, 1994; Beutler & Clarkin, 1990; Lazarus, 1989). A treatment tailoring approach should also be used with spiritual interventions. Because spiritual interventions are not indicated for all clients or for all problems, they should not be applied routinely or uniformly. For example, spiritual interventions may be contraindicated with severely disturbed delusional, psychotic, or obsessive–compulsive clients.

Clients may fail to improve, or, worse yet, ethical violations and negative outcomes might occur if therapists use spiritual interventions indiscriminately or inappropriately (P. S. Richards & Potts, 1995b). Therapists need to decide whether spiritual interventions are indicated, given the client's symptoms, presenting problems, and goals. They also need to determine whether their clients are willing and ready to participate in such interventions. To understand a client's religious and spiritual background, beliefs, and current status is clearly essential if therapists are to integrate spiritual interventions into their treatment plans ethically and effectively. In chapter 7 (see Table 7.1 in particular), we discuss in more depth the types of client, therapist, and process variables that could influence the appropriateness and effectiveness of spiritual interventions that should be considered when conducting a religious–spiritual assessment.

Determining Whether Clients Have Unresolved Spiritual Doubts, Concerns, or Needs That Should Be Addressed in Therapy

According to the theistic, spiritual view of human nature, all human beings have certain spiritual needs and issues: e.g., the need to experience and affirm their eternal spiritual identity and divine worth, to feel connected and in harmony with God and the Spirit of Truth, to feel a transcendent sense of life purpose and meaning, to love and serve God and others altruistically, to spiritually understand suffering and death, to live in harmony with spiritual moral values, and to develop and actualize their spiritual potential. When people have religious and spiritual needs and concerns, the majority of them seek assistance and counsel from their spiritual leaders; however, some do seek help from psychotherapists (Ganje-Fling & McCarthy, 1991).

Although it may often be appropriate for therapists to refer clients who have spiritual issues to their religious leaders, this may not always be in the client's best interest. For example, a client may not feel safe enough to discuss spiritual doubts with his or her religious leader and may prefer to do so with a more neutral, nonjudgmental therapist. In addition, spiritual concerns and needs may be intertwined in complex ways with one's emotional and interpersonal problems (Bergin et al., 1988; P. S. Richards et al., 1989). Thus, when clients present with religious and spiritual concerns, those problems may have psychological and interpersonal roots that need to be addressed. For example, in our clinical experience some clients who have expressed feelings of alienation from and lack of trust in God were abandoned or abused by their parents as children. Their spiritual issues are rooted in the abandonment or abuse and the associated psychological trauma (Ganje-Fling & McCarthy, 1994). Therapists may be more qualified than religious leaders to assist such clients to heal and change.

Therapists also need to be alert to the possibility that when clients present with psychological and interpersonal problems, those problems may have religious or spiritual roots. According to the multisystemic view of human nature discussed in chapter 5, problems in the spiritual system of people's lives may affect their psychological and social functioning. For example, we have observed that clients who struggle emotionally and interpersonally with low self-esteem, shame, lack of self-confidence, and social isolation often lack a sense and assurance of their eternal spiritual nature and divine worth. We believe that the root of their problems is alienation from their core spiritual identity. The most powerful psychological and interpersonal healing and change occurs when these clients receive a spiritual assurance of their divine identity and worth.

Therefore, therapists should avoid compartmentalizing the different systems of human function and working only on psychological and interpersonal issues with clients. To help clients resolve their emotional and interpersonal problems, therapists may frequently need to help clients address their spiritual issues. A religious–spiritual assessment is clearly essential if therapists are to adequately understand and assist clients with their religious and spiritual issues.

CLINICALLY IMPORTANT DIMENSIONS OF RELIGIOUSNESS

What dimensions of religiosity and spirituality should therapists assess? This challenging question defies a simple answer. Although early researchers often used unidimensional and single-item measures when studying religiosity (e.g., religious affiliation, frequency of church attendance), religion is now widely recognized as a complex phenomenon (Bergin, 1983; Smart, 1983, 1994; Spilka, Hood, Hunsberger, & Gorsuch, 2003). During the past 30 years, theorists and researchers have described and operationalized numerous dimensions of religiousness and spirituality. For example, Glock and Stark (1965) described 5 dimensions of religiousness; King and Hunt (1969) described 11; Malony (1985, 1988) described 8; and Smart (1983) described 6. Numerous one- and two-dimensional models of religiousness and spirituality also have been described (e.g., Allen & Spilka, 1967; Allport & Ross, 1967; Ellison, 1983; Fullerton & Hunsberger, 1982; Hood, 1975).

Given this complexity, along with the fact that research and clinical experience with religious–spiritual assessment is still in an early stage, therapists must rely heavily on clinical wisdom and hunches when deciding what religious and spiritual information to seek about their clients. Nevertheless, on the basis of preliminary research and our clinical experience, we briefly discuss what we think are some of the most clinically relevant religious and spiritual dimensions that have been described. We hope that this information will help therapists in their efforts to assess and conceptualize their clients' religiosity and spirituality.

Metaphysical Worldview

A metaphysical worldview is composed of the beliefs a person holds about the universe and the nature of reality. As we discuss in chapter 4, according to Wilhelm Dilthey, there are three major types of metaphysical worldviews: naturalism (e.g., scientific, naturalistic), idealism of freedom (e.g., Western, monotheistic world religions), and objective idealism (e.g., Eastern world religions; Kluback & Weinbaum, 1957; Rickman, 1976). If therapists are to fully understand a client's inner subjective world and empathize with him or her, we believe that it is crucial for them to gain insight into their clients' metaphysical worldview. Therapists should seek to understand their clients' beliefs about questions such as the following: How did human beings come to exist? Is there a Supreme Being or Creator? What is the purpose of life? How should people live their lives to find happiness and peace? What is moral and ethical? Why is there suffering, grief, and pain? Is there life after death? Insight into their clients' beliefs about such questions will help therapists better understand how their clients view themselves, their relationships, and their problems.

Religious Affiliation

The majority of people in the world are affiliated or associated, to one degree or another, with a religious denomination or tradition (D. B. Barrett & Johnson, 2002). Religious affiliation is an important demographic characteristic of clients. Although religious affiliation alone does not tell therapists much about the relative importance of religion in clients' lives, it does provide some basic orienting information as therapists begin to understand their clients. For example, a client may state that his or her religious affiliation is Roman Catholic. Although the therapist knows nothing without further inquiry about what type of Roman Catholic the client is, the therapist does know that the client is not Jewish, Muslim, or Protestant. The therapist has narrowed the assessment field considerably just by finding out the client's religious affiliation. If the therapist is familiar with the client's religious tradition and culture, knowledge of the client's religious affiliation also provides a rich source of insight into the client's religious and cultural background and experiences. Such information should be viewed as a source of tentative hypotheses about the client that can be checked out and explored in more depth if doing so seems clinically relevant.

Religious Orthodoxy

Religious orthodoxy is the degree to which a person believes in and adheres to the traditional doctrines and moral teachings of his or her religion (e.g., Fullerton & Hunsberger, 1982; Stark & Glock, 1968). More specifically, *belief orthodoxy* is the acceptance of the doctrinal beliefs of one's religion, and *behavior orthodoxy* is adherence to the moral teachings and practices of one's religion.

It is important for therapists to assess their clients' levels of religious orthodoxy, because orthodoxy may be related to several important treatment considerations. For example, highly orthodox clients are more likely to prefer therapists who share their religious beliefs than less orthodox individuals (Worthington, 1988; Worthington, Kurusu, McCullough, & Sandage, 1996). Building trust and credibility may be more difficult with highly orthodox clients (Worthington, 1988). Referral to religious leaders or consultation with orthodox therapists may be more necessary with such clients. Orthodox clients also are more likely to view their religious beliefs and lifestyle as being relevant to their presenting problems and concerns than are less orthodox clients. Thus, the exploration of religious and spiritual issues, and the use of religious–spiritual interventions, may be more necessary and appropriate for religiously orthodox clients. Clients who are nonreligious or affiliated with a religion but unorthodox may be more likely to view religion negatively and to resent therapists' attempts to discuss religious issues or use spiritual interventions.

Religious Problem-Solving Style

A person's religious beliefs can influence the manner in which she or he seeks to cope with and solve life's problems and difficulties (e.g., Pargament, 1997; Spilka, Shaver, & Kirkpatrick, 1985). Pargament et al. (1988) described three styles of religious problem solving or coping: self-directing, deferring, and collaborative. In the self-directing style, people believe that it is their own responsibility to resolve their problems; "God is not involved directly in this process. . . . Rather, God is viewed as giving people the freedom and resources to direct their own lives" (Pargament et al., 1988, p. 91). In the deferring style, people "defer the responsibility of problem-solving to God. Rather than actively solve problems themselves, they wait for solutions to emerge through the active efforts of God" (Pargament et al., 1988, p. 92). In the collaborative style, people believe that "responsibility for the problem-solving process is held jointly by the individual and God. . . . Both . . . are viewed as active contributors working together to solve problems" (Pargament et al., 1988, p. 92).

Therapists should assess each client's religious problem-solving style, because this information may help them to determine which therapeutic style (e.g., directive, nondirective, collaborative) and types of interventions may be most appropriate for a given client. For example, deferring clients may defer not only to God, but also to the therapist for resolution of their problems. Therapists may, initially at least, need to be highly directive with deferring clients. When using spiritual (and other) interventions with deferring clients, therapists may also need to strongly emphasize the client's role and responsibility for making these interventions succeed. Self-directing clients may be highly motivated and responsible, but because of their belief that they must resolve their own problems, they may not wish to participate in spiritual interventions that assume that God may actively intervene to assist or guide them: e.g., praying for guidance or seeking a blessing of comfort and healing from their religious leader. Spiritual interventions that require more responsibility and active involvement from the client may work best with self-directing clients. Such clients may also have difficulty accepting active support and assistance from their therapist, and so therapists may, initially at least, need to use a more nondirective therapeutic approach. Collaborative clients may be most open to a wide range of spiritual and secular interventions and may be most able to enter into a collaborative helping relationship with the therapist.

Spiritual Identity

Spiritual identity refers to a person's sense of identity and worth in relation to God and his or her place in the universe. According to our theistic spiritual perspective, people who have a positive sense of their spiritual identity and worth believe that they are eternal spiritual beings who are creations, or children, of God. They believe that they have divine worth and potential, and they feel spiritually connected to God's love. They believe that their eternal potentialities are unlimited and that one purpose of life is to seek to actualize and fulfill their great potential. Such people also believe that their inner spirit, or core identity, is eternal and that their identity and consciousness persist beyond the death of the physical body.

People who lack a positive identity do not feel that they have divine worth or potential. They may or may not believe intellectually that they are creations of God, but in either case, they feel unworthy and worthless. They do not feel God's love in their life, and they doubt whether they have any special potential, worth, or purpose. They may also doubt whether they have an inner spirit that persists beyond the grave.

According to our theistic view of personality, having a positive sense of one's spiritual identity and worth is crucial for healthy development and lifestyle functioning (see chap. 5, this volume). People who have a strong spiritual identity tend to function better emotionally, interpersonally, and spiritually. Some preliminary evidence suggests that religious people who receive an affirmation of their spiritual identity and worth seem to heal more quickly and completely and to make healthy and enduring lifestyle changes (Bergin et al., 1994; P. S. Richards & Potts, 1995a).

Assessing each client's spiritual identity is important for several reasons. First, positive spiritual identity probably bodes well for healing and growth. In our experience, such clients are better able to cope with severe challenges and stresses because of their faith in God's love, in their own capacities, and in the ultimate purpose in life's tests. With such clients, therapists may find that individuals' feelings of spiritual worth can serve as a powerful resource to help them cope with and endure painful challenges.

Second, if a client lacks a positive spiritual identity, therapists may wish to consider the possibility that these deficiencies in identity and worth are at the core of other problems and symptoms. Much has been written over the years about the centrality of identity and self-esteem in psychological and interpersonal functioning (e.g., Erikson, 1968; Rogers, 1961). For religious and spiritual clients, we believe that a deficit in their spiritual identity is significant to diagnosis and treatment. With such clients, therapists may wish to consider using interventions to help clients get more in touch with their spiritual identity and worth (e.g., prayer, meditation, spiritual imagery, spiritual direction).

God Image

God image is a person's perceptions or representations of God (Wulff, 1997). God is perceived by some people as loving, kind, and forgiving, but by others as wrathful, vindictive, and impersonal (P. L. Benson & Spilka, 1973). A number of factors appear to influence people's perceptions of God, including parental relationships, relationships with significant others and groups, self-esteem, religious instruction, and religious practices, although it appears that parental relationships and self-esteem exert the strongest influences. People who experienced loving, nurturing parental relationships and who have positive self-esteem tend to view God as loving, accepting, and forgiving (P. L. Benson & Spilka, 1973; Dickie, Merasco, Geurink, & Johnson, 1993; Wulff, 1997).

There are at least two reasons why therapists should seek to understand how a client perceives or visualizes God when conducting a religious–spiritual assessment. First, if a client has low self-esteem and perceives God to be harsh, vengeful, and impersonal, spiritual interventions that enable him or her to personally feel God's love and support could have powerful healing effects on their sense of self-esteem and worth. In a recent survey of Mormon therapists (P. S. Richards & Potts, 1995a), an increase in clients' self-esteem and feelings of worth was the most frequently reported outcome of spiritual interventions. In the case reports provided by the therapists, several attributed the change in their clients' feelings of self-esteem and self worth to the clients receiving a witness and assurance of God's love and concern (P. S. Richards, 1995). Nevertheless, despite the positive possibilities, much caution should be exercised when using spiritual interventions with clients who perceive God negatively. Such clients may doubt the efficacy of spiritual interventions and may prefer not to participate in them. Negative outcomes may occur if spiritual interventions are attempted and fail (P. S. Richards & Potts, 1995b).

A second reason why therapists should assess how a client perceives God is that this information could help them better understand their clients' psychological and interpersonal problems. According to some object–relations theorists and some research (e.g., Dickie et al., 1993; Grom, cited in Wulff, 1991; Spero, 1992), clients' perceptions of God are intimately connected to their perceptions of parents, significant others, and self. Insight into a client's God image and how it is related to the client's image of self, parents, and significant others will give the therapist a more complete understanding of the client's internalized object relations and potentially more leverage for promoting therapeutic change.

Value–Lifestyle Congruence

Value–lifestyle congruence is the degree to which a person's lifestyle choices and behaviors are congruent with their professed moral, religious, and spiritual values. According to our spiritual view of personality, discussed in chapter 5, as people affirm their spiritual identity and grow in sensitivity to the Spirit of Truth, they internalize and seek to live in harmony with healthy values. Congruence between one's values and lifestyle choices, therefore, is a hallmark of healthy personality and of spiritual development and functioning. A lack of congruence between one's values and lifestyle choices creates guilt and anxiety and may contribute to emotional distur-bance and problems in interpersonal relationships.

With such a view, it is perhaps obvious why it is important to assess the client's degree of value–lifestyle congruence. In the clinical situation, therapists often need to know whether their clients' religious and spiritual beliefs and values are a source of guilt and anxiety or of comfort and strength. Where there is value–lifestyle incongruence, usually there is emotional and interpersonal distress. It may be useful for therapists to help such clients identify and own their incongruencies as well as explore and clarify their values. Sometimes this process affirms new values and lifestyles; other times it strengthens internalization of a client's values and helps him or her turn away from destructive lifestyle choices. Table 8.1 provides an interview and assessment guide for helping therapists to consider whether their clients' values and lifestyles are healthy and adaptive or unhealthy and maladaptive.

Doctrinal Knowledge

Doctrinal knowledge involves people's understanding and knowledge of the doctrines and theology of their religious tradition. Doctrinal or religious knowledge has been viewed by several theorists and researchers as an impor-tant basic dimension of religiosity (e.g., Glock & Stark, 1965; King, 1967). We believe that therapists should assess clients' doctrinal knowledge, because we have found that many clients get into emotional trouble because they misunderstand the doctrines of their religion. As expressed by P. S. Richards et al. (1989),

> Some clients have a tendency to misunderstand or oversimplify church leaders' statements and church doctrines. Some of the clients' misunder-standings seem to be due to a lack of knowledge of the church doctrine. It also appears that problems arise because simplistic religious concepts

TABLE 8.1

Psychospiritual Themes of a Theistic Personality Theory: An Interview and Assessment Guide

Question	Adaptive–healthy faith and spirituality	Maladaptive–unhealthy faith and spirituality
1. Do my client's faith and spirituality promote a mature sense of spiritual identity and purpose or obscure divine potential?	1A. Eternal spiritual identity Love and reverence of God Divine image and worth Meaning and purpose in life Love of humanity God-inspired	1B. Negative aspects of mortal overlay Preoccupation with self Materialistic self-image Nihilism Selfish individualism Hyperspiritual or evil-inspired
2. Do my client's faith and spirituality promote agency and choice or impairment and loss of self-control?	2A. Agency* Internal locus of control Long-term goals and strivings Acceptance of responsibility Anticipation of consequences Self-regulation Good reality testing	2B. Impairment* External locus of control Immediate gratification Denial of responsibility Inability to foresee consequences Addictions Poor reality testing
3. Do my client's faith and spirituality promote moral responsibility or relativism and immorality?	3A. Moral responsibility* Belief in moral universals Attunement to Spirit of Truth* Moral behavior Moral self-esteem	3B. Relativism and uncertainty Belief in moral relativism God-controlled (externalizing or deferring) Immoral behavior Shame
4. Do my client's faith and spirituality promote integrity and congruence or deception?	4A. Integrity Intrinsic personal faith* Truthfulness Sincerity Congruence Authenticity–integrity*	4B. Deception Extrinsic normative faith* Deceitfulness Role-playing Incongruence Manipulation–deception*

5. Do my client's faith and spirituality promote faithful intimacy or infidelity and self-focus?

5A. Faithful intimacy
Nurturing
Tender-protective
Warm–faithful*–intimate*
Caring
Empathic*
Forgiving*
Humble
Assertive

5B. Infidelity and self-focus
Neglectful
Angry–abusive–violent
Antisocial–unfaithful
Sadistic
Insensitive
Unforgiving
Compliant–masochistic
Aggressive or passive

6. Do my client's faith and spirituality promote healthy concern for family and community or selfish individualism?

6A. Marriage, family and community
Interpersonal social orientation
Networking–familial kinship*
Cooperation
Mature self-sacrifice
Altruistic

6B. Alienation and isolation
Narcissistic
Self-aggrandizing
Competitive or individualistic
Self-gratifying
Hedonistic

7. Do my client's faith and spirituality promote benevolent uses of power and influence or authoritarian abuses?

7A. Benevolent power*
Authoritative–affirming
Tolerant
Egalitarian
Facilitating growth

7B. Authoritarian*
Dogmatic–absolutistic–critical
Intolerant–prejudiced
Controlling–dominating
Power-seeking*

8. Does my client's faith and spirituality promote personal growth and change or stagnation?

8A. Growth and change
Actualizing
Growth-oriented*
Change-oriented
Self renewing–repentant
Experiential–creative
Integrates ambiguity and paradox

8B. Stagnation
Perfectionistic
Righteous performances
Rigid
Self-punitive–depressed
Ritualistic–stagnant*
Anxious about the unanticipated

Note. This table is based on the psychospiritual themes described in chapter 5 (see Exhibit 5.2). It may be used by clinicians as an interview and assessment guide for evaluating how healthy and adaptive clients' religious and spiritual values and lifestyles are at the beginning and throughout therapy. It also is a helpful outline for setting therapeutic goals that are in harmony with the values and conceptual framework presented in chapter 5. Data from Bergin (1993).
*Term discussed in chapter 5.

and beliefs which the clients acquired as children, or early in their church membership, have not been critically examined. (p. 518)

The doctrines that cause clients to misunderstand and get into emotional trouble will undoubtedly vary among religious traditions (Lovinger, 1984; P. S. Richards & Bergin, 2000). Therapists who gain an in-depth understanding of the doctrines of their clients' religious traditions will be in the best position to recognize when a client has misunderstood specific doctrines (e.g., Koltko, 1990; P. S. Richards & Bergin, 2000). When working from a denominational therapeutic stance in which they enjoy high credibility and trust with their clients, therapists may greatly help clients by assisting them to examine, challenge, and modify dysfunctional interpretations of religious doctrines. In ecumenical situations, when therapists are not viewed as trusted experts on the client's religious tradition, therapists may still help clients to examine religious beliefs that appear to be dysfunctional. They can do this by referring clients to religious leaders for clarification about specific religious doctrines or by encouraging clients to do some research to determine whether their understanding of a doctrine is accurate.

Religious and Spiritual Health and Maturity

During the past century, a number of theorists and researchers have undertaken the challenge of attempting to distinguish healthy, mature forms of religiosity and spirituality from unhealthy, immature forms (e.g., Allport, 1950, 1959, 1966; Allport & Ross, 1967; Chandler, Holden, & Kolander, 1992; Ellison, 1983; Fowler, 1981; James, 1902/1936; Malony, 1985; Meadow, 1978; Moberg, 1979, 1984). Perhaps the most influential conceptualization of religious and spiritual maturity has been Allport's (1950, 1959, 1966; Allport & Ross, 1967; Donahue, 1985) theory of intrinsic and extrinsic religious orientation. According to Allport and Ross (1967), people with an immature, extrinsic religious orientation "use religion for their own ends:"

> Persons with this orientation may find religion useful in a variety of ways—to provide security and solace, sociability and distraction, status and self-justification. The embraced creed is lightly held or else selectively shaped to fit more primary needs. . . . The extrinsic type turns to God, but without turning away from self. (p. 434)

In contrast, people with a mature, intrinsic orientation "find their master motive in religion:"

> Other needs, strong as they may be, are regarded as of less ultimate significance, and they are, so far as possible, brought into harmony with the religious beliefs and prescriptions. Having embraced a creed the individual endeavors to internalize it and follow it fully. It is in this sense that he lives his religion. (Allport & Ross, 1967, p. 464)

Despite complexities and some controversy about Allport's theory (e.g., Hunt & King, 1971; Kirkpatrick, 1989; Kirkpatrick & Hood, 1990), the conclusion that an intrinsic religious orientation is a mature outlook that tends to be positively associated with a variety of indicators of personality and of emotional and social adjustment has been remarkably consistent and robust (Donahue, 1985; Gartner et al., 1991; Payne et al., 1991). In addition, an extrinsic orientation has usually been uncorrelated or negatively correlated with adjustment (Donahue, 1985; Gartner et al., 1991; Payne et al., 1991).

Allport's theory provides a useful starting point for therapists in considering whether their clients' religious and spiritual orientation is healthy and mature versus unhealthy and immature. Therapists should assess whether their clients are intrinsically or extrinsically religiously motivated, because such information will help give therapists a global understanding of how integrated and mature a client's religious orientation is. Clients who are involved in their religion only because of the social or personal benefits such activity brings may be experiencing a lack of congruence between their beliefs and actions. Such clients may profit from examining their extrinsic religious motivations and involvement and recognizing any emotional conflict that may be associated with it.

Clients who are intrinsically religious are more likely to view their religious beliefs and lifestyle as a source of meaning, support, and strength. Such clients are more likely to benefit from spiritual interventions and from exploring how their religious and spiritual beliefs and community can help them to cope, heal, and grow. This is not to suggest that intrinsic clients' religious beliefs and lifestyles are necessarily uniformly benevolent. People with an overall healthy, intrinsic orientation may nevertheless harbor some unhealthy religious beliefs and tendencies, for example, perfectionistic drives (Batson et al., 1993; Bergin et al., 1988; P. S. Richards et al., 1989; P. S. Richards, Owen, & Stein, 1993). Thus intrinsically religious clients also may benefit from examining how their religious beliefs and lifestyle may be affecting their presenting problems and emotional disturbance.

Since Allport's groundbreaking contributions, several other theorists and researchers have formally proposed and empirically tested theories of religious and spiritual well-being, development, and maturity, such as Fowler's (1981) six-stage model of faith development, Paloutzian and Ellison's (Ellison, 1983; Paloutzian & Ellison, 1979, 1991) two-dimensional model of spiritual well-being, Malony's (1985) eight-dimensional model of Christian maturity, our own theistic model of psychospiritual maturity (see chap. 5 and Exhibit 5.2, this volume), and Pargament's model of religious coping (Pargament et al., 1990). Any or all of these models could prove useful to therapists as they attempt to assess and conceptualize the healthiness and maturity of their clients' religious and spiritual orientations.

In addition to models of religious and spiritual maturity, several abnormal or pathological forms of religious experiences and behavior have been described in the literature and are sometimes observed in clinical situations; for example: demonic possession, scrupulosity ("obsessive overconcern for one's sinfulness"), ecstasy or frenzy, repetitive denominational shifting, acedia ("spiritual languor or depression"), glossolalia (speaking in tongues "when the personal milieu does not esteem this activity"), sudden conversion, and crisis (panic or catastrophe with religious implications; Lovinger, 1984, p. 179, 1996; Pruyser, 1971). Meadow and Kahoe (1984) described a number of additional abnormal religious experiences, including religious delusions, compulsions, and masochism. Media coverage has brought attention to destructive religious behaviors such as mass suicides of religious cult members, ritualistic child abuse, and satanic worship. Finally, the tragedies of September 11, 2001, indelibly imprinted on the world consciousness the reality of terrorism and violence that might have been religiously motivated (e.g., Moghaddam & Marsella, 2003; Pyszczynski, Solomon, & Greenberg, 2003).

Depending on the settings in which they work, therapists may at times be called on to assess whether their clients' religious behaviors and experiences fall into the abnormal and pathological extremes. To make such assessments, therapists must have a sound understanding both of psychopathology and of religious beliefs and behaviors that are considered normative and healthy (as well as abnormal) within the client's religious and cultural tradition. Of course, relying solely on group norms to determine whether a religious belief or behavior is unhealthy or pathological is not sufficient, for some groups engage collectively in religious practices that are unhealthy and pathological (e.g., mass suicides, ritualistic child abuse, terrorism). It is beyond the scope of this book to discuss these extremes in detail, and so we refer readers to Galanter (1996), Lovinger (1984, 1996), Meadow and Kahoe (1984), Meissner (1996), Moghaddam and Marsella (2003), Pruyser (1971), and Pyszczynski et al., (2003) for helpful information about these issues.

THE PROCESS OF RELIGIOUS–SPIRITUAL ASSESSMENT

A religious–spiritual assessment should be embedded in a multilevel, multisystemic assessment strategy. Figure 8.1 illustrates what we mean by this. The circle in Figure 8.1 represents a person, and the divisions within the circle represent the different systems within the person that therapists should assess: the physical, social, behavioral, intellectual, educational–occupational, psychological–emotional, and religious–spiritual systems. When therapists begin to work with a new client, they need to do a brief global assessment of all the major systems mentioned. We refer to this as

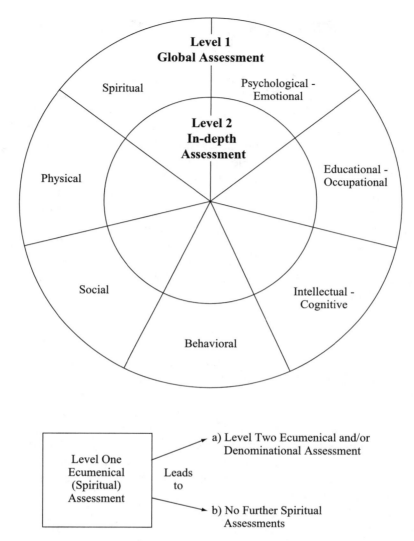

Figure 8.1. A multilevel, multidimensional assessment strategy.

a *Level 1 multisystemic assessment* (represented in Figure 8.1 by the outer ring of the circle). During a Level 1 multisystemic assessment, therapists rely primarily on clients' perceptions and self descriptions of how they are functioning in each system of their lives.

Depending on the client's presenting problems and goals, along with the information obtained during the Level 1 multisystemic assessment, therapists then proceed with more in-depth assessments of the systems that seem clinically warranted. For example, if after completing the Level 1 assessment the client reports that he or she is not experiencing any significant physical problems or symptoms, the therapist would probably not do any further assessment of the client's physical status. If during the Level 1 assessment the client did report that he or she was experiencing significant depression and anxiety and that he or she had some religious concerns (e.g., guilt over violating one's religious values) that seemed to be contributing to these symptoms, the therapist would proceed with more in-depth assessments of both the affective symptoms and the religious issues. More focused, probing questions would be asked during clinical interviews, and the therapist might also wish to have the client complete some standardized assessment measures.

We refer to these more focused, in-depth assessments as *Level 2 assessments* (represented by the inner ring of the circle in Figure 8.1). Therapists can pursue Level 2 assessments in as much depth and detail as they feel is warranted. During Level 2 assessments, therapists do not rely primarily on clients' perceptions and self descriptions of their problems and functioning, but draw more heavily on clinical theory, experience, and objective measures in assessing and conceptualizing client issues. We now discuss Level 1 and Level 2 religious–spiritual assessment approaches in greater detail.

A Level 1 Ecumenical Approach

An ecumenical assessment approach is appropriate for clients of diverse religious and spiritual beliefs and affiliations. During an ecumenical assessment, neither spiritually oriented questions on intake questionnaires and standardized measures nor questions asked by therapists in clinical interviews should be expressed in narrow, denominationally specific language or concepts, but in more general, ecumenical terms. For example, a good ecumenical question might be, "Do you believe in a Supreme Being or Higher Power?" A denominational question might be "Do you believe that Jesus Christ is the Son of God?"

When clients present for treatment, as part of a multisystemic assessment, therapists should conduct a Level 1 ecumenical assessment to gain a global understanding of the client's spiritual worldview and current status. Even when a client belongs to the same religious denomination as the therapist, such an assessment is still needed. Out of respect for individual differences, therapists should not just assume that they understand a client's religious beliefs and values on the basis of religious affiliation alone. Depending on the client's presenting problems and the information obtained in the Level 1 ecumenical assessment, therapists should then either proceed with a more in-depth Level 2 assessment or discontinue any further religious–spiritual assessments.

During a Level 1 multisystemic assessment, it is not feasible to devote a lot of time to making in-depth inquiries about a client's religious and spiritual status—there is too much other information about other systems (e.g., psychological, social, and physical) that also must be gathered to obtain a comprehensive, global understanding of the client. Therapists must quickly collect only that information that will help them to understand their client's spiritual worldview and the extent to which the client's religious and spiritual background and status may be relevant to the presenting problems and treatment planning. Seeking insight into the following seven global assessment questions will help therapists to make such a determination:

1. What is the client's metaphysical worldview (e.g., Western [theistic], Eastern, naturalistic–atheistic, or naturalistic–agnostic)?
2. What were the client's childhood religious affiliation and experiences?
3. What is the client's current religious affiliation and level of devoutness?
4. Does the client believe his or her spiritual beliefs and lifestyle are contributing to his or her presenting problems and concerns in any way?
5. Does the client have any religious and spiritual concerns and needs?
6. Is the client willing to explore his or her religious and spiritual issues and to participate in spiritual interventions?
7. Does the client perceive that his or her religious and spiritual beliefs and community are a potential source of strength and assistance?

Gaining insight into these Level 1 assessment questions need not be difficult or time-consuming for therapists. Currently, the most viable methods for seeking this information are written intake history questionnaires and clinical interviews. As discussed earlier, a Level 1 multilevel assessment should begin on the client's first visit to the psychotherapy office. After the client completes whatever paperwork is necessary to begin treatment (e.g., insurance forms, release of medical information form, and therapist informed consent document), we recommend that therapists ask the client to complete a client intake history questionnaire. Such questionnaires, used routinely by many therapists, generally solicit information from clients about a variety of topics, including client identifying information (e.g., age, gender, and marital status); history and description of presenting problems; psychiatric and counseling history; educational and career history; health and medical history; social and developmental history; and family, marital, and sexual history (e.g., W. H. Cormier & Cormier, 1991; Trzepacz & Baker, 1993).

EXHIBIT 8.1
Religious–Spiritual Client Intake Assessment Questions

1. Are religious or spiritual issues important in your life?
   _____ Yes _____ No _____ Somewhat
2. Do you wish to discuss them in counseling when relevant?
   _____ Yes _____ No
   If not, you do not need to answer the remaining questions about religion and spirituality.
3. Do you believe in God or a Supreme Being? _____ Yes _____ No
   Please elaborate if you wish. _____
   _____
   _____
4. Do you believe you can experience spiritual guidance?
   _____ Yes _____ No
   If so, how often have you had such experiences?
   _____ Often _____ Occasionally _____ Rarely _____ Never
5. What is your current religious affiliation (if any)? _____
6. Are you committed to it and actively involved?
   _____ Yes _____ Somewhat _____ No
7. What was your childhood religious affiliation (if any)? _____
8. How important was religion or spiritual beliefs to you as a child and adolescent?
   _____ Important _____ Somewhat important _____ Unimportant
   Please elaborate if you wish. _____
   _____
   _____
9. Are you aware of any religious or spiritual resources in your life that could be used to help you overcome your problems? _____ Yes _____ No
   If yes, what are they? _____
   _____
10. Do you believe that religious or spiritual influences have hurt you or contributed to some of your problems? _____ Yes _____ No
    If yes, can you briefly explain how? _____
    _____
    _____
11. Would you like your counselor to consult with your religious leader if it appears this could be helpful to you? _____ Yes _____ No _____ Maybe
    If yes, a permission and confidentiality form will be provided for you to sign.
12. Are you willing to consider trying religious or spiritual suggestions from your counselor if it appears that they could be helpful to you? _____ Yes _____ No

To be useful for a Level 1 ecumenical assessment, such questionnaires also must solicit relevant information about clients' religious and spiritual history and status.

Some therapists do not use written questionnaires, but prefer to gather such information during a semistructured clinical interview with clients. We believe that during a Level 1 ecumenical assessment, therapists should use both methods if possible. Therapists can ask clients to complete a written intake history questionnaire and then supplement this information by probing further during the initial clinical interviews. Exhibit 8.1 provides a list of specific religious–spiritual questions that can be included on client history questionnaires or asked by therapists during clinical interviews.

Level 2 Assessment Approaches

A Level 2 religious–spiritual assessment is conducted only if a Level 1 ecumenical assessment shows it to be advisable. Generally speaking, further assessment and exploration of religious and spiritual issues, with the prospective use of spiritual interventions, are indicated for clients who have a religious and spiritual worldview and lifestyle, perceive that their spiritual beliefs are relevant to their presenting problems, and are willing and ready to explore spiritual issues with the therapist.

A Level 2 religious–spiritual assessment can be conducted in an ecumenical or denominationally specific manner. The major difference between these two approaches is that a Level 2 ecumenical assessment approach is used with clients whose religious affiliation and beliefs differ significantly from those of the therapist. A Level 2 denominational assessment approach is appropriate to use only with clients who perceive that the therapist is someone who deeply understands, accepts, and respects their spiritual beliefs (e.g., they belong to the therapist's religious denomination or to some other religious tradition of which the therapist has an in-depth understanding).

When using a Level 2 ecumenical assessment approach, therapists must continue to use language and assessment measures that are ecumenical in nature to avoid confusing or offending their clients. When using a Level 2 denominational assessment approach, therapists can use language and measures that are tailored more specifically to the subtle nuances of the client's religious beliefs and tradition. Aside from these differences, the two assessment approaches have a number of similarities. In both approaches, therapists follow up leads obtained during their Level 1 assessment with more probing, detailed questions and measures. Many of the same dimensions of clients' religiousness and spirituality may be of interest in both approaches. The same basic assessment methods may be used in both: e.g., written questionnaires, clinical interviews, and objective self-report tests.

A variety of assessments may be important to explore with a Level 2 religious–spiritual assessment depending on the client's presenting problems and the results of the Level 1 assessment. The general objective of a Level 2 spiritual assessment is to determine whether the client's religious–spiritual orientation is healthy or unhealthy and what impact it is having on the client's presenting problems and disturbance. Some specific Level 2 assessment questions that we have found clinically useful to pursue are

1. How orthodox is the client in his or her religious beliefs and behavior?

2. What is the client's religious problem-solving style (i.e., deferring, collaborative, or self-directing)?
3. How does the client perceive God (e.g., loving and forgiving versus impersonal and wrathful)?
4. Does the client have a sound understanding of the important doctrines and teachings of his or her religious tradition?
5. Is the client's lifestyle and behavior congruent with his or her religious and spiritual beliefs and values?
6. What stage of faith development is the client in?
7. Does the client have a spiritual assurance of his or her eternal spiritual identity and divine worth?
8. Does the client feel a sense of spiritual well-being, e.g., is his or her relationship with God a source of comfort and strength?
9. Is the client's religious orientation predominantly intrinsic, healthy, and mature or extrinsic, unhealthy, and immature (and in what ways)?
10. In what ways, if any, are the client's religious and spiritual background, beliefs, and lifestyle affecting his or her presenting problems and disturbance?

Currently the most viable method for exploring the Level 2 assessment questions is the clinical interview. When interviewed by Chamberlain, Richards, and Scharman (1996), 13 therapists who were experienced in using a spiritual strategy stated that they preferred clinical interviewing as the method for conducting religious–spiritual assessments. In fact, all the therapists reported that they relied exclusively on clinical interviews when conducting such assessments.

One reason for such an exclusive reliance on clinical interviews is that historically few objective or projective religious and spiritual measures have been available. Although many religious and spiritual measures have been developed over the years by researchers in the psychology and sociology of religion (Gorsuch, 1984; Hill & Hood, 1999), few of them have been standardized for use in clinical situations. Furthermore, most of them were developed within a Christian theological framework, and their suitability for non-Christian clients is unclear (Robinson & Shaver, 1973; Spilka et al., 1985). Finally, religious and spiritual measures are rarely published and distributed commercially, which has limited their accessibility and ease of use for clinicians.

Fortunately, this situation is beginning to change. A recent handbook, *Measures of Religiosity* (Hill & Hood, 1999), contains copies and critical reviews of over 120 measures of different types of religiousness, including religious beliefs, practices, and attitudes; religious orientation; religious development; religious commitment and involvement; religious experience;

religious and moral values; religious coping and problem solving; spirituality and mysticism; God concept; religious fundamentalism; views about death and the afterlife; religious attributions; and forgiveness. A companion volume by the same authors on measures of spirituality is in progress. These two resources should help make religious and spiritual measures more easily accessible to clinicians. In addition, increasing numbers of book chapters and journal articles have been published in recent years that provide helpful perspectives and guidelines for clinicians about religious and spiritual assessment (e.g., Chirban, 2001; Gorsuch & Miller, 1999; Hall, Tisdale, & Brokaw, 1994; Hill & Pargament, 2003; Stanard, Sandhu, & Painter, 2000).

When working with clients in Level 2 ecumenical or denominational assessment situations, therapists may wish to consider using some standardized, objective religious and spiritual measures. In our own work, we sometimes supplement our clinical interview assessments by administering measures of intrinsic and extrinsic religious orientation (Gorsuch & McPherson, 1989) and spiritual well-being (Ellison, 1983). These give us a quick standardized indication of a client's general levels of religious and spiritual maturity and well-being. Copies of these measures were provided in the first edition of this book and are also available in Hill and Hood (1999). Several other religious and spiritual measures have recently been developed that we think are important from a theistic perspective with potential for clinical settings, including the Religious Commitment Inventory (Worthington et al., 2003), the Index of Core Spiritual Experiences (Kass, Friedman, Lesserman, Zuttermeister, & Benson, 1991), and the Spiritual Transcendence Scale (Piedmont, 1999). Copies and brief descriptions of these measures are provided in Exhibits 8.2, 8.3, and 8.4.

Because most religious and spiritual measures have not been adequately validated in clinical situations, therapists should use them only after carefully examining them and personally verifying their suitability for their clients. Even then, therapists should interpret these measures tentatively. Normative data are so limited for most of these measures that sharing normative comparisons with clients should be avoided. At most, these measures should be used only to give therapists some tentative insights into their clients and perhaps as a tool to help clients engage in exploration and self-discovery.

There are increasing numbers of ecumenical measures that are not obviously and exclusively Christian. These include the measures in Exhibits 8.2, 8.3, and 8.4, as well as the *Inventory on Religiousness* (Rayburn, 1997) and *Inventory on Spirituality* (Rayburn & Richmond, 1996). Additional research is needed with most of these measures to ensure their validity for non-Christian clients. Denomination-specific measures for the major non-Christian theistic religious traditions and denominations (e.g., Judaism and Islam), as well as for the Eastern traditions (e.g., Buddhism, Hinduism, and Taoism), are needed as well.

EXHIBIT 8.2
Religious Commitment Inventory (RCI–10)

Directions: The following items deal with various types of religious ideas and social opinions. Please indicate the response you prefer, or most closely agree with, by circling the number corresponding to your choice in the right margin (e.g., 1 = not at all true of me, 2 = somewhat true of me, 3 = moderately true of me, 4 = mostly true of me, 5 = totally true of me).

Scale	Item		
Intrapersonal	1.	I often read books and magazines about my faith.	1 2 3 4 5
Interpersonal	2.	I make financial contributions to my religious organization.	1 2 3 4 5
Intrapersonal	3.	I spend time trying to grow in understanding of my faith.	1 2 3 4 5
Intrapersonal	4.	Religion is especially important to me because it answers many questions about the meaning of life.	1 2 3 4 5
Intrapersonal	5.	My religious beliefs lie behind my whole approach to life.	1 2 3 4 5
Interpersonal	6.	I enjoy spending time with others of my religious affiliation.	1 2 3 4 5
Intrapersonal	7.	Religious beliefs influence all my dealings in life.	1 2 3 4 5
Intrapersonal	8.	It is important to me to spend periods of time in private religious thought and reflection.	1 2 3 4 5
Interpersonal	9.	I enjoy working in the activities of my religious affiliation.	1 2 3 4 5
Interpersonal	10.	I keep well informed about my local religious group and have some influence in its decisions.	1 2 3 4 5

Description and Evaluation: The RCI–10 was developed to be used in research, counseling, and health psychology. It purports to measure "the degree to which a person adheres to his or her religious values, beliefs, and practices and uses them in daily living" (Worthington et al., 2003, p. 85). Factor analyses revealed that the RCI–10 is composed of two subscales: (a) intrapersonal religious commitment and (b) interpersonal religious commitment. High internal consistency reliabilities (ranging from .87 to .96) and test–retest reliabilities (.84) have been reported for the RCI–10's total scale and subscales. The authors have also provided considerable evidence that supports the validity and clinical usefulness of the RCI–10 with both Christian and non-Christian samples. This instrument can be used both as a pretreatment assessment tool to assist in treatment planning and as a therapy outcome measure to assess whether treatment has changed a client's level of religious commitment. Given the amount of work that went into developing this measure, it may now be the preferred choice for researchers and clinicians who desire a brief measure of religious commitment. From "The Religious Commitment Inventory—10: Development, Refinement, and Validation of a Brief Scale for Research and Counseling," by E. L. Worthington Jr., N. E. Wade, T. L. Hight, J. S. Ripley, M. E. McCullough, and J. W. Berry, 2003, *Journal of Counseling Psychology, 50,* pp. 56–58. Copyright 2003 by the American Psychological Association.

Developing valid, clinically relevant religious and spiritual measures will be challenging. To be useful in clinical situations, both ecumenical and denominational measures of religiosity and spirituality must meet accepted professional test standards. For example, such measures must provide (a) evidence of reliability and validity, (b) adequate normative data, (c) evidence and information concerning the test's clinical use and relevance, (d) clear administration and scoring instructions, and (e) a detailed test manual (AERA, 1999). We look forward to the day when measures of religiosity and spirituality that meet such standards are available.

EXHIBIT 8.3
The Spiritual Transcendence Scale (STS)

Scale	Item
C	1. Although dead, images of some of my relatives continue to influence my current life.
PF	2. I meditate and/or pray so that I can reach a higher spiritual plane of consciousness.
PF	3. I have had at least one "peak" experience.
U	4. I feel that on a higher level all of us share a common bond.
U	5. All life is interconnected.
U	6. There is a higher plane of consciousness or spirituality that binds all people.
C	7. It is important for me to give something back to my community.
C	8. I am a link in the chain of my family's heritage, a bridge between past and future.
C	9. I am concerned about those who will come after me in life.
PF	10. I have been able to step outside of my ambitions and failures, pain, and joy to experience a larger sense of fulfillment.
U	11. Although individual people may be difficult, I feel an emotional bond with all of humanity.
C	12. I still have strong emotional ties with someone who has died.
U	13. I believe that there is a larger meaning to life.
PF	14. I find inner strength and/or peace from my prayers or meditations.
U	15. I believe that death is a doorway to another plane of existence.
U	16. I believe there is a larger plan to life.
PF	17. Sometimes I find the details of my life to be a distraction from my prayers and/or meditations.
PF	18. When in prayer or meditation, I have become oblivious to the events of this world.
PF	19. I have experienced deep fulfillment and bliss through my prayers or meditations.
PF	20. I have had a spiritual experience where I lost track of where I was or the passage of time.
PF	21. The desires of my body do not keep me from my prayers or meditations.
C	22. Although there is good and bad in people, I believe that humanity as a whole is basically good.
U	23. There is an order to the universe that transcends human thinking.
U	24. I believe that on some level my life is intimately tied to all of humankind.

Note. PF = prayer fulfillment; C = connectedness; U = universality. *Description and Evaluation:* The STS purports to measure "the capacity of individuals to stand outside of their immediate sense of time and place to view life from a larger, more objective perspective. . . . a person sees a fundamental unity underlying the diverse strivings of nature and finds a bonding with others that cannot be severed, not even by death" (Piedmont, 1999, p. 988). The STS contains three subscales: Universality, Prayer Fulfillment, and Connectedness. Internal consistency reliabilities for these subscales were respectively .85, .85, and .65. Evidence that supports the validity of the STS has been presented, and additional psychometric studies on the STS have been conducted (French & Piedmont, 2004; Piedmont & Leach, 2002). The STS was based on a broad conceptualization of spirituality that may be suitable for diverse faith traditions, including Western (theistic) and Eastern (Piedmont & Leach, 2002), and thus may prove useful as an ecumenical measure of clients' spirituality. The brevity of the STS may also make it feasible to use as a therapy outcome measure in many situations. From "Does Spirituality Represent the Sixth Factor of Personality?" by R. L. Piedmont, 1999, *Journal of Personality, 67*, pp. 985–1013. Copyright © 1999 by Blackwell. Reprinted with permission.

EXHIBIT 8.4
Index of Core Spiritual Experiences (INSPIRIT)

Instructions: The following questions concern your spiritual and religious beliefs and experiences. There are no right or wrong answers. For each question, circle the response that is most true for you.

1. How strongly religious (or spiritually oriented) do you consider yourself to be?

   strong   somewhat strong   not very strong   not at all   can't answer

2. About how often do you spend time on religious or spiritual practices?

   several times per day–several times per week
   once per week–several times per month
   once per month–several times per year
   once a year or less

3. How often have you felt as though you were very close to a powerful spiritual force that seemed to lift you outside yourself?

   never   once or twice   several times   often   can't answer

4. How close do you feel to God?

   extremely close   somewhat close   not very close

   I don't believe in God   can't answer

5. Have you ever had an experience that has convinced you that God exists?

   yes   no   can't answer

6. Indicate whether you agree or disagree with this statement. "God dwells within you."

   definitely disagree   tend to disagree   tend to agree   definitely agree

7. The following list describes spiritual experiences that some people have had. Please indicate if you have had any of these experiences and the extent to which each of them have affected your belief in God.

   The response choices are:
   I had this experience and it:
   4) convinced me of God's existence
   3) strengthened belief in God; or
   2) did not strengthen belief in God
   1) I have never had this experience

   A. An experience of God's energy or presence
   B. An experience of a great spiritual figure (e.g. Jesus, Mary, Elijah, Buddha)
   C. An experience of angels or guiding spirits
   D. An experience of communication with someone who has died
   E. Meeting or listening to a spiritual teacher or master
   F. An overwhelming experience of love
   G. An experience of profound inner peace
   H. An experience of complete joy and ecstasy
   I. A miraculous (or not normally occurring) event
   J. A healing of your body or mind (or witnessed such a healing)
   K. A feeling of unity with the earth and all living beings
   L. A experience with near death or life after death
   M. Other

Description and Evaluation: The INSPIRIT purports to measure whether people (a) view themselves as religious or spiritual, (b) have had core spiritual experiences, and (c) feel a sense of closeness to God. The authors of this measure developed it for the purpose of investigating relationships between spiritual experiences and health outcomes. High internal consistency reliabilities have been reported for the INSPIRIT (.90). Preliminary evidence supporting the validity of the instrument has also been reported. We view this measure as a promising tool for researchers who wish to investigate the relationship between spiritual experiences and mental and physical health. The INSPIRIT may also be useful in clinical situations with religious clients who would like to include an assessment and discussion of their beliefs about God and spiritual experiences as part of therapy. From "Health Outcomes and a New Index of Spiritual Experience," by J. D. Kass, R. Friedman, J. Lesserman, P. Zuttemeister, and H. Benson, 1991, *Journal for the Scientific Study of Religion, 30*, pp. 203–211. Copyright 1991 by Blackwell. Reprinted with permission.

Meta-Empathy and Assessment

For psychotherapists who believe that God can inspire and enlighten human beings, a religious and spiritual assessment will always be more than just gathering and conceptualizing information that has been gathered in intake questionnaires, clinical interviews, and objective or projective assessment measures. As we discuss in chapters 5 and 6, for such therapists, a spiritual assessment includes an effort to seek and remain open to spiritual impressions and insights about clients and their problems that may come from the divine source. Meta-empathy, the capacity to receive felt impressions and insights about clients that go beyond ordinary clinical hypothesizing or hunches (Chamberlain et al., 1996; C. Rogers, personal communication, June 9, 1986; West, 2000), is not well understood or often reported. Nevertheless, we are convinced that such experiences are real. As therapists engage in the process of client assessment and conceptualization, we hope that they will take the time, on occasion, to pray and contemplate about their clients. As they do, they may experience spiritual impressions and insights that deepen their understanding of their clients and increase their ability to help them.

ASSESSING THE OUTCOMES OF PSYCHOTHERAPY

We believe that the outcomes of psychotherapy should be evaluated multidimensionally. We are not, of course, the first to advocate such an evaluation approach; a gradual movement in this direction has occurred over several decades. As expressed by Kazdin (1994),

> There is general consensus that outcome assessment needs to be multi-faceted, involving different perspectives (e.g., patients, significant others, mental health practitioners), characteristics of the individual (e.g., affect, cognitions, and behavior), domains of functioning (e.g., work, social, marital adjustment), and methods of assessment (e.g., self-report, direct observation). (p. 40)

Lambert and Hill (1994) noted that there has been much variation in the criteria therapists and researchers have used to evaluate the outcomes of therapy. Psychological symptoms such as depression, anxiety, low self-esteem, phobias, compulsions, personality disorders, and schizophrenia have been assessed the most frequently, as well as interpersonal and social adjustment (Lambert & Hill, 1994). An important contribution of the theistic, spiritual strategy to psychotherapy outcome research is the view that an evaluation of clients' religious and spiritual status and functioning is crucial for an adequate assessment of outcome. Therapists and researchers should not ignore this dimension when assessing therapy outcome, but should assess it along with other clinically important criteria regardless of the therapy approach (secular or spiritual) that is being evaluated.

There are several important reasons why researchers should assess how therapy affects clients' religiousness and spirituality. Do secular psychotherapies undermine and weaken clients' spiritual beliefs and faith, as some religious people have claimed? Do spiritually oriented psychotherapies strengthen clients' faith and spirituality, as some have suggested? As many religiously committed people hesitate to seek psychotherapy from secular therapists, fearing that it will undermine their religious faith and values (Bergin, 1991; P. S. Richards & Bergin, 2000; Worthington, 1986), it would seem important for psychotherapy researchers to address these questions. Documenting that psychotherapy does not necessarily undermine clients' faith and spirituality could increase the trust leaders and members of traditional religious communities have for mental health professionals. It could also lead to greater numbers of referrals from religious leaders and increased mental health service utilization rates from members of their congregations.

From an empirical perspective, assessing clients' spiritual outcomes is in line with suggestions from leading psychotherapy researchers who have advocated a multifaceted approach to outcome assessment (e.g., Kazdin, 1994; Lambert & Hill, 1994). With several extant multidimensional models of mental health giving notable attention to spirituality (e.g., Jung, 1933; Maslow, 1964; May, 1982; Myers, Sweeney, & Witmer, 2000; Myers, 1988; P. S. Richards & Bergin, 1997), the need to assess spiritual outcomes seems clear. But despite the widespread use of multidimensional assessments of clients' psychological, social, and physical functioning, the religious and spiritual outcomes of psychotherapy have to date been largely neglected (P. S. Richards & Bergin, 1997).

A related reason to assess the spiritual outcomes of mental health treatment is to determine whether improvements in spiritual well-being are associated with better treatment outcomes in other domains of clients' functioning. Some health professionals have suggested that improvements in faith and spirituality during treatment may be associated with better and more enduring emotional, social, familial, and work outcomes (Benson, 1996; Bergin, 1991; P. S. Richards & Bergin, 1997). The possibility of spiritual growth as a catalyst in promoting and maintaining other positive changes in clients' lives is intriguing. Spiritual outcome measures are needed to investigate this possibility.

Unfortunately, few therapists or researchers have used religious or spiritual outcome measures in evaluating the effects of psychotherapy. Perhaps this neglect of the spiritual dimension in psychotherapy outcome research is not surprising, given the historical exclusion of religion and spirituality in the professions of psychology and psychotherapy (Bergin,

1980a). Another reason for this neglect is undoubtedly the limited number of empirically proven religious and spiritual outcome measures. Although researchers in the psychology of religion have developed numerous measures of religiousness and spirituality during the past few decades (Gorsuch, 1984; Hill & Hood, 1999), few of these have been validated for use in clinical settings.

The most widely used measure of spirituality in recent years, the Spiritual Well-Being Scale (SWBS; Ellison, 1983; Ellison & Smith, 1991), has been used as a therapy outcome measure in a number of studies. It is brief, and it correlates positively with a variety of physical and mental health indicators, which makes it appealing as an outcome measure. However, with some religiously devout clients the SWBS is subject to ceiling effects, which could limit its usefulness in some situations for detecting positive changes during treatment (e.g., Hall, Tisdale, & Brokaw, 1994; P. S. Richards, Hardman, & Berrett, 2001).

Most existing measures of religiousness and spirituality were not specifically designed as psychotherapy outcome measures (Hill & Hood, 1999) and thus may lack the sensitivity to change needed from such measures (Lambert & Hill, 1994). Though not true of all existing measures, until research is conducted in clinical settings their sensitivity to change will remain unclear. Thus reliable, valid, and clinically useful spiritual outcome measures need to be developed (P. S. Richards & Bergin, 1997).

To help meet the need for religious and spiritual therapy outcome measures, we, along with our colleagues, have developed an English and German version of the Theistic Spiritual Outcome Survey (TSOS; P. S. Richards, Smith, Schowalter, et al, in press). The TSOS is theoretically grounded in a theistic view of spirituality, thus in general harmony with the beliefs of many devout Christians, Jews, and Muslims. This perspective of spirituality includes several dimensions or components: (a) faith in God's existence and loving influence; (b) awareness of one's spiritual identity and purpose as a creation of God; (c) love for other people, including a desire to promote their welfare; and (d) feelings of moral congruence, worthiness, and self-acceptance.

A 17-item version of the TSOS was found to have adequate reliability and validity in a sample of college students. Three factors emerged from the analyses that corresponded to subscales labeled Love of God, Love of Others, and Love of Self. Correlations with measures of psychological outcomes were statistically significant. In subsequent analyses, the TSOS was administered over an 8-week period to a sample of inpatient women with eating disorders and to two samples from inpatient psychological clinics in Germany. The analyses resulting from these studies also supported the reliability, validity, and clinical usefulness of the scale. Overall, the findings affirmed the use of the TSOS as a spiritual outcome scale in psychotherapy

EXHIBIT 8.5
Theistic Spiritual Outcome Survey (TSOS)

Directions: Please help us understand how you have been feeling spiritually this past week, including today. Carefully read each item below and fill in or mark the circle that best describes how you felt.

Name _____ ID # _____

Age: _____   Gender: F   M

Religious Preference: _____

Session # _____   Date ___/___/___

	Never	Rarely	Sometimes	Frequently	Almost Always
1. I had feelings of love toward others.	O	O	O	O	O
2. I felt there is a spiritual purpose for my life.	O	O	O	O	O
3. I felt good about my moral behavior.	O	O	O	O	O
4. I wanted to make the world a better place.	O	O	O	O	O
5. I felt peaceful.	O	O	O	O	O
6. I felt appreciation for the beauty of nature.	O	O	O	O	O
7. I felt like praying.	O	O	O	O	O
8. I felt spiritually alive.	O	O	O	O	O
9. I felt worthy.	O	O	O	O	O
10. My behavior was congruent with my values.	O	O	O	O	O
11. I felt love for all of humanity.	O	O	O	O	O
12. I had faith in God's will.	O	O	O	O	O
13. I felt like helping others.	O	O	O	O	O
14. I felt God's love.	O	O	O	O	O
15. I praised and worshipped God.	O	O	O	O	O
16. I felt forgiveness toward others.	O	O	O	O	O
17. I loved myself.	O	O	O	O	O

Description and Evaluation: The TSOS purports to measure the spiritual outcomes of psychotherapy from a theistic spiritual perspective, which is defined as "attunement with God, the Spirit of Truth, of the Divine Intelligence that governs the universe" (Richards & Bergin, 1997, p. 77). The TSOS is composed of three subscales, which were labeled *Love of God, Love of Others, and Love of Self*. The TSOS has adequate internal consistency reliabilities (.90 for total scale; .93 for Love of God; .80 for Love of Others; and .80 for Love of Self) in a sample of college students. Evidence that supports its validity and usefulness as a psychotherapy outcome measure has also been reported in American and German clinical samples (Richards, Smith, et al., in press; Schowalter, Richard, Senst, & Murken, in press). The TSOS has potential as a therapy outcome measure because of its brevity and apparent sensitivity to change. Research on the TSOS with a wider range of religious denominations and clinical populations is needed before we can endorse it for widespread use. From "Development and Validation of the Spiritual Outcome Scale," by P. S. Richards, T. B. Smith, M. Schowalter, M. Richard, M. E. Berrett, and R. K. Hardman, *Psychotherapy Research* (in press). Copyright 1998 by P. Scott Richards, PhD 328 MCKB, BYU, Provo, Utah 84602 (801) 378-4868; e-mail: Scott_Richards@byu.edu research, although additional validation work is still needed (P. S. Richards, Smith, Schowalter, et al., in press). A copy of the English version of the TSOS is provided in Exhibit 8.5.

In this chapter we have identified several assessment measures that could also be used for outcome research (e.g., the Age Universal Intrinsic–Extrinsic Scale, the Spiritual Well-Being Scale, the Religious Problem Solving Scale, the Religious Commitment Scale, the Index of Core Spiritual Experiences, and the Spiritual Transcendence Scale). More research is needed on these measures before they can be confirmed as sensitive and valid outcome measures. At present, as long as they are interpreted cautiously, they can at least provide researchers with some "semi-standardized" ways of assessing the impact of therapy on clients' religiosity and spirituality.

CONCLUSION

Compared with the domains of intellectual, personality, and psychopathology assessment, for which volumes on theory and research have been published and numerous standardized, commercially published tests are available, religious–spiritual assessment is in its infancy. Much more theoretical and research work is obviously needed on religious–spiritual assessment approaches and methods. We hope that during the next decade a greater variety of reliable and valid religious and spiritual assessment and outcome measures will be developed and become more widely available for research and clinical purposes.

9

RELIGIOUS AND SPIRITUAL PRACTICES AS THERAPEUTIC INTERVENTIONS

The everlasting God . . . the Creator of the ends of the earth . . . giveth power to the faint; and to them that have no might he increaseth strength.

Even the youths shall faint and be weary, and the young men shall utterly fall: But they that wait upon the LORD shall renew their strength; they shall mount up with wings as eagles; they shall run, and not be weary; and they shall walk, and not faint.

—Isaiah 40:28–31
Holy Bible, King James Version

What religiously oriented psychotherapists often refer to as *spiritual interventions* are actually practices, traditions, or rituals that religious believers have been engaged in for centuries (e.g., prayer, meditation, scripture reading, repentance, forgiveness). In this chapter, we describe a number of such practices that have therapeutic potential in ecumenical therapy and across a variety of denominational situations. We also offer some clinical suggestions for implementing these practices appropriately in therapy.

These practices have endured because, in different ways, they express and respond to people's deepest needs, concerns, and problems. Research indicates that there is significant healing power in some of them (e.g., H. Benson, 1996; Borysenko & Borysenko, 1994; Krippner & Welch, 1992; W. R. Miller & Martin, 1988). We briefly discuss this evidence in the sections that follow. Spiritual practices can be used as adjunctive interventions in therapy to assist clients in their efforts to cope, heal, and grow. In chapter 10, we describe and provide specific examples of how therapists have applied these practices in therapy.

PRAYER

The word *prayer* was defined by James (1902/1936) as "every kind of inward communication or conversation with the power recognized as divine" (p. 454). Prayers can be offered verbally or nonverbally (Meadow & Kahoe, 1984). Prayer is advocated by all the Western (theistic) world religious traditions and by several of the Eastern traditions (e.g., Hinduism, Mahayana Buddhism, Religious Taoism, and Shintoism), although the specific forms of prayer advocated vary from religion to religion.

A variety of different forms of prayer have been described in religious and psychological literature, including the following:

> [There are prayers of] *petition*, asking something for one's self, and *intercession* (asking something for others). There are also prayers of *confession*, the repentance of wrongdoing and the asking of forgiveness; *lamentation*, crying in distress and asking for vindication; *adoration*, giving honor and praise; *invocation*, summoning the presence of the Almighty; and *thanksgiving*, offering gratitude. (Dossey, 1993, p. 5; see also Finney & Malony, 1985a; Heiler, 1932/1958; Meadow & Kahoe, 1984; Poloma & Pendleton, 1991; D. G. Richards, 1991)

Thus prayers can differ across a variety of dimensions, including what the purpose of the prayer is, how formal the prayer is, who is being prayed to, and what people are doing and thinking during the prayer. Many forms of prayer have in common that they are efforts at communion with a higher power and that they are based on the faith that such worship enhances life and/or the ability to cope.

Considerable research has been done to investigate the effects of prayer on physical and psychological health. A number of researchers have attempted to determine whether prayer on behalf of people who do not know they are being prayed for promotes their physical and psychological healing (e.g., Butler, Stout, & Gardner, 2002; Byrd, 1988; Collipp, 1969; Dossey, 1993; Finney & Malony, 1985a; Joyce & Welldon, 1965; Sicher, Targ, Moore, & Smith, 1998). Although there is some intriguing evidence that anonymous intercessory prayer can have positive effects on those being prayed for, overall this domain of research remains controversial and inconclusive (Dossey, 1993; Everly & Lating, 2002; McCullough, 1995; Remle & Koenig, 2001; Tan & Dong, 2001;). There is no doubt, however, that people who pray do believe that prayer helps them physically and psychologically. Whether this is because of the placebo effect, the "relaxation response," the power of the mind–body connection, or a transcendent healing influence remains scientifically uncertain (H. Benson, 1996; Borysenko, 1993; Dossey, 1993; McCullough, 1995), but among people of devout faith, scientific certainty is of limited import. There is also some evidence that different types of prayer may have different effects on people's emotional well-being and life satisfaction (e.g., Duckro & Magaletta, 1994; Finney & Malony, 1985c; McCullough, 1995; Poloma & Pendleton, 1991; D. G. Richards, 1991; Butler et al., 2002; McCullough & Larson, 1999). For example, people who only practice ritual prayer are more likely to be sad, lonely, depressed, and tense, whereas those who engage in meditative and colloquial prayer are more likely to be associated with well-being and happiness (Poloma & Pendleton, 1991).

Research has revealed that in their professional work, spiritually oriented psychotherapists sometimes (a) pray silently for clients during or outside of therapy sessions, (b) pray vocally with clients during sessions, and (c) encourage clients to pray by themselves outside of therapy sessions (Ball & Goodyear, 1991; Chamberlain, Richards, & Scharman, 1996; Jones, Watson, & Wolfram, 1992; Magaletta & Brawer, 1998; P. S. Richards & Potts, 1995b; Worthington, Dupont, Berry, & Duncan, 1988). The cited studies have provided evidence that therapists engage in or encourage clients to engage in petitionary and intercessory prayers, but we do not know whether therapists engage in or encourage other forms of prayer. Finney and Malony (1985b) suggested that therapists may wish to encourage clients to engage in contemplative prayer. Given the preliminary evidence that different forms of prayer may be associated differentially with well-being and life satisfaction, it would seem important for therapists to give careful consideration to what forms of prayer they encourage or engage in with clients.

Therapists who believe in God and think that God can enlighten and guide people would be wise to regularly pray for God's inspiration and guidance to assist them in their work with clients. Prayer and transcendent guidance should not be viewed as a substitute for therapists' professional competency and psychological health. Nevertheless, for therapists who have good psychological health and sound professional competencies and ethics, prayer and spiritual guidance can be an added resource to help them assist their clients. From time to time in therapy, such therapists may experience intuitive insights, impressions, and promptings that help them to guide clients through critical change moments (Chamberlain et al., 1996; McMinn, 1996). No one should presume, however, that God is obliged to respond to human petitions in the time, place, or manner they desire.

It may be appropriate at times for therapists to encourage religious clients to turn to God through prayer for assistance, strength, and wisdom. Even therapists who do not believe in God or prayer themselves need to remember that clients' perceived relationships with God can be a great source of strength and comfort to them. In their darkest hours, many people are sustained by their belief that God is there and loves them (Duncan,

Eddy, & Haney, 1981; McCullough & Larson, 1999). Prayer is one religious practice that helps many people feel God's love and healing power, and so encouraging clients who are struggling with serious problems to pray for strength, comfort, and wisdom could be a powerful intervention for helping them cope and heal.

We have some serious reservations about therapists praying with clients during therapy sessions. In the studies that have distinguished between client and therapist praying individually or together, praying with clients during sessions has been found to be rare (Jones et al., 1992; P. S. Richards & Potts, 1995b; Shafranske & Malony, 1990). In P. S. Richards and Potts's (1995b) survey of Mormon therapists, 33 therapists mentioned specifically that they believed psychotherapists should not pray with clients during sessions. In general, we tend to agree with this position.

Praying with clients during sessions increases the risk that role boundaries will become confused. Clients may find it more difficult to keep clear in their minds the differences between the roles of professional therapists and religious leaders. The danger of potentially unhealthy transference issues arising in therapy also is greater. We suspect that clients who have unresolved issues of anger toward or dependency on God and religious authorities are more likely to project these issues onto the therapist if their therapist prays with them. We recognize that, when such transference issues arise during therapy, they can be used to a therapeutic advantage, but we believe the risks may outweigh the potential benefits.

We are not saying that therapists should never pray with their clients during therapy sessions. Praying with clients may be more appropriate in some settings and with some types of clients than with others. For example, therapists who practice in religious settings (e.g., parochial universities or church social service agencies) may find that it is expected, comfortable, and helpful to pray with clients individually or in group sessions. Therapists in private practice settings who work with generally well-functioning religiously devout clients also may find that praying with clients can be helpful. In some inpatient settings in which religious services are included as part of the treatment milieu, it also may be appropriate. However, therapists in such situations who pray with their clients should be alert to the possible dangers of doing so.

Finally, when praying with clients or encouraging clients to pray, therapists need to make sure that they work within their clients' religious belief systems so that they do not impose their own beliefs about and practices of prayer on their clients. In denominational therapeutic situations, with clients who do not understand how to pray but who would like to learn, it may be appropriate for therapists to teach clients about prayer and explain how it could help them. In ecumenical therapy situations, it may be appropriate for therapists to explore clients' beliefs about prayer and to encourage them to pray for help with their problems. However, if in an ecumenical situation a client lacks an understanding of prayer, we believe that, in general, it may be most appropriate for the therapist to avoid teaching the client about prayer and to refer the client to his or her religious leaders or members of the client's religious community for such instruction and guidance. Such a practice will reduce the possibility that therapists will impose their own beliefs about prayer on clients who are of different religious faiths.

CONTEMPLATION AND MEDITATION

The word *contemplate* is defined in the *American Heritage Dictionary of the English Language* (American Heritage Dictionaries, 1992) as "to consider carefully and at length; meditate on or ponder" (p. 406). According to J. P. Miller (1994), "Contemplation includes meditation as well as spontaneous and unstructured moments when we experience a connection with the unity of things . . . . Meditation is a form of contemplation that involves concentrated practice" (pp. 2–3). Meditation was defined by J. C. Smith (1975) as a "family of mental exercises that generally involve calmly limiting thought and attention. Such exercises vary widely and can involve sitting still and counting breaths, attending to a repeated thought, or focusing on virtually any simple external or internal stimulus" (p. 558). Specific types of meditation include vipassana (insight), mindfulness, transcendental, Zen, visualization, and devotional meditation (H. Benson, 1996; Borysenko & Borysenko, 1994; Carlson, Bacaseta, & Simanton, 1988; Hirai, 1989; J. P. Miller, 1994; Sweet & Johnson, 1990; Thomson, 2000). J. P. Miller (1994) categorized meditation approaches into four general types: intellectual (i.e., a focus on awareness and discrimination), emotional (i.e., connection with the heart), physical (i.e., involvement with various forms of movement), and action–service (i.e., orientation toward service).

Many forms of contemplation and meditation have come directly from the Eastern religious traditions, most notably Hinduism, Jainism, and Buddhism. Some writers have expressed concerns that the passive forms of meditation (i.e., those that encourage shutting down of mental activity) advocated by some Eastern traditions may not be compatible with the Western (theistic) religious traditions (e.g., Carlson et al., 1988; McLemore, 1982). However, other writers have pointed out similarities between Eastern and Western forms of contemplation, meditation, imagery, and centering prayer (e.g., Carlson et al., 1988; Finney & Malony, 1985b). Martin and Carlson (1988) suggested that there is a relationship between relaxation, meditation, and some forms of prayer; we would add contemplation and spiritual imagery to this list. All of these spiritual practices require a trusting, passive attitude of release and surrender of control, isolation from distracting environmental noise, active focus or repetition of thoughts, task awareness, and muscle relaxation (Martin & Carlson, 1988; Payne, Bergin, & Loftus, 1992). Tan and Dong (2001) distinguished Eastern forms of meditation from Western or Judeo–Christian forms:

> In some Eastern traditions, meditation offers a means of transcending the illusions of daily life, becoming more conscious of one's immediate experience, or achieving a state of nonjudgmental detachment . . . . From a [Western] perspective, meditation is a means of seeking attachment to God and entering into his presence. Through meditation, the individual may receive specific direction, a word of comfort, or increased peace from spending time with God. (p. 300)

Research has revealed that psychotherapists occasionally recommend or practice contemplation, meditation, and spiritual imagery with clients, although, these interventions are used less frequently than most other spiritual strategies (Ball & Goodyear, 1991; Jones et al., 1992; P. S. Richards & Potts, 1995b; Sweet & Johnson, 1990; Worthington et al., 1988). Given the relatively large amount of empirical evidence that such practices can have significant healing effects on the mind and body (H. Benson, 1996; Borysenko & Borysenko, 1994), it is surprising that they are not used more frequently in psychotherapy. Perhaps most psychotherapists have more training in and comfort with secularized versions of these practices, such as biofeedback, progressive muscle relaxation, and hypnosis.

On the basis of his clinical practice as a physician, H. Benson (1996) concluded that interventions designed to promote the relaxation response are more powerful when they draw on people's deepest religious and spiritual convictions. He referred to this as "the faith factor" and indicated that it appears that people's faith in an "eternal or life-transcending force" enhances "the average effects of the relaxation response" (H. Benson, 1996, pp. 151, 155). Carlson et al. (1988) also found evidence of this in an empirical study that compared the relative effectiveness of devotional meditation and progressive muscle relaxation. Individuals who engaged in devotional meditation reported less anger, anxiety, and muscle tension than did those who engaged in progressive muscle relaxation. Thus, there is reason to believe that spiritual practices such as meditation, contemplation, and religious imagery could have more powerful healing effects with religious and spiritual clients than secular interventions that may purge all religious and spiritual content or meaning. More comparative studies are needed, but in the meantime we believe that therapists should be more open to encouraging or using contemplation, meditation, and spiritual imagery with their religious and spiritual clients.

Contemplation, meditation, and spiritual imagery may be especially indicated in therapy with spiritually devout clients who are at risk physically and psychologically because of Type A coronary-prone behavior pattern (Martin & Carlson, 1988). Clients who are struggling with stress-related problems such as reactive depression, anxiety, panic attacks, adjustment disorders, and posttraumatic stress disorder, as well as those who have health problems such as hypertension, cardiovascular conditions, cancer, and weakened autoimmune systems may also benefit psychologically, spiritually, and physically from such practices (H. Benson, 1996; Martin & Carlson, 1988; Seeman, Dubin, & Seeman, 2003; Remle & Koenig, 2001). Of course, many psychotherapy clients, to one degree or another, struggle with higher-than-normal levels of emotional distress, and therefore it may be that some form of contemplation, meditation, or spiritual imagery could be beneficial for most clients, and especially those who are religiously and spiritually devout. Clients who are active, busy, and performance-focused may not find contemplative practices appealing. However, such clients may benefit most from practices that help them to slow down, focus inwardly, and get more in touch with their emotional and spiritual feelings (H. Benson, 1996; Borysenko & Borysenko, 1994; J. P. Miller, 1994; Seeman, Dubin, & Seeman, 2003).

Therapists need to be sure that the forms of contemplation, meditation, and spiritual imagery they encourage or use with clients are consistent with clients' values. Some Eastern forms of meditation, for example, may be viewed negatively by some Christian clients (McLemore, 1982). Selecting forms of meditation that are more active and Bible-centered may be essential with such clients. Therapists who are working in a denominational therapeutic stance and thus have an in-depth knowledge of their clients' religious beliefs should not find it difficult to tailor contemplative practices to fit the beliefs of their clients. In ecumenical situations, therapists will need to rely heavily on their clients' input to help them select forms of contemplation, meditation, and spiritual imagery with which clients feel comfortable. In ecumenical situations, therapists might want to encourage clients to engage in these practices outside of sessions to reduce the possibility of therapist value imposition and client discomfort. Because of the amount of time contemplation and meditation can take, therapists should limit how much in-session time is spent engaging in these practices. Clients who understand how to engage in contemplative practices and appreciate their purpose and possible benefits should be encouraged to engage in these practices outside therapy.

READING SACRED WRITINGS

All the major world religious traditions have some type of text or writings that devout followers view as sacred and as a source of spiritual wisdom and insight (Nigosian, 1994; see also chap. 4, this volume). According to Whiting (1983),

> Holy books are usually ones which contain teaching revealed by God or gods and so they are of very special value to their religions. . . .
>
> Holy books are usually given a place of honour in the worship building and may be ceremoniously carried in during services. Readings from them are considered most important and a sermon (instructive talk) may be based on some passage from them. . . .
>
> The contents of holy books are varied. They are likely to contain some historical facts as well as biographies of leading characters, rules to be followed, songs or poems to be recited, and myths. (p. 46)

All of the major theistic world religious traditions teach that God, the Supreme Being, has revealed himself and his words to human beings through that tradition's scriptures or sacred writings (McCasland, Cairns, & Yu, 1969; Smart, 1994; Whiting, 1983). For example, Jews believe that God revealed himself and his law to Moses, as recorded in the Torah. Jews also revere the Talmud, which is "a huge collection of traditions to explain the Torah, as well as the oral law handed down by word of mouth from previous generations" (Whiting, 1983, p. 57). Christians believe that God revealed himself and his will through his son, Jesus Christ, as recorded in the Holy Bible (particularly the New Testament). Some Christian denominations also believe in other sacred writings: for example, members of the Church of Jesus Christ of Latter-Day Saints accept the Bible, but also the Book of Mormon as a record of God's revelations to prophets of the appearance of the resurrected Christ in ancient America (Ulrich, Richards, & Bergin, 2000). Muslims believe that Allah (God) revealed his eternal speech and words to human beings through the angel Gabriel to Mohammed, as recorded in the Qur'an. Zoroastrians believe that God revealed himself to human beings in the Avesta. Sikhs believe that God revealed himself through gurus whose inspired words, along with those of other holy men, are recorded in the Guru Granth Sahib.

The major Eastern world religious traditions view their sacred writings as a source of spiritual and moral wisdom, although not all of them claim that these writings are necessarily a revelation from God or the gods. For example, in Hinduism there are two types of sacred writings: Sruti (hearings) and Smriti (memory). The Sruti, which include the Vedas, Brahmanas, Aranqakas, and Upanishads, are viewed as wisdom the "rishis (holy men) heard from the gods" (Whiting, 1983, pp. 46–47; Roger R. Keller, personal communication, March 12, 1997). The Smriti are long collections of stories that "were remembered from generation to generation and then written down by wise men" (Whiting, 1983, p. 47). They are considered less authoritative than the Sruti. Buddhists have several sacred writings, including the

Tripitaka, which are the scriptures of the Theravada Buddhists (Nigosian, 1994; Whiting, 1983). The Tripitaka contains teachings of Buddha and his followers, as well as stories about Buddha. Mahayana Buddhists accept the Tripitaka, but they also accept many other sacred texts that contain sayings, rules, and stories (Nigosian, 1994; Whiting, 1983). In Jainism there are two canons of sacred writings: those of the Svetambaras and Digambaras (Nigosian, 1994). The Svetambara canon consists of 45 texts that deal with matters such as the origin of the universe, astronomy, geography, doctrines, and rules on ascetic life (Nigosian, 1994). The Digambara canon "consists of two major works that address the doctrines of karma and passions" (Nigosian, 1994, p. 162). The Jain canons are thought to contain the basic teachings of Mahavira (Jainism's founder) and those of his followers.

This brief description of the sacred writings of some of the world's major religious traditions illustrates the great diversity among these traditions about texts or writings viewed as sacred or holy. Not only do the major religions differ in what writings they consider to be sacred, but individuals within each tradition differ in the degree of orthodoxy with which they view their tradition's sacred writings. Some people who are highly orthodox view their tradition's sacred writings as infallible, as literally and completely the word of God. At the other extreme are religious believers who might view the sacred writings of their tradition as a source of spiritual wisdom, insight, and poetic metaphors for how to live, but nevertheless as the fallible writings of human beings, subject to errors, myths, and false traditions. Religious and spiritual people also differ in how frequently they read or study the sacred texts of their traditions. Some study the scriptures daily, whereas others never actually read their tradition's sacred writings but rely on memories, cultural traditions, or the teachings and interpretations of their spiritual leaders.

People also differ in the purpose for which they read sacred writings. Some believers study their tradition's scriptures for intellectual reasons, to gain a more complete doctrinal understanding of their tradition's theology or philosophy. Others find comfort, insight, enjoyment, and a sense of identity and meaning as they read the narrative stories and myths found in these writings. Many also read and reflect on sacred writings because they feel that doing so brings them into the presence of the divine (i.e., they feel a sense of spiritual communion and enlightenment). Regardless of how infallible or fallible people consider the sacred writings of their tradition, or how frequently or in what manner they read these writings, a belief most religious people share is that their tradition's sacred writings can be a source of understanding, instruction, guidance, comfort, insight, and enlightenment (Nigosian, 1994; Smart, 1993, 1994; Whiting, 1983). An indication of the social and psychological importance of sacred writings was disclosed in a survey some years ago in the United States by the Book of the Month Club and the Library of Congress's Center for the Book (U.S. Library of Congress, 1991). When asked what book had most influenced their lives, respondents identified the Bible more frequently than any other book. Even Albert Ellis (1993), who is an atheist, acknowledged that the Bible has been the single most significant self-help book in human history. It is unfortunate that mental health professionals generally have been slow to recognize or acknowledge this pervasive influence.

Research has revealed that religious psychotherapists are using scriptures and sacred writings in therapy in a number of different ways and that they are doing so frequently. Therapists have (a) quoted scriptures[1] to clients, (b) interpreted scriptures for clients, (c) made indirect reference to scriptures while discussing or teaching religious concepts, (d) related stories from the scriptures, (e) encouraged clients to memorize scriptures, (f) encouraged clients to read and study scriptures outside therapy sessions, and (g) used scriptures to challenge clients' dysfunctional or irrational beliefs (Ball & Goodyear, 1991; Jones et al., 1992; Propst, 1980; Propst, Ostrom, Watkins, Dean, & Mashburn, 1992; P. S. Richards & Potts, 1995b; Tan, 1987; Worthington et al., 1988). Overall it appears that some variation of scriptural discussion, interpretation, and study is engaged in more frequently during psychotherapy than any other spiritual intervention (Ball & Goodyear, 1991; Jones et al., 1992; Moon, Willis, Bailey, & Kwasny, 1993; P. S. Richards & Potts, 1995b; Worthington et al., 1988). This prevalence is interesting, especially considering that little research has been done to evaluate the effects of reading or studying scriptures or sacred writings.

Cognitive therapy treatment approaches that have included scriptures to help challenge dysfunctional beliefs have been successful at reducing clients' depression (e.g., Pecheur & Edwards, 1984; Propst, 1980; Propst et al., 1992). In addition, scriptural readings and reflections, combined with prayer and quiet time, have been shown to help reduce anger, anxiety, and muscle tension (e.g., Carlson et al., 1988). However, in all these studies, scripture reading was just one part of a multifaceted treatment program; thus it is impossible to isolate the effects of the scriptural interventions. Making reference to scriptures was the most frequently reported "effective" spiritual intervention in the case reports of 215 Mormon therapists (P. S. Richards & Potts, 1995b). Despite these suggestive findings, we are aware of little conclusive evidence that reading, studying, interpreting, discussing, or reflecting on scriptures and other sacred writings have beneficial psychological or physical effects. We believe that such practices and interventions are often therapeutic, but clearly research is needed to explore how this may be so.

---

[1] We use the term *scriptures* as a convenience to include both canonized texts such as the Bible and Qur'an as well as other sacred or inspirational writings that do not have such a formal status.

It appears that sacred writings can be used for a variety of purposes in therapy, such as helping clients (a) challenge and modify their dysfunctional beliefs; (b) reframe and understand their problems and lives from an eternal, spiritual perspective; (c) clarify and enrich their understanding of the doctrines of their religious tradition; (d) strengthen their sense of spiritual identity and life purpose; and (e) seek God's enlightenment, comfort, and guidance. Before implementing a spiritual intervention involving sacred writings in some way, therapists, of course, should accurately assess their clients' beliefs and feelings about these sacred writings. Therapists should use only scriptural interventions that are compatible with their clients' spiritual beliefs.

Therapists should avoid getting into scriptural or theological debates with their clients. Some clients would probably enjoy such power struggles, but others may be deeply offended by them. Scriptural debates could lead to unethical value imposition by the therapist. Thus, in our opinion, such debates are rarely appropriate or helpful. We believe that when questioning clients' scriptural understandings or offering their own scriptural interpretations, therapists should do so nondogmatically, emphasizing that they do not speak with any official authority (cf. Lovinger, 1984).

When their clients' scriptural understandings seem dysfunctional, therapists may find it best to refer such clients to their religious leaders for doctrinal discussions and clarification. This is most effective when the therapist has permission to converse with or sit in with the leader. If client and therapist are of the same belief system, it may be appropriate for therapists to invite clients to explore specific writings relevant to their misunderstandings, being cautious not to set themselves up as authorities.

It appears that most religiously oriented therapists have used scriptures as a cognitive intervention to influence and modify clients' religious understandings and cognitions (see also Table 10.2 in chap. 10 of this volume for an example of a biblical scripture used by Propst for this purpose). We believe that scriptures also have much potential as affective and transcendent interventions. The stories and narratives in sacred writings can be powerful metaphors for connecting with clients affectively and spiritually. Much has been written in recent years about the power of metaphors and stories in psychotherapy (e.g., Barker, 1996; Kopp, 1995; Lieblich, McAdams, & Josselson, 2004; Mills & Crowley, 1986; Siegelman, 1990; Vitz, 1990, 1992a, 1992b), and scriptural stories are some of the most powerful and meaningful in all of literature.

Many religious people believe that sacred writings help them communicate with God and know God's will for them. It may be appropriate for therapists to encourage such individuals to read, ponder, and reflect on the scriptures, seeking transcendent insight into their problems and concerns. Of course, such an intervention could be misused. Some clients have been told by family or religious leaders, "If you'll just read the scriptures and pray, everything will be fine." Reading scriptures and praying about problems may help many, but such practices should not be recommended as a magical cure for all of life's problems. If clients do read the scriptures seeking enlightenment and feel that they have not gained such insight, therapists need to be prepared to help clients deal with such "failures."

REPENTANCE, ATONEMENT, AND FORGIVENESS

Repentance, atonement, and forgiveness may be the most powerful change process handed down to us by religious traditions. The three major theistic world religions, Christianity, Islam, and Judaism all subscribe to a theology and practice of repentance, atonement, and forgiveness. Repentance can be viewed as a prelude to forgiveness—that is, in repentance, people seek forgiveness from God or from those they have hurt or offended, and it includes reform in thought, feeling, and action (McCullough, Sandage, & Worthington, 1997; McCullough & Worthington, 1994a, 1994b; Payne et al., 1992).

The word *repent* is defined in the *American Heritage Dictionary of the English Language* as "to feel remorse, contrition, or self-reproach for what one has done or failed to do" and "to make a change for the better as a result of remorse or contrition for one's sins" (American Heritage Dictionaries, 1992, p. 1530). Repentance from sin (transgression of God's laws or commands) requires that a person give up and turn away from attitudes and behaviors that are wrong, bad, or alien to the godly prescribed lifestyle. In the deeper sense, this entails a "change of heart" in that one's basic motives are purged of carnal, selfish, or worldly desire. This is not an easy process, but the personal work it requires is reminiscent of the principles that have guided psychotherapeutic change from its inception to the present time.

The essence of it is that one must sacrifice and exercise agency via self-control; that is, give up some pleasure or satisfaction that is harmful to self and/or others for the sake of a higher goal. The satisfaction to be yielded can be as simple as the determination to always be right in a marital argument and as complex as overcoming a lifelong addiction. A person is motivated to do such courageous things by the belief that God wills it. One has to *recognize* that his or her way of being is foreign to his or her faith. This brings about *remorse*, which leads to *reform* and, ultimately, making *restitution*, which leads to *reconciliation* with God and others.

The spiritual energy behind repentance or the quest to be reconciled with the God one worships should not be underestimated. It can be an immeasurable power for good; that is, for the constructive changes all therapists cherish. When motivated by faith in God and the blessings that flow from obedience to God's commandments, it produces tremendous energy in the change process.

Naturally, this process is motivated not only by the desire to please God or to be reconciled with other people—both positive aims—but also by guilt. In this sense guilt is friendly—that is, it impels one to do the right thing in order to be relieved of the pain of conscience. This is a critical contribution of religion to therapy, and one not to be dismissed. The history of psychotherapy is replete with efforts to relieve guilt without repentance, one of the truly negative effects of professional change technology (Bergin, 1980a; Mowrer, 1961, 1967). It was a major error to confuse "neurotic guilt" with "moral guilt" and then to excuse them both. No one wants to make life worse for the perfectionistic, obsessional, guilt-ridden client who is overcontrolled by an excessive superego; but the fear of doing so has led to therapeutic pampering of a vast clientele of person's suffering from true guilt (Mowrer, 1961, 1967).

The great contribution of theism to the guilty is the promise of atonement and forgiveness. To atone means to compensate for the negative effects of an action. Repentance is one way of atoning. Another way is by suffering the consequences of one's sin (in religious context) or one's crime (in civil context) (see Oaks, 2002). In either case the demands of justice are met by punishment. Theistic religions teach that God's justice may be moderated or even totally avoided through forgiveness that follows from contrition, faith, repentance, or other rituals. For example, Christians believe that Jesus Christ forgives sin under such conditions and is considered to be the Savior in that by faith in Him, salvation from the punishments of divine justice is granted. For the believing Christian, faith in Christ should not be ignored or underestimated in its power for change.

When treating theistic clients, teachings concerning repentance and atonement lead naturally to the topic of forgiveness. The word *forgive* is defined in the *American Heritage Dictionary of the English Language* (American Heritage Dictionaries, 1992) as "to excuse for a fault or an offense; pardon" and "to renounce anger or resentment against" (p. 713). All theistic world religions teach that people should forgive those who have harmed or offended them and seek forgiveness for wrongdoings (R. R. Keller, personal communication, May 8, 1996). There are, of course, differences in the specific beliefs about to whom, when, and how forgiveness should be granted and sought. For example, within the Christian tradition, believers are told to forgive "all enemies and offenders in an unqualified way" (Payne et al., 1992, p. 183). In the Jewish tradition, it may not be viewed as desirable to "forgive people who do not acknowledge the injury, or even worse, rationalize their injurious behavior as having been deserved" (Lovinger, 1990, p. 177). In some religious traditions (e.g., Catholic, Latter-Day Saint), confession to church authorities is viewed as a necessary step in seeking forgiveness for some infractions, whereas in other traditions confession to religious authorities is not viewed as necessary.

From a religious perspective, forgiveness is viewed as an act that has important spiritual consequences. For example, within the Christian tradition, forgiveness is thought to restore people's relationship with God and help them to qualify for salvation through Jesus Christ (McCullough & Worthington, 1994b). From a psychological perspective, writers have suggested that forgiveness can (a) promote positive changes in affective well-being, (b) affect physical and mental health, (c) restore a sense of personal power, and (d) allow reconciliation between the offended and offender (Bergin, 1988; McCullough & Worthington, 1994a, 1994b). Hope (1987) suggested that by choosing to forgive, people increase their options and freedom to grow. When seeking forgiveness, people take responsibility for their wrongdoings and thus make it easier for those they have hurt to heal (Worthington & Drinkard, 2000).

Research reveals that encouraging forgiveness is one of the spiritual interventions most frequently used by psychotherapists (Ball & Goodyear, 1991; DiBlasio, 1992; DiBlasio & Benda, 1991; DiBlasio & Proctor, 1993; Freedman & Enright, 1996; Jones et al., 1992; Moon et al., 1993; P. S. Richards & Potts, 1995b; Worthington et al., 1988); however, they sometimes give insufficient attention to the vital role of repentance and atonement in this process. Therapists have encouraged clients to forgive (a) parents and others who have hurt, abused, or offended them; (b) themselves for their own mistakes and transgressions; and (c) to accept forgiveness from others and from God. A growing body of research supports the belief that forgiveness is an important component of interpersonal and psychological healing (Enright & Fitzgibbons, 2000; Freedman & Enright, 1996; Hebl & Enright, 1993; Sanderson & Linehan, 1999; Worthington, Kurusu, McCullough, & Sandage, 1996; McCullough, Pargament & Thoreson, 2000; Worthington, Berry, & Parrott, 2001). We believe that forgiveness is a powerful healing practice, and we endorse its careful use in psychotherapy.

Forgiveness can be encouraged without any reference to religious or spiritual concepts; indeed, DiBlasio (1993; DiBlasio & Benda, 1991) found that therapists' religious beliefs were weakly or completely unrelated to their attitudes about the importance and usefulness of forgiveness in therapy. However, consistent with H. Benson's (1996) assertion that connecting people's religious and spiritual beliefs to relaxation techniques can enhance the potency of the relaxation response, the effectiveness of forgiveness may be enhanced by relating it to clients' deeply held beliefs. Bergin's (1988) transitional figure technique illustrates what we mean. Bergin suggested encouraging a client to become a transitional person in the history of his or her family, absorbing the pain of past victimization, stopping its transmission into future generations, forgiving perpetrators, and adopting a redemptive role between previous ancestors and future progeny. With devout Christian clients, the parallels between a client's redemptive role in the family and the redemptive role of Jesus Christ can be discussed explicitly to strengthen clients' sense of purpose, meaning, and resolve.

Before therapists encourage clients to forgive others or to seek forgiveness from others, we believe it is crucial that they assess clients' readiness for such an intervention. Forgiveness is a spiritual and emotional process that takes time—sometimes a lot of time. Individuals who have been abused and severely hurt by others must often go through stages in the healing process: (a) acknowledging shock and denial; (b) developing awareness and recognition that they have been abused and offended; (c) experiencing feelings of hurt, grief, anger and having the opportunity to safely express these feelings to others; (d) receiving validation that they have been wronged and, if possible, to see justice done and restitution occur; (e) attaining boundary repair (i.e., the opportunity to affirm and ensure that the abuse or offenses will not happen again); and (f) the ability to let go, forgive, and move on with life. If therapists encourage clients to forgive others before they have had the opportunity to appropriately work through such phases in the healing process, considerable emotional and spiritual harm could be done. When people attempt to forgive prematurely, the process cannot be completed and unresolved feelings of pain, grief, guilt, shame, and anger may continue to create problems for them in their lives (Enright, 2001; Enright & Fitzgibbons, 2000).

We have found that some clients, because of feelings of religious obligation, have prematurely attempted to forgive those who have offended them. Some devoutly religious clients with whom we have worked have said that they felt unworthy and unrighteous because they were not able to forgive others more quickly. We have found it helpful to teach such clients that forgiveness involves a process of reconciliation that often takes considerable time and may require real or imagined encounters with the perpetrators of their pain. With such clients, we have found that reframing the client's dilemma in the following manner has sometimes been helpful: "It isn't that you haven't forgiven your [parents], it's just that you are still involved in the process of forgiving. You are part way through the process, and hopefully our work together will help you eventually complete that process. In the meantime, it appears that you still have a lot of hurt, grief, and anger that you need to talk about and work through." Reconciliation between the offender and offended is the ideal but is not always possible. In such cases, the needed inward reconciliation can be facilitated by faith in God's ultimate justice and mercy.

Therapists also should be careful not to encourage clients to seek forgiveness before they have truly taken responsibility for their own behavior and done all they can to make restitution for their own wrongdoings. If clients who have wronged others have not yet fully owned and taken responsibility and do not yet have a sincere desire to make restitution to whatever extent possible, then any attempts to confess and ask for forgiveness may be wasted. Even worse, the victim may be further harmed by premature or insincere forgiveness solicitations. Thus therapists need to be cautious not to encourage clients to forgive others or seek forgiveness prematurely. Often, most of the work therapists must do is to help clients work through the painful and difficult initial stages of healing, such as shock and denial, awareness and recognition, hurt, grief, anger, rage, and shame. By the time it is appropriate to encourage clients to forgive others or to seek forgiveness, most of the difficult therapeutic work should have been done. See Carter, McCullough, Sandage, and Worthington (1994); Enright (2001); Enright and Fitzgibbons (2000); Ganje-Fling and McCarthy (1994); Hope (1987); McCullough et al. (1997); McCullough and Worthington (1994a, 1994b); and McCullough, Pargament, and Thoreson (2000) for additional clinically useful information about the process and role of forgiveness in healing. Freedman and Enright's (1996) work with incest survivors is a compelling example.

WORSHIP AND RITUAL

The word *worship* is defined in *The American Heritage Dictionary of the English Language* as "the reverent love and devotion accorded a deity" (American Heritage Dictionaries, 1992, p. 2059). The word *ritual* is defined as "the body of ceremonies or rites used in a place of worship" or a "ceremonial act or a series of such acts" (American Heritage Dictionaries, 1992, p. 1557). Not all rituals are oriented toward a deity (R. R. Keller, personal communication, March 12, 1997). All the major world religious traditions encourage their followers to engage in various acts of private and public worship or ritual (Parrinder, 1961; Smart, 1983; Whiting, 1983). Believers can worship in many ways:

> I can worship God in my heart and you cannot in any obvious way see that is going on. But it is also typical and somehow more basic for worship to take a partly outward form. Worshippers bow down, or kneel, or stand up and sing. More elaborately they may pay their reverence to God or a god by making a sacrifice or going on a pilgrimage. Ritual is often assisted by various external visible means, such as the use of candles, flags, chapels, temples, statues, icons, and so on. Look at a cathedral and you are, so to speak, looking at an act of worship frozen into stone. Look at a crucifix and you are looking at a feeling of faith congealed into wood and metal. And music, that wonderful and wordless

way of expressing feelings, can be audible adoration, a flow of sound dedicated to sacred things. (Smart, 1983, pp. 130–131)

The theistic world religious traditions promote and support their followers' need to worship and engage in rituals in a number of ways:

1. *Providing places of worship:* temples, shrines, mosques, churches, and synagogues;
2. *Conducting and promoting religious rituals:* engaging in special prayers; reciting vows; singing hymns; performing ritualistic acts such as bowing and kneeling; bathing and washing; fasting or abstaining from food, water, or sexual relations; lighting candles; partaking of sacramental emblems such as bread and wine; and practicing baptism;
3. *Sponsoring and supporting religious festivals:* Divali or Festival of Lights (in Hinduism, a new year festival in which Vishnu and his bride are welcomed into every house and light or good overcomes darkness or evil); Wesak (in Theravada and Mahayana Buddhism, a festival that commemorates Buddha's birth, enlightenment, and entry into nirvana); Pesach, or Passover (in Judaism, the eight-day Feast of the Unleavened Bread, which marks God's passing over the Jews in Egypt, sparing their firstborns during the plagues, and their freedom from enslavement in about 1300 B.C.); Easter (in Christianity, to commemorate the resurrection of Jesus Christ); Ramadan Fast and Id al Fitr (in Islam, the fast held during the ninth month of the Islamic year marking the time when Mohammed received Allah's first revelation of the Qur'an; Id al Fitr is a celebration marking the end of Ramadan); and
4. *Requiring, encouraging, or permitting religious pilgrimages:* journeys to holy places (Hindus make pilgrimages to the city of Benares and bathe in the River Ganges, Muslims make a pilgrimage to the city of Mecca, and many Jews and Christians make pilgrimages to Israel and Jerusalem).

From a spiritual perspective, acts of worship and ritual can serve a number of purposes for believers: (a) expressing one's devotion, love, and respect toward God or the gods; (b) committing or recommitting oneself to a spiritual and moral life; (c) demonstrating devotion and piety to other members of one's religious community; (d) offering penitence and sacrifice for sins or wrongdoings; (e) demonstrating one's solidarity with other members of the religious community; and (f) seeking spiritual enlightenment, guidance, and healing (Smart, 1983, 1993, 1994). Acts of worship and ritual may also be psychologically and physically healing (Tan & Dong, 2001).

H. Benson (1996) suggested that worship services "are full of potentially therapeutic elements—music, aesthetic surroundings, familiar rituals, prayer and contemplation, distraction from everyday tensions, the opportunity for socializing and fellowship, and education" (p. 176). H. Benson (1996) also described why he believed religious rituals can be therapeutic:

> There is something very influential about invoking a ritual that you may first have practiced in childhood, about regenerating the neural pathways that were formed in your youthful experience of faith. In my medical practice, this has proven true. . . . Even if you experience the ritual from an entirely different perspective of maturity and life history, the words you read, the songs you sing, and the prayers you invoke will soothe you in the same way they did in what was perhaps a simpler time in your life. Even if you don't consciously appreciate that there is any real drama or emotion attached to the ritual, the brain retains a memory of the constellation of activities associated with the ritual, both the emotional content that allows the brain to weigh its importance and the nerve cell firings, interactions, and chemical releases that were first activated. (p. 177)

Research reveals that psychotherapists do not often encourage clients to engage in acts of worship and ritual (Ball & Goodyear, 1991; Jones et al., 1992; P. S. Richards & Potts, 1995b; Tan, 1987; Worthington et al., 1988; Griffith & Griffith, 2002). Religious rituals such as anointing with oil, laying on of hands, blessings, encouraging clients to attend worship services, and fasting tend to be rarely or infrequently used or mentioned. Of course, there are many other acts of religious worship and ritual besides those that have been included to date in surveys of therapists. Perhaps these surveys have not given therapists an adequate opportunity to indicate acts of worship and ritual they encourage clients to perform. A more careful examination of this question is needed, but for now the best evidence we have suggests that acts of worship and religious ritual are not frequently recommended by therapists. This seems unfortunate, because some forms of religious worship and ritual may promote better physical and psychological health (e.g., H. Benson, 1996; Gartner, Larson, & Allen, 1991; Matthews, Larson, & Barry, 1993–1995). On the other hand, many clients engage in such rituals regularly, but their significance is rarely discussed in the clinical situation. Discussing them may enhance the healing significance of both the rituals themselves and the therapy sessions.

Forms of worship and ritual that help clients to affirm their spiritual heritage, identity, worth, life purpose, and involvement with their religious community may be especially helpful for clients who struggle with a lack of life structure, purpose, and meaning or who struggle with guilt, shame, alienation, anxiety, depression, and grief. Such forms of worship and ritual can also help people integrate and cope with major life transitions such as marriage; poor health; death; divorce; and the birth, growth, and departure of children. Of course, we recognize that acts of worship and ritual also can be promoted and used in extreme, rigid, perfectionistic, and shaming ways that could harm people physically and psychologically. Thus we do not indiscriminately endorse all acts of worship and ritual for use in psychotherapy, but we believe that therapists should consider carefully those that could have healing properties. When such forms of worship and ritual are identified, therapists and researchers should test and evaluate them in clinical situations. In a discussion about therapists' role in ritual, Griffith and Griffith (2002) suggested that

> [Therapists] help people to notice, honor, and make space for important rituals and ceremonies in their lives, staying curious about what the person's experience is and how that may be relevant to the work of the therapy. Our role is to support the person in "holding the mystery" as he or she participates in, learns from, and draws strength from a ritual or ceremony. When such forms of worship and ritual are identified, therapists and researchers should test and evaluate them in clinical situations. (p. 177)

In both ecumenical and denominational therapeutic situations, therapists should be cautious about engaging in acts of religious worship or ritual with clients during therapy sessions, because this could confuse role boundaries (see chap. 7, this volume). For example, we think that therapists should normally not give clients blessings (laying on of hands) or pray with them. There may be some exceptions to this, such as in therapy settings clearly affiliated with a religious institution. Also, in some inpatient settings in which clients do not have normal access to their religious community, it may be appropriate to provide opportunities for worship and ritual on the unit. In such situations, therapists may wish or need to lead or participate in such experiences or services. If they participate, therapists should carefully define their roles in relation to their clients' spiritual leaders.

Therapists also should be cautious about participating with their clients in acts of religious worship or ritual outside of therapy sessions (e.g., attending church or synagogue with clients), because the religious leader–therapist role boundaries can be confused and crossed. Therapists should normally encourage clients to engage in religious worship and rituals outside of therapy sessions, in private, with family members, or with religious leaders and other members of their religious community. If therapists believe that it may be appropriate to engage in religious worship or ritual with a particular client, we recommend that they consult with professional colleagues before doing so to ensure that they fully examine and minimize the potential risks.

In both denominational and ecumenical therapy situations, therapists may find it helpful to explore with clients whether there are acts of religious worship or ritual that clients might find meaningful and therapeutic. In denominational therapeutic situations, therapists may teach clients how to engage in different religious practices and rituals if clients do not understand, clarifying why these practices may be beneficial. In ecumenical situations, they should avoid the risk of teaching religious practices that are not consistent with clients' religious beliefs by referring clients to their religious leaders for instruction. Therapists should, of course, teach clients only religious practices that are clearly consistent with clients' religious beliefs.

FELLOWSHIP AND SERVICE

The word *fellowship* is defined in the *American Heritage Dictionary of the English Language* (American Heritage Dictionaries, 1992) as the "condition of sharing similar interests, ideals, or experiences, as by reason of profession, religion, or nationality" (p. 670). The word *service* is defined as an "act of assistance or benefit to another or others; a favor" (American Heritage Dictionaries, 1992, p. 1649). All the major world religious traditions encourage their followers to engage in fellowship with members of their religious community and to perform (and be the recipients of) various acts of altruistic service (Nigosian, 1994; Smart, 1993, 1994; Whiting, 1983). According to H. Benson (1996), fellowship activities may take many forms:

> Be it weekly church or synagogue services, daily masses or temples devoted to prayer several times each day, be it Bible study or bingo night, confirmation classes, preparation for bar mitzvah or bat mitzvah, potluck suppers or youth groups, marriage encounter weekends or church camps, Sunday school or soup kitchens, religious institutions ensure that their members get ample doses, not just of faith but of healthy social interactions. (p. 181)

Altruistic service can take many forms, including, for example, giving food to the hungry, donating clothing and money to the poor, visiting the sick, providing emotional support to those who are discouraged or grieving, and serving in volunteer positions in one's religious community. The donation of money in the form of tithes or offerings is often a tangible mode of anchoring one's contribution to the larger community and its welfare. The specific types of fellowship and service and the frequency with which they are engaged in or received by followers varies somewhat in different religious traditions. The basic need for fellowship, mutual support, and service, however, is universal among human beings, and all the great world religious traditions encourage and provide opportunities for expressing and fulfilling these needs.

From a spiritual perspective, fellowship, support, and altruistic service have a number of potential benefits in believers' lives:

1. strengthening them spiritually when their faith is weak and in times of trial;
2. fortifying them against worldly (evil) influences and pressures;
3. helping them to avoid self-preoccupation and to forget their own self interests or place their own problems in a broader social and spiritual perspective;
4. teaching them to be unselfish and loving;
5. helping them feel a sense of belonging and social acceptance;
6. endowing them with a sense of purpose and meaning;
7. filling their hearts with joy and love for their fellow human beings;
8. helping them to feel a sense of harmony with God; and
9. providing them with extra help in coping with stress, death, disease, and trauma (Pargament, 1996).

Considerable evidence shows that fellowship and altruistic service have beneficial physical and psychological effects. For example, Levin (1994) concluded that epidemiological studies suggest that the social support and fellowship provided by religion "serve to buffer the adverse effects of stress and anger, perhaps via psychoneuroimmunologic pathways" (p. 9). In the *Healing Power of Doing Good*, Luks (1993) reported the results of a survey of thousands of volunteers across the United States. He found that people who helped other people consistently reported better health than people who did not and that many believed that their health improved when they started to do volunteer work. The vast majority of those surveyed said that helping others gave them a physical sensation or rush, including a sudden warmth, increased energy, a sense of euphoria, and greater calm and relaxation. Results of numerous other studies suggest that the social support and fellowship opportunities provided by religious communities contribute to better physical and psychological health and to decreased mortality rates (e.g., H. Benson, 1996; Berkman & Syme, 1979; Martin & Carlson, 1988; Oman, Thoresen, & McMahon, 1999; Pargament, 1996; Payne, Bergin, Bielema, & Jenkins, 1991; Spiegel, Bloom, Kraemer, & Gottheil, 1989).

Research is unclear about how often psychotherapists encourage clients to engage in mutual fellowship or altruistic service. P. S. Richards and Potts (1995b) found that Mormon therapists they surveyed frequently used interventions involving the client's religious community. Using the religious community occasionally was reported in two studies of Protestant therapists by Ball and Goodyear (1991). However, the way clients' religious communities were used is unclear in all three of these studies. We do not know to what extent clients were encouraged to engage in fellowship with members of their religious community or to perform and receive altruistic service. Little and Robinson (1988) reported that one component of their moral reconation group treatment approach for offenders was requiring participants to engage in community service. Tan (1996) encouraged therapists to consider referring their clients to groups within their religious community for fellowship and support. To our knowledge, however, no other empirical studies have investigated how frequently therapists encourage the use of fellowship and altruistic service as an intervention. The best evidence we have seems to indicate that psychotherapists do not often encourage clients to engage in fellowship with members of their religious community or to perform and accept acts of altruistic service. We are not sure why this is the case, but we believe it is unfortunate, considering the potential healing power of such activities.

Therapists could more routinely consider ways that they can involve clients in fellowship and service activities within their religious communities. Such interventions may be particularly helpful with clients who are socially isolated, lonely, depressed, or experiencing major life changes (e.g., death of a loved one, divorce, or loss of a job). With suicidal clients, the social support and concern that may be available within the religious community could help save their lives. Not all clients, of course, will necessarily need or benefit from involvement in fellowship or service. Some clients we have worked with are already overinvolved in their religious communities, even to the point of being burned out from fellowship and service. Such clients may need help in reducing the degree of involvement in their religious communities so that they have more time to attend to their own needs and growth. Some clients have been abused or otherwise hurt by members of their religious community. They may need, at least temporarily, to distance themselves from their community while they work through feelings of hurt, grief, anger, and rage. Thus, interventions that provide opportunities to engage in fellowship and to receive and give altruistic service are not indicated for all clients, but such interventions may greatly assist many in coping with, reframing, and resolving their problems.

We recognize that it is not necessarily easy to enlist the appropriate support of clients' religious communities or to find appropriate ways to involve clients in fellowship and service. Many clients do feel isolated from their community and will resist therapists' efforts to get them more involved in it. In addition, therapists need to be cautious about how and with whom they involve their clients in the religious community. Although many people in such communities have good intentions and would be willing to engage in fellowship and provide service to needy individuals, not all of these people are capable of providing quality help. Some of them are needy or disturbed themselves and could exploit or otherwise relate in harmful ways to clients, as has been noted in cases of clergy abuse of children or exploitation of adults for financial or sexual gain.

As this discussion illustrates, therapists need to investigate situations carefully before attempting to involve their clients in religious fellowship or service. They should seek to understand the intricacies of their clients' religious communities, developing contacts with religious leaders and helping professionals who they can trust and with whom they can consult (Tan & Dong, 2001). Therapists should always be sure that they fully understand clients' perceptions and feelings about their religious communities before deciding whether to attempt to involve them in fellowship, service, or both. Of course, therapists should also obtain written consent from clients before they make contacts in the religious community on behalf of their clients.

SEEKING SPIRITUAL DIRECTION

Spiritual direction was described by Ganje-Fling and McCarthy (1991) as "a relationship which has as its major objective the on-going development of the spiritual self" (p. 104). Worthington et al. (1996) defined it as "guided reflection about the spiritual aspect's of one's life" (p. 465). Believers in all the world religious traditions at times seek guidance and direction from their religious and spiritual leaders such as their priest, minister, pastor, rabbi, bishop, guru, spiritual director, elder, or prophet (R. R. Keller, personal communication, May 8, 1996). The focus of the direction varies somewhat from religion to religion: in some traditions guidance focuses exclusively on spiritual matters, whereas in others it also may include temporal concerns of an emotional, physical, familial, financial, or career nature. The duration of the spiritual direction may also vary, ranging from one or two brief meetings to extended periods of training and instruction. The degree of formality also may vary, ranging from informal, optional, unstructured, and spontaneous to formal, required, structured, and planned.

Although seeking spiritual direction and guidance from religious leaders is a time-honored practice in the world religious traditions, research investigating its spiritual and psychological effects is relatively rare. Some surveys indicate that people generally believe that they are helped with emotional problems by clergy and by mutual help or support groups, many of which are sponsored by religious organizations (Bergin & Lambert, 1978; Lambert & Bergin, 1994). A well designed, controlled outcome study on the treatment of depression showed that the efficacy of clergy counseling was equivalent to that of professional therapists (Propst et al., 1992). It would seem that believers might benefit in a variety of ways spiritually and psychologically from seeking spiritual guidance and direction from their spiritual leaders, including, for example, receiving (a) increased spiritual enlightenment and growth; (b) absolution from sin and relief from guilt and shame; (c) advice and information about how to cope with and overcome emotional, marital, and family challenges and problems; (d) social support and acceptance; and (e) financial and temporal assistance. We hope that research on the effects of spiritual direction will be conducted so that psychotherapists might better understand the potential benefits of this practice for their clients.

Research also is unclear about how often psychotherapists refer clients to religious or spiritual leaders for direction and guidance. P. S. Richards and Potts (1995b) found that Mormon therapists occasionally referred clients to religious leaders for blessings (laying on of hands). In addition, Ball and Goodyear (1991) found that some Protestant therapists occasionally referred clients to their pastor for guidance about specific spiritual questions. We are not aware of any other studies that provide insight on how frequently therapists refer clients to their religious leaders for spiritual direction. Thus the evidence to date suggests that therapists do this only occasionally. This is unfortunate, considering the potential benefits to clients of working cooperatively with religious leaders.

Although in general therapists should do more collaborative work with clients' religious leaders by consulting with and referring to them, we recognize that doing so may not always be in the clients' best interests. We have worked with some clients who seemed to be experiencing emotional problems at least partially resulting from poor advice and counsel given to them by their religious leaders. Not all leaders are helpful to their followers. Some leaders use shame and even abuse their followers; some provide simplistic, unhelpful advice. In addition, not all clients are ready to seek spiritual direction. Some clients have unresolved anger and resentment toward religious leaders or institutions and would react negatively to a suggestion to seek direction from them. Thus therapists need to use caution, including a careful assessment of clients' feelings toward their religious leaders, before recommending to clients that they seek spiritual direction. In addition, whenever possible therapists should attempt to get personally acquainted with clients' spiritual advisors to determine how helpful they might be. Of course, therapists should always obtain a written release from the client before such a consultation. In chapter 7, in the section titled "Displacing or Usurping Religious Authority," we offer specific suggestions about how therapists can go about consulting with clients' religious leaders. Tan (2003) also recently provided a helpful overview concerning the practice of spiritual direction and ethical considerations associated with its application.

If these cautions are followed, religious personnel can often be a great help to clients and to the therapy process. They can provide meaningful spiritual and emotional guidance and comfort. They also can be powerful allies in encouraging people to get the psychological help they need. Without such encouragement, many clients would not be willing to enter psychotherapy in the first place. Because of their spiritual authority, religious leaders often have more credibility and leverage with clients than do therapists, and they can get clients to comply with therapeutic recommendations when therapists might not. In addition, many of them can quickly mobilize social and financial resources in their religious community on clients' behalf. They also can be a valuable source of diagnostic and assessment information by providing therapists with helpful history and insight into clients' functioning outside therapy. Finally, when it is time for therapists to terminate with clients, religious leaders can be of valuable assistance in setting up social support to help clients maintain the progress they have made in therapy. Thus, in this day of managed care and briefer therapy, consulting with and referring clients to spiritual advisors may be interventions that therapists should use more often.

MORAL INSTRUCTION

One of the major functions of all the world religious traditions is to transmit religious, moral, and ethical values from one generation to another (Smart, 1983, 1993, 1994). Leaders of religions instruct their followers in the values of that tradition, and adults instruct children and adolescents. This is done in a variety of ways, which includes telling religious and moral stories and myths, studying and discussing religious and moral guidelines found in sacred texts, and through modeling or providing examples (Smart, 1993, 1994).

There is considerable agreement among the world religions about the general religious and moral values that need to be transmitted from generation to generation. According to Smart (1983), "The major faiths have much in common as far as moral conduct goes. Not to steal, not to lie, not to kill, not to have certain kinds of sexual relations—such prescriptions are found across the world" (p. 117). Dong Sull Choi, a world religion scholar, similarly affirmed that general moral principles that all of the theistic world religions endorse include do not kill, do not lie, do not steal, do not covet, honor one's parents, love all people, do not worship idols, and do not take oaths (D. S. Choi, personal communication, October 9, 1996). There is, however, much variety in the specific interpretations of these religious and moral values (D. S. Choi, personal communication, October 9, 1996; Smart, 1983, 1993, 1994). There also is some variation in the manner in which the religious and moral rules and values are viewed:

> There are different models of virtue. For the Jew and Muslim, for instance, the rules are part of the fabric of divinely instituted law. . . . Obedience to the rules is obedience to God. . . . In Buddhism the rules

of morality are part of the "eightfold path" which leads to ultimate liberation. It is not that God has to be obeyed, but rather that, as part of the general effort at self-purification, it is wise to be good. The model for the monotheist is the obedient person of faith, such as Abraham. The model Buddhist is the person of superior insight. (Smart, 1983, pp. 117–118)

Transmission of religious and moral rules and values is essential for the survival of societies and human life:

[Such values and rules] are found across the world because such rules are necessary if there is to be a society at all. The widespread breaking of these rules would lead to chaos. Society can exist only where such wrong acts are in the minority. (Smart, 1983, p. 117)

Not only does the transmission of moral values and rules help to preserve societies, but, as discussed in chapter 5 of this volume, moral values are essential for the healthy psychosocial and spiritual functioning of human beings. One of the hallmarks of healthy functioning is the capacity to self-regulate in a consistent and healthy manner (Bergin, 1985, 1991; Jensen & Bergin, 1988), and without a set of guiding moral and ethical values, people have no basis for this regulation (Bergin, 1985, 1991).

Many people recognize that the religious and moral rules and values taught by the great world religious traditions are "recipes for living that have been evolved, tested, and winnowed through hundreds of generations of human social history" (Campbell, 1975, p. 1103). In addition, many people view these religious and moral rules and values as God-given or as laws that are a "part of the nature of the world" and "fabric of the cosmos" (Smart, 1983, p. 118). Such a view tends to increase people's commitment to their religious and moral values and may increase their ability to self-regulate. As expressed by Bergin (1985),

Self-regulation can never be optimally successful unless a commitment is made to values, and that commitment can be stronger and more lasting if the client feels that he or she is committing to something that is lawful and moral; not just because somebody said so but because it is built into the universe and is part of our nature. (p. 26)

Thus, it may be that people's religious and spiritual beliefs can enhance their commitment and capacity to regulate their behavior in healthy ways. The finding that religious people tend to have lower rates of alcoholism, drug abuse, divorce, suicide, delinquency, and sexual promiscuity (e.g., Gartner et al., 1991; Payne et al., 1991) is consistent with this idea.

Research reveals that some psychotherapists do occasionally engage in religious and moral values instruction, clarification, or correction with their clients (Ball & Goodyear, 1991; Jones et al., 1992; Moon et al., 1993; P. S. Richards & Potts, 1995b). For example, the second most frequently used intervention reported by Christian therapists in Ball and Goodyear's (1991) study was teaching religious concepts, which included engaging in values clarification with clients. Christian psychologists surveyed by Jones et al. (1992) said that they confronted approximately 27% of their clients about sinful life patterns. P. S. Richards and Potts (1995b) found that Mormon therapists occasionally confronted clients about discrepancies between their religious values and behaviors. Christian therapists surveyed by Moon et al. (1993) said they encouraged approximately 25% of their clients to be obedient to God's will. Despite these studies and despite research that reveals that the majority of therapists do believe that values are important for mentally healthy lifestyles and for guiding and evaluating psychotherapy (Jensen & Bergin, 1988), researchers know little about how therapists go about engaging in religious and moral value instruction, clarification, or correction with clients, nor do they know the frequency of use or effectiveness of such interventions.

Therapists should be sensitive to value issues throughout the course of therapy, although explicit value discussions with clients should not be overemphasized (Bergin, 1991). Nevertheless, we believe that on certain occasions during therapy therapists should actively endorse values that they believe are healthy and that they should explicitly own their values and the consensus religious and psychotherapeutic values mentioned in chapter 6 of this volume. These occasions are described briefly in Exhibit 9.1 and are discussed in more detail by P. S. Richards, Rector, and Tjeltveit (1999), who also describe a number of values assessment and intervention techniques that therapists may find helpful.

We recognize dangers in suggesting that therapists engage in religious and moral value discussions with clients. The greatest danger is that therapists could, knowingly or unknowingly, impose private beliefs that are irrelevant to mental health on vulnerable clients. As we discuss in chapter 6, such a practice is inappropriate and unethical. Bergin (1991) acknowledged that it is a delicate and challenging task for therapists to manage values issues in therapy, and he suggested that

> The therapy process can best be compared with that of good parenting: Trust is established; guided growth is stimulated; values are conveyed in a respectful way; the person being influenced becomes stronger, more assertive, and independent; the person learns ways of clarifying and testing value choices; the influencer decreases dependency, nurturance and external advice; and the person experiments with new behaviors and ideas until he or she becomes more mature and autonomous. (p. 397)

EXHIBIT 9.1
Occasions During Therapy When Therapists May Wish to Explicitly Own and Endorse Values That They Believe Are Healthy

1. During informed consent, therapists may wish to disclose the values that influence the goals they pursue and the approach they use.
2. When asking clients to complete assessment measures, therapists may wish to explain why they believe these particular measures are valuable (i.e., what assessment information they value).
3. When helping clients to set goals for therapy, therapists may wish to explain why they believe the goals they endorse are valuable to pursue.
4. Before implementing therapeutic interventions, therapists may wish to explain why they believe the intervention will be helpful (i.e., what valued outcome it might promote).
5. When deciding whether to terminate therapy, therapists may wish to explain what criteria (valued outcomes) they use to judge whether therapy has been successful.
6. When major value conflicts between the therapist and client become apparent that could threaten the therapeutic relationship or jeopardize mutual collaboration on therapeutic goals, therapists may wish to explicitly disclose and own their values while reaffirming clients' rights to differ.
7. When therapists perceive that clients' value choices are contributing to their emotional or relationship problems, therapists may wish to help clients explicitly examine the value choices and suggest more healthy alternatives.
8. When clients admit confusion about what their values really are or manifest discrepancies between their professed values and behavior, therapists may wish to explicitly help clients examine and explore their confusion and incongruencies.
9. When clients lack an understanding of mentally healthy values, therapists may wish to explicitly teach what psychotherapists tend to regard as mentally healthy values.
10. When clients lack an understanding of their religious (or cultural) tradition's values, therapists may wish to explicitly teach clients what the values are (if they know), or they should encourage clients to seek this information from religious leaders or other members of their religious community.

Bergin (1991) also cautioned that

> A strong interest in value discussions . . . can be problematic if it is overemphasized. It would be unethical to trample on the values of clients, and it would be unwise to focus on value issues when other issues may be at the nucleus of the disorder, which is frequently the case in the early stages of treatment. It is vital to be open about values but not coercive, to be a competent professional and not a missionary for a particular belief, and at the same time to be honest enough to recognize how one's value commitments may or may not promote health. (p. 399)

In theory, therapists historically have eschewed the role of moral guide or teacher, although the impossibility of them fully avoiding this role is now widely acknowledged (e.g., Bergin et al., 1996; London, 1986; Lowe,

1976; Smith & Slife, in press; Tjeltveit, 1999; Woolfolk, 1998). As we suggest in chapter 6, therapists need to more fully accept that they function as moral guides or teachers and think carefully about how they can function ethically and effectively in this role without becoming missionaries or usurping clerical functions. Ultimately, we believe that therapists will find that they can better help clients overcome unhealthy lifestyle behaviors if they use clients' religious and spiritual beliefs and values to help motivate and reinforce clients' efforts to change and self-regulate. To this end, we hope that a wider variety of interventions that help therapists in their efforts to provide religious and moral value clarification, correction, and instruction to clients will be designed.

CONCLUSION

We do not claim to have described all religious and spiritual practices that could be useful in psychotherapy, but we have described several promising ones that could have wide application in ecumenical and numerous denominational therapy situations. There may be some therapeutic religious practices that are unique to individual religious traditions. We hope that therapists who have an expertise in specific traditions will identify and apply in therapy those religious and spiritual practices that have the greatest therapeutic value for clients from those traditions.

Many of the religious or spiritual practices we describe in this chapter have now been adapted or used in psychotherapy. In chapter 10 we describe the variety of ways that contemporary psychotherapists have used spiritual interventions. Given the creativity of psychotherapists, we anticipate that the development of religious and spiritual interventions to help clients cope, heal, and grow will continue.

10

SPIRITUAL INTERVENTIONS USED BY CONTEMPORARY PSYCHOTHERAPISTS

Cognitive restructuring could be defined as a type of spiritual transformation of the mind—a spiritual exercise.

—L. Rebecca Propst

In this chapter we describe and give specific examples of how therapists have adapted or applied the religious and spiritual practices described in chapter 9 to the psychotherapy situation. Some spiritual practices are used in therapy in the same way that they might be used by religious leaders in religious settings (e.g., encouraging clients to pray for guidance in overcoming their problems). Other theistic spiritual practices have been adapted or partially integrated with secular concepts or techniques so that the practice is used in therapy somewhat differently from how it typically would be practiced within the religious community (e.g., asking clients to read specific spiritual literature to challenge and modify their irrational cognitions). Ultimately, however, most spiritual interventions that have been used in therapy can be traced to some religious or spiritual practice that is advocated by one or more of the world religions.

We first describe some of the specific purposes of using a theistic approach. We then review the empirical literature to determine which theistic spiritual interventions therapists have used, how frequently they have used them, and what percentage of therapists use them. We discuss several schemes for classifying theistic spiritual interventions and briefly describe a number of them specifically. We also briefly discuss how these techniques have been used with different theoretical orientations, treatment modalities, clinical issues, and special populations. We discuss when spiritual methods are contraindicated, and then we offer some general process suggestions. We conclude by briefly discussing research concerning the efficacy of theistic spiritual interventions and treatment approaches.

PURPOSE OF THEISTIC SPIRITUAL INTERVENTIONS

In Exhibit 10.1 we briefly summarize the views of some of the major psychotherapy traditions regarding the general purpose of interventions in therapy and compare their views about interventions with those of the theistic, spiritual strategy. The general purpose of religious and spiritual interventions is to facilitate and promote clients' religious and spiritual coping, growth, and well-being. We believe that clients who are growing in spiritually healthy ways are more likely to function effectively in the other areas of their lives.

In addition to the general purpose stated earlier, there are more specific reasons why therapists may want to use a theistic approach. For example, such approaches can be used to help clients to more effectively or fully

1. experience and affirm their eternal spiritual identity and divine worth;
2. seek guidance and strength from God to assist them in their efforts to cope, heal, and grow;
3. obtain social, emotional, and material support from their religious community and leaders;
4. examine and modify dysfunctional religious and spiritual beliefs and practices;
5. reframe or understand their problems from an eternal, spiritual perspective;
6. explore and work through religious and spiritual doubts and concerns;
7. forgive and heal, both emotionally and spiritually, regarding past abuse and pain;
8. accept responsibility and make restitution for their own harmful and selfish behaviors that have hurt others; and
9. grow in faith and commitment to their religious and spiritual beliefs and values.

Undoubtedly there are other reasons therapists may want to use a theistic approach, but to enumerate all of them is beyond the scope of this chapter. The most important point we emphasize here is that such interventions enable therapists to intervene directly in and use the religious–

EXHIBIT 10.1
Comparison of Therapeutic Techniques in the Major Psychotherapy Traditions and in Theistic Psychotherapy

Psychodynamic	Behavioral	Cognitive	Humanistic	Family systems	Theistic
The major interventions are the analysis and interpretation of free-association material, dreams, resistance, and transference. The purpose of these interventions is to promote client insight into unconscious dynamics and to help clients work through core conflicts and defenses so they can resolve their symptoms and function better in their lives.	Major interventions include relaxation training, systematic desensitization and other exposure methods, token economies and other reinforcement techniques, modeling, assertiveness training, and self-monitoring. The purpose of these techniques is to help people change their symptomatic behavior without necessarily analyzing the past or the dynamics thereof.	Examples of major techniques include examining and challenging irrational or dysfunctional cognitions, teaching the A–B–C model, employing rational–emotive imagery, and using shame attacking exercises. These are viewed as highly important for helping clients to modify their irrational or dysfunctional cognitions, which in turn can modify affects and behaviors.	Techniques are viewed as being secondary to the therapeutic relationship. Major interventions are relationship skills, nonjudgmentalness, communicating warmth, empathy, and authenticity. The purpose of relationship skills is to provide a therapeutic climate that allows the client to deeply explore their beliefs, values, meaning feelings, and interpersonal conflicts.	Examples of major interventions include family sculpting, genograms, teaching communication skills, utilizing paradoxical intention, reframing, and detriangulating. Techniques are viewed as highly important for perturbing, or creating change in the family system. Diagnosis and treatment assume that disorders are systemic and reflect dysfunctions in systems of interaction.	Examples of major interventions include cognitive restructuring of irrational religious beliefs, transitional figure technique, forgiveness, meditation and prayer, scripture study, blessings, participating in religious services, employing spiritual imagery, keeping a journal about spiritual feelings, repenting, and using the client's religious support system. Interventions are viewed as highly important for facilitating and promoting clients' religious and spiritual coping, healing, and growth and for helping clients to draw on the spiritual resources in their lives.

spiritual system of their clients therapeutically. None of the mainstream psychotherapy traditions have developed interventions for this purpose, and so the theistic spiritual strategy contributes uniquely to the profession in this regard (Bergin, 1988; Bergin & Payne, 1991).

VARIETY AND PREVALENCE OF SPIRITUAL INTERVENTIONS AND SPIRITUALLY ORIENTED PSYCHOTHERAPISTS

A number of survey studies during the past 15 years have documented that professionals use a variety of spiritual interventions in psychotherapy and have looked into the percentage of psychologists and psychotherapists who do so. For example, a 1985 national survey of psychotherapists in psychiatry, clinical psychology, marriage and family therapy, and clinical social work conducted by Jensen, Bergin, and Greaves (1990) revealed that 17% of eclectic therapists included a religious–transpersonal component in their overall integrative approach. Although this study did not provide specific information about what types of interventions were used or how frequently the therapists used them, it did suggest that even 20 years ago a sizable number of mainstream psychotherapists were attempting to integrate a spiritual component into their therapeutic approach.

Shafranske and Malony (1990) surveyed members of the American Psychological Association's (APA's) Division 12 (Society of Clinical Psychology) and asked them to indicate which of six religious interventions they had used in therapy. They found that a large majority (91%) of the clinical psychologists indicated that they believe it is important to inquire about their clients' religious backgrounds. Sizable proportions of them also reported the use of other spiritual techniques in their practices, including religious language or concepts (57%), recommending participation in religion (36%), using or recommending religious or spiritual books (32%), praying privately for a client (24%), and praying with a client (7%).

Ball and Goodyear (1991) asked doctoral-level clinical members of the Christian Association for Psychological Studies (CAPS) to list interventions that they had used with Christian clients that they regarded as "distinct to Christian counseling" (p. 146). Of the 174 CAPS members who responded, 153 (87%) indicated that they use religious interventions in their practices. The respondents listed and described 436 interventions, which were then grouped by raters into 15 clusters or categories. The most frequently mentioned spiritual interventions were prayer, teaching of religious concepts, and making reference to scripture. On the other hand, integration techniques, scripture memorization, anointing with oil, confrontation and challenge, and screening and intake were rarely used.

P. S. Richards and Potts (1995a, 1995b) conducted a national survey of 215 members of the Association of Mormon Counselors and Psychotherapists, asking them to indicate how frequently they had used various religious and spiritual interventions during the past year in their professional practices. Approximately 90% of the psychotherapists indicated they had used one or more religious and spiritual interventions during the past year. A large number indicated that they occasionally or often encouraged forgiveness (91%), used the religious community as a resource (86%), prayed privately for clients (82%), taught spiritual concepts (85%), encouraged clients to pray privately (73%), encouraged clients to confess (65%), and made reference to scripture (64%). A small number indicated that they occasionally engaged in in-session prayer with clients (17%), gave blessings to their clients (10%), and encouraged clients to memorize scriptures (14%).

Shafranske (2000, 2001) conducted national surveys of 242 psychologists who belonged to Division 22 (Rehabilitation Psychology) of the APA and 111 psychiatrists who belonged to the American Psychiatric Association, asking them to indicate how often they used various spiritual interventions. Overall, the results were startling, in that approximately 78% of the psychologists and 50% of the psychiatrists indicated that they sought to assess their clients' religious backgrounds. A sizable number of the respondents also said that they explored clients' religious beliefs (~ 45%); referred clients to chaplains, ministers, or rabbis (~ 35%); and used religious language or concepts (~ 30%). Fewer said that they prayed privately for clients (~ 18%), engaged in personal religious self-disclosure (~ 16%), recommended meditation and other religious practices (~ 10%), and recommended religious books (~ 6%).

Raphel (2001) surveyed members of the American Counseling Association (ACA), the APA, the National Association of Social Workers (NASW), and the American Association of Pastoral Counselors (AAPC) about their use of spiritual interventions in treatment. She divided her participants into three subgroups for statistical comparisons: (a) participants who belonged to a mainstream mental health organization that does not identity itself as having a religious or spiritual focus; (b) participants who belonged to a division within a mainstream mental health organization that identifies itself as religious or spiritual in focus; and (c) participants who belonged to the AACP. She found that sizable percentages of the therapists in all three groups reported that they sometimes conducted spiritual assessments (25.2% to 48.9%), prayed privately for their clients (44.6% to 86.8%), encouraged their clients to pray (54.5% to 71.9%), used religious and spiritual language during therapy (79.0% to 94.0%), recommended spiritual readings (30.6% to 66.3%), and made reference to biblical quotations and stories (32.8% to 54.2%). As anticipated, a larger percentage of therapists who belonged to organizations with a religious or spiritual focus tended to use spiritual interventions compared to those with less interest or involvement in religion.

The studies just described document and provide insight into the variety of theistic spiritual practices that have been used by licensed therapists in clinical and counseling psychology, clinical social work, psychiatry, and marriage and family therapy. They also provide evidence that sizable percentages of practitioners (30% to 90%, depending on the group surveyed and the technique at issue) now incorporate spiritual interventions into their practices. Higher percentages of psychotherapists who are personally religious tend to use spiritual interventions, compared to therapists who are less religious, and they tend to use a wider variety of such interventions (Raphel, 2001; Shafranske, 2000, 2001). These studies and others (e.g., Chamberlain, Richards, & Scharman, 1996; Payne, Bergin, & Loftus, 1992) have revealed that most psychotherapists do not use theistic spiritual interventions exclusively but as part of an eclectic, integrative approach that includes mainstream secular therapeutic approaches.

Past research on theistic spiritual interventions has primarily surveyed Roman Catholic, Mainline Protestant, Jewish, and Latter-Day Saint therapists, but more recent national surveys have included therapists from a greater diversity of backgrounds, including Unitarians, Quakers, Evangelicals, Buddhists, and Christian Scientists (Raphel, 2001; Shafranske, 2000, 2001). Thus it is clear that the use of various theistic spiritual interventions within the psychotherapy profession as a whole is a growing phenomenon.

In Table 10.1 we provide definitions and examples of various interventions that have been reported in the literature. Currently it appears that those most frequently used tend to be praying privately (or silently) for clients, teaching religious and spiritual concepts, encouraging forgiveness, taking a history of clients' religious and spiritual backgrounds, and making reference to scriptures. Less frequently used are spiritual meditation, religious relaxation and imagery, in-depth religious–spiritual assessments, and vocal therapist–client in-session prayer. Rarely used methods include blessings (e.g., laying on of hands and anointing with oil), scripture memorization, prayer for direct divine healing, and exorcism from the demonic (Ball & Goodyear, 1991; Jones, Watson, & Wolfram, 1992; Raphel, 2001; P. S. Richards & Potts, 1995b; Shafranske, 2000, 2001; Shafranske & Malony, 1990; Worthington, Dupont, Berry, & Duncan, 1988; Worthington, Kurusu, McCullough, & Sandage, 1996).

CATEGORIES OF SPIRITUAL INTERVENTIONS

We now discuss several ways that the variety of religious and spiritual techniques described earlier can be conceptualized or categorized so that

TABLE 10.1
Definitions and Examples of Various Theistic Interventions

Intervention	Definition	Examples of intervention
Therapist prayer	Therapist silent prayer	Prayer to help clients develop a bigger picture of their suffering and look beyond their current circumstances
Teaching spiritual concepts	Information concerning theological issues and spiritual concepts	Teaching an awareness of scriptural promises of peace, love, and faith; help clients view self worth based on what God says about them
Reference to scripture	Direct quotation or citation of scripture to establish a point	Instruction by scripture to counter inappropriate feelings such as perfectionistic striving; therapist cites references to Christ's emotions to help clients feel at ease about their problems
Spiritual self-disclosure	Therapist self-disclosing or modeling spiritual experiences or behaviors in an attempt to influence the client	Therapist shares aspects of his or her own spiritual experience; therapist attempts to model grace and affirmation
Spiritual confrontation	Interventions that confront a client concerning religious or spiritual beliefs and values	Therapist asks clients in bad relationships what they think the Bible says about the relationship; therapist gently confronts clients about the incongruencies between their professed religious values and their current behavior
Spiritual assessment	Use of the initial counseling session as a way to assess the client's religious and spiritual status	Therapist takes a history of the client's spiritual development when he or she first sees him or her; therapist gives clients the Spiritual Well-Being Scale to assess how they feel about their relationship with God
Religious relaxation or imagery	The use of guided imagery, meditation, or relaxation with direct reference to spiritual concepts	During guided imagery, therapist asks clients to visualize being embraced by and speaking to Jesus; therapist uses imagery and metaphor in biblical stories for relaxation
Therapist and client prayer	Vocal in-session prayer with client	Therapist prays on behalf of clients that they will have the strength to deal with strong, painful feelings; therapist invites the client to pray at the beginning of a session to petition God's guidance and help during the session
Blessing by therapist	Use of priesthood blessings (laying on of hands) in session to help client cope or work through impasses	Therapist lays hands on a client's head, blessing him or her that he or she might receive comfort, strength, and insight
Encouragement for forgiveness	Discussion of the concept of forgiveness with client, encouraging client to forgive parents or others	Therapist discusses how to seek forgiveness when a client reports guilt about a behavior or feeling; therapist uses forgiveness in restoring broken relationships

(continued)

TABLE 10.1 (Continued)

Intervention	Definition	Examples of intervention
Use of religious community	Use of the client's religious community as an extratherapy resource	Therapist refers to a pastor for specific spiritual or theological questions; therapist sends a person to a Christian attorney for information
Client prayer	Encouragement of client private prayers	Therapist encourages client to pray for help to know how to better relate to his or her spouse; therapist suggests that a client pray for strength to resist whenever he feels tempted to view pornography
Encouragement of client confession	Encouragement of the client to confess violations of moral code to appropriate persons and to seek repentance	Therapist suggests that a client admit that he was overly harsh and emotionally abusive to his children and ask them to forgive him; therapist supports a client in her decision to confess a sexual transgression to her religious leader
Referral for blessing	Advice to client to request priesthood blessing from home teacher or religious leader to help client cope and work through impasses	Therapist suggests that a client seek a blessing from her spiritual leader for assistance in gaining the emotional and spiritual strength to cope with the death of her child
Religious journal writing	Suggestion that client keep journal concerning spiritual struggles, insights, and experiences	Therapist assigns journal keeping of answered prayer; therapist suggests to some clients that they record spiritual insights or impressions they have
Spiritual meditation	Encouraging meditation about spiritual matters to promote client spiritual growth	Therapist suggests meditation or meditative imagery focusing on Christ and his love; therapist suggests quiet times when the client can ponder and contemplate about his or her life and God's will for her
Religious bibliotherapy	Use of religious and spiritual literature	Therapist encourages clients to read the Book of Job in the Bible; therapist gives some clients tapes or articles of talks by leaders in the church
Scripture memorization	Interventions specifically using client memorization of scriptures to affect change	Therapist suggests scripture memorization for thought stopping of obsessive clients for coping during panic attacks
Dream interpretation	Helping clients in exploration of and interpretation of the religious and spiritual significance of their dreams	Therapist helps clients explore the spiritual themes present in their dreams; therapist helps a client decide whether his dream was a "message from God" or simply a reflection of his emotional and spiritual conflicts

Note. Definitions and examples were adapted from two sources: Ball and Goodyear (1991), reprinted here by permission from the Christian Association for Psychological Studies; From "Using Spiritual Interventions in Psychotherapy: Practices, Successes, Failures, and Ethical Concerns of Mormon Psychotherapists," by P. S. Richards and R. W. Potts, *Professional Psychology: Research and Practice, 26*, pp. 163–170. Copyright 1995 by the American Psychological Association.

therapists will better understand the types of theistic spiritual techniques that are available to them. We limit our descriptions to several categorization schemes that may have some clinical relevance and utility. Specific examples of applications of spiritual interventions are provided in Table 10.1, in the section on treatment package approaches, and in the case studies provided in chapter 11.

Religious Versus Spiritual Interventions

One way of categorizing interventions is according to whether they are "religious" or "spiritual." This is difficult to differentiate precisely, because the terms *religious* and *spiritual* are interrelated; however, they can be distinguished along several dimensions (e.g., denominational versus ecumenical, external versus internal, cognitive and behavioral versus affective, ritualistic versus spontaneous, public versus private). We define *religious interventions* as those that are more structured, behavioral, denominational, external, cognitive, ritualistic, and public. Examples of religious interventions include quoting or paraphrasing scriptures; encouraging clients to attend church, engage in religious rituals and traditions, and use resources available within the institution; and suggesting that clients read (and possibly reinterpret) scriptures or the writings of their religious leaders. We define *spiritual interventions* as those that are more experiential, transcendent, ecumenical, cross-cultural, internal, affective, spontaneous, and personal. Examples of spiritual interventions include private prayer, spiritual meditation, spiritual imagery that is personally meaningful to the client, forgiveness, and spiritual journals. Distinguishing between religious and spiritual interventions is helpful because of the somewhat imprecise and overlapping nature of these categories; other schemes for categorizing and conceptualizing them are also needed.

In-Session Versus Out-of-Session Interventions

Another way of categorizing interventions is according to whether they are used in or out of the session (e.g., P. S. Richards & Potts, 1995b). *In-session interventions* are those that therapists or clients actually carry out during the therapy session. Examples include offering vocal or silent in-session prayers, teaching clients spiritual concepts, quoting or paraphrasing scriptures, confronting clients about discrepancies between their religious beliefs and behaviors, and using guided religious or spiritual imagery activities during the session. *Out-of-session interventions* are those that are prescribed or suggested as homework activities for clients. Out-of-session interventions, of course, must be recommended and discussed during the therapy session, but the actual activity or experience occurs outside the session without the therapist. Examples include suggesting that clients attend religious worship services, encouraging them to pray and meditate privately during the week, encouraging them to confess violations of their moral code to their religious leader, suggesting that they request help and support from their religious leaders or congregants, and asking them to keep a journal about their spiritual struggles, experiences, and insights.

P. S. Richards and Potts (1995b) found that Mormon therapists reported that, on the average, they used out-of-session approaches more frequently than in-session ones. The reason was unclear, but the researchers speculated that the therapists believed out-of-session methods to be less risky because there is less chance that therapists will cross role boundaries by engaging in religious activities that would be more appropriately performed by the client's religious leader or that would cause the client to perceive the therapist as a religious authority. When recommending out-of-session processes, therapists can convey support of clients' spiritual beliefs and growth with less risk of influencing or coercing clients into spiritual activities that are alien to them. The risk of coercion is also lower with out-of-session techniques because clients can more comfortably choose not to participate in them.

This is not to say that we believe out-of-session processes should always be preferred over in-session ones. The little research evidence available suggests that in-session interventions can be highly effective (e.g., P. S. Richards & Potts, 1995b). Therapists should simply keep in mind that in-session interventions may be somewhat more risky than out-of-session interventions with some clients.

Denominational Versus Ecumenical Interventions

Another useful way of categorizing interventions is according to whether they are denominational or ecumenical. We define *denominational interventions* as those that contain theological content or religious practices that make them suitable only for clients who belong to a particular religious tradition. Within denominations, numerous subcategories could be created, such as for Jewish clients (e.g., Orthodox, Conservative, and Reformed), Christians (e.g., Roman Catholic, Greek Orthodox, Lutheran, Baptist, Mormon, Seventh-Day Adventist), Muslims (e.g., Sunni, Shi'ah), and so on. Examples of denominational interventions include encouraging Jewish clients to attend their synagogue, using spiritual imagery focusing on Jesus with Christian clients, and discussing verses from the Qur'an with Muslim clients.

Many practices can be adapted and used in denominationally specific manners across a variety of different denominations (Lovinger, 1984). For example, when working with Jewish clients, therapists may discuss with them scriptures from the Torah, and therapists working with Christian clients may discuss New Testament scriptures with them. Therapists who have an in-depth knowledge of several religious traditions may find that they can apply the same practices (e.g., discussing scriptural teachings) with clients from each of these traditions by adapting the content to suit each client. Generally speaking, however, therapists should use interventions in a denominational manner only when they have adopted a denominational therapeutic stance, as discussed in chapter 6 of this volume.

We define *ecumenical interventions* as those that do not contain doctrine or practices that would identify with a specific tradition. The content and meaning of an ecumenical approach is general, flexible, and as universal as possible so that it can be used with clients from a variety of traditions. Examples include encouraging theistic clients to pray or commune with their God or Higher Power, suggesting that clients keep a journal in which they record their spiritual experiences and insights, and using spiritual imagery experiences that ask clients to supply their own spiritual images (H. Benson, 1996). We recognize that it may be almost impossible for approaches to be completely ecumenical, because almost all contain some content or meaning that could exclude some clients. Nevertheless, some interventions are clearly more ecumenical than others. If therapists are careful to use general and nondenominational language, many interventions that are typically denominationally therapeutic may be suitable when working from an ecumenically therapeutic stance.

Transcendent Versus Nontranscendent Interventions

Another useful way of categorizing religious and spiritual interventions is according to whether they are transcendent or nontranscendent. We define *transcendent interventions* as those that assume and petition transcendent spiritual influences on behalf of clients or the therapy process. Transcendent interventions require that the client, the therapist, or both believe in God and in the reality of transcendent influences. Examples include client or therapist prayer, blessings from religious leaders, and spiritual meditation when such practices are engaged in with the intent of seeking spiritual guidance, enlightenment, and strength.

Examples of *nontranscendent interventions* include discussing clients' understanding of scriptures, confronting discrepancies between clients' professed religious values and their behaviors, assessing clients' religious and spiritual background and status, encouraging clients to forgive others, referring clients to their religious community, and keeping a spiritual journal. Of course, some nontranscendent approaches could be used with the hope that the client will be blessed with transcendent assistance (e.g., a therapist may encourage a client to read scriptures with the hope that the client will have a transcendent spiritual experience while doing so). Thus some interventions could be viewed as either transcendent or nontranscendent depending on the purpose or intent for which they are used.

Affective, Behavioral, Cognitive, and Interpersonal Interventions

Another useful way of categorizing religious and spiritual interventions is according to the primary modality (e.g., affective, behavioral, cognitive, or interpersonal) through which the intervention is intended to affect the client. Such a classification scheme also has been useful for categorizing the interventions of the mainstream psychotherapy traditions (e.g., L. S. Cormier, Cormier, & Weisser, 1984; L. S. Cormier & Hackney, 1987).

We define *affective spiritual interventions* as those that are designed to help clients by changing their religious and spiritual feelings and emotions. Clients who are emotionally sensitive and expressive, who use their emotions in problem solving and decision making, may be the most receptive to affective interventions (L. S. Cormier & Hackney, 1987). Examples of affective spiritual interventions include client prayer, spiritual imagery, blessings, spiritual journals, and spiritual contemplation and meditation.

We define *behavioral spiritual interventions* as those that are designed to help clients by changing their religious and spiritual practices and lifestyle. Clients who have a strong goal orientation and who like to be actively doing something may be the most receptive to behavioral techniques (L. S. Cormier & Hackney, 1987). Examples of behavioral spiritual techniques include encouraging clients to participate in religious practices and rituals (e.g., attending worship services, visiting a temple or shrine, or participating in a religious festival), urging clients to read and memorize scriptures, pointing out discrepancies between clients' professed religious values and their behaviors, modeling spiritual values, and encouraging clients to confess and forsake unhealthy and sinful behaviors.

We define *cognitive spiritual interventions* as those that are designed to help clients by changing their religious and spiritual religious beliefs and understandings. Clients who are logical and rational in their problem-solving approach—who find ideas, theories, and concepts appealing—may be most receptive to cognitive interventions (L. S. Cormier & Hackney, 1987). Examples are teaching and discussing spiritual concepts, paraphrasing and interpreting scriptures, and assigning scriptural study homework.

We define *interpersonal spiritual interventions* as those that are designed to help clients by changing the amount and nature of their involvement with members of their religious community. Clients who have good social skills and are open to relationships with other people may be the most receptive to interpersonal interventions (L. S. Cormier & Hackney, 1987). Examples include encouraging clients to engage in fellowship with members of their religious community, to provide service to people in need, and to serve in ecclesiastical or volunteer positions in their religious congregation.

Because of the complex interplay among affect, behavior, cognitions, and interpersonal relationships, it is often difficult to know what type of intervention will be most helpful for a given client. Just because a client may be receptive to techniques that use a certain modality does not mean that they will be effective. Interventions that clients are initially the least receptive to may help them the most. For example, clients who are socially unskilled and interpersonally isolated may find interpersonal spiritual techniques threatening and difficult to participate in, but extremely beneficial.

Summary

None of the categorization schemes we have described is meant to be *the* correct one. Each of these schemes has some advantages and limitations. We hope that these schemes will be studied empirically to evaluate their clinical usefulness. Perhaps other clinically relevant categorization schemes will be proposed and tested. Ultimately, perhaps the ideal classification scheme would be one that categorizes them according to the type of client problems or issues with which the method is effective. For example, it would be useful to have a categorization scheme that indicates which interventions are most likely to help clients to (a) develop a healthier sense of self-esteem and identity, (b) overcome depression and suicidal ideation, (c) improve their marital relationship, and so on.

APPLICATIONS OF SPIRITUAL INTERVENTIONS IN CLINICAL PRACTICE

Theistic approaches have been widely used in clinical practice during the past decade. Descriptions and clinical examples of how such approaches can be integrated with various therapeutic traditions, treatment modalities, and clinical issues are provided in P. S. Richards and Bergin (2004) and Sperry and Shafranske (2005). It is not possible to describe in detail in this volume the variety of ways that theistic approaches have been used, but we make note of some of these trends and provide citations to relevant sources.

Integration With Mainstream Theoretical Orientations

Spiritual perspectives and interventions have now been incorporated into most mainstream theoretical orientations. For example, a number of scholars have attempted to incorporate theistic perspectives into the psychoanalytic tradition (e.g. Genia, 1995; Jung, 1990; Klostreich, 2001; Northcut,

2000; Rizzuto, 1996; Shafranske, 2004, 2005; Spero, 1990; R. A. Watson, 2000). Corbett and Stein (2005) discussed Jungian approaches to spiritual psychotherapy. O'Connell (1997) and R. E. Watts (2000) described how Adlerian therapy is amenable to working with spiritual clients. Several writers have described how theistic approaches may be integrated into behavior therapy (e.g., Martin & Booth, 1999; W. R. Miller & Martin, 1988). Propst (1996) described a religious group cognitive therapy approach. Nielsen, Johnson, and Ellis (2001) described how to use spiritual concepts and principles with rational–emotive behavior therapy. Table 10.2 provides examples from their book of "religiously integrated" rational–emotive behavior therapy disputations.

Kaplan (1999), Thorne (1998), and West (2004) have sought to bring spiritual perspectives into person-centered therapy. Elkins (2005) described a humanistic approach to spiritually oriented therapy. Mahrer (1996) described how an existential–humanistic therapist could work with religious clients and religious material. L. Miller (2005) described a spiritually oriented interpersonal psychotherapy approach. Hinterkopf (2005) expanded the experiential focusing approach to apply it to spirituality. Harris (2000) discussed the spiritual dimensions of the practice of Gestalt therapy. Steinfeld (2000) explained how constructivism can create a context for spiritually oriented psychotherapy. Trautmann (2003) wrote about the place of spirituality in transactional analysis. In conclusion, we anticipate that the integration of spiritual perspectives and interventions with other therapeutic traditions will continue. We welcome this trend if it is done thoughtfully and carefully, with attention given to the possible theological, philosophical, theoretical, and clinical implications of such integrative efforts.

Applications in Various Therapeutic Modalities

It appears that theistic spiritual interventions have been used most frequently in a treatment tailoring fashion during individual psychotherapy with adult clients (Ball & Goodyear, 1991; Chamberlain et al., 1996; Jones et al., 1992; Payne et al., 1992; P. S. Richards & Potts, 1995b; Worthington et al., 1996). However, these interventions are being used with increasing frequency in group therapy, marriage and family therapy, and child and adolescent therapy.

Group Therapy

Numerous descriptions of the application of theistic approaches in group therapy are now available (e.g., Chew, 1998; Freeman, Wofson, & Affolter, 1998; Hiatt, 1999; Jacques, 1998; Little & Robinson, 1988; Ogden, 2001; Propst, 1980; P. S. Richards, Owen, & Stein, 1993; Rodriguez, 2001).

TABLE 10.2
Examples of Religiously Integrated Rational–Emotive Behavior Therapy Disputation Techniques

Disputation style	Disputation strategies				
	Theological	Religious evidence	Religiously functional	Religious dissonance	Religious alternative
"Self-rating" beliefs					
Didactic	Look, if you're God's creation, it just doesn't make sense for you to call yourself a basket case or a weakling ... or some other insulting name.	Christ said, "If you have done it to the least ... you've done it unto me" (Matthew 25:40). That means that He considers all people to be of equal value with *Him!*	You know, when you call yourself names it *de*-motivates you where right and wrong are concerned. You feel *less* like going to church and *more* like breaking commandments.	You forgive Peter for denying Christ—and remember, Peter saw miracles. So apply that kind of forgiveness to yourself. Be fair with yourself!	I suggest that you memorize and tell yourself, over and over again, what Peter said, "God hath showed me that I should not call any man common or unclean" (Acts 10:28).
Socratic	If the Bible says "All have sinned and fall short of the glory of God" (Romans 3:23), help me understand how *you* are especially deserving of damnation when *you* sin?	What did Jesus say about the worth of sinners? The lost sheep? The lost coin? The prodigal son? What do these parables (all in Luke 15) say about your worth?	What does it do for you or for God when you down-rate yourself? Does it help you help others or pray or go to church or repent? Does it do any good for His works?	Do you believe what Christ said, "He who is without sin among you, let him first cast a stone" (John 8:7)? Why are you so set on clobbering yourself?	Instead of the unbiblical notion that you are no good or less human when you err (sin), what is a more truthful and biblically correct thing you could tell yourself?
"Awfulizing" beliefs					
Metaphorical	The death of Jesus on the cross was first viewed as catastrophic, but we now see it as an important gift! What seems awful at first may not seem awful later.	Martyrs of the early church welcomed suffering if it brought God glory. Perhaps they would view what you call "terrible" as an opportunity or privilege.	When the Jews were enslaved in Egypt, some probably said "this is awful," and others said "The Lord will deliver us." Who do you imagine felt better?	If an earth-covering flood was not a catastrophe but part of God's plan, how likely is it that this thing you face is a true catastrophe?	In the lion's den, what might Daniel have said (and to God) instead of "this is awful!"

(continued)

TABLE 10.2 (Continued)

Disputation style	Theological	Religious evidence	Disputation strategies			
			Religiously functional	Religious dissonance	Religious alternative
"Awfulizing" beliefs					
Therapist Self-Disclosure	I used to say that various things were terrible or awful until I realized that God may have designed them that way for His purposes.	Practically nothing is 100%, bad and nothing is more than 100% bad. No matter what is wrong, I could be facing it without God. That would be worse!	When I tell myself something in my life is awful or catastrophic, I find it only helps me to become immobilized, angry, and distant from God.	When I start believing something is awful, I close my eyes and imagine walking through it without God. Suddenly, whatever it is seems less bad!	When anything seems awful to me, I imagine Christ putting a nail-pierced hand on my shoulder and smiling kindly and I realize nothing I face is especially awful!
Humorous	During the "awful" storm on the Sea of Galilee, Jesus slept peacefully while the disciples fretted. Might your own "catastrophe" make Jesus sleepy as well?	Yes, I'm certain the martyred saints of the church would agree that your situation is the worst *any* Christian has *ever* faced. You win the Holy All-time Awful Award (HAAA!).	How exactly does your catastrophizing chant ("This is awful") help your spiritual walk and promote your faith in God?	If *this* is awful, then it could not be worse, so I guess that means this is worse than roasting in hell for eternity?	Lord, I know things could be worse, much worse, but how about no more "opportunities" for growth like this one for awhile?

Note. Adapted from *Counseling and Psychotherapy With Religious Persons: A Rational Emotive Behavior Therapy Approach,* by S. L. Nielsen, B. W. Johnson, and A. Ellis, 2001, Mahwah, NJ: Erlbaum. Copyright 2001 by Erlbaum. Reprinted with permission.

For example, Propst (1980, 1988, 1996) pioneered efforts to integrate religious and spiritual interventions with cognitive group psychotherapy. Propst (1988) developed a cognitive therapy group treatment protocol for depression that includes religious rationales for the treatment approach, religious arguments to counter dysfunctional thoughts, religious imagery procedures, and religious motivations for behavior change. These interventions can be used in both group and individual psychotherapy. Propst and colleagues have conducted two well-designed outcome studies that have provided evidence that religious cognitive therapy with religious clients is as effective, and sometimes more effective, than standard cognitive therapy (Propst, 1980; Propst, Ostrom, Watkins, Dean, & Mashburn, 1992).

Propst's writings have stimulated other efforts in theory and research. For example, Tan and colleagues have critiqued and provided guidelines for a biblical (Christian) cognitive therapy approach (e.g., Craigie & Tan, 1989; Tan, 1987). Pecheur and Edwards (1984) empirically compared a religious (Christian) cognitive–behavioral treatment approach with a secular one. They found that the religious cognitive–behavioral treatment was significantly more effective than the waiting list control group, although it was equivalent to the secular approach. Johnson and colleagues developed a treatment protocol for Christian rational–emotive behavior therapy and compared it with secular rational–emotive behavior therapy (W. B. Johnson, 1993a; W. B. Johnson, Devries, Ridley, Pettorini, & Peterson, 1994; W. B. Johnson & Ridley, 1992; Nielsen, Johnson, & Ridely, 2000). They found that both religious and secular forms of rational–emotive behavior therapy were equally effective with depressed Christian clients. P. S. Richards et al. (1993) pilot-tested a religiously oriented group therapy cognitive approach for perfectionistic Latter-Day Saint students. They found that, by the end of treatment, the students had experienced significant reductions in depression and perfectionism as well as increases in self-esteem and existential and religious well-being. Thus, research provides support for the efficacy of religious cognitive therapy group approaches and incentive for further efforts to refine and evaluate them (McCullough, 1999).

Marriage and Family Therapy

There has been a rather dramatic increase in theistic approaches to marital and family therapy during the past decade (e.g., Anderson & Worthen, 1997; Becvar, 1997; Blanton, 2002; Butler, Gardner, & Bird, 1998; Butler & Harper, 1994; Butler, Stout, & Gardner, 2002; Dollahite, Slife, & Hawkins, 1998; Frame, 2000; Griffith, 1986; Harris, 2002; Lantz, 2002; L. Sperry & Giblin, 1996; Nakhaima & Dicks, 1995; Walsh, 1999; Worthington, 1989b, 1990). L. Sperry and Giblin (1996) provided a helpful description of an eclectic, ecumenical marriage and family therapy approach that includes an overview of relevant theory and concepts from the secular literature, a discussion of religious beliefs and practices that may influence therapy, techniques for assessing religion and spirituality, and descriptions of religious and spiritual interventions that the authors believe are suitable for couples and families. Spiritual interventions they recommend include prayer; exploration of spiritual content in dreams; discussion of scriptures; forgiveness and acceptance; spiritual bibliotherapy; and the infusion of spiritual content into gestalt, empty-chair, and letter-writing techniques.

Butler and Harper (1994) described three ways in which couples may triangulate with God when they are not well-differentiated. First, both wife and husband may claim to one another that they are on God's side, using scriptures and revelatory experiences against the other partner; second, couples may project responsibility for marital problems onto God; and third, one or both parties may "manage their anxiety by distancing from their marital partner and striving for surrogate intimacy with God" (p. 238). Butler and Harper assert, however, that when each party is well-differentiated, the presence of God in the relationship can allow couples to turn to God for assistance in taking responsibility for their part in marital discord, reconciliation, and inspiration in problem solving.

Worthington (1989b, 1990) described a Christian marriage counseling approach. Suitable for committed Christian couples, Worthington's approach integrates Christian perspectives and spiritual interventions (e.g., praying, quoting, and explaining biblical scriptures, and encouraging forgiveness) with secular marital therapy concepts and techniques (e.g., from the systemic and structural marital therapy traditions).

Child and Adolescent Therapy

Descriptions of the use of spiritual interventions with children and adolescents are becoming more common (e.g., Josephson & Dell, 2004; Koepfer, 2000; Lonborg & Bowen, 2004; Maples, 2001; L. Miller, 2004; Sweeney & Landreth, 1993; Wells, 1999). For example, Wells (1999) provided a helpful review of theory and research on religious development in children, including discussions of Elkind's (1978, 1982) work on children's understanding of prayer and institutional identification, Fowler's (1981, 1991) faith development theory, Oser's (1991) descriptions of children's religious thinking, and Tamminen's (1991) research on the religious development of Finnish children and youth. Wells (1999) also discussed implications of this theory and research for clinicians, suggesting that religious and spiritual interventions may be the most useful for children and adolescents with internalizing (mood) disorders and adjustment disorders. He discussed the coping value of religious beliefs and suggested that spiritual interventions such as prayer, meditation, participation in religious rituals, and useful religious metaphors and narratives may be therapeutic with children and adolescents (see also Coles, 1990; Keith-Lucas, 1992; Komp, 1993).

L. Miller (2004, 2005) described the use of a theistic interpersonal group psychotherapy approach for the treatment of depressed, pregnant African American adolescents in Harlem, New York. Slife, Mitchell, and Whoolery (2004) described a theistic community–wilderness treatment approach for conduct-disordered and antisocial adolescents. Hardman, Berrett, and Richards (2004) described a theistic inpatient treatment program for female adolescents (and adults) with eating disorders. Lovinger and Lovinger (2004) described their theistic–psychodynamic approach with a 7-year-old girl and 9-year-old boy with learning problems, impulsivity, and noncompliance.

Theistic approaches that make use of play, art, stories, dance or movement, games, drama or role-playing, imagery, puppets, and music also may be useful for children and younger adolescents (Bradley & Gould, 1993; Sweeney & Landreth, 1993). Given that the major psychosocial tasks of adolescence concern issues of identity, meaning, values, and sexuality (Erikson, 1968; Havighurst, 1972), methods that help adolescents to affirm their sense of identity, worth, and belonging and that clarify and internalize healthy values may be useful for them. Prayer, meditation, spiritual literature and music, fellowship and service with peers in the religious community, and spiritual direction from leaders may be helpful in this regard. There is reason to believe that such interventions also may help prevent common problems of adolescence, such as substance abuse, promiscuity and pregnancy, sexually transmitted diseases, depression and suicide, violence, delinquency, and gang involvement (Pargament, 1996; Payne et al., 1992).

Applications With Various Clinical Issues and Populations

Theistic approaches have now been used with a variety of clinical issues and populations, including addictions (Ringwald, 2002), anxiety disorders (Killmer, 2002), eating disorders (Jersild, 2001; Manley & Leichner, 2003; P. S. Richards et al., 1997), stress (Everly & Lating, 2002), attention deficit and hyperactivity disorder (Stein, 2003), compulsive gambling (Ciarrocchi, 2002), dependency (Brown & Peterson, 1990; Hopson, 1996; Page & Berkow, 1998; Sandoz, 2001), dissociative disorders (Rosik, 2000), trauma (Barnette, 2001; Ferch & Ramsey, 2003; Grame, Tortorici, Healey, Bede, Dillingham, & Winklebaur, 1999; D. Miller & Guidry, 2002; Sparr & Fergueson, 2000; Wilson & Moran, 1998), antisocial and psychopathic personality disorders (Martens, 2003), self-injurers (J. A. Watts, 2000), transplant survivors (Sears & Wallace, 2001), postpartum depression (Steinfeld,

1999), sadomasochism (Southern, 2002), veterans (Moran, 2000), and cancer (Cole & Pargament, 1999). It is not possible in this book to describe all of these applications, but we briefly describe several examples used in the treatment of addictions, heart disease, and eating disorders.

Addictions

Spirituality is central to most treatment programs for addictions, including alcohol, drug, and sexual addictions (Ringwald, 2002). The 12-step program of Alcoholics Anonymous (AA) is the largest and most influential self-help group in contemporary society (McCrady & Delaney, 1995). AA estimates that they have approximately 87,000 groups in 150 countries and more than 1.7 million members worldwide (Alcoholics Anonymous World Services, 1990). Numerous other fellowships that subscribe to the AA 12-step model of recovery have been created, such as Narcotics Anonymous, Gamblers Anonymous, and Sex and Love Addictions Anonymous. Although empirical evidence that supports the effectiveness of 12-step programs is relatively sparse (Hopson, 1996; McCrady & Delaney, 1995), 12-step programs do enjoy considerable acceptance among helping professionals. Many therapists look to 12-step groups as a source of assistance and support for their clients and as an important supplement to professional treatment (Castaneda & Galanter, 1987; Hopson, 1996; McCrady & Delaney, 1995; Ringwald, 2002).

It is well known that the 12-step program of AA, and many other 12-step programs, is based on a spiritual worldview (Hopson, 1996; Ringwald, 2002). The 12-step program of AA starts with the assumption that to recover from alcoholism, people must humble themselves before God, or their Higher Power, and acknowledge that they need God's assistance. As can be seen in Exhibit 10.2, the entire 12-step process is a spiritual model of healing and recovery. As explained by Hopson (1996),

> The 12-step programs view spirituality in recovery from addiction as the basis of a lifestyle change. Rather than denying the reality of his or her condition, the addict must begin to see the addiction as destructive to the self. Spirituality involves an assertion of the will to bring one's behavior in line with the reality of one's condition. Acknowledgment of one's helplessness leads to the recognition that one must turn to something outside the self to begin the process of recovery (Buxton, Smith, & Seymour, 1987, p. 280). That something outside the self that will support recovery is the higher power. Recovery is made possible at the junction between the surrendered self and the higher power. The quest that has compelled someone to use a substance is redirected toward the beneficent higher power. (pp. 536–537)

Religious and spiritual interventions that are potentially used to facilitate the recovery process in 12-step programs include confessing, making

EXHIBIT 10.2
The Twelve Steps of Alcoholics Anonymous

1. We admitted we were powerless over alcohol—that our lives had become unmanageable.
2. Came to believe that a Power greater than ourselves could restore us to sanity.
3. Made a decision to turn our will and our lives over to the care of God *as we understood Him.*
4. Made a searching and fearless moral inventory of ourselves.
5. Admitted to God, to ourselves, and to another human being the exact nature of our wrongs.
6. Were entirely ready to have God remove all these defects of character.
7. Humbly asked Him to remove our shortcomings.
8. Made a list of all persons we had harmed, and became willing to make amends to them all.
9. Made direct amends to such people wherever possible, except when to do so would injure them or others.
10. Continued to take personal inventory and when we were wrong promptly admitted it.
11. Sought through prayer and meditation to improve our conscious contact with God *as we understood Him,* praying only for knowledge of His will for us and the power to carry that out.
12. Having had a spiritual awakening as the result of these steps, we tried to carry this message to alcoholics, and to practice these principles in all our affairs.

Note. From Alcoholics Anonymous World Services (AAWS; 1980). Reprinted with permission of Alcoholics Anonymous World Services, Inc. Permission to reprint the Twelve Steps does not mean that AAWS has reviewed or approved the contents of this publication, nor that AAWS agrees with the views expressed herein. AA is a program of recovery from alcoholism *only*—use of the Twelve Steps in connection with programs and activities that are patterned after AA, but which address other problems, or in any other non-AA context, does not imply otherwise.

restitution, seeking forgiveness from God and others, engaging in prayers of petition and invocation, meditating, and serving others. Some 12-step groups also use scriptural interventions—that is, they make explicit connections between the Bible and the 12 steps (Friends in Recovery, 1994; McCrady & Delaney, 1995).

Another creative way of helping chemically dependent adults to explore spiritual issues is through the use of puppet therapy, an approach that was recently developed and empirically evaluated by Vizzini (2003). Secular 12-step programs also have been developed for clients and therapists who have less interest in a theistic, spiritual approach (Dupont & McGovern, 1994).

Type A Personality and Heart Disease

Numerous treatment programs have been developed to help people modify Type A coronary prone behavior pattern and heart disease. Some of these treatment programs have integrated religious and spiritual interventions into the treatment package (e.g., Friedman et al., 1984; Ornish, 1990;

Powell & Thoresen, 1987). Perhaps the best known of these is Ornish's (1990) "Opening Your Heart" program (Friend, 1995). Ornish's program has received national attention because well-designed research studies have proved that it can stop and even reverse coronary heart disease (Friend, 1995; Ornish, 1990).

Ornish's (1990) treatment program is more than just a medical intervention—it seeks to help people physically, psychologically, and spiritually. As explained by Ornish (1990),

> Physically, this program can help you begin to open your heart's arteries and to feel stronger and more energetic, freer of pain. Emotionally, it can help you open your heart to others and to experience greater happiness, intimacy, and love in your relationships. Spiritually, it can help you open your heart to a higher force (however you experience it) and to rediscover your inner sources of peace and joy. (p. 3)

Ornish's (1990) program, which encourages patients to engage in comprehensive lifestyle changes, includes a number of treatment components: low-fat diet, smoking cessation program, exercise program, techniques for reducing stress, interventions for improving communication and intimacy with others, and methods for seeking spiritual communion with God or a Higher Power. Spiritual practices and interventions that are used in Ornish's program include yoga; "inner teacher" visualization; encouragement for altruism, compassion, and forgiveness; meditation; and prayer or devotion (Ornish, 1990).

Ornish (1990) believed that the spiritual component of treatment is essential for treatment success:

> Your mind, body, and spirit are all intimately interconnected. Because of this, coronary heart disease occurs on emotional and spiritual levels as well as physical ones. The Opening Your Heart program is designed to address *all* of these levels, not just the physical ones.
>
> If we limit our treatments only to the physical heart, then the disease tends to come back again and again—or the treatments may be worse than the illness. If we also address the emotional and spiritual dimensions, then the physical heart often begins to heal as well. (p. 250)

In recent years, numerous physicians have discussed the potential health benefits of spiritual beliefs and practices such as meditation, imagery, and prayer (e.g., H. Benson, 1996; Borysenko & Borysenko, 1994). Exhibit 10.3 provides examples of two meditation techniques from Borysenko and Borysenko's (1994) book, *The Power of the Mind to Heal: Renewing Body, Mind, and Spirit.*

EXHIBIT 10.3
Meditation Scripts From Borysenko and Borysenko (1994)

Meditation Script

Holy moment meditation

"Take a few letting-go breaths, and remember a time when you felt present in the moment—absorbed in a sunset, marveling at fresh-fallen snow, enchanted by the smile of a baby. . . . If several memories come, choose just one. . . .

Enter the memory with all of your senses. Remember the sights and colors. . . . the fragrances. . . . the position and movement of your body . . . the emotional or felt sense. . . .

Let the memory go and meditate on the feelings that remain—the stillness and joy of your own Higher Self."

TONGLEN: The meditation of forgiveness and compassion

"Close your eyes and take a stretch and a few letting-go breaths. . . . Begin to notice the flow of your breathing, allowing your body to relax and your mind to come to rest. . . .

Imagine a Great Star of Light above your head, and feel it washing over you like a waterfall and running through you like a river runs through the sand at its bottom. . . . Allow it to carry away any fatigue, pain, illness, or ignorance. . . . See these wash through the bottom of your feet into the earth for transformation. As you are washed clean, notice that the light within your heart begins to shine very brightly. . . .

Now imagine yourself as a child, choosing whatever age seems most relevant to you at this time. . . . You, better than anyone, know the pain in your heart at that time. Breathe it in as a black smoke (or dark clouds), and breathe out the light in your heart to yourself. . . .

Imagine yourself as you are right now, as if you could see yourself in a mirror. See whatever pain or illness you have as a black smoke around your heart. Inhale the smoke and exhale the light of your Higher Self. . . . Fill your heart with light. . . .

Bring to mind a person that you love. . . . Think about the pain or illness that might be in their heart. . . . Inhale that pain as a black smoke, and exhale the light of your own true nature back into their heart.

Bring to mind someone whom you are ready to forgive. Imaging them in as much detail as you can. Imagine their pain, illness, or illusion as a black smoke around their heart. . . . Breathe in the smoke, and breathe back the light of your own true nature into their heart.

Think of someplace in the world where there is suffering. If possible, bring a specific example of that suffering to mind—a starving child, a grieving parent . . . . Breathe in the pain of that suffering as a black smoke, and let it part the clouds of darkness around your own heart. Breathe out the light of your Higher Self.

End with a prayer or a short period of mindful meditation. You may also want to dedicate the fruits of this meditation to alleviate the suffering of all beings:

> May all beings be happy.
> May all be free from suffering.
> May all know the beauty of their own true nature.
> May all beings be healed."

Note. From *The Power of the Mind to Heal: Renewing Body, Mind, and Spirit* (p. 127, 172–174), by J. Borysenko and M. Borysenko, 1994, Carlsbad, CA: Hay House. Copyright 1994 by Hay House. Reprinted with permission from Hay House, Inc.

Eating Disorders

Until recent years little was known about the relationship between spirituality and eating disorders (Kroll & Sheenan, 1989; Mitchell, Erlander, Pyle, & Fletcher, 1990). But recently an increasing number of studies have provided evidence that faith and spirituality are important in eating disorder etiology and recovery (Hall & Cohn, 1992; Rorty, Yager, & Rossotto, 1993; P. S. Richards, Hardman, & Berrett, 2001; Smith, Hardman, Richards, & Fischer, 2003). Several contemporary eating disorder treatment programs now include spiritual perspectives and interventions as part of their treatment programs (e.g., Jersild, 2001; P. S. Richards et al., 1997).

The Center for Change, a private inpatient care facility in Utah, is an example of a contemporary eating disorder treatment program that includes a strong spiritual component. The Center's program is grounded in current research findings and accepted clinical guidelines for treating eating disorders (P. S. Richards, Hardman, Berrett, & Carter, in press; Striegel-Moore & Smolak, 2001). A medical assessment of each client is completed upon admission. Throughout the treatment program, the physician oversees the physical aspects of recovery, including the medical progress of each client, diet, and weight gain. In addition, at the time of admission, a psychiatrist, psychologist, or social worker gathers an eating disorder history and assesses the patient's emotional condition.

Patients participate in a variety of needed therapies to ensure comprehensive treatment and progress toward recovery. These include (a) individual psychotherapy sessions; (b) group psychotherapy and body image groups; (c) experiential and expressive activities, including music, dance, movement, and recreation therapies; (d) family counseling; (e) nutrition monitoring and counseling; (f) medical evaluations and treatment; (g) eating disorder education classes on a variety of topics, including diet and nutrition, self-esteem, healthy exercise, assertiveness, and communication skills; and (h) individualized academic management and tutoring.

During treatment, patients are encouraged to explore their own spiritual beliefs and to draw on their faith to assist in their recovery. Therapists at the center feel that, as patients align their behavior with their own spiritual beliefs, they benefit from improved confidence, self-respect, and peace of mind. Patients are invited to explore spiritual issues related to their recovery if they desire during their individual psychotherapy sessions.

To further facilitate spiritual exploration and healing, patients attend a weekly 60-minute spiritual exploration and growth group, and they read a self-help workbook, which includes scriptural and other spiritual readings and educational materials about topics such as faith in God, spiritual identity, grace, forgiveness, repentance, prayer, and meditation (P. S. Richards, Hardman, & Berrett, 2000; P. S. Richards et al., in press). Patients use the structure of the workbook and support of the group to help them come to an understanding of their own spiritual beliefs and convictions and to include those understandings in their recovery program.

Patients participate in a biweekly, 12-step group that is adapted for women with eating disorders. They are also given opportunities during the treatment program to attend religious services of their choice and to engage in altruistic acts of service within the center and community. Two research studies conducted at Center for Change have provided evidence that spiritual growth and healing during treatment is positively associated with better patient outcomes (P. S. Richards, Hardman, & Berrett, 2001; Smith et al., 2002).

Applications to Multicultural and Special Populations

Recognizing that religion and spirituality are important aspects of diversity has led therapists to incorporate spiritual perspectives and interventions into treatment with various multicultural and special client populations (P. S. Richards & Bergin, 2000; Smith & Richards, 2002). For example, spiritually oriented treatment approaches have been used with most racial–ethnic minority groups, including African Americans (Davis-Russell; 2002; Nwadiora, 1996), Latinos (Baez & Hernandez, 2001), Asian Americans (Tan & Dong, 2000), and Native Americans (Trujillo, 2000). Spiritual approaches have also been used with members of most religious traditions, including a wide range of Christians (P. S. Richards & Bergin, 2000), Jews (Frankel, 2001; Hartsman, 2002; L. Miller & Lovinger, 2000; Rabinowitz, 2000), Muslims (Hedayat-Diba, 2000), Buddhists (Brazier, 1995; Eigen, 1998; Epstein, 1995; Fredenberg, 2002; Magdid, 2002; Manne-Lewis, 1996; G. Watson, Batchelor, & Claxton, 2000; Welwood, 2000; Wray, 1986), and Hindus (Sharma, 2000). Spiritual approaches have also been used with elderly people (Koenig, Larson, & Matthews, 1996; Ramsey & Blieszner, 2000); gays, lesbians, and bisexuals (Davidson, 2000; Arguelles & Rivero, 1997; Perlstein, 1996); women (Funderburk & Fukuyama, 2001); and gifted individuals (Chauvin, 2000).

RESEARCH ON SPIRITUALLY ORIENTED TREATMENT APPROACHES

Empirical research on religious and spiritual issues in mental health and psychotherapy has increased rapidly during the past two decades. In a comprehensive *Psychological Bulletin* review, Worthington, Kurusu, McCullough, and Sandage (1996) examined 148 empirical studies on religion and psychotherapy, which provided considerable insight into "(a) religion and mental health, (b) religion and coping with stress, (c) religious people's views of the world, (d) preferences and expectations about religion and counseling, and (e) religious clients' responses to counseling" (p. 451). They also concluded that the methodological quality of this research has improved to the point of approaching "current secular standards, except in outcome research" (Worthington et al., 1996, p. 448). Since publication of the Worthington et al. review, there have been several updates of the research literature in this domain, including a meta-analysis of religiously accommodative outcome studies (McCullough, 1999) and several narrative reviews (e.g., Oman & Thoresen, 2001; Worthington & Sandage, 2001a, 2001b). Exhibit 10.4 summarizes some of the major conclusions from these publications.

Although relatively few experimental therapy outcome studies of religious and spiritual therapies have been conducted, their number is increasing (Worthington & Sandage, 2001a, 2001b). Six experimental outcome studies have compared standard and religiously accommodative versions of cognitive, cognitive–behavioral, or rational–emotive behavior therapy (Hawkins, Tan, & Turk, 1999; McCullough, 1999). In general, they have provided evidence that theistic cognitive therapy that makes use of scriptures, religious imagery, and references to Christian theology tends to be equal to standard cognitive therapy at reducing depression and superior at increasing spiritual well-being. Three experimental outcome studies have also investigated the effectiveness of a Muslim-accommodative cognitive therapy approach for anxiety and depression (Azhar, Varma, & Dharap, 1994; Azhar & Varma, 1995a, 1995b). They provided evidence that those clients who received the religiously accommodative treatment approach tended to have better outcomes than those who received a standard secular treatment, although weaknesses in methodology call for tentativeness about these findings.

Several other recent outcome studies of spiritual treatment approaches with other clinical issues and populations have been conducted, including a spiritual growth group for eating disorder inpatients (P. S. Richards et al., 2001), a spiritually integrated reminiscence group for assisted-living facility adults (Emery, 2003), a religiously integrated forgiveness group for college women who had been wronged in romantic relationships (Rye & Pargament, 2002), a spiritually informed cognitive–behavioral stress management workshop for college students (Nohr, 2001), a spiritually focused therapy group for cancer patients (Cole, 2000), a spiritually focused puppet therapy for adults with chemical dependency (Vizzini, 2003), and a psycho–spiritual manualized individual therapy intervention for female sexual abuse survivors (Murray-Swank & Pargament, 2004). These studies, in general, have found that theistic integrative interventions are equivalent to and sometimes more effective than standard secular treatment approaches for religious clients.

EXHIBIT 10.4
Major Conclusions From Reviews of Research on Religion and Psychotherapeutic Processes

1. Most research has been done on potential, not actual, clients, although this has begun to change in recent years.
2. Numerous studies have investigated the relation between religion and mental health, personality, social behavior, and coping. Generally, these studies provide considerable evidence that religion can be beneficial. Certain types of religiousness (e.g., intrinsic) appear to be healthier than others (e.g., extrinsic).
3. A number of studies have been done on how religious beliefs and values influence expectations and preferences in counseling. Generally, religiously devout clients prefer and trust counselors with similar religious beliefs and values.
4. A sizable number of studies have examined the religious beliefs and practices of psychotherapists. Psychotherapists tend, on average, to be less religious than clients, although not as much as was previously believed. Religious therapists are more likely to view religion as being relevant to treatment and to use spiritual interventions.
5. Large numbers of clergy provide mental health therapy, and in some localities clergy are more popular as a source of counseling than are mental health professionals. Little is known empirically about the effectiveness of the counseling provided by clergy, spiritual directors, and chaplains, but some research indicates that clergy with backgrounds in mental health do well.
6. A few studies have been done on whether the religion of the therapist, client, or both influences clinical judgment. This research has been inconclusive, and more studies are needed.
7. Several studies have investigated the referral practices of mental health professionals and clergy. Generally, mental health professionals rarely refer clients to clergy. Clergy refer difficult cases to mental health professionals, particularly when they know and agree with the professional's religious values.
8. Many studies have been conducted on prayer, forgiveness, and meditation. In general, this research provides support for the therapeutic use of these practices.
9. Approximately 10 outcome studies have examined the effectiveness of religious cognitive therapy interventions. Generally, they have shown that religious cognitive therapy is as effective as secular cognitive or rational–emotive behavior therapy and sometimes slightly more effective for reducing symptoms of depression and anxiety. Nonreligious therapists have successfully used religious cognitive therapy. Religious clients tend to prefer religiously accommodative cognitive therapy approaches.
10. Increasing numbers of studies have investigated the effectiveness of spiritual treatment approaches with a variety of other clinical issues and populations (e.g., eating disorders, addictions, sexual abuse survivors, cancer patients). Preliminary evidence indicates that spiritual approaches may be effective with a diversity of clinical issues and populations.
11. Generally, the methodological rigor of outcome studies on spiritual treatment approaches needs improvement. In particular, large-scale controlled comparative outcome studies are needed.

Collectively, they represent a growing body of evidence that spiritual treatment approaches may be effective with a variety of clinical issues and populations.

We hope that the number and quality of carefully designed experimental outcome studies on theistic approaches with a variety of clinical issues and populations will continue to increase. We agree with W. B. Johnson (1993b), who described a number of important methodological criteria or standards that theistic psychotherapy outcome researchers should seek to achieve, including

1. treatment manuals,
2. multiple therapists,
3. therapists trained to criteria,
4. evaluation of therapist competence,
5. establishment of internal validity,
6. consistent verification of treatment integrity,
7. homogeneous subject samples,
8. clinical samples,
9. multiple channels of measurement,
10. evaluation of clinical significance, and
11. follow-up assessment.

There is a great need for such studies (McCullough, 1999; Worthington & Sandage, 2001a), particularly given the current climate of managed care accountability and the push for empirically supported treatments. We also hope that more single-subject, discovery-oriented, and qualitative studies in this domain will be conducted. We expect that within the next decade the efficacy of theistic spiritual treatment approaches will be solidly evaluated by both quantitative and qualitative empirical research.

CONCLUSION

During the past two decades, religious and spiritual interventions have been integrated into psychotherapy practice by large numbers of licensed mental health professionals. Most practitioners use theistic approaches in an integrative way, incorporating them along with mainstream secular interventions. We are impressed by therapists' creativity and by the variety of ways that they have used theistic spiritual interventions in an ethical way to assist their clients. We anticipate that the creative development and application of spiritual interventions will continue.

Despite the progress that has been made, much work remains to be done in this domain. There is still much that is not known or understood about theistic interventions, including questions about prevalence, appropriateness, process, and outcome. For example, What types of methods are different types of clients most comfortable with? When and how can specific practices be implemented ethically and effectively? Are theistic spiritual interventions more effective than secular interventions, and if so, when? What types of theistic approaches are most effective with what types of clients and problems? How can spiritual fads, excesses, and inappropriate commercializing be curbed while responsible experimentation continues? These and many other questions need further investigation.

V

RESEARCH AND
FUTURE DIRECTIONS

11

A THEISTIC, SPIRITUAL VIEW OF SCIENCE AND RESEARCH METHODS

I want to know how God created this world . . . I want to know His thoughts, the rest are details.

—Albert Einstein

If a theistic framework is to take its place alongside other major theories of personality and psychotherapy, it is crucial for those with interests in it to subject their ideas and practices to the scrutiny of empirical research. As we have noted throughout this book, there is much that is not known in this domain. For example, in what ways do different religious and spiritual beliefs influence personality development? When and how do spiritual practices promote physical and psychological healing? What types of spiritual interventions are most effective with what types of clients and problems? If psychologists are to gain more insight into these and many other important questions, much research is needed.

We recognize that there are major challenges associated with conducting research on spiritual phenomena. The study of such phenomena was excluded from psychological science more than 100 years ago, because many researchers believed that it was impossible to study "subjective" and "invisible" experiences. More recently, some theorists have raised concerns that the assumptions and methods of traditional science may preclude the valid study of spiritual phenomena (e.g., Slife, Hope, & Nebeker, 1999).

We agree that existing research methodologies are, and perhaps always will be, fundamentally limited for studying spiritual phenomena. Perhaps science will never allow researchers to fully unlock the complexities and mysteries of this domain. We think, however, that research *can* help psychologists to learn a great deal more than is currently known. As long as researchers recognize the limitations that their assumptions and research methodologies impose on their knowledge (Howard, 1986; Slife et al., 1999) and avoid the mistaken view that a phenomenon that cannot be directly observed with our senses or measurement instruments is therefore not real, they can proceed with the research enterprise, gaining what understanding and knowledge they can from it.

Another challenge of conducting research on spirituality is that, for most of the 20th century, there were biases in the professorate that have made it difficult for graduate students and scholars to pursue research in this domain. In order to be accepted into graduate school, obtain their degrees, and find employment after graduation, young scholars were forced to channel their interests in more "acceptable" (i.e., naturalistic or secular) directions (Bergin, 1980a). In addition, funding for research about spiritual phenomena and mainstream publication outlets were scarce.

Fortunately, although such biases still exist, as we discuss in chapter 3, the *Zeitgeist* in the natural and behavioral sciences is now more open to the investigation of spiritual phenomena. There are growing numbers of established scholars in this domain, and opportunities for publication, funding, and mentoring are growing. We hope that these trends continue.

In this chapter, we further discuss *scientific theism*, a topic we briefly introduce in chapter 4. We first briefly review the major "ways of knowing" available to human beings. We then describe a theistic view of epistemology and discuss its implications for our understanding of the scientific process. We define and discuss methodological pluralism and explain our reasons for endorsing it. We conclude by briefly describing major quantitative and qualitative research designs and the contributions they can make to the study of a theistic framework in personality and psychotherapy.

SCIENTIFIC THEISM

We have decided to use the term *scientific theism* as the label for our theistic view of science and scholarship. Our scientific theism is similar, though not identical, to other perspectives of theistic science that have been proposed, including Johnson's and Plantinga's *theistic realism* (P. E. Johnson, 1993; Plantinga, 1991a, 1991b) and Griffin's and Whitehead's *naturalistic theism* (Griffin, 2000, 2001). According to scientific theism, God exists, is the creator of the universe and life, and communicates with human beings through spiritual means (Bergin, 1980a). Furthermore, the most valid and useful scientific theories and methods are those that acknowledge and provide insight into the role of divine intelligence in the origins and operations of the universe and the life within it, including human development, personality, and therapeutic change.

Scientific theism rejects *atheistic scientific naturalism* (Griffin, 2000). Atheistic naturalists attempt to "explain and interpret the objective world as if reference to God is irrelevant or superfluous . . . God's current activities are [also] presumed to be irrelevant to designing and conducting studies" (Slife, 2004, p. 5–6). Atheistic naturalists, along with many other scientists, also often assume that the scientific method "provides a value-free, transparent method or logic that does not affect the outcome of investigation" (Slife, 2004, p. 11).

In contrast, scientific theism asserts that it is unnecessary and unhelpful to exclude spiritual explanations and influences from science. Scientific theism invites scientists to bring faith in God and spiritual influences and realities back into scientific theory, discovery, and methodology (O'Grady & Richards, 2003, 2004). Furthermore, we assume that all scientific inquiry, including our own, is value-laden. The scientific method is grounded in value-laden naturalistic assumptions that may constrain scientists from discovering and fully understanding spiritual realities (Slife et al., 1999; Slife, 2004). Scientific theism helps to illuminate how naturalistic assumptions have biased scientific inquiry and thereby have constrained scientists from adequately studying and understanding spiritual realities. We expand further on these themes below.

Ways of Knowing

As we discuss in chapter 2, *epistemology* is the branch of philosophy that concerns itself with the nature and sources of knowledge (Percesepe, 1991). Most philosophers agree that there are a limited number of "ways of knowing" or sources of knowledge (e.g., Madsen, 1995; Percesepe, 1991). The most commonly acknowledged sources include *authority, sense experience/empiricism, reason,* and *intuition/inspiration* (Madsen, 1995; Percesepe, 1991).

Authority

One way for us to gain knowledge is to seek it from experts or "authorities" in a given field, whether scientific, religious, or legal. One advantage of relying on authority is that we can learn from the experience, knowledge, and insights of others, which can save us a great deal of time and effort. A major disadvantage of relying on authorities is that they can be wrong. History is replete with examples of religious and scientific "authorities" who were mistaken in their understandings of the world.

Sense Experience/Empiricism

Another way to gain knowledge is to observe the world with the senses: seeing, hearing, touching, tasting, and smelling it (Percesepe, 1991). People who believe that the best way to gain knowledge of the world is through sensory experience are called *empiricists* (Percesepe, 1991). Modern science is based on a belief in empiricism. One advantage of relying on sensory experience as a source of knowledge is that such knowledge is grounded in observable facts. When people have observed a phenomenon for themselves (e.g., that the Earth is round), they no longer need to rely on the opinions of others or on logic or intellectual speculation.

One major disadvantage of relying on sense experience is the impossibility of observing all phenomena in the world and universe, even with the aid of observation and measurement instruments. Clark (1971) pointed out that

> The five senses have their limitations. The unreliability of touch is exemplified by the "burn" which cold metal can give. Taste is not only notoriously subjective—"one man's meat, another man's poison"—but is also governed, to an extent not yet fully known, by genetic inheritance. So, too, smell is an indicator whose gross incapacity in humans is thrown into relief by insects that can identify members of their species at ranges of up to a mile. Sound is hardly any better. The pattern of "reality" heard by the human is different from that heard by the dog— witness the "soundless" dog whistles of trainers; while the "real" world of the near sightless bat is one in which "real" objects are "seen"—and avoided—by ultrasonic waves which play no part in the construction of the external human world.
>
> And sight . . . is perhaps the most illusory of all senses. . . . All that unaided human physiology allows in the visual search for the world around—comes through only a narrow slit in a broad curtain . . . The landscape seen with human eyes is dramatically different, yet no more "real," than the scene captured on the infrared plate and showing a mass of detail beyond human vision. . . .
>
> Thus the human species is unconsciously and inevitably selective in describing the nature of the physical world in which it lives and moves. (pp. 91–92)

Another disadvantage of relying only on sense experience as a source of knowledge is that observations and facts alone are not meaningful (Percesepe, 1991). People's sensory experiences and observations need to be organized and interpreted, and to do this people must use their reasoning abilities and prior knowledge. During this process people's conceptual schemas and limitations influence and bias their interpretations of their experiences and observations.

Reason

People can also gain knowledge through thought or reason. Philosophers who believe reason is the primary source of knowledge are called *rationalists* (Percesepe, 1991). Rationalism is "the view that the human mind is sufficient in itself to discover truth by apprehending relations of ideas" (Percesepe, 1991, p. 161). One advantage of using reason as a source of knowledge is that people do not have to rely on the opinions of others; they can think things through for themselves. In addition, reasoning about an issue gives people a way to gain understanding about a phenomenon when they are unable to use their senses to observe the truth about it.

One major disadvantage of relying only on reason as a source of knowledge is that it is possible to "construct a rationalistic system of beliefs that is internally consistent, noncontradictory, *and completely unrelated to the world we live in!*" (Percesepe, 1991, p. 163). Another disadvantage is that human reasoning and judgment capacities may be fundamentally limited. Human reasoning about complex phenomena may be more likely to result in errors than in sound judgment or knowledge (Faust, 1984).

Intuition and Inspiration

Another way to gain knowledge is through intuition and inspiration. According to Percesepe (1991),

> [Intuition] may be defined as the ability to have direct, immediate knowledge of something without relying on the conscious use of reason or sense perception. In its most general sense, it may simply mean a direct, unmediated, privileged knowledge of one's own personhood. In its strongest sense intuition can mean a type of mystical experience that gives a person direct access to a higher way of knowledge. (p. 164)

Percesepe (1991) provided examples of intuition, including the "experience of the lived body," the "rapid insight that specialists often display in their field," "artistic and religious experiences," and "our knowledge of good and evil" (pp. 164–165). One advantage of intuition as a source of knowledge is that it seems to allow people access to knowledge that is not available through rational or empirical means. Another is that intuitive insights or hunches often are experienced as holistic and integrative, affecting those who experience them in powerful and meaningful ways.

A disadvantage of intuitive ways of knowing is that they can "land us in a mystical nowhere-land" (Percesepe, 1991, p. 165) totally cut off from reality. Not all intuitive experiences can be trusted as valid; some may be delusions or hallucinations. In addition, intuitive ways of knowing are not well understood, controlled or used easily, or easy to verify or replicate publicly.

In the behavioral sciences, sense experience, or empiricism, has been viewed historically as the most valid way of knowing, although the importance of reason in the research enterprise has been acknowledged. Scientific and psychological "authorities," such as prominent leaders in the field, have also frequently been viewed as important sources of knowledge, but religious "authorities," such as scriptures and the words of religious leaders, have been spurned. Intuition also has been almost totally disregarded as a way of knowing in the behavioral sciences.

A Theistic View of Epistemology

An important contribution that the theistic, spiritual worldview makes to the understanding of epistemology is that it affirms that religious authority, intuition, and inspiration can be valid sources of knowledge. As we discuss in chapter 4, according to the theistic worldview, God has spiritually inspired and enlightened prophets and other holy men and women. Scriptures are thought to contain a record of the inspiration and revelation that God has given in the past to such persons, and many believers therefore view them as a valid source of knowledge and truth. Many also accept the words of modern-day spiritual leaders as inspired and authoritative. Many people also view inspiration through God's spirit to individual lay believers as a valid source of truth or way of knowing. All of this we support and keep distinct from the pseudo-inspiration of fanatical and deluded religiosity that is alien to the historic spirit of both science and benevolent, mature religious traditions.

Although the theistic world religions may teach that religious authority, intuition, and inspiration are the trustworthiest ways of knowing, they do not discount all other ways of gaining knowledge and understanding. According to the theistic worldview, people can learn and know much through their sensory experiences and reason. The belief that sense experience and reason are the only legitimate or valid ways of knowing does conflict with the theistic worldview. Strict empiricism and rationalism, therefore, are rejected. A pluralistic view of how humans gain knowledge is most consistent with the theistic worldview. Authority, sense experience, reason, intuition, and inspiration all provide ways of gaining understanding and knowledge, although, as discussed earlier, each has its limitations. Inspiration from God is the most valued, authoritative source of personal knowledge, including scientific creativity, although theistic scientists recognize that in the public and scientific domains, knowledge claims must also be submitted to rational and empirical scrutiny (Bergin, 1979). We will say more about this below.

A Theistic View of the Scientific Process

An important contribution of the theistic view of epistemology to our understanding of the scientific process is that it affirms that intuitive, inspirational ways of knowing may be a part of the scientific discovery process. According to the theistic worldview, many great ideas, creations, and discoveries are gifts from God. Through intuition and inspiration, God enlightens human beings to make great discoveries and creations to benefit humanity.

The traditional view of the scientific process has been that scientists (a) use reason to formulate theories and hypotheses and (b) test their theories and hypotheses through sensory observation (collecting empirical data). Sensory observations are thought to lead to theory refinement and to further hypotheses generation. Scientists may to some extent rely on authority in the sense that they build on the theories and research of other authorities in the field; however, sensory (empirical) observation is viewed as the primary epistemological method. Intuitive, inspirational processes are generally deemphasized or ignored entirely.

The academic world has taken considerable interest in the question of where great ideas and scientific discoveries come from (Bergin, 1979). For example, 70 years ago, in *The Art of Thought*, Graham Wallas (1926), a professor emeritus at the University of London, examined this question and concluded that there are "three stages in the formation of a new thought" (p. 80): the preparation, incubation, and illumination stages.

Wallas described the *preparation stage* as a "hard, conscious, systematic, and fruitless analysis of the problem" (p. 81). During this stage, scientists become interested in a topic or problem and learn all they can about it, and they think about it and examine it from various perspectives. During the *incubation stage*, the scientist does "not voluntarily or consciously think on a particular problem, and . . . a series of unconscious and involuntary . . . mental events may take place during that period" (p. 86). During this stage, the scientist relaxes (e.g., goes for a walk, goes sailing, takes a nap) and allows the brain to digest what he or she has learned. Wallas (1926) described the *illumination stage* as "the appearance of the 'happy idea' together with the psychological events which immediately preceded and accompanied that appearance" (p. 80). Wallas further explained that the flashes of insight that come in the illumination stage often are preceded by feelings of "intimation" that the flash of insight is coming. Wallas (1926) also described a *verification stage*, a period that follows the formation of the new thought "in which both the validity of the idea [is] tested, and the idea itself [is] reduced to exact form" (p. 81).

Neal E. Miller, a National Science Medal winner, described two phases of the scientific process: discovery and proof (Bergin & Strupp, 1972). As can be seen in the following statement, Miller's discovery phase seems to correspond well with the first three stages of Wallas's (1926) model:

> During the discovery or exploratory phase, I am interested in finding a phenomenon, gaining some understanding of the most significant conditions that affect it. . . . During this phase I am quite free-wheeling and intuitive—follow hunches, vary procedures, try out wild ideas, and take short-cuts. During it, I usually am not interested in elaborate controls. (Miller, quoted in Bergin & Strupp, 1972, p. 348)

Miller's proof phase seems to correspond with Wallas's (1926) verification stage:

> After I believe I have discovered a phenomenon and understand something about it comes the next phase of convincingly and rigorously proving this to myself and to the rest of the scientific community. . . . During this phase it is essential to use the controls that demonstrate that the phenomenon really is what one thinks it is. (Miller, quoted in Bergin & Strupp, 1972, p. 348)

Many scientists, musicians, and artists have described the intuitive, inspirational nature of the illumination or discovery phases of the scientific and artistic processes. For example, Helmholtz, the great German physicist, explained that, after investigating "in all directions," his most important new thoughts came to him "unexpectedly without effort, like inspiration" (quoted in Wallas, 1926, p. 80). In Albert Einstein's biography, R. W. Clark wrote that "Today, two-thirds of a century after Einstein posted the manuscript of his paper to *Annalen der Physik,* the dust is still stirred by discussion of what inspired him" (Clark, 1971, p. 74). Einstein once reflected on the fact that even in his youth he had intimations of his later concepts. He also said that

> When I examine myself and my methods of thought I come to the conclusion that the gift of fantasy has meant more to me than my talent for absorbing positive knowledge. . . . The mind can proceed only so far upon what it knows and can prove. There comes a point where the mind takes a higher plane of knowledge, but can never prove how it got there. All great discoveries have involved such a leap. (quoted in Clark, 1971, pp. 87, 622)

Mozart amazed his friends with flashes of insight and intuitions (Percesepe, 1991). Kekule von Stadonitz, the German chemist who was a founder of structural organic chemistry and introduced the cyclic structure of benzene, "had a visionary experience in which he perceived the ends of swirling molecules bending and touching one another to form a ring" (Bergin, 1979, p. 451). In discussing inspirational dreams, the prominent psychiatrist Kenneth Colby stated that "in the final analysis no one knows where great ideas come from—they are a gift from God" (quoted in Bergin & Strupp, 1972, pp. 280–281).

Many modern-day scientists believe in God. A 1997 survey found that 39% of American scientists believed in "a God to whom one may pray in expectation of receiving an answer" (Barbour, 2000, p. 1). There is also evidence that many theistic natural and behavioral scientists believe that God can inspire their scientific and scholarly endeavors. For example, O'Grady and Richards (2003, 2004) surveyed theistic natural and behavioral scientists in the United States and invited them to share their views about the role of inspiration in science and scholarship. They found that the majority of the respondents believe that God inspires scientists and researchers in their research and scholarship. The respondents described various occasions during the scientific process when they had experienced inspiration, including while (a) choosing a research topic, (b) choosing collaborators, (c) conceptualizing and organizing the study, (d) problem solving or seeking to understand a phenomenon, and (e) writing scholarly manuscripts.

Respondents shared specific ways in which inspiration enriched their scholarship. For example, one professor stated that his longest research contract came as a result of an idea he was praying about while jogging. Another science professor said that said that during a time of heightened spiritual awareness, he made a discovery that had been overlooked by scientists for nearly 20 years. Another said that she felt "incremental illuminations" guiding her as she put her findings into writing. A behavioral science professor said, "Several articles I have written deal with how to understand human relationships. When I started, I knew the received understanding was wrong, but I didn't know how to articulate it and make my argument. As I worked on it, I received inspiration concerning how I would make my arguments" (O'Grady & Richards, 2003, p. 11). The respondents in these two studies shared many other experiences where they felt that they were inspired in their research and scholarly endeavors.

The respondents also shared their views about how scientists can prepare and qualify for divine assistance in their scientific endeavors. These suggestions included (a) being humble, (b) living virtuous lives, (c) having altruistic motives for their scientific and scholarly endeavors, (d) working hard on the problems at hand, (e) praying, and (f) listening to and writing down ideas that come to mind. Many of the respondents shared their view that in addition to rigorous intellectual and academic preparation, scientists should consider spiritual preparation and faith in God as an additional way to magnify their research efforts (O'Grady & Richards, 2003, 2004).

We do not, of course, expect all behavioral scientists to accept the idea that God inspires scientists in their scholarly endeavors. It certainly is possible to accept the well-documented fact that the scientific process involves creative, intuitive processes without attributing such creativity and intuitive insights to transcendent spiritual influences. For such researchers, the theistic view of the scientific process can simply serve as a reminder to them that the scientific process cannot easily be reduced to reason and empirical observations alone and that the creative, intuitive aspects of this process must be acknowledged and should perhaps be valued. For researchers who believe in the theistic view that intuition and inspiration are at the core of scientific discovery and scholarship, it would seem that they should more consistently exercise faith in God and humbly seek for such enlightenment in their research and scholarly endeavors. We have on occasions felt inspiration in our own scholarly endeavors and so we are convinced that such experiences are real and that they can help scientists gain new insights and deeper understanding.

We recognize, of course, that in the public and scientific domains scholars cannot make knowledge claims based solely on their intuitive and inspirational experiences. Such insights must be subjected to the tests of rational scrutiny and empirical testing. Thus, in the scientific process, the intuitive, inspirational stage of inquiry must be followed by the verification or proof stage (Miller, quoted in Bergin & Strupp, 1972, p. 348; Wallas, 1926). Scientists may rely heavily on intuitive and inspirational sources of insight and understanding in their personal lives and at various stages of the scientific and scholarly process, but when making knowledge claims in the public domain, reason and empirical evidence are absolutely essential (Bergin, 1979). Claims to inspiration cannot trump reason and empirical observation in professional scientific endeavors.

Theistic Realism

As we discuss in chapter 2, the behavioral sciences were built on a 19th-century view of science and thus adopted classical realism, positivism, and empiricism as working assumptions. These assumptions have been challenged and found to be wanting (Kuhn, 1970; Lakatos & Musgrave, 1970; Manicas & Secord, 1983; Polanyi, 1962). It is now recognized that science is a value- and theory-laden process, that complete objectivity is impossible, and that scientific theories cannot be easily verified or falsified (Kuhn, 1970; Lakatos & Musgrave, 1970; Polanyi, 1962). Several scholars also have pointed out that the research methodologies themselves can limit or distort one's understanding of the world (Howard, 1986; Slife et al., 1999). As expressed by Howard (1986), "It is simply not true that experimental methodology affords researchers a set of glasses through which the world may be glimpsed as it truly exists" (p. 20).

Although we accept this revised view of science and its methods, we do not agree with some relativists who believe that there are no criteria of truth and that it is impossible to establish that some theories, ideas, practices, or behaviors are better than others (Slife & Williams, 1995). We agree with Manicas and Secord (1983) that "there is a world that exists independently of cognizing experience. Since our theories are constitutive of the known world but *not* of the *world*, we may always be wrong, but *not* anything goes" (p. 401). Howard (1986) suggested that commonsense knowledge and scientific knowledge are both

> stationed on a continuum anchored at one end by total skepticism or solipsism, in which we give up knowing or science, and anchored at the other end by total credulity. Ordinary knowing and science are in between these extremes and somehow combine a capacity for focused distrust and revision with a belief in the common body of knowledge claims. It follows from *this imperfect yet improvable* view of scientific knowledge that the cumulative revision of scientific knowledge becomes possible through a process of trusting (tentatively at least) the great bulk of current scientific and commonsense belief ("knowledge") and using it to discredit and revise one aspect of scientific belief. (pp. 20–21)

It also is important to note that such critiques of scientific models and of classical realism began not long after Newton established the "laws" of the physical universe. In the 19th century, many sophisticated scientists and philosophers proposed essentially the same arguments against classical realism stated today by some postmodernists. Indeed, it was the critical and original work of Kirchhoff, Mach, Maxwell, and others that laid the foundation of relativity theory; then came quantum mechanics, and the mechanical picture of the universe disintegrated. Much of philosophy and science during most of the 20th century has been devoted to creating alternative views.

Who can question the greatness of the contributions of Newton and his contemporaries and followers who laid the foundation of modern science and technology? Indeed, it is ironic that some people with theistic and spiritual perspectives are so quick to criticize the modernist–Newtonian worldview when Newton, the great originator, was himself a devoted theistic Christian who believed that his work was inspired by God. He always believed that his work on nature was only a small part of God's picture of the universe, never the full picture. He maintained that God's power, influence, and presence are behind and in the phenomena of nature (Burtt, 1955).

It is thus possible through spiritual and other means to gain valid understanding and knowledge about the world and about spiritual realities, but researchers' understanding and knowledge will always be incomplete and somewhat limited by their culture and context, and it should always be held tentatively. However, researchers need not lapse into extreme relativism or nihilism, i.e., the belief that all values are baseless and that nothing can be authentically known or communicated. By seeking knowledge and understanding through reason, sensory experience, authority, intuition, and inspiration, human beings can advance in their understanding and knowledge of truth. Thus, according to theistic realism, the scientific process at its best combines all four major ways of knowing rigorously and creatively.

Methodological Pluralism

We believe that the professions of psychology and psychotherapy need to embrace a methodologically pluralistic approach to research. The term *methodological pluralism* refers to the practice of using a wide range of research philosophies, designs, methods, and strategies, including quantitative and qualitative ones (Greenberg, Elliot, & Lietaer, 1994; Kazdin, 1994; Slife & Gantt, 1999). Such an approach is more consistent with a theistic view of epistemology than is strict empiricism, and we think that it also is more consistent with current views in the philosophy of science.

To some extent, a movement toward methodological pluralism has already begun in psychology and psychotherapy. The postmodern critiques of 19th and 20th century science have broken down the rigid adherence to traditional experimental and quantitative research designs and methodologies. Qualitative, ethnographic, naturalistic, and phenomenological methodologies have been proposed and are being used with increasing frequency (e.g., Kirk & Miller, 1986; Lincoln & Guba, 1985; Reichardt & Cook, 1979). We think that this is fortunate, because such approaches hold considerable promise for broadening and deepening the understanding of human beings and the complexities of personality, psychotherapy, and therapeutic change. We endorse these methodologies as long as they are used carefully and rigorously. We also endorse the continued use of traditional quantitative methodologies, including experimental, quasi-experimental, correlational, survey, single-subject, process, and discovery-oriented designs.

We recognize that some scholars view the quantitative (modernistic) and qualitative (postmodern) research paradigms as being philosophically incompatible (e.g., Lincoln & Guba, 1985). Lincoln and Guba's (1985) book *Naturalistic Inquiry* provides a helpful discussion of the assumptions of the positivistic and naturalistic (postmodern) paradigms. Table 11.1, reprinted from *Naturalistic Inquiry,* briefly contrasts some of the assumptions of these two paradigms. Although these paradigms are based on seemingly conflicting assumptions about the nature of the world and science (Lincoln & Guba, 1985; Slife et al., 1999), we think that these assumptions and

TABLE 11.1
Contrasting Positivistic and Postmodern Axioms

Axiom	Positivist paradigm	Postmodern paradigm
The nature of reality	Reality is single, tangible, and fragmentable	Realities are multiple, constructed, and holistic
The relationship of knower to the known	Knower and known are independent, a dualism	Knower and known are interactive, inseparable
The possibility of generalization	Time- and context-free generalizations (nomothetic statements) are possible	Only time- and context-bound working hypotheses (idiographic statements) are possible
The possibility of causal linkages	There are real causes, temporally precedent to or simultaneous with their effects	All entities are in a state of mutual simultaneous shaping so that it is impossible to distinguish causes from effects
The role of values	Inquiry is value-free	Inquiry is value-bound

Note. Adapted from *Naturalistic Inquiry* (p. 37), by Y. S. Lincoln and E. G. Guba, 1985, Beverly Hills, CA: Sage. Copyright 1985 by Sage Publications. Reprinted with permission.

methods are not necessarily mutually exclusive. Each paradigm offers different language, "lenses," and methods through which researchers can seek to study and understand the world (Slife & Gantt, 1999).

As researchers embrace a methodologically pluralistic approach to the research enterprise, it is important for them to understand the underlying assumptions of the quantitative (modernistic) and qualitative (postmodern) paradigms and consider how these may limit or filter what they can know (Howard, 1986; Slife et al., 1999; Spackman & Williams, 2001). Slife and his colleagues have also provided helpful critiques of the assumptions of naturalistic, modernistic science, as well as some alternative assumptions associated with postmodernism (Slife, 2004; Slife & Gantt, 1999). Table 11.2 summarizes some of these viewpoints and their implications for psychotherapy researchers. Slife and his colleagues have also discussed why scientific methods that are based on the philosophical assumptions of modernistic naturalism may be problematic for researchers interested in theistic spirituality (Slife, 2004; Slife et al., 1999). For example, Slife et al. (1999) explained that modernistic science assumes that if a phenomenon cannot be operationalized, repeated or replicated, and reduced into smaller parts, factors, or dimensions, its reality or truth status is suspect. They pointed out that such methodological requirements are based on the assumptions of universalism, materialism, and atomism, assumptions that are not necessarily true. They also argued that these assumptions create difficulties for researchers who study spirituality with modernistic methods, because the researchers must alter their conceptions of spirituality to fit the assumptions of the modernistic

TABLE 11.2
The Description, Problems, and Alternatives of Five Major Assumptions of Naturalism

Naturalistic assumptions	Description	Problems	An alternative
Objectivism—constrains therapy innovation and favors objectivist therapy strategies (empirically supported treatments, eclecticism)	The objective (natural) world of therapy occurs outside our subjectivity, and thus in a value-free world without meanings and morality. Scientific methods reveal this world through a relatively value-free logic that does not affect the outcome of the investigation and thus does not favor one type of therapy over another.	Philosophers of science have shown that scientific methods are underlaid with unproven and uninvestigated assumptions and values. There is no empirical justification for empiricism. The positive empirical evaluations of some therapies may be the result of systematic bias rather than efficacy without such bias.	*Continental philosophy:* Quantitative and qualitative researchers should critically examine the values inherent in the logic of their methods. Therapists who deny their own inescapable values risk imposing them (without awareness) on clients. Therapists should embrace their own values for therapeutic opportunities.
Materialism—accounts for many research practices and the increasing biologization of disorders and treatment	Matter is what is important and sufficient for understanding. Hence, nonobservable constructs are operationalized (translated into the material and thus observable), and psychotherapy is increasingly biologized (with treatment and diagnosis becoming increasingly medical and biological).	All findings that use operationalizations are, at best, the findings of manifestations rather than the findings of the intended phenomenon of study. Researchers often confuse the process of operationalization, which presumes no cause or basis, with the process of identification, which presumes that the cause or basis is matter.	*Holism:* Biological factors are necessary but not sufficient conditions for behavior, cognition, and even the body, accounting for materialist findings but implying the existence of nonmaterialist factors. Empirical research on agency and spirituality suggests the availability of nonmaterialistic necessary conditions.
Hedonism—dominates conceptions of therapy outcome, human nature, and human relationships	All living things seek pleasure and avoid pain, with all higher animals ultimately concerned with benefits to the self (e.g., psychoanalytic pleasure principle, behavioral reinforcement, humanistic self-actualization, cognitive rationality). Helping others and suffering are only important as means to self-benefits (e.g., well-being).	If the hedonism of therapy theory is correct, therapists and clients are capable only of a sophisticated selfishness. They can help others, but only when it ultimately benefits themselves. If therapists and clients are capable of altruism, then a core aspect of many therapy theories is wrong or severely limited in its applicability.	*Altruism:* A primary outcome of therapy is a wider sense of purpose, including ultimate concern and action for the sake of others. Even a willingness to suffer for others or for cherished values, leading to deeper meaning, should be embraced. Mainstream theories of therapy will need to be significantly revised.

Atomism—accounts for emphasis on individual diagnosis and treatment as well as relativistic moral values	The natural world is comprised of self-contained "atoms" (molecules, cells), each with its own properties and qualities contained therein. In the social sciences, this means the qualities of each person originate from the self-contained individual, requiring the therapist to work within the needs and moral framework of the client.	Qualities of the self are never independent of the contexts "outside" individuals, serving as the impetus for the family therapy and social constructionist movements. Paradoxes also challenge the individualism and relativism of traditional therapy, questioning the self-containment of client needs and moral values.	*Contextualism:* At least some of the properties and qualities of things (e.g., diagnoses) come from outside the thing—in its context. None of the variables or events that science studies is self-contained. Diagnostic and outcome measures would need to be interpersonal and relational rather than personal and individual.
Universalism—explains emphasis on theoretical principles, standardized diagnoses, and manualized techniques	The most fundamental and natural things are the things that do not change—the things that are universal across both time and space. True social science knowledge approximates this universality—through standardization, generalization, and replication. The ideal is a matching of diagnostic and treatment "universals."	Emphasis on standardization and generalization discounts qualitative differences between and among clients. Some important information involves nongeneralizable, nonreplicable, and even completely unique and one-time events (e.g., trauma, "spiritual" events), but universalism leads therapists away from this vital information.	*Hermeneutics:* The changeable is at least as fundamental as the unchangeable. We should search for contextual patterns of change in experiences, meanings, and relationships, rather than context-free laws, principles, or theories. This is not relativism but a changeable truth that is linked to lived experience and cultural context.

Note. From "Theoretical Challenges to Therapy Practice and Research: The Constraint of Naturalism" (pp. 44–83), by B. D. Slife, in M. J. Lambert (Ed.), *Bergin and Garfield's Handbook of Psychotherapy and Behavior Change*, 5th ed., 2004, New York: Wiley. Copyright 2004 by Wiley. Reprinted with permission.

methods (e.g., that spiritual phenomena must be operationalizable, replicable, and capable of being subdivided into smaller parts, factors, or dimensions).

Slife et al. (1999) argued that assumptions of postmodernism such as lived experience, radical holism, and contextualism may be more compatible with theistic views. They pointed out that theistic conceptualizations of spirituality tend to be contextual, holistic, and transcendent, and they suggested that a methodological pluralism that includes qualitative research methods may allow researchers to investigate spirituality in a more valid manner (Slife et al., 1999; Slife & Gantt, 1999). They encouraged spirituality researchers to consider carefully the assumptions they are adopting and their conceptual costs before deciding what methods to use in their study of spiritual phenomena.

We wish to emphasize that, in our view, quantitative research methods clearly do not need to be discarded in the study of spirituality. Although such methods may in some ways distort and limit the understanding of spiritual phenomena, they also can help researchers to learn much in this domain. As long as researchers keep in mind the advantages and limitations of both quantitative and qualitative methodologies as they use them, progress can be made, and they can avoid discounting or ignoring phenomena that do not conform to their methodological assumptions.

In saying this, we wish to make it clear that we do not endorse what Spackman and Williams (2001) have called *naive methodological pluralism*, which holds that "no method is inherently superior to any other" regardless of the particular phenomenon being studied, and that "the ontological status of the subject of study is unimportant" (p. 401). We also recognize that both quantitative and qualitative methods can be used in ways that ignore or rule out theistic spiritual realities. When researchers start with naturalism as their grounding assumption, theistic spiritual realities are ruled out of science, *ipso facto*, regardless of whether the methods selected by researchers are quantitative or qualitative. Naturalistic assumptions, once accepted, play out at every stage of the scientific and scholarly process. Theistic perspectives of reality get excluded from theories and research hypotheses. No consideration is given to whether the research design and measuring instruments remain sensitive or open to theistic realities. Interpretations of research findings get framed in naturalistic ways.

We agree with Spackman and Williams (2001) that neither quantitative nor qualitative methods are inherently superior to the other, and that the choice of methodology should depend on the research questions and the ontological status of the subject matter. Our theistic view of methodological pluralism also emphasizes that researchers must remain open and sensitive to theistic spiritual realities, or to a theistic ontology, when formulating their theories, hypotheses, and research designs. We encourage theistic researchers to remain "open to God" and to the possibility of discovering and understanding spiritual phenomena. We also encourage them to seek inspiration, along with their reasoning and empirical observations, as they engage in the process of discovery and scholarship.

MAJOR RESEARCH DESIGNS AND THEIR CONTRIBUTIONS TO A THEISTIC PSYCHOLOGY AND PSYCHOTHERAPY

We now briefly describe some of the major quantitative and qualitative research designs and discuss how they can contribute to the study of a spiritual strategy in personality and psychotherapy. We do not describe the various research designs in detail, because this has been done in numerous books and articles (e.g., Borg & Gall, 1989; Denzin & Lincoln, 1994; Greenberg, 1986; Heppner, Kivlighan, & Wampold, 1992; Kazdin, 1994; Kendall, Holmbeck, & Verduin, 2004; J. M. Morse & Field, 1995; Ray & Ravizza, 1988; Rice & Greenberg, 1984). Our purpose is to briefly describe the defining characteristics of the major designs, their main strengths and weaknesses, and the types of research questions regarding a spiritual strategy that they are most suitable for investigating. Although it is too simplistic to classify research designs exclusively into quantitative and qualitative categories because some research designs (e.g., survey, single-subject, and discovery-oriented) combine elements of both paradigms, we group them in this manner for convenience and to highlight which paradigm (positivistic or postmodern) each design has been predominantly associated with historically.

Quantitative Research Designs

There are several quantitative research designs. In Table 11.3 we summarize the key characteristics of six designs that we believe have the potential for furthering the understanding of a spiritual strategy: analogue, survey, experimental (including quasi-experimental), correlational, single-subject, and discovery-oriented designs. Research on religious and spiritual issues in mental health and psychotherapy has been dominated by analogue, survey, correlational, and experimental designs. We expect that such designs will continue to make valuable contributions to the advancement of a theistic framework for psychology and psychotherapy.

Given that relatively few experimental therapy outcome studies of religious and spiritual therapies have been conducted (McCullough, 1999; Worthington, Kurusu, McCullough, & Sandage, 1996), we suggest that there is a great need for more of them. Therapy outcome studies using rigorous experimental designs are time-consuming and expensive, but they are

TABLE 11.3
Comparison of Major Quantitative Research Designs or Strategies

Design or strategy	Defining characteristic	Types of research questions	Type of data	Major advantages	Major limitations
Analog	Simulation of psychotherapy, does not study actual therapy situations	Causal questions; how do different therapist, client, or process variables affect therapy process and outcomes (e.g., client religiosity)?	Quantitative measures and ratings from trained judges	Rigorous experimental control is possible; good for addressing causal questions about the relationship between religiosity and therapy outcomes and processes	Limited external (ecological) validity; generalizing to real therapy situations is difficult
Survey	Participants are contacted by phone or mail and asked to describe their beliefs, attitudes, and practices	Good for describing therapists' and clients' attitudes, beliefs, and behaviors (e.g., clients' religious beliefs and practices)	Relatively brief, researcher-constructed questionnaires	Good for describing the self-reported religious and spiritual characteristics, beliefs, and behaviors of a population	Relies only on self-report data with all of its potential distortions; cannot establish causality
Correlational	The relationship between two or more variables explored through correlational statistics or causal–comparative methods	What is the relationship between variables (e.g., what is the relationship between religious devoutness and various indicators of mental health)?	Quantitative measures	Good for exploring associations among religious and mental health variables when experimental manipulations of variables is not possible	Cannot establish causal relationships
Therapy outcome study (experimental)	Random assignment to treatment conditions and control groups used in actual therapy situations	Are spiritual treatment approaches effective? Which spiritual treatments are most effective with what clients and problems?	Quantitative outcome measures and ratings from trained judges	Can demonstrate treatment effects and differences between various spiritual therapy approaches and between spiritual and secular approaches	Difficult to conduct in real therapy situations: expensive, time-consuming, difficult to control all confounding variables, and ethical concerns with using control groups

	Description	Research questions	Measures	Strengths	Limitations
Single subject	Study one client at a time; take repeated outcome and process measurements over the course of treatment	Did a specific spiritual intervention work? What components of a spiritual approach were most effective? What in-session spiritual interventions or processes were associated with what outcomes?	Quantitative outcome and process measures and ratings from trained judges	High ecological validity; feasible for therapists to use in clinical settings; can demonstrate treatment effects of spiritual interventions and isolate the effects of specific spiritual components of treatment	Limited external and internal validity unless the design is repeated many times with many clients and therapists
Discovery-oriented or change process	Study significant "change" events in therapy and their immediate and long-term impact on process and outcome	How did an in-session spiritual event or intervention affect the immediate (and long-term) processes and outcomes of therapy?	Quantitative and qualitative process and outcome measures or descriptions of clients and therapists	Clinically relevant; good for understanding important spiritual "change events" in therapy	Limited internal and external validity; exploratory and descriptive in nature

Note. Sources consulted: Borg and Gall (1989); Greenberg (1986); Heppner, Kivlighan, and Wampold (1992); Kazdin (1994); Ray and Ravizza (1988); and Rice and Greenberg (1984).

essential for investigating outcome questions such as: Are spiritual treatment approaches and interventions effective? What types of changes do they promote? Are spiritual treatment approaches more or less effective than secular ones? Is psychotherapy more effective when secular and spiritual approaches are integrated? With what types of clients and problems are spiritual interventions most effective?

We think that single-subject and discovery-oriented research designs (Greenberg, 1986; Kazdin, 1994; Mahrer, 1988) also have great potential for contributing to the advancement of a spiritual strategy. Although these designs are more limited in terms of traditional notions of internal and external validity, they are more feasible to carry out in clinical settings because they are less intrusive, ethically problematic, costly, and time-consuming. They also are more clinically relevant in that they allow the exploration of research questions that are more meaningful to psychotherapists (Barlow, Hayes, & Nelson, 1984; Greenberg, 1986; Kazdin, 1994; Mahrer, 1988).

Single-subject designs could prove especially useful for evaluating the effectiveness of religious and spiritual interventions. Psychotherapists in clinical settings can use these designs relatively easily to evaluate their own practices. In a single-subject study, the client serves as his or her own control. By measuring changes in the client's symptoms or problems over time, the therapists can see the impact of the treatment (Kazdin, 1994). If therapists who use spiritual interventions in clinical settings are willing to invest the relatively small amount of effort needed to administer repeated outcome measures to their clients during the course of treatment, they could document the effectiveness of their own work and contribute to the establishment of a large database on the outcomes of spiritual interventions. Perhaps this will be most feasible if practicing clinicians collaborate with scholars in academic and research settings. Both clinicians and scholars would benefit from such collaboration, and the database on theistic psychotherapy would grow rapidly.

Qualitative Research Designs

There are numerous overlapping qualitative research designs or strategies and many ways of categorizing them (Denzin & Lincoln, 1994). In Table 11.4 we present five major qualitative research strategies that we think have considerable potential for contributing to the understanding of a spiritual strategy: phenomenology, ethnography, grounded theory, biographical, and case study. We limit our discussion to these strategies because of space limitations; in doing so, however, we are not ruling out the possibility that other strategies will prove useful in the study of a spiritual strategy.

TABLE 11.4
Comparison of Major Qualitative Research Designs or Strategies

Design or strategy	Defining characteristic	Types of research questions	Type of data	Major advantages	Major limitations
Phenomenology	Studies the meaning of people's experiences	Meaning questions (e.g., the meaning of clients' spiritual experiences)	Audiotaped or videotaped conversations; written anecdotes of personal experiences	Can give insight into the meaning that clients give to their religious and spiritual experiences in life and to spiritually healing experiences in therapy	Limited generalizability
Ethnography	Studies people's values, beliefs, and cultural practices	Descriptive questions about the values, beliefs, and practices of cultural group (e.g., clients' spiritual beliefs, values, and practices)	Unstructured interviews; participant observation; field notes	Can provide rich, detailed description and insight into the religious and spiritual values, beliefs, and practices of clients, therapists, and therapeutic groups and communities	Limited generalizability
Grounded theory	Studies people's experiences over time	Process questions that ask about experiences over time (e.g., how do clients change spiritually during therapy?)	Interviews (audio or video recorded); participant observation; memos, diaries	Can provide rich, detailed description and insight into the emotional, religious, and spiritual changes that clients experience during the course of therapy	Limited generalizability; amount of change is not quantifiable
Biographical	Documents the history of a person's life	What can be learned from this person's life (e.g., about the role of religion and spirituality in the person's functioning, growth, and healing)?	Letters, journals, memoirs, documents, interviews	Can provide rich insight into how religious and spiritual beliefs and practices affect human development, emotional functioning, and social relationships	May be difficult to establish the factual status of the materials used; biases of the biographer can distort the truthworthiness of the account

(continued)

TABLE 11.4 (Continued)

Design or strategy	Defining characteristic	Types of research questions	Type of data	Major advantages	Major limitations
Case study	Studies a person or group	What can be learned from the treatment of this person or group (e.g., what role did spiritual interventions play in their healing)?	Clinical observations and recollections, case notes, client history, client self-reports, and reports of significant others	Can provide rich insight into clients' religious and spiritual issues, the process and course of treatment, and the perceived effects of specific spiritual interventions	Limited generalizability; biases of the therapist can distort the trustworthiness of the report; outcomes are not objectively measured and documented

Note. Sources consulted: Borg and Gall (1989); Denzin and Lincoln (1994); J. M. Morse and Field (1995); L. M. Smith (1994); and Stake (1994).

A relatively small number of qualitative studies have been done on religious and spiritual issues in mental health and psychotherapy, although we are aware of an increasing number of them that have been done in recent years (e.g., Bergin et al., 1994; Chamberlain et al., 1996; Mattson & Scharman, 1994; O'Grady & Richards, 2004; Preece, 1994; Scharman, 1994; White, 2002). Like the rest of the behavioral sciences, spirituality research has relied on quantitative methods almost exclusively (Slife et al., 1999; Worthington et al., 1996). This seems unfortunate, because such methods may, to some extent, limit and distort the understanding of spiritual phenomena (Slife et al., 1999). Quantitative research has provided considerable insight into clients' symptoms and behaviors and into therapeutic processes and outcomes, but it has not provided much insight into clients' inner, subjective worlds. We think that this is where qualitative designs will contribute the most to a spiritual strategy and to mainstream psychology and psychotherapy. Such studies will help researchers better understand clients' inner worlds, or "lived experience," thereby enabling them to understand and empathize with them more fully.

Phenomenological, ethnographic, grounded theory, biographical, and case study strategies hold considerable promise for helping researchers to gain richer, more in-depth insight into clients' religious and spiritual perceptions, experiences, understandings, feelings, beliefs, values, desires, and practices, and similarly into how their spirituality is intertwined with their emotions and behavior. These strategies also hold promise for yielding considerable insight into the spiritual nature and processes of therapeutic change and healing, as viewed from the perspectives of clients and therapists. Biographical and case study strategies have been used for a long time in psychology and psychotherapy (L. M. Smith, 1994; Stake, 1994) and have considerable potential for providing insight into religious and spiritual development and functioning over the life span as well as during therapy.

Qualitative studies are not easy to do. They are time-consuming, laborious, and challenging to report. However, many of the methods used for data collection in qualitative research are highly similar to the methods used as part of clinical practice, such as unstructured interviews, participant observation (in therapy groups), audiotaped conversations, field (case) notes, and diaries (Denzin & Lincoln, 1994). With some training in qualitative methods and permission from clients, much of what therapists do in psychotherapy could serve as data for qualitative studies (W. Miller & Crabtree, 1994). We hope that during the next decade many psychotherapists, perhaps in collaboration with scholars in academic and research positions, will study spiritual issues in personality and psychotherapy creatively and rigorously using qualitative methods.

CONCLUSION

We think that a theistic view and approach for science, or *scientific theism*, is an essential part of a comprehensive framework for psychology and psychotherapy. The conceptual and methodological constraints of a naturalistic scientific framework must be superseded if theistic behavioral scientists and mental health professionals are to succeed in their efforts to adequately understand the role of faith and spirituality in human development, healing, and therapeutic change.

Scientific theism makes conceptual space for God and spiritual realities in the study of health and human welfare. It opens the door to a truly dialogical, mutually beneficial relationship between science and religion. Much work needs to be done to fully establish a theistic viewpoint and scholarly approach before it will take its place as an influential alternative to the naturalistic scientific framework. However, the *Zeitgeist* is ripe for this to happen. We hope that theistic scientists and scholars of diverse spiritual backgrounds will join with us in the effort to fully develop and establish a theistic approach to science and scholarship.

12

DIRECTIONS FOR THE FUTURE

[I]f science and religion are so broadly similar, and not arbitrarily limited in their domain, they should at some time converge. I believe this convergence is inevitable . . . .

—Charles H. Townes
Nobel Laureate in Physics

In this chapter we discuss what we believe are the needs and directions for the advancement of a theistic framework for psychology and psychotherapy. We briefly summarize highlights in the progress that has been made during the last decade. We discuss some pressing theoretical and research questions that need investigation. We also discuss and make recommendations for multicultural education and clinical training. Finally, we briefly discuss a number of domains in which a theistic framework is beginning to make important contributions to practice, including psychotherapy, medicine, health psychology, education and prevention, and religious institutions.

THEORY AND RESEARCH

Theory and research relevant to a theistic framework for psychology and psychotherapy have increased greatly during the past decade. As we discuss in chapter 10, there has been an explosion of articles, books, and research studies about the theory and practice of religiously accommodative and spiritually oriented psychotherapies (e.g., McCullough, 1999; W. R. Miller, 1999; P. S. Richards & Bergin, 2000, 2004; Shafranske, 1996; Sperry & Shafranske, 2005; Worthington, Kurusu, McCullough, & Sanders, 1996; Worthington & Sandage, 2001a). Despite impressive

EXHIBIT 12.1
Proposed Research Agenda on Religion, Mental Health, and Psychotherapy

Research Agenda

1. Research on actual clients should be a priority.
2. More research needs to be done to determine more fully why religion sometimes has positive or negative effects. What forms of religiosity and spirituality are healthy, and what forms are unhealthy? How does religion help people to cope, change, and heal?
3. Studies that document clients' reactions to spiritual interventions are needed (e.g., What type of clients feel comfortable with spiritual interventions? When do they feel comfortable with them? With what types of spiritual interventions are clients most comfortable?).
4. Therapy outcome studies of specific spiritual interventions and of spiritual–secular integrative treatment approaches are badly needed.
5. Studies of inpatient treatment programs are needed.
6. Studies of religiously and spiritually oriented group therapy and psychoeducational groups are needed.
7. More research on the effectiveness of counseling by clergy, chaplains, and lay religious counselors is needed.
8. Research is needed on brief forms of religious counseling.
9. More research on religious counseling with religiously and culturally diverse groups is needed.
10. More research on religious clients, religious counselors, and religious and spiritual interventions is needed.

Note. Data from Worthington, Kurusu, McCullough, and Sandage (1996).

progress, many pressing questions still need to be answered. In their 1996 *Psychological Bulletin* review, Worthington et al. (1996) recommended a research agenda regarding religiously accommodative and spiritual psychotherapies that remains timely today. In Exhibit 12.1 we summarize these recommendations.

Perhaps the most pressing need is for more outcome studies with actual clients on specific spiritual interventions and on spiritual–secular integrative treatment approaches (McCullough, 1999; P. S. Richards & Bergin, 2000; Sperry & Shafranske, 2005; Worthington et al., 1996; Worthington & Sandage, 2001a, 2001b). Studies that document the effectiveness of spiritual treatment approaches are essential if a theistic psychotherapy framework is to achieve credibility in mainstream psychotherapy. We hope that practitioners and researchers interested in a spiritual strategy will join together in such efforts. We also endorse the call by Worthington et al. (1996) for more research on psychotherapy with religiously and culturally diverse groups. Most theory and research in this domain has focused on the Judeo–Christian religious traditions and Western (Euro–American) cultures (P. S. Richards & Bergin, 2000). We hope that theorists and researchers with interests and expertise in diverse religions and cultures will contribute to the literature in this domain.

Much scholarly work has also been done during the past two decades in the psychology of religion, which has great relevance to a theistic framework for psychology and psychotherapy. Progress has been made in conceptualizing and measuring religion and spirituality, including the publication of a handbook of religious and spiritual measures (Hill & Hood, 1999). In addition to textbooks on the psychology of religion, chapters on the psychology of religion are beginning to appear in introductory psychology texts, which is helping to stimulate increased teaching of psychology of religion (Hester, 2002). Emmons and Paloutzian (2003) characterized this progress in the following manner:

> The psychology of religion ... has emerged as a strong research enterprise whose ... scholars produce an impressive body of research, whose research will further develop internationally and cross-culturally, and whose importance is only going to increase.
>
> We think ... that the field has changed to such a degree ... that a new concept is needed to guide it. We call it the *multilevel interdisciplinary paradigm*. This paradigm recognizes the value of data at multiple levels of analysis while making nonreductive assumptions concerning the value of spiritual and religious phenomena. ... The field has made great strides in its efforts to say something important to the rest of psychology, and we think what has come before is only a platform and that the field is now poised, ready to begin. (p. 395)

Research in the psychology of religion interfaces with and influences scholarship in personality psychology (e.g., the study of spiritual transcendence, ultimate concerns, and spiritual transformation), developmental psychology (e.g., the study of religious and spiritual development), positive psychology (e.g., the study of virtues such as gratitude, forgiveness, humility), psychotherapy (e.g., the study of spirituality, health, and healing), and many other areas of psychology. Emmons and Paloutzian (2003) discuss these trends and other promising research directions.

There are also a number of other topics relevant to a theistic, spiritual strategy where recent progress has been made (see the citations below) but need continued scholarly attention. These include

1. implications of the theistic worldview for human personality (e.g., Emmons, 1999; Kirkpatrick, 1999; Pargament, 1999; Piedmont, 1999);
2. implications of the theistic worldview for psychotherapy (e.g., Sperry & Shafranske, 2005; P. S. Richards & Bergin, 2004);
3. the nature of spirit, spirituality, and spiritual well-being (e.g., Zinnbauer, Pargament, & Scott, 1999);

4. the nature of religious and spiritual development across the life span (e.g., Poll & Smith, 2003);
5. the major spiritual needs and issues of human beings (e.g., Emmons, 1999; Emmons & Paloutzian, 2003; Pargament, 1999);
6. the prevalence and role of intuition, inspiration, and divine intervention in therapeutic change and healing (O'Grady & Richards, 2004);
7. the prevalence and role of intuition and inspiration in scientific discovery and research (O'Grady & Richards, 2003, 2004);
8. the nature, prevalence, effects, and meaning of spiritual and mystical experiences (e.g., Fox, 2003; Cardena, Lynn, & Krippner, 2000; Greyson, 2000; Ring & Cooper, 1999);
9. the implications and usefulness of epistemological and methodological pluralism (e.g., Slife & Gantt, 1999; Spackman & Williams, 2001);
10. the conflicts and potential compatibility between the assumptions and methodologies of scientific modernism and postmodernism (e.g., Slife, 2004; Slife & Gantt, 1999);
11. the development of reliable, valid, and clinically useful assessment and outcome measures of religious and spiritual orientation and functioning that are applicable with clients from diverse religious and cultural backgrounds (e.g., Hill & Hood, 1999; Piedmont, 1999; P. S. Richards, Smith, Schowalter, Richard, Berrett, & Hardman, in press; Worthington et al., 2003); and
12. the development and application of research methodologies, procedures, and designs that allow researchers to study spiritual phenomena validly (Slife, 2004; Slife et al., 1999).

As evident, there is no shortage of fascinating and challenging projects for philosophers, theorists, and researchers in this domain during the decades ahead. We hope that individuals who have influence at the highest levels of academic, government, business, and religious institutions and societies will use it to help gain financial and political support for these efforts. We are pleased that private sources of funding for research and education about science and religion and spirituality and health have increased dramatically during the past decade, due in large part to the generosity of Sir John Templeton and his foundation (John Templeton Foundation, n.d.). We are also pleased that federal grant money for research in this domain is also becoming increasingly available.

MULTICULTURAL EDUCATION AND CLINICAL TRAINING

As we discuss in chapter 3, for many years religion and spirituality were neglected as aspects of diversity in multicultural scholarship and training. During the past decade this has changed to some degree. For example, religion is now recognized as one type of diversity in the American Psychological Association's (APA's) ethical guidelines (American Psychological Association [APA], 2002a) and in the APA's *Guidelines on Multicultural Education, Training, Practice, and Organizational Change for Psychologists* (APA, 2002b). Growing numbers of multicultural books and journal articles are giving at least some attention to religious and spiritual aspects of diversity. Furthermore, many prominent multicultural scholars, and a majority of mental health professionals, now acknowledge that religion and spirituality are important aspects of multicultural diversity (Crook-Lyon, O'Grady, & Richards, 2004; Sue, Bingham, Porche-Burke, & Vasquez, 1999).

Despite the growing recognition that religion and spirituality are multicultural issues, most graduate training programs in the mental health professions still do not systematically address these topics (Bergin, 1983; D. R. Bishop, Avila-Juarbe, & Thumme, 2003; P. S. Richards & Bergin, 2000; Shafranske, 1996, 2000). Schulte, Skinner, & Claiborn (2002) recently explored the types of training currently offered in counseling psychology programs in the United States. Eighty-two percent of respondents said that their training programs offered no courses with a specifically religious or spiritual theme. Percentages did increase when respondents were asked if their programs offered a course that included religion or spirituality in the content: 25% offered two or more courses, and 28% offered one course. Only 13% of respondents reported that students in their program received training about religious and spiritual development.

Brawer, Handal, Fabricatore, Roberts, and Wajda-Johnston (2002) conducted a similar study that surveyed directors of clinical training at APA-accredited clinical programs within the United States and Canada. Only 13% of the training directors indicated that their programs offered a specific course in religion and spirituality. The frequency that these courses were offered ranged from once a year to once every other year. Twenty-two percent of training directors indicated that there was a faculty member in their program who identified him- or herself as having spirituality and religion as a major area of interest. Nearly half of the respondents reported awareness of at least one student having an interest in these areas.

In a recent national survey of members of APA's Divisions 12 (Society of Clinical Psychology), 36 (Psychology of Religion), and 45 (Society for the Psychological Study of Ethnic Minority Issues), as well as members of the American College Counseling Association, Crook-Lyon et al. (2004)

found that whereas over 82% of the respondents agreed that "religious and spiritual issues should be included in the multicultural movement," and over 61% of them agreed that "religious and spiritual issues should be taught in multicultural courses," 55.4% of them believed that "religious and spiritual issues are not adequately addressed in graduate training programs."

The findings of these studies document that there is currently a gap between professional beliefs and practice in regard to the inclusion of religion and spirituality in multicultural training. The majority of professionals now believe religion and spirituality are important aspects of diversity and that training programs should give these topics attention, but relatively few programs are doing so. There may be several reasons for this. The first is a practical issue. The course content of graduate training programs in the mental health professions must be responsive to the requirements of accrediting bodies and licensure or certification boards. Meeting these demands often leaves little room for adding content to the curricula. Consistent with this, a small percentage of professionals (16.9%) surveyed by Crook-Lyon et al. (2004) indicated concern that if religion and spirituality were added to the multicultural curricula, it would "water-down" or weaken the treatment given to other aspects of diversity.

There may also be other issues that create resistance to more fully incorporating religion and spirituality into multicultural training. For example, some professionals in academic and other training settings have no or little experience with religious or spiritual feelings or concerns, either personally or professionally, and have no idea how to provide training or supervision in this domain. Other professionals think the "aims of many religious groups are not in harmony with the aims of multiculturalism" and that the "spiritual and religious teachings are dismissive of cultural differences" (Crook-Lyon et al., 2004). Distrust between different "stakeholders" in the multicultural field, therefore, may be contributing to the gap between professional beliefs and training in this domain. We hope that such barriers to incorporating religious and spiritual aspects of diversity into multicultural education and training will be overcome.

In chapter 7 we offer several recommendations about how therapists who are interested in implementing a spiritual strategy in their work can obtain the specialized training and knowledge that they need to work more sensitively and effectively with religious and spiritual clients (e.g., reading books on the psychology of religion, taking classes in world religions, and attending workshops on spiritual issues in healing and psychotherapy). Here we do not speak to individual therapists about education and training. Rather, we want to make recommendations for professional organizations and graduate training programs about the religious and spiritual content that is needed in educational and clinical training experiences. Adopting these recommendations is essential if the gap between professional beliefs and educational practice in this domain is to be achieved.

Shafranske and Malony (1996) proposed "a number of measures to redress and remedy the current status of training" (p. 576) on religious issues in their concluding chapter of a book published by the APA, *Religion and the Clinical Practice of Psychology* (Shafranske, 1996). They opined that the ideal curriculum would include four components: "a 'values in psychological treatment' component, a 'psychology of religion' component, a 'comparative-religion' component, and a 'working with religious issues' component" (Shafranske & Malony, 1996, p. 576). Their recommendations are still current.

Values in Psychological Treatment

This component of the training model would include studies in (a) the philosophy and epistemology of science and (b) the role of values in theory, research, professional acculturation, and clinical practice. As described by Shafranske and Malony (1996),

> In essence, we are calling for and envision a curriculum that addresses the underlying value commitments that establish the canon of science and influence its application within clinical practice. Such an investigation will include a philosophical inquiry into the nature of facts, scientific practices, models of validation and falsification, and the assumptions on which clinical theories and treatments are based. . . . [It] would also include an investigation of the role of personal values of the clinician as they are expressed in clinical thinking and practice. (pp. 577–578)

Shafranske and Malony (1996) expressed their belief that "this is critical for the profession of psychology and essential 'if a constructive relationship for religion with the science and profession of psychology' (Jones, 1996) is to be achieved" (pp. 577–578). We agree with them. Such studies are essential to help theorists, researchers, and clinicians become more aware of underlying and often hidden assumptions and values, those of the profession as well as their own. An awareness of these assumptions and values can help therapists be more aware of how such factors might influence, limit, and bias their views of the world, their clients, and their professional work.

Psychology of Religion

This component of the training model would include studies in the psychology and sociology of religion. Shafranske and Malony (1996) commented on the importance of this component:

Many clinicians have not gone much deeper than a cursory reading of Freud and, perhaps, William James and are mostly unaware of the rich tradition of psychological interest in religion. . . . An exposure to the psychology of religion provides a fascinating history of American psychology in addition to its examination of essential issues concerning religion in individual and cultural experience. (p. 579)

Comparative Religions

This component of the training model would include studies in comparative world religions. Shafranske and Malony (1996) acknowledged the great diversity in religions and spiritual perspectives. They also wrote,

There is a need for clinicians to have some appreciation of the variety. If nothing else, such a study would keep therapists from premature claims that they knew what was or was not orthodoxy for other traditions. In addition, an understanding of religious diversity would assist the clinician in making determinations regarding particular beliefs and practices in respect to normative religious practice in a given faith community. . . . Such knowledge is required for a clinical assessment to be proffered. Moreover, such a study might provoke a greater appreciation for the ways in which various religious traditions provide guidelines for well-being and fulfilling life adjustment. (p. 580)

Clinical Training

This component of the training model includes instruction and supervision in working with religious issues in therapy, including (a) assessment of clients' religiousness and spirituality as related to their mental health and (b) appropriate treatment of religious issues and use of spiritual interventions in psychotherapy. Shafranske and Malony (1996) pointed out that there are several excellent resources available to assist in such training. They also pointed out that support for this component of training

appears to be developing in a number of professional associations. . . . The Office of Accreditation [of the APA] includes religion as one aspect of multicultural sensitivity that site visitors take into consideration in evaluating a program's education in cultural diversity. The American Psychiatric Association recommends, as well, that religion be considered in the evaluation and treatment of patients within residency training. (p. 581)

Shafranske and Malony's (1996) recommendations are excellent. We also appreciate the suggestions offered by Brawer et al. (2002). They respond to the request of training directors and students for curriculum guidelines regarding spiritual and religious issues (Young, Cashwell, Wiggins-Frame,

& Belaire, 2002; D. R. Bishop et al., 2003; Brawer et al., 2002) by offering the following guidelines. They recommend that training directors

1. enhance their awareness of, and sensitivity to, issues of religion and spirituality and develop an academic environment that encourages students to gain knowledge and personal understanding of these issues;
2. be knowledgeable of religious systems, including traditions, language, and culture, and assessment measures;
3. integrate training in religion and spirituality into already existing courses;
4. encourage faculty members who share an interest in religion and spirituality to identify themselves as mentors for current students and potential applicants;
5. invite guest speakers knowledgeable in the areas of spirituality and religion;
6. make books and publications on religious and spiritual issues available to students; and
7. inform students about conferences that examine issues of spirituality and religion.

We wish that every graduate training program in the mental health professions would incorporate these recommendations. Some training in religious and spiritual aspects of diversity can take place in existing multicultural classes. Most programs also require a course in counseling theories, and spiritual perspectives could also receive some coverage in such courses. Some of the leading introductory textbooks on counseling and psychotherapy now devote space to the topics of religion and spirituality (e.g., Corey, 2005; Ivey, Ivey, Myers, & Sweeney, 2005), which should make it easier for instructors to include this as a component of their classes. It is also essential that graduate students receive supervision from supervisors with expertise in religious issues and diversity (D. R. Bishop et al., 2003).

We hope that many training program administrators will find ways to offer more than minimal training and supervision in this domain of practice. Several programs have shown that it is possible to offer an entire course that explores religious and spiritual issues in mental health and psychotherapy. There are now numerous books available, including this one, that would be useful in such a course (e.g., G. Miller, 2003; W. R. Miller, 1999; P. S. Richards & Bergin, 2000, 2004; Sperry & Shafranske, 2005). As documented in the reference list in this book, numerous scholarly articles are also available.

Many programs, particularly those accredited by the APA, already offer a class or classes that introduce students to the history and theoretical and philosophical foundations of the behavioral sciences. With relatively minimal effort, such courses could, as recommended by Shafranske and Malony (1996), include an examination of how the foundational metaphysical and epistemological ideas in the behavioral sciences compare with those of the world's religious traditions. A careful examination of students' personal values and worldviews should be a required experience in multicultural and ethics classes as well as an ongoing concern during practica and internships.

Many universities offer courses in comparative world religions and in the psychology and sociology of religion. Thus many graduate training programs in the behavioral sciences would not need to design their own classes on these topics. They could simply require or encourage their students to take these classes as electives. When such courses are not available or feasible to design, students could be required or encouraged to complete independent readings on these topics for academic credit. Finally, we encourage both students and faculty to pursue continuing education to train them on religious and diversity issues throughout their careers by attending workshops and conventions, reading books and articles, and consulting with colleagues who have expertise in this domain.

We are pleased with the progress that has been made in bringing religious and spiritual aspects of diversity and psychotherapy practice into training during the past decade. For example, Larson, Lu, and Swyers (1996) developed a model curriculum about spirituality for psychiatry training, which has helped lead to the adoption of courses about spirituality by the majority of U.S. medical schools (Puchalski, Larson, & Lu, 2000). The Association for Religious, Value, and Spiritual Issues in Counseling (ASERVIC), a division of the American Counseling Association, has published professional practice guidelines for counselors concerning religion and spirituality (Young et al., 2002). Discussions are also under way in the Executive Committee of Division 36 (Psychology of Religion) of APA concerning the possibility of developing professional practice guidelines for psychologists who work with religious and spiritual clients. We hope that these trends continue. We also hope that accrediting organizations, including the APA, will soon require all graduate training programs in the mental health professions to provide a substantial training component in religious and spiritual aspects of diversity and practice.

PRACTICE

In this book we focus on describing a spiritual strategy for use in the practice of counseling and psychotherapy. It is in the practice of psychotherapy that the spiritual strategy has perhaps the most potential for enhancing professional practice, including individual, marital, family, and group therapies. However, there are reasons to believe that spiritual perspectives and interventions will make important contributions to practice in a number of other professional domains.

Behavioral Medicine and Health Psychology

As we discuss briefly in chapter 5, spiritual perspectives and interventions have already proved helpful in the field of medicine. There is evidence that spiritual beliefs and interventions can aid in the prevention and healing of a variety of physical diseases and can help people cope with chronic pain, illness, and death and dying (Benson, 1996; Borysenko & Borysenko, 1994; Ornish, 1990; B. S. Siegel, 1986). More and more, physicians are recognizing this fact and are incorporating spiritual interventions into their work (Benson, 1996; Borysenko & Borysenko, 1994; Koenig, McCullough, & Larson, 2001; Ornish, 1990; B. S. Siegel, 1986) and into their training programs. Five years ago, only 3% of medical schools surveyed offered training courses in religious and spiritual issues, whereas today 30% of those same schools do (Brawer et al., 2002). For these reasons, we expect that spiritual perspectives and interventions will continue to make significant contributions to practice in the medical profession.

We also think that a spiritual strategy has much potential for contributing to the profession of health psychology (Koenig et al., 2001; Plante & Sherman, 2001; Smith, 2001; Martin & Carlson, 1988). Spiritual perspectives have had a relatively minor influence in the health psychology profession to date, as evidenced by the neglect of religious and spiritual issues in most publications on health psychology (e.g., G. D. Bishop, 1994). However, in a recent book chapter, Smith (2001) discussed the relevance of religion and spirituality for health psychology and pointed out some promising directions for future research and practice.

Values and Lifestyle Education

In our view, a theistic spiritual approach also holds promise for enhancing the health education and illness prevention efforts of schools and public health education agencies. According to the theistic view of personality, values play a crucial role in the development of healthy behavior and lifestyles. The often-repeated empirical finding that spiritual values and practices are positively associated with better physical and mental health and improved coping provides support for this hypothesis (e.g., Koenig et al., 2001; Plante & Sherman, 2001). This research therefore provides both theoretical and empirical justification for healthy lifestyle values education efforts.

We recognize that there are difficulties with teaching lifestyle values in a pluralistic society and that such efforts will likely encounter strong resistance from some. We are not saying that schools and public health agencies should promote religion. Nevertheless, lifestyle values and practices that health professionals have documented to be, through clinical practice and empirical research, helpful for promoting physical and mental health should be endorsed and taught in schools and by public health agencies. Such lifestyle values and practices should be taught and promoted in an ecumenical, multiculturally sensitive, and noncoercive manner. These healthy lifestyle values and practices should be taught regardless of whether they had their origins in the world's religious traditions, medicine, or the mental health professions.

Congregation Development as Community Psychology

We think that a spiritual strategy also holds promise for strengthening and enhancing the psychosocial climate and well-being of religious institutions and their members. It is well known that religious institutions potentially provide much social, emotional, and spiritual support to their members (Pargament, 1996). However, the psychosocial climate of religious institutions is not always positive (Pargament, Silverman, Johnson, Echemendia, & Snyder, 1983). Many people experience religious institutions as impersonal, frustrating, oppressive, rigid, shaming, or discriminatory (Pargament et al., 1983; Silverman, Pargament, Johnson, Echemendia, & Snyder, 1983). In addition, as expressed by Pargament et al. (1991), "churches and synagogues present the full range of problems . . . , from the mental health concerns of individual members, the conflicts of leaders and clergy, and questions about particular programs to issues of organizational survival, direction and growth" (p. 394).

The historical alienation between religion and the mental health professions has kept religious leaders from seeking assistance from mental health professionals, but this has begun to change (Pargament et al., 1991). By becoming sensitive to religious issues, incorporating spiritual strategies into practice, and establishing trust and credibility with leaders in religious communities, mental health professionals open opportunities to provide a variety of psychological services to such communities, including psychotherapy and organizational consultation. The Congregation Development Program developed by Pargament et al. (1991) demonstrates how mental health professionals with expertise in religious and spiritual issues can consult with and assist religious institutions and their members. More recently, Plante

(1999) described his experience in developing a working relationship with both clergy and parishioners of the Roman Catholic Church.

Pastoral Counseling

Historically, pastoral counseling has had numerous successes in integrating psychological knowledge within the role and repertoire of clergy (e.g., Collins, 1988; Estadt, Blanschette, & Compton, 1983; W. R. Miller & Jackson, 1985; Wicks, Parsons, & Capps, 1985). As a theistic, spiritual strategy develops within mainstream psychology, the overlap between pastoral and clinical counseling will expand. Competition between the two may create unhealthy rivalry or confusion in role boundaries (see chap. 7, this volume); however, a collaborative stance could greatly enhance the roles of both clergy and mental health professionals. Such collaboration might enable sharing information, working together to help specific clients, collaborating on designing therapeutic congregational structures and processes, joining efforts in outcome research, and many additional benefits. Much thought and research within community psychology and the prevention movement have already been accomplished (Pargament, Maton, & Hess, 1992; Pargament et al., 1991), but adding a spiritual dimension *within* psychological theory and practice could further enhance the synergy between the pastoral and clinical models of helping (Lyall, 1995; Topper, 2003).

CONCLUSION

A spiritually open *Zeitgeist* now exists in the sciences and health professions. The movement to integrate spiritual perspectives and interventions into mainstream psychology and psychotherapy has matured and continues to gain momentum. We agree with Jones (1994), who argued that religious worldviews can contribute to the progress of psychological science and practice "by suggesting new modes of thought . . . and new theories" (p. 194). We think that the theistic worldview, in particular, contributes important insights into previously neglected aspects of human nature, personality, therapeutic change, and the practice of psychotherapy.

The most serious deficiency in modern mainstream theories of personality and psychotherapy has been their neglect of God and the human spirit. We are pleased that this is being rectified. A theistic strategy for psychotherapy will enhance the ability of mental health professionals to understand and work more sensitively and effectively with their clients. We hope that this book and its companion volume of case studies will assist in achieving this important goal.

In a recent edited book called *Judeo–Christian Perspectives on Psychology: Human Nature, Motivation, and Change,* which was published by the APA, William R. Miller (2005, p. 15) asked, "Dare we develop a theistic psychology?" Our response is a resounding Yes. Let us dare to develop both a theistic psychology and a theistic psychotherapy and bring them to a place of equality and influence within the professional and academic mainstreams. The time is ripe for such an achievement. We invite theistic psychologists and psychotherapists from diverse theistic spiritual traditions to join in this important work.

REFERENCES

Adorno, T. W., Frenkel-Brunswik, E., Levinson, D. J., & Sanford, R. N. (1950). *The authoritarian personality*. New York: Norton.

Alcoholics Anonymous World Services. (1980). *Alcoholics Anonymous*. New York: Author.

Alcoholics Anonymous World Services. (1990). *Alcoholics Anonymous 1989 membership survey*. New York: Author.

Allen, R. O., & Spilka, B. (1967). Committed and consensual religion: A specification of religion–prejudice relationships. *Journal for the Scientific Study of Religion, 6*, 191–206.

Allport, G. W. (1950). *The individual and his religion: A psychological interpretation*. New York: Macmillan.

Allport, G. W. (1959). Religion and prejudice. *Crane Review, 2*, 1–10.

Allport, G. W. (1966). The religious context of prejudice. *Journal for the Scientific Study of Religion, 5*, 447–457.

Allport, G. W., & Ross, J. M. (1967). Personal religious orientation and prejudice. *Journal of Personality and Social Psychology, 5*, 432–443.

Alston, W. P. (1991). *Perceiving God: The epistemology of religious experience*. Ithaca, NY: Cornell University Press.

American Association for Marriage and Family Therapy. (2001). *AAMFT code of ethics*. Alexandria, VA: Author.

American Counseling Association. (1995). *Code of ethics and standards of practice*. Alexandria, VA: Author.

American Educational Research Association, American Psychological Association, & National Council on Measurement in Education. (1999). *Standards for educational and psychological testing*. Washington, DC: American Educational Research Association.

American Heritage Dictionaries. (1992). *American Heritage Dictionary of the English language* (3rd ed.). Boston: Houghton Mifflin.

American Psychiatric Association. (1994). *Diagnostic and statistical manual of mental disorders* (4th ed.). Washington, DC: Author.

American Psychiatric Association. (2001). *The principles of medical ethics with annotations especially applicable to psychiatry* [includes November 2003 amendments]. Washington, DC: Author.

American Psychological Association. (1981). *Ethical principles of psychologists* (Rev. ed.). Washington, DC: Author.

American Psychological Association. (1992). Ethical principles of psychologists and code of conduct. *American Psychologist, 47*, 1597–1611.

American Psychological Association. (2002a). *Ethical principles of psychologists and code of* conduct. Washington, DC: Author. Retrieved January 5, 2005, from http://www.apa.org/ethics

351

American Psychological Association. (2002b). *Guidelines on multicultural education, training, practice, and organizational change for psychologists.* Washington, DC: Author. Retrieved from http://www.apa.org/about/division/guide.html

Anderson, D. A., & Worthen, D. (1997). Exploring a fourth dimension: Spirituality as a resource for the couple therapist. *Journal of Marital and Family Therapy, 23*(1), 3–12.

Antoun, R. T., & Hegland, M. E. (Eds.). (1987). *Religious resurgence: Contemporary cases in Islam, Christianity, and Judaism.* Syracuse, NY: Syracuse University Press.

Appleyard, B. (1992). *Understanding the present: Science and the soul of modern man.* New York: Doubleday.

Arguelles, L., & Rivero, A. (1997). Spiritual emergencies and psycho-spiritual treatment strategies among gay/homosexual Latinos with HIV disease. In M. P. Levine, P. M. Nardi, & J. H. Gagnon (Eds.), *In changing times: Gay men and lesbians encounter HIV/AIDS* (pp. 83–98). Chicago: University of Chicago Press.

Association for Spiritual, Ethical, Religious, and Value Issues in Counseling. (n.d.). ASERVIC Web site. Retrieved February 21, 2005, from http://www.aservic.org/

Azhar, M. Z., & Varma, S. L. (1995a). Religious psychotherapy as management of bereavement. *Acta Psychiatrica Scandinavia, 91,* 223–235.

Azhar, M. Z., & Varma, S. L. (1995b). Religious psychotherapy in depressive patients. *Psychotherapy and Psychosomatics, 63,* 165–173.

Azhar, M. Z., Varma, S. L., & Dharap, A. S. (1994). Religious psychotherapy in anxiety disorder patients. *Acta Psychiatrica Scandinavia, 90,* 1–3.

Baez, A., & Hernandez, D. (2001). Complementary spiritual beliefs in the Latino community: The interface with psychotherapy. *American Journal of Orthopsychiatry, 71,* 408–415.

Ball, R. A., & Goodyear, R. K. (1991). Self-reported professional practices of Christian psychologists. *Journal of Psychology and Christianity, 10,* 144–153.

Bandura, A. (1969). *Principles of behavior modification.* New York: Holt, Rinehart & Winston.

Bandura, A. (1986). *Social foundations of thought and action: A social cognitive theory.* Englewood Cliffs, NJ: Prentice Hall.

Bandura, A. (1997). *Self-efficacy: The exercise of control.* New York: W. H. Freeman.

Barbour, I. G. (1990). *Religion in an age of science: The Gifford lectures 1989–1991* (Vol. 1). San Francisco: Harper & Row.

Barbour, I. G. (2000). *When science meets religion: Enemies, strangers, or partners?* New York: HarperCollins.

Barker, P. (1996). *Psychotherapeutic metaphors: A guide to theory and practice.* New York: Brunner/Mazel.

Barlow, D. H., Hayes, S. C., & Nelson, R. O. (1984). *The scientist practitioner: Research and accountability in clinical and educational settings.* Elmsford, NY: Pergamon Press.

Barnette, V. (2001). Resolving PTSD through time limited dynamic psychotherapy. *Journal of College Student Psychotherapy, 16*(1–2), 27–41.

Barrett, D. B. (1996). Religion: World religious statistics. In *Encyclopedia Britannica Book of the Year* (p. 298). Chicago: Encyclopedia Britannica.

Barrett, D. B., & Johnson, T. M. (2002). Religion. In *Britannica Book of the Year* (p. 303). Chicago: Encyclopedia Britannica.

Batson, C. D., Schoenrade, P., & Ventis, W. C. (1993). *Religion and the individual: A social–psychological perspective.* New York: Oxford University Press.

Bechtel, W. (1988). *Philosophy of science: An overview for cognitive science.* Hillsdale, NJ: Erlbaum.

Beck, A. T. (1976). *Cognitive therapy and the emotional disorders.* Madison, CT: International Universities Press.

Beckwith, B. P. (1985). *The decline of U.S. religious faith 1912–1984 and the effects of education and intelligence on such faith.* Palo Alto, CA: Author.

Becvar, D. S. (1997). *Soul healing: A spiritual orientation in counseling and therapy.* New York: Basic Books.

Beit-Hallahmi, B. (1974). Psychology of religion 1880–1930: The rise and fall of a psychological movement. *Journal of the History of the Behavioral Sciences, 10,* 84–90.

Bennett, W. J. (1993). *The book of virtues.* New York: Simon & Schuster.

Benor, D. J. (1992). *Healing research: Vol. 1. Research in healing.* Munich, Germany: Helix.

Benson, H. (1996). *Timeless healing: The power and biology of belief.* New York: Scribner.

Benson, P. L., & Spilka, B. (1973). God image as a function of self-esteem and locus of control. *Journal for the Scientific Study of Religion, 12,* 297–310.

Bergin, A. E. (1969). A self-regulation technique for impulse-control disorders. *Psychotherapy: Theory, Research and Practice, 6,* 113–118.

Bergin, A. E. (1979). Bringing the restoration to the academic world: Clinical psychology as a test case. *Brigham Young University Studies, 19,* 449–473.

Bergin, A. E. (1980a). Psychotherapy and religious values. *Journal of Consulting and Clinical Psychology, 48,* 75–105.

Bergin, A. E. (1980b). Religious and humanistic values: A reply to Ellis and Walls. *Journal of Consulting and Clinical Psychology, 48,* 642–645.

Bergin, A. E. (1980c). Behavior therapy and ethical relativism: Time for clarity. *Journal of Consulting and Clinical Psychology, 48,* 11–13.

Bergin, A. E. (1983). Religiosity and mental health: A critical reevaluation and meta-analysis. *Professional Psychology: Research and Practice, 14,* 170–184.

Bergin, A. E. (1985). Proposed values for guiding and evaluating counseling and psychotherapy. *Counseling and Values, 29,* 99–116.

Bergin, A. E. (1988). Three contributions of a spiritual perspective to counseling, psychotherapy, and behavior change. *Counseling and Values, 32,* 21–31.

Bergin, A. E. (1991). Values and religious issues in psychotherapy and mental health. *American Psychologist, 46,* 394–403.

Bergin, A. E. (1993). *Adaptive/healthy versus maladaptive/unhealthy religious lifestyles.* Unpublished manuscript, Brigham Young University, Provo, UT.

Bergin, A. E. (2002). *Eternal values and personal growth: A guide on your journey to spiritual, emotional, and social wellness.* Provo, UT: Brigham Young University Studies.

Bergin, A. E., & Garfield, S. L. (Eds.). (1994). *Handbook of psychotherapy and behavior change* (4th ed.). New York: Wiley.

Bergin, A. E., & Jensen, J. P. (1990). Religiosity of psychotherapists: A national survey. *Psychotherapy, 27,* 3–7.

Bergin, A. E., & Lambert, M. J. (1978). The evaluation of therapeutic outcomes. In S. L. Garfield & A. E. Bergin (Eds.), *Handbook of psychotherapy and behavior change: An empirical analysis* (2nd ed., pp. 137–189). New York: Wiley.

Bergin, A. E., Masters, K. S., & Richards, P. S. (1987). Religiousness and mental health reconsidered: A study of an intrinsically religious sample. *Journal of Counseling Psychology, 34,* 197–204.

Bergin, A. E., Masters, K. S., Stinchfield, R. D., Gaskin, T. A., Sullivan, C. E., Reynolds, E. M., et al. (1994). Religious life-styles and mental health. In L. B. Brown (Ed.), *Religion, personality, and mental health* (pp. 69–93). New York: Springer-Verlag.

Bergin, A. E., & Payne, I. R. (1991). Proposed agenda for a spiritual strategy in personality and psychotherapy. *Journal of Psychology and Christianity, 10,* 197–210.

Bergin, A. E., Payne, I. R., & Richards, P. S. (1996). Values in psychotherapy. In E. Shafranske (Ed.), *Religion and the clinical practice of psychology* (pp. 297–325). Washington, DC: American Psychological Association.

Bergin, A. E., Stinchfield, R. D., Gaskin, T. A., Masters, K. S., & Sullivan, C. E. (1988). Religious life styles and mental health: An exploratory study. *Journal of Counseling Psychology, 35,* 91–98.

Bergin, A. E., & Strupp, H. H. (1972). *Changing frontiers in the science of psychotherapy.* Chicago: Aldine-Atherton.

Berkman, L. F., & Syme, S. L. (1979). Social networks, host resistance, and mortality: A nine year follow-up study of Alameda County residents. *American Journal of Epidemiology, 109,* 186–204.

Bertens, H. (1995). *The idea of the postmodern.* New York: Routledge.

Beutler, L. E. (1972). Value and attitude change in psychotherapy: A case for dyadic assessment. *Psychotherapy, 9,* 262–267.

Beutler, L. E., & Clarkin, J. (1990). *Systematic treatment selection: Toward targeted therapeutic interventions.* New York: Brunner/Mazel.

Bishop, D. R., Avila-Juarbe, E., & Thumme, B. (2003). Recognizing spirituality as an important factor in counselor supervision. *Counseling and Values, 48,* 34–46.

Bishop, G. D. (1994). *Health psychology: Integrating mind and body.* Boston: Allyn & Bacon.

Blackmore, S. (1993). *Dying to live: Near-death experiences.* New York: Prometheus Books.

Blanton, P. G. (2002). The use of Christian mediation with religious couples: A collaborative language systems perspective. *Journal of Family Psychotherapy, 13*, 291–307.

Boorstien, S. (2000). Transpersonal psychotherapy. *American Journal of Psychotherapy, 54*(3), 409–423.

Borg, W. R., & Gall, M. D. (1989). *Educational research: An introduction* (5th ed.). New York: Longman.

Boring, E. G. (1950). *A history of experimental psychology* (2nd ed.). New York: Appleton-Century-Crofts.

Borysenko, J. (1993). *Fire in the soul: A new psychology of spiritual optimism*. New York: Warner Books.

Borysenko, J., & Borysenko, M. (1994). *The power of the mind to heal: Renewing body, mind, and spirit*. Carlsbad, CA: Hay House.

Bowlby, J. (1969). *Attachment and loss: Volume 1. Attachment*. New York: Basic Books.

Boyce, M. (1979). *Zoroastrians: Their religious beliefs and practices*. New York: Routledge.

Boyce, M. (1984). *Textual sources for the study of Zoroastrianism*. Dover, NH: Manchester University Press.

Bradley, L. J., & Gould, L. J. (1993). Individual counseling: Creative interventions. In A. Vernon (Ed.), *Counseling children and adolescents* (pp. 83–117). Denver, CO: Love.

Brawer, P. A., Handal, P. J., Fabricatore, A. N., Roberts, R., & Wajda-Johnston, V. A. (2002). Training and education in religion/spirituality within APA-accredited clinical psychology programs. *Professional Psychology: Research and Practice, 33*, 203–206.

Brazier, D. (1995). *Zen therapy*. London: Constable.

Brown, H. P., & Peterson, J. H. (1990). Rationale and procedural suggestions for defining and actualizing spiritual values in the treatment of dependency. *Alcoholism Treatment Quarterly, 7*(3), 7–46.

Brown, V. L., Jr. (1981). *Human intimacy: Illusion and reality*. Salt Lake City, UT: Parliament.

Brush, S. G. (1988). *The history of modern science: A guide to the second scientific revolution, 1800–1950*. Ames: Iowa State University Press.

Buber, M. (1996). *I and thou* (W. Kaufmann, Trans.). New York: Simon & Schuster. (Original work published 1923)

Bullis, R. K. (2001). *Sacred calling, secular accountability: Law and ethics in complementary and spiritual counseling*. Philadelphia: Brunner-Routledge.

Burns, D. (1980). *Feeling good: The new mood therapy*. New York: Morrow.

Burns, E. M., & Ralph, P. L. (1974). *World civilizations: Their history and their culture* (5th ed.). New York: Norton.

Burtt, E. A. (1955). *The metaphysical foundations of modern physical science*. Garden City, NY: Doubleday.

Butler, M. H., Gardner, B. C., & Bird, M. H. (1998). Not just a time-out: Change dynamics of prayer for religious couples in conflict situations. *Family Process, 37*, 451–478.

Butler, M. H., & Harper, J. M. (1994). The divine triangle: God in the marital system of religious couples. *Family Process, 33*, 277–286.

Butler, M. H., Stout, J. S., & Gardner, B. C. (2002). Prayer as a conflict resolution ritual: Clinical implications of religious couples' report of relationship softening, healing perspective, and change responsibility. *American Journal of Family Therapy, 30*, 19–37.

Buxton, M. E., Smith, D. E., & Seymour, R. B. (1987). Spirituality and other points of resistance to the 12-step recovery process. *Journal of Psychoactive Drugs, 19*, 275–286.

Byrd, R. C. (1988). Positive therapeutic effects of intercessory prayer in a coronary care unit. *Southern Medical Journal, 81*, 826–829.

Campbell, D. T. (1975). On the conflicts between biological and social evolution and between psychology and moral tradition. *American Psychologist, 30*, 1103–1126.

Capra, F. (1983). *The Tao of physics: An exploration of the parallels between modern physics and Eastern mysticism* (2nd ed.). Boulder, CO: Shambhala.

Cardena, E., Lynn, S. J., & Krippner, S. (Eds.). (2000). *Varieties of anomalous experience: Examining the scientific evidence*. Washington, DC: American Psychological Association.

Carlson, C. R., Bacaseta, P. E., & Simanton, D. A. (1988). A controlled evaluation of devotional meditation and progressive relaxation. *Journal of Psychology and Theology, 16*, 362–368.

Carmody, D. L., & Carmody, J. T. (1989). *Christianity: An introduction* (2nd ed.). Belmont, CA: Wadsworth.

Carter, E. F., McCullough, M. E., Sandage, S. J., & Worthington, E. L., Jr. (1994, August). *What happens when people forgive? Theories, speculations, and implications for individual and marital therapy*. Paper presented at the 102nd Annual Convention of the American Psychological Association, Los Angeles.

Castaneda, R., & Galanter, M. (1987). A review of treatment modalities for alcoholism and their outcome. *American Journal of Social Psychiatry, 7*, 237–244.

Chadwick, B. (1993). Religiosity and delinquency among LDS adolescents. *Journal for the Scientific Study of Religion, 32*, 51–67.

Chalfant, H. P., Heller, P. L., Roberts, A., Briones, D., Aguirre-Hochbaum, S., & Farr, W. (1990). The clergy as a resource for those encountering psychological distress. *Review of Religious Research, 31*, 305–313.

Chamberlain, R. B., Richards, P. S., & Scharman, J. S. (1996). Using spiritual perspectives and interventions in psychotherapy: A qualitative study of experienced AMCAP therapists. *Association of Mormon Counselors and Psychotherapists Journal, 22,* 29–74.

Chandler, C. K., Holden, J. M., & Kolander, C. A. (1992). Counseling for spiritual wellness: Theory and practice. *Journal of Counseling and Development, 71,* 168–175.

Chausse, M. (2003, March). Event to teach health and spirit integration. *Research News and Opportunities in Science and Theology, 3*(7), 5, 33.

Chauvin, J. C. (2000). Spirituality, psychotherapy, and the gifted individual. *Advanced Development, 9,* 123–135.

Chew, J. (1998). *Women survivors of childhood sexual abuse: Healing through group work: Beyond survival.* Binghamton, NY: Haworth Press.

Chirban, J. T. (2001). Assessing religious and spiritual concerns in psychotherapy. In T. G. Plante & A. C. Sherman (Eds.), *Faith and health: Psychological perspectives* (pp. 265–290). New York: Guilford Press.

Church of Jesus Christ of Latter-Day Saints. (1979). *The holy bible: Authorized King James version.* Salt Lake City, UT: Author.

Ciarrocchi, J. W. (2002). Counseling problem gamblers: A self-regulation manual for individual and family therapy. *Family Therapy, 29,* 183.

Citizens Commission on Human Rights International. (1997). *Creating evil: Psychiatry destroying religion.* Los Angeles: Author. Retrieved February 21, 2005, from http://www.cchr.org/religion/page00.htm

Clark, M. E. (1998). Human nature: What we need to know about ourselves in the twenty-first century. *Zygon, 33,* 645–659.

Clark, R. W. (1971). *Einstein: The life and times.* New York: World.

Clayton, P. (2003, October). A program ends, the quest for science-and-religion continues. *Research News and Opportunities in Science and Theology, 4*(2), 2–3, 33.

Cole, B., & Pargament, K. (1999). Re-creating your life: A spiritual/psychotherapeutic intervention for people diagnosed with cancer. *Psycho-Oncology, 8,* 395–407.

Cole, B. S. (2000). The integration of spirituality and psychotherapy for people confronting cancer: An outcome study. *Dissertation Abstracts International, 61* (02), 1075B.

Coles, R. (1990). *The spiritual life of children.* Boston: Houghton Mifflin.

Collins, G. R. (1977). *The rebuilding of psychology: An integration of psychology and Christianity.* Wheaton, IL: Tyndale House.

Collins, G. R. (1988). *Christian counseling: A comprehensive guide* (Rev. ed.). Dallas, TX: Word.

Collipp, P. J. (1969). The efficacy of prayer: A triple blind study. *Medical Times, 97,* 201–204.

Corbett, L., & Stein, M. (2005). Contemporary Jungian approaches to spiritually oriented psychotherapy. In L. Sperry & E. P. Shafranske (Eds.), *Spiritually oriented psychotherapy* (pp. 51–73). Washington, DC: American Psychological Association.

Corey, G. (2005). *Theory and practice of counseling and psychotherapy* (7th ed.). Pacific Grove, CA: Brooks/Cole.

Corey, G., Corey, M. S., & Callanan, P. (2003). *Issues and ethics in the helping professions* (6th ed.). Pacific Grove, CA: Brooks/Cole.

Cormier, L. S., Cormier, W. H., & Weisser, R. J. (1984). *Interviewing and helping skills for health professionals.* Belmont, CA: Wadsworth.

Cormier, L. S., & Hackney, H. (1987). *The professional counselor: A process guide to helping.* Englewood Cliffs, NJ: Prentice Hall.

Cormier, W. H., & Cormier, L. S. (1991). *Interviewing strategies for helpers: Fundamental skills and cognitive behavioral interventions.* Pacific Grove, CA: Brooks/Cole.

Coulson, W. R., & Rogers, C. R. (1968). *Man and the science of man.* Columbus, OH: Charles E. Merrill.

Covey, S. R. (1989). *The seven habits of highly effective people.* New York: Simon & Schuster.

Crabb, L. J., Jr. (1982). *The marriage builder: A blueprint for couples and counselors.* Grand Rapids, MI: Zondervan.

Craigie, F. C., Jr., & Tan, S. Y. (1989). Changing resistant assumptions in Christian cognitive–behavioral therapy. *Journal of Psychology and Theology, 17,* 93–100.

Crook-Lyon, R., O'Grady, K. A., & Richards, P. S. (October 1, 2004). *Training in spiritual knowledge, skills, and awareness.* Paper presented at the semi-annual convention of the Association of Mormon Counselors and Psychotherapist, Salt Lake City, UT.

Davis-Russell, E. (2002). Religiosity and racial identity attitudes: Clinically relevant factors in psychotherapy with African Americans. In E. Davis-Russell (Ed.), *The California school of professional psychology handbook of multicultural education, research, intervention, and training* (pp. 263–276). San Francisco: Jossey-Bass.

Davidson, M. G. (2000). Religion and spirituality. In R. M. Perez & K. A. DeBord et al. (Eds.), *Handbook of counseling and psychotherapy with lesbian, gay, and bisexual clients* (pp. 409–433). Washington, DC: American Psychological Association.

Davies, P. (1988). *The cosmic blueprint.* New York: Simon & Schuster.

Davies, P. (1992). *The mind of God: The scientific basis for a rational world.* New York: Simon & Schuster.

Davies, P. (1999). *The 5th miracle: The search for the origin and meaning of life.* New York: Touchstone.

Day, J. M., & Tappan, M. B. (1996). The narrative approach to moral development: From the epistemic subject to dialogical selves. *Human Development, 39,* 67–82.

Dembski, W. A. (2001). *No free lunch: Why specified complexity cannot be purchased without intelligence.* Lanham, MD: Rowman & Littlefield.

Dembski, W. A. (Ed.). (2004). *Uncommon descent: Intellectuals who find Darwinism unconvincing.* Wilmington, DE: ISI Books.

Denzin, N. K., & Lincoln, Y. S. (Eds.). (1994). *Handbook of qualitative research.* Thousand Oaks, CA: Sage.

DiBlasio, F. A. (1992). Forgiveness in psychotherapy: Comparison of older and younger therapists. *Journal of Psychology and Christianity, 11,* 181–187.

DiBlasio, F. A. (1993). The role of social workers' religious beliefs in helping family members forgive. *Families in Society, 74,* 163–170.

DiBlasio, F. A., & Benda, B. B. (1991). Practitioners, religion and the use of forgiveness in the clinical setting. *Journal of Psychology and Christianity, 10,* 166–172.

DiBlasio, F. A., & Proctor, J. H. (1993). Therapists and the clinical use of forgiveness. *American Journal of Family Therapy, 21,* 175–184.

Dickie, J. R., Merasco, D. L., Geurink, A., & Johnson, M. (1993, August). *Mother, father, God: Children's perceptions of nurturing authority figures.* Paper presented at the 101st Annual Convention of the American Psychological Association, Toronto.

Dickson, P. (1995). The phenomenology of evil. *Journal of Value Inquiry, 29,* 5–12.

Dilthey, W. (1978). *Dilthey's philosophy of existence: Introduction to* Weltanschauungslehre (W. Kluback & M. Weinbaum, Trans.). Westport, CT: Greenwood Press.

Dittes, J. E. (1971). Religion, prejudice, and personality. In M. Strommen (Ed.), *Research on religious development: A comprehensive handbook* (pp. 355–390). New York: Hawthorn Books.

Dixon, T. (2002). Scientific atheism as a faith tradition. *Studies in History, Philosophy, Biology, and Biomedical Science, 33,* 337–359.

Doherty, W. I. (1995). *Soul searching: Why psychotherapy must promote moral responsibility.* New York: Basic Books.

Dollahite, D., Slife, B., & Hawkins, A. (1998). Family generativity and generative counseling: Helping families keep faith with the next generation. In D. P. McAdams & D. S. Aubin (Eds.), *Generativity and adult development: How and why we care for the next generation* (pp. 449–481). Washington, DC: American Psychological Association.

Donahue, M. J. (1985). Intrinsic and extrinsic religiousness: Review and meta-analysis. *Journal of Personality and Social Psychology, 48,* 400–419.

Dossey, L. (1993). *Healing words: The power of prayer and the practice of medicine.* San Francisco: HarperCollins.

Drakeman, D. L. (1991). *Church–state constitutional issues: Making sense of the establishment clause.* Westport, CT: Greenwood Press.

Duckro, P. N., & Magaletta, P. R. (1994). The effect of prayer on physical health: Experimental evidence. *Journal of Religion and Health, 33,* 211–219.

Duncan, H. D., Eddy, J. P., & Haney, C. W. (1981). Using religious resources in crisis intervention. *Counseling and Values, 25,* 178–191.

Dupont, R. L., & McGovern, J. P. (1994). *A bridge to recovery: An introduction to 12–step programs.* Washington, DC: American Psychiatric Association.

Eccles, J., & Robinson, D. N. (1984). *The wonder of being human: Our brain and our mind*. New York: Free Press.

Edwards, P. (Ed.). (1967). *The encyclopedia of philosophy* (Vol. 6). New York: Macmillan Free Press.

Eigen, M. (1998). One reality. In A. Molino (Ed.), *The couch and the tree: Dialogues in psychoanalysis and Buddhism* (pp. 217–230). New York: North Point Press.

Eisenberg, N., & Miller, P. A. (1987). The relation of empathy to prosocial and related behaviors. *Psychological Bulletin, 101*, 91–119.

Elkind, D. (1978). *The child's reality: Three developmental themes*. Hillsdale, NJ: Erlbaum.

Elkind, D. (1982). Piagetian psychology and the practice of child psychiatry. *Journal of the American Academy of Child Psychiatry, 21*, 435–445.

Elkins, D. (2005). A humanistic approach to spiritually oriented psychotherapy. In L. Sperry & E. P. Shafranske (Eds.), *Spiritually oriented psychotherapy* (pp. 131–151). Washington, DC: American Psychological Association.

Elkins, D. N. (1995). Psychotherapy and spirituality: Toward a theory of the soul. *Journal of Humanistic Psychology, 35*, 78–98.

Ellis, A. (1971). *The case against religion: A psychotherapist's view*. New York: Institute for Rational Living.

Ellis, A. (1973). *Humanistic psychotherapy: The rational–emotive approach*. New York: Julian Press.

Ellis, A. (1980). Psychotherapy and atheistic values: A response to A. E. Bergin's "Psychotherapy and Religious Values." *Journal of Consulting and Clinical Psychology, 48*, 635–639.

Ellis, A. (1986). Fanaticism that may lead to a nuclear holocaust: The contributions of scientific counseling and psychotherapy. *Journal of Counseling and Development, 65*, 146–151.

Ellis, A. (1993). The advantages and disadvantages of self-help therapy materials. *Professional Psychology: Research and Practice, 24*, 335–339.

Ellis, A. (1996, August). Discussant. In A. P. Jackson & S. L. Neilsen (Chairs), *Religiously oriented REBT: Reconciling the sacred and the profane*. Symposium conducted at the 104th Annual Convention of the American Psychological Association, Toronto.

Ellison, C. W. (1983). Spiritual well-being: Conceptualization and measurement. *Journal of Psychology and Theology, 11*, 330–340.

Ellison, C. W., & Smith, J. (1991). Toward an integrative measure of health and well-being. *Journal of Psychology and Theology, 19*, 35–48.

Ellsworth, S. G. (1995). *How I got this way and what to do about it*. Draper, UT: Author.

Emery, E. E. (2003). Living history-spiritually . . . or not? A comparison of conventional and spiritually integrated reminiscence groups. *Dissertation Abstracts International, 63*, 4898B.

Emmons, R. A. (1999). *The psychology of ultimate concerns: Motivation and spirituality in personality*. New York: Guilford Press.

Emmons, R. A., & Crumpler, C. A. (2000). Classical sources of human strength: A psychological analysis. *Journal of Social and Clinical Psychology, 19*, 56–69.

Emmons, R. A., & Paloutzian, R. F. (2003). The psychology of religion. *Annual Review of Psychology, 54*, 377–402.

Emmons, R. A., & Shelton, C. M. (2002). Gratitude and the science of positive psychology. In C. R. Snyder & S. J. Lopez (Eds.), *Handbook of positive psychology* (pp. 459–471). New York: Oxford University Press.

Enright, R. D. (2001). *Forgiveness is a choice: A step-by-step process for resolving anger and restoring hope*. Washington, DC: American Psychological Association.

Enright, R. D., & Fitzgibbons, R. P. (2000). *Helping clients forgive: An empirical guide for resolving anger and restoring hope*. Washington, DC: American Psychological Association.

Epstein, M. (1995). *Thoughts without a thinker: Psychotherapy from a Buddhist perspective*. New York: Basic Books.

Erikson, E. H. (1963). *Childhood and society* (2nd ed.). New York: Norton.

Erikson, E. H. (1968). *Identity: Youth and crisis*. New York: Norton.

Ermarth, M. (1978). *Wilhelm Dilthey: The critique of historical reason*. Chicago: University of Chicago Press.

Estadt, B. K., Blanschette, M., & Compton, J. R. (1983). *Pastoral counseling*. Englewood Cliffs, NJ: Prentice Hall.

Etzioni, A. (1994). *The spirit of community: The reinvention of American society*. New York: Simon & Schuster.

Everly, G. S., & Lating, J. M. (2002). *A clinical guide to the treatment of the human stress response* (2nd ed.). New York: Kluwer Academic.

Faiver, C., Ingersoll, R. E., O'Brien, E. M., & McNally, C. (2001). *Explorations in counseling and spirituality: Philosophical, practical, and personal reflections*. Belmont, CA: Thomson Learning-Brooks/Cole.

Farah, C. E. (1994). *Islam: Beliefs and observances* (5th ed.). Hauppauge, NY: Barron's Educational Series.

Faulconer, J. E., & Williams, R. N. (1985). Temporality in human action: An alternative to positivism and historicism. *American Psychologist, 40*, 1179–1188.

Faust, D. (1984). *The limits of scientific reasoning*. Minneapolis: University of Minnesota Press.

Fennema, J., & Paul, I. (Eds.). (1990). *Science and religion: One world changing perspectives on reality*. Norwell, MA: Kluwer Academic.

Ferch, S. R., & Ramsey, M. I. (2003). Sacred conversation: A spiritual response to unavoidable suffering. *Canadian Journal of Counseling, 37*(1), 16–27.

Finney, J. R., & Malony, H. N. (1985a). Empirical studies of Christian prayer: A review of the literature. *Journal of Psychology and Theology, 13*, 104–115.

Finney, J. R., & Malony, H. N. (1985b). Contemplative prayer and its use in psychotherapy: A theoretical model. *Journal of Psychology and Theology, 13*, 172–181.

Finney, J. R., & Malony, H. N. (1985c). An empirical study of contemplative prayer as an adjunct to psychotherapy. *Journal of Psychology and Theology, 13*, 284–290.

Fischer, L., & Sorenson, G. P. (1985). *School law for counselors, psychologists, and social workers*. New York: Longman.

Flowers, R. B. (1994). *That godless court?: Supreme court decisions on church–state relationships*. Louisville, KY: Westminster John Knox Press.

Fowler, J. W. (1981). *Stages of faith: The psychology of human development and the quest for meaning*. New York: Harper & Row.

Fowler, J. W. (1991). Stages in faith consciousness. In F. K. Oser & W. G. Scarlett (Eds.), *Religious development in childhood and adolescence* (pp. 27–45). San Francisco: Jossey-Bass.

Fowler, J. W. (1996). Pluralism and oneness in religious experience: William James, faith-development theory, and clinical practice. In E. P. Shafranske (Ed.), *Religion and the clinical practice of psychology* (pp. 165–186). Washington, DC: American Psychological Association.

Fox, M. (2003). *Religion, spirituality, and the near-death experience*. London: Routledge.

Frame, M. W. (2000). Constructing religious/spiritual genograms. In R. E. Watts (Ed.), *Techniques in marriage and family counseling. The family psychology and counseling series* (Vol. 1, pp. 69–74). Alexandria, VA: American Counseling Association.

Frame, M. W. (2003). *Integrating religion and spirituality into counseling: A comprehensive approach*. Pacific Grove, CA: Thomson Learning-Brooks/Cole.

Frankel, E. (2001). Kabbalah as sacred psychology. *Women and Therapy, 24*, 55–73.

Frankl, V. E. (1959). *Man's search for meaning*. New York: Washington Square Press.

Fredenberg, J. R. (2002). The Buddhist psychologist: An exploration into spirituality and psychotherapy (Doctoral Dissertation, Chicago School of Professional Psychology, 2002). *Dissertation Abstracts International, 63*(4), 2055B.

Freedman, S. R., & Enright, R. D. (1996). Forgiveness as an intervention goal with incest survivors. *Journal of Consulting and Clinical Psychology, 64*, 983–992.

Freeman, D. W., Wofson, R., & Affolter, H. U. (1998). Spiritual dimensions of a mind–body group for people with severe mental illness. In R. D. Fallot (Ed.), *Spirituality and religion in recovery from mental illness. New directions for mental health services* (pp. 57–67). San Francisco: Jossey-Bass/Pfeiffer.

French, A. C., & Piedmont, R. L. (2004, March 19 & 20). *An evaluation of the reliability and validity of the revised Spiritual Transcendence Scale—Short form*. Poster session presented at the annual APA Division 36 Mid-Winter Conference on Religion and Spirituality, Columbia, MD.

Freud, S. (1927). *The future of an illusion*. Garden City, NY: Doubleday.

Freud, S. (1961). *The future of an illusion* (J. Strachey, Ed. & Trans.). New York: Norton. (Original work published 1927)

Friedman, M., Thoresen, C. E., Gill, J. J., Powell, L., Ulmer, D., Thompson, L., et al. (1984). Alteration of Type A behavior and reduction in cardiac recurrences in postmyocardial infarction patients. *American Heart Journal, 108*, 237–248.

Friend, T. (1995, September 20). Patient calls Ornish program miraculous. *USA Today*, pp. 1–2.

Friends in Recovery. (1994). *The twelve steps for Christians: Based on biblical teachings* (Rev. ed.). San Diego, CA: RPI.

Fromm, E. (1956). *The art of loving*. New York: Harper & Row.

Fukuyama, M., & Sevig, T. (1999). *Integrating spirituality into multicultural counseling*. Thousand Oaks, CA: Sage.

Fuller, A. R. (1986). *Psychology and religion: Eight points of view* (2nd ed.). Lanham, MD: University Press of America.

Fullerton, J. T., & Hunsberger, B. (1982). A unidimensional measure of Christian orthodoxy. *Journal for the Scientific Study of Religion, 21*, 317–326.

Funderburk, J. R., & Fukuyama, M. A. (2001). Feminism, multiculturalism, and spirituality: Convergent and divergent forces in psychotherapy. *Women and Therapy, 24*(3–4), 1–18.

Galanter, M. (1996). Cults and charismatic groups. In E. Shafranske (Ed.), *Religion and the clinical practice of psychology* (pp. 269–296). Washington, DC: American Psychological Association.

Gallup, G. H. (2003, January 7). Public gives organized religion its lowest rating. *Gallup Poll Tuesday Briefing*, pp. 1–2. (Available from The Gallup Organization, 502 Carnegie Center, Suite 300, Princeton, NJ 08540)

Gallup Organization. (1993). Report on trends. *Gallup Poll Monthly, 331*, 36–38.

Ganje-Fling, M. A., & McCarthy, P. R. (1991). A comparative analysis of spiritual direction and psychotherapy. *Journal of Psychology and Theology, 19*, 103–117.

Ganje-Fling, M., & McCarthy, P. R. (1994, April). *Impact of childhood sexual abuse on client spiritual development: Counseling implications*. Paper presented at the annual convention of the American Counseling Association, Minneapolis, MN.

Gardner, H. (1985). *The mind's new science: A history of the cognitive revolution*. New York: Basic Books.

Garfield, S. L., & Bergin, A. E. (Eds.). (1986). *Handbook of psychotherapy and behavior change* (3rd ed.). New York: Wiley.

Gartner, J., Larson, D. B., & Allen, G. D. (1991). Religious commitment and mental health: A review of the empirical literature. *Journal of Psychology and Theology, 19*, 6–25.

Genia, V. (1995). *Counseling and psychotherapy for religious clients: A developmental approach*. Westport, CT: Praeger.

Gergen, K. J. (1982). *Toward transformation in social knowledge*. New York: Springer-Verlag.

Gergen, K. J. (1985). The social constructionist movement in modern psychology. *American Psychologist, 40,* 266–275.

Giberson, K. (2003, September). Science-and-religion is alive and well. *Research News and Opportunities in Science and Theology, 4*(1), 4.

Giberson, K. W., & Yerxa, D. A. (2002). *Species of origins: America's search for a creation story.* Lanham, MD: Rowman & Littlefield.

Gillham, J. E., & Seligman, M. E. P. (1999). Footsteps on the road to positive psychology. *Behaviour Research and Therapy, 37,* S163–S173.

Gilligan, C. (1982). *In a different voice: Psychological theory and women's development.* Cambridge, MA: Harvard University Press.

Glock, C. Y., & Stark, R. (1965). *Religion and society in tension.* Chicago: Rand McNally.

Gorsuch, R. (1968). The conceptualization of God as seen in adjective ratings. *Journal for the Scientific Study of Religion, 7,* 56–64.

Gorsuch, R. L. (1984). Measurement: The boon and bane of investigating religion. *American Psychologist, 39,* 228–236.

Gorsuch, R. L. (2002). The pyramid of sciences and of humanities: Implications for the search for religious "truth." *American Behavioral Scientist, 45,* 1822–1838.

Gorsuch, R. L., & McPherson, S. E. (1989). Intrinsic/extrinsic measurement: I/E-revised and single-item scales. *Journal for the Scientific Study of Religion, 28,* 348–354.

Gorsuch, R. L., & Miller, W. R. (1999). Assessing spirituality. In W. R. Miller (Ed.), *Integrating spirituality into treatment: Resources for practitioners* (pp. 47–64). Washington, DC: American Psychological Association.

Grame, C. J., Tortorici, J. S., Bede, J., Healey, B. J., Dillingham, J. H., & Winklebaur, P. (1999). Addressing spiritual and religious issues of clients with a history of psychological trauma. *Bulletin of the Menninger Clinic, 63*(2), 223–239.

Greeley, A. M. (1975). *The sociology of the paranormal, a reconnaissance.* Beverly Hills, CA: Sage.

Greenberg, L. (1986). Change process research. *Journal of Consulting and Clinical Psychology, 54,* 4–9.

Greenberg, L., Elliott, R., & Lietaer, G. (1994). Research on experiential psychotherapies. In A. E. Bergin & S. L. Garfield (Eds.), *Handbook of psychotherapy and behavior change* (4th ed., pp. 509–539). New York: Wiley.

Greyson, B. (2000). Near-death experiences. In E. Cardena, S. J. Lynn, & S. Krippner (Eds.), *Varieties of anomalous experience: Examining the scientific evidence* (pp. 315–352). Washington, DC: American Psychological Association.

Griffin, D. R. (1989). *God and religion in the postmodern world: Essays in postmodern theology.* Albany: State University of New York Press.

Griffin, D. R. (2000). *Religion and scientific naturalism: Overcoming the conflicts.* Albany: State University of New York Press.

Griffin, D. R. (2001). *Reenchantment without supernaturalism: A process philosophy of religion.* London: Cornell University Press.

Griffin, D. R., Cobb, J. B., Ford, M. P., Gunter, P. A., & Ochs, P. (1993). *Founders of constructive postmodern philosophy: Pierce, James, Bergson, Whitehead, and Hartshorne*. Albany: State University of New York Press.

Griffith, J. L. (1986). Employing the God–family relationship in therapy with religious families. *Family Process, 25*, 609–618.

Griffith, J. L., & Griffith, M. E. (2002). *Encountering the sacred in psychotherapy: How to talk with people about their spiritual lives*. New York: Guilford Press.

Groth-Marnat, G. (1989). The near-death experience: A review and critique. *Journal of Humanistic Psychology, 29*, 109–133.

Gurman, A. S., & Kniskern, D. P. (1981). *Handbook of family therapy*. New York: Brunner/Mazel.

Haidt, J. (2001). The emotional dog and its rational tail: A social intuitionist approach to moral judgment. *Psychological Review, 108*, 814–834.

Hall, C. S., & Lindzey, G. (1978). *Introduction to theories of personality* (3rd ed.). New York: Wiley.

Hall, C. S., Lindzey, G., & Campbell, J. B. (1998). *Theories of personality* (4th ed.). New York: Wiley.

Hall, L., & Cohn, L. (1992). *Bulimia: A guide to recovery*. Carlsbad, CA: Gurze Books.

Hall, T. W., Tisdale, T. C., & Brokaw, B. F. (1994). Assessment of religious dimensions in Christian clients: A review of selected instruments for research and clinical use. *Journal of Psychology and Theology, 22*, 395–421.

Hardman, R. K., Berrett, M. E., & Richards, P. S. (2004). A theistic inpatient treatment approach for eating-disorder patients: A case report. In P. S. Richards & A. E. Bergin (Eds.), *Casebook for a spiritual strategy in counseling and psychotherapy* (pp. 55–73). Washington, DC: American Psychological Association.

Harris, E. S. (2000). God, Buber and the practice of Gestalt therapy. *Gestalt Journal, 23*(1), 39–62.

Harris, R. (2002). *Christ-centered therapy: Empowering the self*. New York: Haworth Press.

Hartsman, E. E. (2002). Jewish anthropology: The stuff between. In R. P. Olsen (Ed.), *Religious theories of personality and psychotherapy: East meets west* (pp. 245–211). New York: Haworth Press.

Havighurst, R. (1972). *Developmental tasks and education*. New York: McKay.

Hawkins, R. S., Tan, S. Y., & Turk, A. A. (1999). Secular versus Christian inpatient cognitive–behavioral therapy programs: Impact on depression and spiritual well-being. *Journal of Psychology and Theology, 27*, 309–318.

Hay, D., & Morisy, A. (1978). Reports of ecstatic, paranormal, or religious experience in Great Britain and the United States: A comparison of trends. *Journal for the Scientific Study of Religion, 17*, 255–268.

Hearnshaw, L. S. (1987). *The shaping of modern psychology*. New York: Routledge & Kegan Paul.

Hebl, J., & Enright, R. D. (1993). Forgiveness as a psychotherapeutic goal with elderly females. *Psychotherapy, 30*, 658–667.

Hedayat-Diba, Z. (2000). Psychotherapy with Muslims. In P. S. Richards & A. E. Bergin (Eds.), *Handbook of psychotherapy and religious diversity* (pp. 289–314). Washington, DC: American Psychological Association.

Heiler, F. (1958). *Prayer* (S. McComb, Ed. & Trans.). New York: Oxford University Press. (Original work published 1932)

Helminiak, D. A. (1996). *The human core of spirituality: Mind as psyche and spirit.* Albany: State University of New York Press.

Henning, L. H., & Tirrell, F. J. (1982). Counselor resistance to spiritual exploration. *Personnel and Guidance Journal, 61,* 92–95.

Heppner, P. P., Kivlighan, D. M., Jr., & Wampold, B. E. (1992). *Research design in counseling.* Pacific Grove, CA: Brooks/Cole.

Herlihy, B., & Golden, L. (1990). *Ethical standards casebook* (4th ed.). Alexandria, VA: American Association for Counseling and Development Press.

Hesse, M. (1980). *Revolutions and reconstructions in the philosophy of science.* Bloomington: Indiana State University Press.

Hester, M. (2002). Psychology of religion: Then and now. In *The teaching of psychology: A tribute to Wilbert McKeachie and Charles Brewer.* Mahwah, NJ: Erlbaum.

Hetherington, E. M., Parke, R. D., & Locke, V. O. (1999). *Child psychology: A contemporary viewpoint.* New York: McGraw-Hill.

Hiatt, J. F. (1999). A transpersonal care program in an institutional setting. *Psychiatric Annals, 29,* 480–483.

Hill, C. H., & Hood, R. W. (1999). *Measures of religiosity.* Birmingham, AL: Religious Education Press.

Hill, P. C., & Pargament, K. I. (2003). Advances in the conceptualization and measurement of religion and spirituality. *American Psychologist, 58,* 64–74.

Hill, P. C., Pargament, K. I., Hood, R. W., McCullough, M. E., Swyers, J. P., Larson, D., et al. (2000). Conceptualizing religion and spirituality: Points of commonality, points of departure. *Journal for the Theory of Social Behaviour, 30*(1), 51–77.

Hillner, K. P. (1984). *History and systems of modern psychology: A conceptual approach.* New York: Gardner Press.

Hinterkopf, E. (2005). The experiential focusing approach. In L. Sperry & E. P. Shafranske (Eds.), *Spiritually oriented psychotherapy* (pp. 207–233). Washington, DC: American Psychological Association.

Hirai, T. (1989). *Zen meditation and psychotherapy.* Tokyo: Japan Publications.

Hirschberg, C., & Barasch, M. I. (1995). *Remarkable recovery.* New York: Riverhead.

Hoge, D. R. (1996). Religion in America: The demographics of belief and affiliation. In E. P. Shafranske (Ed.), *Religion and the clinical practice of psychology* (pp. 21–41). Washington, DC: American Psychological Association.

Honer, S. M., & Hunt, T. C. (1987). *Invitation to philosophy: Issues and options* (5th ed.). Belmont, CA: Wadsworth.

Hood, R. W., Jr. (1975). The construction and preliminary validation of a measure of reported mystical experience. *Journal for the Scientific Study of Religion, 14*, 29–41.

Hood, R. W., Jr. (Ed.). (1995). *Handbook of religious experience.* Birmingham, AL: Religious Education Press.

Hood, R. W., Jr., Spilka, B., Hunsberger, B., & Gorsuch, R. L. (1996). *The psychology of religion: An empirical approach.* New York: Guilford Press.

Hope, D. (1987). The healing paradox of forgiveness. *Psychotherapy, 24*, 240–244.

Hopson, R. E. (1996). The 12-step program. In E. P. Shafranske (Ed.), *Religion and the clinical practice of psychology* (pp. 533–558). Washington, DC: American Psychological Association.

Horner, D., & Vandersluis, P. (1981). Cross-cultural counseling. In G. Althen (Ed.), *Learning across cultures* (pp. 25–38). Washington, DC: National Association for Foreign Student Affairs.

Howard, G. S. (1985). The role of values in the science of psychology. *American Psychologist, 40*, 255–265.

Howard, G. S. (1986). *Dare we develop a human science?* Notre Dame, IN: Academic.

Howard, G. S., & Conway, C. G. (1986). Can there be an empirical science of volitional action? *American Psychologist, 41*, 1241–1251.

Hudgins, H. C., Jr., & Vacca, R. S. (1995). *Law and education: Contemporary issues and court decisions* (4th ed.). Charlottesville, VA: Michie Law.

Hunt, R. A., & King, M. B. (1971). The intrinsic–extrinsic concept: A review and evaluation. *Journal of the Scientific Study of Religion, 10*, 339–356.

Hunter, C. G. (2003). *Darwin's proof: The triumph of religion over science.* Grand Rapids, MI: Brazo Press.

Ibrahim, F. A. (1985). Effective cross-cultural counseling and psychotherapy: A framework. *Counseling Psychologist, 13*, 625–638.

Ibrahim, F. A. (1991). Contribution of cultural worldview to generic counseling and development. *Journal of Counseling and Development, 70*, 13–19.

Ivey, A., Ivey, M., Myers, J., & Sweeney, T. (2005). *Developmental counseling and therapy: Promoting wellness over the lifespan.* New York: Lahaska Press/ Houghton Mifflin.

Jacobs, L. (1984). *The book of Jewish beliefs.* New York: Behrman House.

Jacques, J. (1998). Working with spiritual and religious themes in group therapy. *International Journal of Group Psychotherapy, 48*(1), 69–83.

James, W. (1936). *The varieties of religious experience.* New York: Modern Library. (Original work published 1902)

James, W. (1947). The moral philosopher and the moral life. In W. James, *Essays on faith and morals* (pp. 184–215). New York: Longmans, Green.

Jensen, J. P., & Bergin, A. E. (1988). Mental health values of professional therapists: A national interdisciplinary survey. *Professional Psychology: Research and Practice, 19*, 290–297.

Jensen, J. P., Bergin, A. E., & Greaves, D. W. (1990). The meaning of eclecticism: New survey and analysis of components. *Professional Psychology: Research and Practice, 21,* 124–130.

Jersild, A. (2001). Field mice and mustard seeds: Approaching spirituality as a therapeutic tool. *Eating Disorders: The Journal of Treatment and Prevention, 9,* 267–273.

John Templeton Foundation. (n.d.). Retrieved February 9, 2005, from http://www.templeton.org

Johnson, P. E. (1993). *Reason in the balance: The case against naturalism in science, law, and education.* Downers Grove, IL: InterVarsity Press.

Johnson, W. B. (1993a). Christian rational–emotive therapy: A treatment protocol. *Journal of Psychology and Christianity, 12,* 254–261.

Johnson, W. B. (1993b). Outcome research and religious psychotherapies: Where are we and where are we going? *Journal of Psychology and Theology, 21,* 297–308.

Johnson, W. B. (2004). Rational emotive behavior therapy for disturbance about sexual orientation (pp. 247–265). In P. S. Richards & A. E. Bergin (Eds.), *Casebook for a spiritual strategy in counseling and psychotherapy.* Washington, DC: American Psychological Association.

Johnson, W. B., Devries, R., Ridley, C. R., Pettorini, D., & Peterson, D. R. (1994). The comparative efficacy of Christian and secular rational–emotive therapy with Christian clients. *Journal of Psychology and Theology, 22,* 130–140.

Johnson, W. B., & Ridley, C. R. (1992). Brief Christian and non-Christian rational–emotive therapy with depressed Christian clients: An exploratory study. *Counseling and Values, 36,* 220–229.

Jones, S., & Butman, R. (1991). *Modern psychotherapies: A comprehensive Christian appraisal.* Downers Grove, IL: InterVarsity Press.

Jones, S. L. (1994). A constructive relationship for religion with the science and profession of psychology: Perhaps the boldest model yet. *American Psychologist, 49,* 184–199.

Jones, S. L. (1996). A constructive relationship for religion with the science and profession of psychology: Perhaps the boldest model yet. In E. P. Shafranske (Ed.), *Religion and the clinical practice of psychology* (pp. 113–147). Washington, DC: American Psychological Association.

Jones, S. L., Watson, E. J., & Wolfram, T. J. (1992). Results of the Rech Conference Survey on religious faith and professional psychology. *Journal of Psychology and Theology, 20,* 147–158.

Josephson, A. M., & Dell, M. L. (2004). Religion and spirituality in child and adolescent psychiatry: A new frontier. *Child and Adolescent Psychiatric Clinics of North America, 13,* 1–15.

Joyce, C. R. B., & Welldon, R. M. C. (1965). The objective efficacy of prayer: A double-blind clinical trial. *Journal of Chronic Disease, 18,* 367–377.

Judd, D. K. (1985). *Religiosity and mental health: A literature review 1928–1985.* Unpublished master's thesis, Brigham Young University, Provo, UT.

Judy, D. H. (1996). Transpersonal psychotherapy with religious persons. In B. W. Scotton et al. (Eds.), *Textbook of transpersonal psychiatry and psychology* (pp. 293–301). New York: Basic Books.

Jung, C. G. (1933). *Modern man in search of a soul*. New York: Harcourt, Brace, & World.

Jung, C. G. (1938). *Psychology and religion*. New Haven, CT: Yale University Press.

Jung, C. (1990). *The basic writings of C. G. Jung*. Princeton, NJ: Princeton University Press.

Kalb, C. (2003, November 10). Faith and healing. *Newsweek*, 44–56.

Kantrowitz, B., King, P., Rosenberg, D., Springen, K., Wingert, P., Namuth, T., et al. (1994, November 28). In search of the sacred. *Newsweek*, 52–62.

Kaplan, M. (1996, June 24). Ambushed by spirituality. *Time*, 62.

Kaplan, P. (1999). Letting in the light: One person's experience of a person-centered process. (Doctoral dissertation, Union Institute, 1999). *Dissertation Abstracts International, 60*(2), 0833B.

Karier, C. J. (1986). *Scientists of the mind: Intellectual founders of modern psychology*. Chicago: University of Illinois Press.

Kass, J. D., Friedman, R., Lesserman, J., Zuttermeister, P., & Benson, H. (1991). Health outcomes and a new index of spiritual experience. *Journal for the Scientific Study of Religion, 30,* 203–211.

Kaufmann, Y. (1989). Analytical psychotherapy. In R. J. Corsini & D. Wedding (Eds.), *Current psychotherapies* (4th ed., pp. 119–152). Itasca, IL: F. E. Peacock.

Kazdin, A. E. (1994). Methodology, design, and evaluation in psychotherapy research. In A. E. Bergin & S. L. Garfield (Eds.), *Handbook of psychotherapy and behavior change* (4th ed., pp. 19–71). New York: Wiley.

Keith-Lucas, A. (1992). Encounters with children: Children and religion. *Residential Treatment for Children and Youth, 10,* 65–73.

Keith-Spiegel, P., & Koocher, G. (1985). *Ethics in psychology: Standards and cases*. New York: Random House.

Keller, R. R. (2000). Religious diversity in North America. In P. S. Richards & A. E. Bergin (Eds.), *Handbook of psychotherapy and religious diversity* (pp. 27–55). Washington, DC: American Psychological Association.

Kelly, E. W. (1993, March). *The status of religious and spiritual issues in counselor education*. Paper presented at the annual convention of the American Counseling Association, Atlanta, GA.

Kelly, E. W. (1994). The role of religion and spirituality in counselor education: A national survey. *Counselor Education and Supervision, 33,* 227–237.

Kelly, E. W. (1995). *Religion and spirituality in counseling and psychotherapy*. Alexandria, VA: American Counseling Association.

Kendall, P. C., Holmbeck, G., & Verduin, T. (2004). Methodology, design, and evaluation in psychotherapy research. In M. J. Lambert (Ed.), *Bergin and*

Garfield's handbook of psychotherapy and behavior change (5th ed., pp. 16–43). New York: Wiley.

Kessell, P., & McBrearty, J. F. (1967). Values and psychotherapy: A review of the literature. *Perceptual and Motor Skills, 25*(Suppl. 2–U25), 669–690.

Killmer, J. M. (2002). The treatment of anxiety disorders in devout Christian clients. *Journal of Family Psychotherapy, 13,* 308–327.

King, M. B. (1967). Measuring the religious variable: Nine proposed dimensions. *Journal for the Scientific Study of Religion, 6,* 173–190.

King, M. B., & Hunt, R. A. (1969). Measuring the religious variable: Amended findings. *Journal for the Scientific Study of Religion, 8,* 321–323.

Kirk, J., & Miller, M. L. (1986). *Reliability and validity in qualitative research.* Beverly Hills, CA: Sage.

Kirkpatrick, L. A. (1989). A psychometric analysis of the Allport-Ross and Feagin measures of intrinsic–extrinsic religious orientation. *Research in the Social Scientific Study of Religion, 1,* 1–31.

Kirkpatrick, L. A. (1999). Attachment and religious representations and behavior. In J. Cassidy & P. R. Shaver (Eds.), *Handbook of attachment: theory, research, and clinical applications* (pp. 803–822) New York: Guilford Press.

Kirkpatrick, L. A., & Hood, R. W., Jr. (1990). Intrinsic–extrinsic religious orientation: The boon or bane of contemporary psychology of religion? *Journal for the Scientific Study of Religion, 29,* 442–462.

Kirschenbaum, H., & Henderson, V. (Eds.). (1990). *The Carl Rogers reader.* London: Constable.

Kitchener, R. F. (1980a). Ethical relativism and behavior therapy. *Journal of Consulting and Clinical Psychology, 48,* 1–7.

Kitchener, R. F. (1980b). Ethical relativism, ethical naturalism, and behavior therapy. *Journal of Consulting and Clinical Psychology, 48,* 14–16.

Klostreich, E. A. (2001). The theory of Christian psychology. (Doctoral dissertation, The Union Institute, 2001). *Dissertation Abstracts International, 62*(7-B), 3381B.

Kluback, W., & Weinbaum, M. (1957). *Dilthey's philosophy of existence: Introduction to* Weltanschauungslehre. Westport, CT: Greenwood Press.

Kluckhohn, C. (1951). Values and value orientations in the theory of action. In T. Parsons & F. A. Shields (Eds.), *Toward a general theory of action* (pp. 388–433). Cambridge, MA: Harvard University Press.

Kluckhohn, C. (1956). Toward a comparison of value-emphasis in different cultures. In L. D. White (Ed.), *The state of social sciences* (pp. 116–132). Chicago: University of Chicago Press.

Kluckhohn, F. R., & Strodtbeck, F. L. (1961). *Variations in value orientations.* Evanston, IL: Row, Peterson.

Kluger, J., & Chu, J. (2004, October 25). Is God in our genes? *Time, 164,* pp. 62–71.

Koch, S. (1959–1963). *Psychology: A study of a science* (Vols. 1–6). New York: McGraw-Hill.

Koch, S. (1981). The nature and limits of psychological knowledge: Lessons of a century of science. *American Psychologist, 36,* 257–269.

Koenig, H. G. (1997). *Is religion good for your health? The effects of religion on physical and mental health.* New York: Haworth Press.

Koenig, H. G. (1998). *Handbook of religion and mental health.* San Diego, CA: Academic Press.

Koenig, H. G. (1999). *The healing power of faith.* New York: Simon & Schuster.

Koenig, H. G., Larson, D. B., & Matthews, D. A. (1996). Religion and psychotherapy with older adults. *Journal of Geriatric Psychiatry, 29,* 155–184.

Koenig, H. G., McCullough, M. E., & Larson, D. B. (2001). *Handbook of religion and health.* New York: Oxford University Press.

Koepfer, S. R. (2000). Drawing on the spirit: Embracing spirituality in pediatrics and pediatric art therapy. *Art Therapy, 17*(1), 188–194.

Kohlberg, L. (1981). *Essays on moral development: The philosophy of moral development: Moral stages and the idea of justice.* New York: Harper & Row.

Koltko, M. E. (1990). How religious beliefs affect psychotherapy: The example of Mormonism. *Psychotherapy, 27,* 132–141.

Koltko-Rivera, M. E. (2004). The psychology of worldviews. *Review of General Psychology, 8,* 3–58.

Komp, D. M. (1993). *A child shall lead them: Lessons in hope from children with cancer.* Grand Rapids, MI: Zondervan.

Kopp, R. R. (1995). *Metaphor therapy: Using client-generated metaphors in psychotherapy.* New York: Brunner/Mazel.

Krasner, L. (1962). The therapist as a social reinforcement machine. In H. H. Strupp & L. Luborsky (Eds.), *Research in psychotherapy* (Vol. 2, pp. 61–94). Washington, DC: American Psychological Association.

Krippner, S., & Achterberg, J. (2000). Anomalous healing experiences. In E. Cardena, S. J. Lynn, & S. Krippner (Eds.), *Varieties of anomalous experience: Examining the scientific evidence* (pp. 353–395). Washington, DC: American Psychological Association.

Krippner, S., & Welch, P. (1992). *Spiritual dimensions of healing.* New York: Irvington.

Kroll, J. R., & Sheehan, W. (1989). Religious beliefs and practices among 52 psychiatric inpatients in Minnesota. *American Journal of Psychiatry, 146,* 67–72.

Kuhn, T. (1970). *The structure of scientific revolutions* (2nd ed.). Chicago: University of Chicago Press.

Lakatos, I., & Musgrave, A. (Eds.). (1970). *Criticism and the growth of knowledge.* New York: Cambridge University Press.

Lambert, M. J. (Ed.). (2004). *Bergin and Garfield's handbook of psychotherapy and behavior change* (5th ed.). New York: Wiley.

Lambert, M. J., & Bergin, A. E. (1994). The effectiveness of psychotherapy. In A. E. Bergin & S. L. Garfield (Eds.), *Handbook of psychotherapy and behavior change* (4th ed., pp. 143–189). New York: Wiley.

Lambert, M. J., & Hill, C. E. (1994). Assessing psychotherapy outcomes and processes. In A. E. Bergin & S. L. Garfield (Eds.), *Handbook of psychotherapy and behavior change* (4th ed., pp. 72–113). New York: Wiley.

Lantz, J. (2002). Meaning-centered marital and family therapy: Learning to bear the beams of love. *Family Therapy. 29*(3), 190.

Larson, D. B., & Larson, S. (1994). *The forgotten factor in physical and mental health: What does the research show?* Rockville, MD: National Institute for Healthcare Research.

Larson, D. B., Lu, F. G., & Swyers, J. P. (Eds.). (1996). *Model curriculum for psychiatry residency training programs: Religion and spirituality in clinical practice*. Rockville, MD: National Institute for Healthcare Research.

Larson, D. B., Lu, F. G., & Swyers, J. P. (1997). *Model curriculum for psychiatric residency training programs: Religion and spirituality in clinical practice, a course outline*. Rockville, MD: National Institute for Healthcare Research.

Larson, D. B., Pattison, E. M., Blazer, D. G., Omran, A. R., & Kaplan, B. H. (1986). Systematic analysis of research on religious variables in four major psychiatric journals, 1978–1982. *American Journal of Psychiatry, 143,* 329–334.

Larson, D. B., Sherrill, K. A., Lyons, J. S., Craige, F. C., Thielman, S. B., Greenwold, M. A., et al. (1992). Dimensions and valences of measures of religious commitment found in the American Journal of Psychiatry and the Archives of General Psychiatry, 1978–1989. *American Journal of Psychiatry, 149,* 557–559.

Larson, D. B., Swyers, J. P., & McCullough, M. E. (1997). *Scientific research on spirituality and health: A consensus report*. Rockville, MD: National Institute for Healthcare Research.

Laudan, L. (1984). *Science and values: The aims of science and their role in scientific debate*. Berkeley: University of California Press.

Lazarus, A. A. (1973). Multimodal behavior therapy: Treating the BASIC I.D. *Journal of Nervous and Mental Disease, 156,* 404–411.

Lazarus, A. A. (1976). *Multimodal behavior therapy*. New York: Springer Publishing.

Lazarus, A. A. (1989). Multimodal therapy. In R. J. Corsini & D. Wedding (Eds.), *Current psychotherapies* (4th ed., pp. 503–544). Itasca, IL: F. E. Peacock.

Leahey, T. H. (1991). *A history of modern psychology*. Englewood Cliffs, NJ: Prentice Hall.

Levin, J. (2001). *God, faith, and health: Exploring the spirituality–healing connection*. New York: Wiley.

Levin, J. S. (1994). Investigating the epidemiologic effects of religious experience. In J. S. Levin (Ed.), *Religion in aging and health: Theoretical foundations and methodological frontiers* (pp. 3–17). Thousand Oaks, CA: Sage.

Levin, J. S. (1995, April). *Epidemiology of religion*. Paper presented at a conference of the National Institute for Healthcare Research, Leesburg, VA.

Lewis, C. S. (1991). *The four loves*. New York: Harcourt. (Original work published 1960)

Liebert, R. M., & Liebert, L. L. (1998). *Liebert & Spiegler's personality strategies and issues* (8th ed.). Pacific Grove, CA: Brooks/Cole.

Lieblich, A., McAdams, D. P., & Josselson, R. (2004). *Healing plots: The narrative basis of psychotherapy*. Washington, DC: American Psychological Association.

Lincoln, Y. S., & Guba, E. G. (1985). *Naturalistic inquiry*. Beverly Hills, CA: Sage.

Little, G. L., & Robinson, K. D. (1988). Moral reconation therapy: A systematic step-by-step treatment system for treatment resistant clients. *Psychological Reports, 62,* 135–151.

Lomax, J. W., Karff, R. S., & McKenny, G. P. (2002). Ethical considerations in the integration of religion and psychotherapy: Three perspectives. *Psychiatric Clinics of North America, 25,* 547–559.

Lonborg, S. D., & Bowen, N. A. (2004). Counselors, communities, and spirituality: Ethical and multicultural considerations. *Professional School Counseling, 7,* 318–325.

London, P. (1964). *Modes and morals of psychotherapy*. New York: Holt, Rinehart & Winston.

London, P. (1986). *The modes and morals of psychotherapy* (2nd ed.). New York: McGraw-Hill.

Lovinger, R. J. (1984). *Working with religious issues in therapy*. Northvale, NJ: Jason Aronson.

Lovinger, R. J. (1990). *Religion and counseling: The psychological impact of religious belief*. New York: Continuum.

Lovinger, R. J. (1996). Considering the religious dimension in assessment and treatment. In E. Shafranske (Ed.), *Religion and the clinical practice of psychology* (pp. 327–364). Washington, DC: American Psychological Association.

Lovinger, R. J., & Lovinger, S. L. (2004). Religious cross-matches between therapists and clients. In P. S. Richards & A. E. Bergin (Eds.), *Casebook for a spiritual strategy in counseling and psychotherapy* (pp. 267–284). Washington, DC: American Psychological Association.

Lowe, C. M. (1976). *Value orientations in counseling and psychotherapy: The meanings of mental health* (2nd ed.). Cranston, RI: Carroll Press.

Lucas, C. (1985). Out at the edge: Notes on a paradigm shift. *Journal of Counseling and Development, 64,* 165–172.

Ludwig, T. M. (1996). *The sacred paths: Understanding the religions of the world* (2nd ed.). Englewood Cliffs, NJ: Prentice Hall.

Luks, A. (1993). *The healing power of doing good*. New York: Ballantine Books.

Lundin, R. W. (1985). *Theories and systems of psychology* (3rd ed.). Lexington, MA: Heath.

Lyall, D. (1995). *Counselling in the pastoral and spiritual context*. Buckingham, England: Open University Press.

Maddux, J. E. (2002). Stopping the "madness": Positive psychology and the deconstruction of the illness ideology and the *DSM*. In C. R. Snyder & S. J.

Lopez (Eds.), *Handbook of positive psychology* (pp. 13–25). New York: Oxford University Press.

Madsen, T. G. (1995). On how we know. In *Brigham Young University 1994–95 devotional and fireside speeches*. Provo, UT: Brigham Young University Publications and Graphics.

Magaletta, P., & Brawer, P. (1998). Prayer in psychotherapy: A model for its use, ethical considerations, and guidelines for practice. *Journal of Psychology and Theology, 26,* 322–330.

Magdid, B. (2002). *Ordinary mind: Exploring the common ground of Zen and psychotherapy.* Somerville, MA: Wisdom.

Mahler, M., Pine, F., & Bergman, A. (1975). *The psychological birth of the human infant: Symbiosis and individuation.* New York: Basic Books.

Mahrer, A. (1988). Discovery-oriented research. *American Psychologist, 43,* 694–702.

Mahrer, A. R. (1996). Existential–humanistic psychotherapy and the religious person. In E. P. Shafranske (Ed.), *Religion and the clinical practice of psychology* (pp. 433–460). Washington, DC: American Psychological Association.

Malony, H. N. (1985). Assessing religious maturity. In E. M. Stern (Ed.), *Psychotherapy and the religiously committed patient* (pp. 25–33). New York: Haworth Press.

Malony, H. N. (1988). The clinical assessment of optimal religious functioning. *Review of Religious Research, 30,* 3–17.

Manicas, P. T., & Secord, P. F. (1983). Implications for psychology of the new philosophy of science. *American Psychologist, 38,* 399–413.

Manley, R. S., & Leichner, P. (2003). Anguish and despair in adolescents with eating disorders: Helping to manage suicidal ideation and impulses. *Crisis, 24*(1), 32–36.

Maples, M. F. (2001). Spirituality: Its place in counseling children. In D. S. Sandhu (Ed.), *Elementary school counseling in the new millennium* (pp. 223–237). Alexandria, VA: American Counseling Association.

Martens, W. H. (2003). Spiritual psychotherapy for antisocial and psychopathic personalities: Some theoretical building blocks. *Journal of Contemporary Psychotherapy, 33,* 205–218.

Martin, J. E., & Booth, J. (1999). Behavioral approaches to enhance spirituality. In W. R. Miller (Ed.), *Integrating spirituality into treatment: Resources for practitioners* (pp. 161–175). Washington, DC: American Psychological Association.

Martin, J. E., & Carlson, C. R. (1988). Spiritual dimensions of health psychology. In W. R. Miller & J. E. Martin (Eds.), *Behavior therapy and religion* (pp. 57–110). Newbury Park, CA: Sage.

Maslow, A. (1964). *Religion, values, and peak experiences.* Columbus: Ohio State University Press.

Maslow, A. (1970). *Motivation and personality* (Rev. ed.). New York: Harper & Row.

Maslow, A. H. (1968). *Toward a psychology of being* (2nd ed.). New York: Van Nostrand.

Maslow, A. H. (1971). *The farther reaches of human nature*. New York: Viking Press.

Mason, S. F. (1962). *A history of the sciences*. New York: Macmillan.

Matarazzo, J. D. (1985). Psychotherapy. In G. A. Kimble & K. Schlesinger (Eds.), *Topics in the history of psychology* (Vol. 2, pp. 219–250). Hillsdale, NJ: Erlbaum.

Matthews, D. A., Larson, D. B., & Barry, C. P. (1993–1995). *The faith factor: An annotated bibliography of clinical research on spiritual subjects* (Vols. 1–3). Rockville, MD: National Institute for Healthcare Research.

Mattson, R., & Scharman, J. S. (1994). Divorce in Mormon women: A qualitative study. *Association of Mormon Counselors and Psychotherapists Journal, 20*, 29–60.

May, R. (Ed.). (1961). *Existential psychology*. New York: Random House.

May, R. (1982). *The will and spirit: A contemplative psychology*. San Francisco: Harper & Row.

May, R., Angel, E., & Ellenberger, H. (1958). *Existence*. New York: Basic Books.

McCasland, S. V., Cairns, E. G., & Yu, D. C. (1969). *Religions of the world*. New York: Random House.

McClenon, J. (1984). *Deviant science: The case of parapsychology*. Philadelphia: University of Pennsylvania Press.

McClenon, J. (2002). *Wondrous healing: Shamanism, human evolution, and the origin of religion*. Dekalb: Northern Illinois University Press.

McCrady, B. S., & Delaney, S. I. (1995). Self-help groups. In R. K. Hester & W. R. Miller (Eds.), *Handbook of alcoholism treatment approaches* (2nd ed., pp. 160–175). Boston: Allyn & Bacon.

McCrady, B. S., & Miller, W. R. (1993). *Research on Alcoholics Anonymous: Opportunities and alternatives*. New Brunswick, NJ: Rutgers Center for Alcohol Studies.

McCullough, M. E. (1995). Prayer and health: Conceptual issues, research review, and research agenda. *Journal of Psychology and Theology, 25*, 15–29.

McCullough, M. E. (1999). Research on religion-accommodative counseling: Review and meta-analysis. *Journal of Counseling Psychology, 46*, 92–98.

McCullough, M. E., & Larson, D. B. (1999). Prayer. In W. R. Miller (Ed.), *Integrating spirituality into treatment: Resources for practitioners* (pp. 85–110). Washington, DC: American Psychological Association.

McCullough, M. E., Pargament, K. I., & Thoresen, C. E. (Eds.). (2000). *Forgiveness: Theory, research, and practice*. New York: Guilford Press.

McCullough, M. E., Sandage, S. J., & Worthington, E. L., Jr. (1997). *To forgive is human*. Downers Grove, IL: InterVarsity Press.

McCullough, M. E., & Worthington, E. L., Jr. (1994a). Encouraging clients to forgive people who have hurt them: Review, critique, and research prospectus. *Journal of Psychology and Theology, 22*, 15–29.

McCullough, M. E., & Worthington, E. L., Jr. (1994b). Models of interpersonal forgiveness and their applications to counseling: Review and critique. *Counseling and Values, 39,* 2–14.

McCullough, M. E., & Worthington, E. L., Jr. (1999). Religion and the forgiving personality. *Journal of Personality, 67,* 1141–1164.

McGrath, A. (1999). *Science and religion: An introduction.* Oxford, England: Blackwell.

McLemore, C. (1982). *The scandal of psychotherapy.* Wheaton, IL: Tyndale House.

McMinn, M. R. (1996). *Psychology, theology, and spirituality in Christian counseling.* Wheaton, IL: Tyndale House.

Meadow, M. J. (1978). The cross and the seed: Active and receptive spiritualities. *Journal of Religion and Health, 17,* 57–69.

Meadow, M. J. (1982). True womanhood and women's victimization. *Counseling and Values, 26,* 93–101.

Meadow, M. J., & Kahoe, R. D. (1984). *Psychology of religion: Religion in individual lives.* New York: Harper & Row.

Meichenbaum, D. (1977). *Cognitive behavior modification: An integrative approach.* New York: Plenum Press.

Meissner, M. W. (1996). The pathology of beliefs and the beliefs of pathology. In E. Shafranske (Ed.), *Religion and the clinical practice of psychology* (pp. 241–267). Washington, DC: American Psychological Association.

Merriam-Webster, Inc. (2004). *Merriam-Webster's collegiate dictionary* (11th ed. p. 1128). Springfield, MA: Author.

Messer, S. B., Sass, L. A., & Woolfolk, R. L. (1988). *Hermeneutics and psychological theory: Interpretive perspectives on personality, psychotherapy, and psychopathology.* New Brunswick, NJ: Rutgers University Press.

Miller, D., & Guidry, L. (2002). Addiction and trauma recovery: Healing the body, mind and spirit. *Psychotherapy: Theory, Research, Practice, Training, 39,* 269–270.

Miller, G. (2003). *Incorporating spirituality into counseling and psychotherapy: Theory and technique.* Hoboken, NJ: Wiley.

Miller, J. P. (1994). *The contemplative practitioner: Meditation in education and the professions.* Westport, CT: Bergin & Garvey.

Miller, K. R. (1999). *Finding Darwin's God: A scientist's search for common ground between God and evolution.* New York: HarperCollins.

Miller, L. (2004). A spiritual formulation of interpersonal psychotherapy for depression in pregnant girls. In P. S. Richards & A. E. Bergin (Eds.), *Casebook for a spiritual strategy in counseling and psychotherapy* (pp. 75–86). Washington, DC: American Psychological Association.

Miller, L. (2005). Interpersonal psychotherapy from a spiritual perspective. In L. Sperry & E. P. Shafranske (Eds.), *Spiritually oriented psychotherapy* (pp. 153–175). Washington, DC: American Psychological Association.

Miller, L., & Lovinger, R. (2000). Psychotherapy with conservative and reform Jews. *Handbook of psychotherapy and religious diversity* (pp. 259–286). Washington, DC: American Psychological Association.

Miller, L., Richards, P. S., & Keller, R. R. (2000). Religion and optimism. In E. C. Chang (Ed.), *Optimism and pessimism: Implications for theory, research, and practice.* Washington, DC: American Psychological Association.

Miller, W., & Crabtree, B. (1994). Clinical research. In D. Denzin & Y. S. Lincoln (Eds.), *Handbook of qualitative research* (pp. 340–352). Thousand Oaks, CA: Sage.

Miller, W. R. (1999). *Integrating spirituality into treatment: Resources for practitioners.* Washington, DC: American Psychological Association.

Miller, W. R. (2005). What is human nature? Reflections from Judeo–Christian perspectives (pp. 11–29). In W. R. Miller & H. D. Delaney (Eds.), *Judeo-Christian perspectives on psychology: Human nature, motivation, and change.* Washington, DC: American Psychological Association.

Miller, W. R., & C'deBaca, J. (1994). Quantum change: Toward a psychology transformation. In T. Heatherton & J. Weinberger (Eds.), *Can personality change?* (pp. 253–280). Washington, DC: American Psychological Association.

Miller, W. R., & Jackson, K. A. (1985). *Practical psychology for pastors.* Englewood Cliffs, NJ: Prentice Hall.

Miller, W. R., & Martin, J. E. (Eds.). (1988). *Behavior therapy and religion: Integrating spiritual and behavioral approaches to change.* Newbury Park, CA: Sage.

Miller, W. R., & Thoresen, C. E. (2003). Spirituality, religion, and health: An emerging research field. *American Psychologist, 58,* 24–35.

Mills, J. C., & Crowley, R. J. (1986). *Therapeutic metaphors for children and the child within.* New York: Brunner/Mazel.

Mitchell, J. E., Erlander, M., Pyle, R. L., & Fletcher, L. A. (1990). Eating disorders, religious practices and pastoral counseling. *International Journal of Eating Disorders, 9,* 589–593.

Moberg, D. O. (Ed.). (1979). *Spiritual well-being: Sociological perspectives.* Lanham, MD: University Press of America.

Moberg, D. O. (1984). Subjective measures of spiritual well-being. *Review of Religious Research, 25,* 351–364.

Moghaddam, F. M., & Marsella, A. J. (Eds.). (2003). *Understanding terrorism: Psychosocial roots, consequences, and interventions.* Washington, DC: American Psychological Association.

Moody, R. (1975). *Life after life.* New York: Bantam Books.

Moon, G. W., Willis, D. E., Bailey, J. W., & Kwasny, J. C. (1993). Self-reported use of Christian spiritual guidance techniques by Christian psychotherapists, pastoral counselors, and spiritual directors. *Journal of Psychology and Christianity, 12,* 24–37.

Moran, L. A. (2000). Transpersonal psychiatry at a VA medical center. *Psychiatric Services, 51,* 530–531.

Morse, J. M., & Field, P. A. (1995). *Qualitative research methods for health professionals* (2nd ed.). Thousand Oaks, CA: Sage.

Morse, M. (1994a). *Parting visions: Uses and meanings of pre-death, psychic, and spiritual experiences*. New York: Villard.

Morse, M. L. (1994b). Near death experiences and death-related visions in children: Implications for the clinician. *Current Problems in Pediatrics, 24*, 55–83.

Mosak, H. H. (1989). Adlerian psychotherapy. In R. J. Corsini & D. Wedding (Eds.), *Current psychotherapies* (4th ed., pp. 65–116). Itasca, IL: F. E. Peacock.

Mowrer, O. H. (1961). *The crisis in psychiatry and religion*. Princeton, NJ: Van Nostrand.

Mowrer, O. H. (Ed.). (1967). *Morality and mental health*. Chicago: Rand McNally.

Moyers, W. (1996, October 11–13). America's religious mosaic. *USA Weekend*, pp. 4–5.

Murray, D. J. (1988). *A history of Western psychology* (2nd ed.). Englewood Cliffs, NJ: Prentice Hall.

Murray-Swank, N. A., & Pargament, K. I. (2004, March 19 & 20). *Solace for the soul: A journey towards wholeness*. Paper presented at the annual APA Division 36 Mid-Winter Conference on Religion and Spirituality, Columbia, MD.

M. W. H. (1986, November). Letter of the month. *Minnesota Psychological Association Newsletter*, 10.

Myers, J. E., Sweeney, T. J., & Witmer, J. M. (2000). The wheel of wellness counseling for wellness: A holistic model for treatment planning. *Journal of Counseling and Development, 78*, 251–266.

Myers, L. J. (1988). *Understanding an Afrocentric world view: Introduction to an optimal psychology*. Dubuque, IA: Kendall/Hunt.

Nakhaima, J. M., & Dicks, B. H. (1995). Social work practice with religious families. *Families International, 76*, 360–368.

National Association of Social Workers. (1999). *Code of ethics of the National Association of Social Workers*. Washington, DC: Author.

Neimeyer, R. A., & Mahoney, M. J. (Eds.). (1995). *Constructivism in psychotherapy*. Washington, DC: American Psychological Association.

Nielsen, L. S. (2004). A Mormon rational emotive behavior therapist attempts Qur'anic rational emotive behavior therapy. In P. S. Richards & A. E. Bergin (Eds.), *Casebook for a spiritual strategy in counseling and psychotherapy* (pp. 213–230). Washington, DC: American Psychological Association.

Nielsen, N. C., Jr., Hein, N., Reynolds, F. E., Miller, A. L., Karff, S. E., Cowan, A. C., et al. (1988). *Religions of the world* (2nd ed.). New York: St. Martin's Press.

Nielsen, S. L., Johnson, B. W., & Ellis, A. (2001). *Counseling and psychotherapy with religious persons: A rational emotive behavior therapy approach*. Mahwah, NJ: Erlbaum.

Nielsen, S. L., Johnson, W. B., & Ridely, C. R. (2000). Religiously sensitive rational emotive behavior therapy: Theory, techniques, and brief excerpts from a case. *Professional Psychology: Research and Practice, 31*(1), 21–28.

Nigosian, S. A. (1994). *World faiths* (2nd ed.). New York: St. Martin's Press.

Nohr, R. W. (2001). Outcome effects of receiving a spiritually informed vs. a standard cognitive–behavioral stress management workshop. *Dissertation Abstracts International, 61*(7), 3855B.

Norcross, J. C. (Ed.). (1986). *Handbook of eclectic psychotherapy.* New York: Brunner/Mazel.

Norcross, J. C., & Goldfried, M. R. (Eds.). (1992). *Handbook of psychotherapy integration.* New York: Basic Books.

Northcut, T. (2000). Constructing a place for religion and spirituality in psychodynamic practice. *Clinical Social Work Journal, 28*(2), 155–169.

Nwadiora, E. (1996). Therapy with African American families. *Western Journal of Black Studies, 20,* 117–124.

Oaks, D. H. (2002). *With full purpose of heart.* Salt Lake City, UT: Deseret Book.

O'Connell, W. E. (1997). The radical metaphors of Adlerian psychospirituality. *Individual Psychology: Journal of Adlerian Theory Research and Practice, 53*(1), 33–41.

Ogden, G. (2001). Integrating sexuality and spirituality: A group therapy approach to women's sexual dilemmas. In P. J. Kleinplatz (Ed.), *New directions in sex therapy: Innovations and alternatives* (pp. 322–346). New York: Brunner-Routledge.

O'Grady, K. A., & Richards, P. S. (2003, March 28–29). *The role of inspiration in scientific scholarship and discovery.* Paper presented at the annual APA Division 36 Mid-Winter Conference on Religion and Spirituality, Columbia, MD.

O'Grady, K. A., & Richards, P. S. (2004, July). *Professionals' perceptions of the role of inspiration in science and psychotherapy.* Paper presented at the annual convention of the American Psychological Association, Honolulu, HI.

Oman, D., & Thoresen, C. E. (2001, August 24–28). *Using intervention studies to unravel how religion affects health.* Paper presented at the annual convention of the American Psychological Association, San Francisco.

Oman, D., Thoreson, C. E., McMahon, K. (1999). Volunteerism and mortality among the community-dwelling elderly. *Journal of Health Psychology, 4*(3), 301–316.

Orlinsky, D. E., Grawe, K., & Parks, B. K. (1994). Process and outcome in psychotherapy: *Noch einmal.* In A. E. Bergin & S. L. Garfield (Eds.), *Handbook of psychotherapy and behavior change* (4th ed., pp. 270–376). New York: Wiley.

Ornish, D. (1990). *Dr. Dean Ornish's program for reversing heart disease: The only system scientifically proven to reverse heart disease without drugs or surgery.* New York: Ballantine Books.

Oser, F. K. (1991). The development of religious judgment. In F. K. Oser & W. G. Scarlett (Eds.), *Religious development in childhood and adolescence* (pp. 5–25). San Francisco: Jossey-Bass.

Packer, M. J. (1985). Hermeneutic inquiry in the study of human conduct. *American Psychologist, 40,* 1081–1093.

Page, R., & Berkow, D. N. (1998). Group work as facilitation of spiritual development for drug and alcohol abusers. *Journal for Specialists in Group Work*, *23*, 285–297.

Palmer, S. J., & Keller, R. R. (1989). *Religions of the world: A Latter-Day Saint view*. Provo, UT: Brigham Young University Press.

Palmer, S. J., Keller, R. R., Choi, D. S., & Toronto, J. A. (1997). *Religions of the world: A Latter-Day Saint view* (2nd ed.). Provo, UT: Brigham Young University Press.

Paloutzian, R. F., & Ellison, C. W. (1979, September). Developing a measure of spiritual well-being. In R. F. Paloutzian (Chair), *Spiritual well-being, loneliness, and perceived quality of life*. Symposium conducted at the 87th Annual Convention of the American Psychological Association, New York.

Paloutzian, R. F., & Ellison, C. W. (1991). *Manual for the Spiritual Well-Being Scale*. Nyack, NY: Life Advances.

Pargament, K. I. (1996). Religious methods of coping: Resources for the conservation and transformation of significance. In E. Shafranske (Ed.), *Religion and the clinical practice of psychology* (pp. 215–239). Washington, DC: American Psychological Association.

Pargament, K. I. (1997). *The psychology of religion and coping: Theory, research, practice*. New York: Guilford Press.

Pargament, K. I. (1999). The psychology of religion and spirituality? Yes and no. *International Journal for the Psychology of Religion*, *9*, 3–16.

Pargament, K. I., Echemendia, R. J., Johnson, S., Cook, P., McGrath, C., Myers, J. G., et al. (1987). The conservative church: Psychosocial advantages and disadvantages. *American Journal of Community Psychology*, *15*, 269–286.

Pargament, K. I., Ensing, D. S., Falgout, K., Olsen, H., Reilly, B., Van Haitsma, K., et al. (1990). God help me: (I): Religious coping efforts as predictors of the outcomes to significant negative life events. *American Journal of Community Psychology*, *18*, 793–824.

Pargament, K. I., Falgout, K., Ensing, D. S., Reilly, B., Silverman, M., Van Haitsma, K., et al. (1991). The Congregation Development Program: Database consultation with churches and synagogues. *Professional Psychology: Research and Practice*, *22*, 393–404.

Pargament, K. I., Kennell, J., Hathaway, W., Grenvengoed, N., Newman, J., & Jones, W. (1988). Religion and the problem-solving process: Three styles of coping. *Journal for the Scientific Study of Religion*, *27*, 90–104.

Pargament, K. I., & Mahoney, A. (2002). Spirituality: Discovering and conserving the sacred. In C. R. Snyder & S. J. Lopez (Eds.), *Handbook of positive psychology* (pp. 646–659). New York: Oxford University Press.

Pargament, K. I., Maton, K. I., & Hess, R. E. (Eds.). (1992). *Religion and prevention in mental health: Research, vision and action*. New York: Haworth Press.

Pargament, K. I., & Park, C. L. (1995). Merely a defense? The variety of religious means and ends. *Journal of Social Issues*, *51*, 13–32.

Pargament, K. I., Silverman, W., Johnson, S., Echemendia, R., & Snyder, S. (1983). The psychological climate of religious congregations. *American Journal of Community Psychology, 11*, 351–381.

Pargament, K. I., Sullivan, M. S., Balzer, W. E., Van Haitsma, K. S., & Raymark, P. H. (1995). The many meanings of religiousness: A policy capturing approach. *Journal of Personality, 63*, 953–983.

Park, C. L. (2003). The psychology of religion and positive psychology. *American Psychological Association Division 36 (Psychology of Religion) Newsletter, 28*, 1–8.

Parrinder, G. (1961). *Worship in the world's religions.* London: Faber & Faber.

Patterson, C. H. (1958). The place of values in counseling and psychotherapy. *Journal of Counseling Psychology, 5*, 216–223.

Paul, E. R. (1992). *Science, religion, and Mormon cosmology.* Chicago: University of Chicago Press.

Payne, I. R., Bergin, A. E., Bielema, K. A., & Jenkins, P. H. (1991). Review of religion and mental health: Prevention and the enhancement of psychosocial functioning. *Prevention in Human Services, 9*, 11–40.

Payne, I. R., Bergin, A. E., & Loftus, P. E. (1992). A review of attempts to integrate spiritual and standard psychotherapy techniques. *Journal of Psychotherapy Integration, 2*, 171–192.

Peacocke, A. (2001). *Paths from science towards god: The end of all our exploring.* Oxford, England: Oneworld.

Pecheur, D. R., & Edwards, K. J. (1984). A comparison of secular and religious versions of cognitive therapy with depressed Christian college students. *Journal of Psychology and Theology, 12*, 45–54.

Peck, M. S. (1978). *The road less traveled: A new psychology of love, traditional values, and spiritual growth.* New York: Simon & Schuster.

Peck, M. S. (1983). *People of the lie.* New York: Simon & Schuster.

Percesepe, G. (1991). *Philosophy: An introduction to the labor of reason.* New York: Macmillan.

Perlstein, M. (1996). Integrating a gay, lesbian, or bisexual person's religious and spiritual needs and choices into psychotherapy. In C. J. Alexander (Ed.), *Gay and lesbian mental health: A sourcebook for practitioners* (pp. 173–188). New York: Harrington Park.

Peterson, C. (2000). The future of optimism. *American Psychologist, 55*, 44–55.

Piedmont, R. L. (1999). Does spirituality represent the sixth factor of personality? Spiritual transcendence and the Five-Factor model. *Journal of Personality, 67*, 985–1013.

Piedmont, R. L., & Leach, M. M. (2002). Cross-cultural generalizability of the Spiritual Transcendence Scale in India: Spirituality as a universal aspect of human experience. *American Behavioral Scientist, 45*, 1888–1901.

Plante, T. G. (1999). A collaborative relationship between professional psychology and the Roman Catholic Church: A case example and suggested principles for success. *Professional Psychology: Research and Practice, 30*, 541–546.

Plante, T. G., & Sherman, A. C. (Eds.). (2001). *Faith and health: Psychological perspectives*. New York: Guilford Press.

Plantinga, A. (1984). Advice to Christian philosophers. *Faith and Philosophy, 1,* 253–271.

Plantinga, A. (1991a). When faith and reason clash: Evolution and the Bible. *Christian Scholar's Review, 21,* 8–32.

Plantinga, A. (1991b). Evolution, neutrality, and antecedent probability: A reply to McMullin and Van Till. *Christian Scholar's Review, 21,* 80–109.

Plantinga, A. (1993). *Warrant and proper function*. New York: Oxford University Press.

Plantinga, A., & Wolterstorff, N. (Eds.). (1983). *Faith and rationality: Reason and belief in God*. Notre Dame, IN: University of Notre Dame Press.

Pojman, L. P. (1999). *Philosophy: The quest for truth* (4th ed.). Belmont, CA: Wadsworth.

Polanyi, M. (1962). *Personal knowledge: Towards a post-critical philosophy*. Chicago: University of Chicago Press.

Polkinghorne, J. (1998). *Belief in God in an age of science*. New Haven, CT: Yale University Press.

Polkinghorne, J. (2002). *Science and religion: Where have we come from and where are we going?* Plenary address delivered at the inaugural meeting of the International Society for Science and Religion, Granada, Spain.

Polkinghorne, J. C. (1990). A revived natural theology. In J. Fennema & I. Paul (Eds.), *Science and religion: On world-changing perspectives on reality* (pp. 87–97). Norwell, MA: Kluwer Academic.

Poll, J. B., Richards, P. S., & Smith, T. B. (2004, July 29). *Longitudinal study of spiritual identity development and altruism*. Paper presented at the annual convention of the American Psychological Association, Honolulu, HI.

Poll, J. B., & Smith, T. B. (2003). The spiritual self: Toward a conceptualization of spiritual identity development. *Journal of Psychology and Theology, 31,* 129–142.

Poloma, M. M., & Pendleton, B. F. (1991). The effects of prayer and prayer experiences on measures of general well-being. *Journal of Psychology and Theology, 19,* 71–83.

Ponterotto, J. G., Casas, J. P., Suzuki, L. A., & Alexander, C. M. (Eds.). (1995). *Handbook of multicultural counseling*. Thousand Oaks, CA: Sage.

Ponterotto, J. G., Suzuki, L. A., & Meller, P. J. (Eds.). (1996). *Handbook of multicultural assessment*. San Francisco: Jossey-Bass.

Pope, E. (1989, October). [Letter to the editor]. *Central Washington University Observer*, p. 2.

Pope, K. S. (1985). Dual relationships: A violation of ethical, legal, and clinical standards. *California State Psychologist, 20,* 3–5.

Popper, K. R. (Ed.). (1972). *Objective knowledge*. Oxford, England: Clarendon Press.

Popper, K. R., & Eccles, J. C. (1977). *The self and its brain*. New York: Springer Publishing.

Powell, L. H., & Thoresen, C. E. (1987). Modifying the Type A behavior pattern: A small group treatment approach. In J. A. Blumenthal & D. C. McKee (Eds.), *Applications in behavioral medicine and health psychology: A clinician's source book* (pp. 171–207). Sarasota, FL: Professional Resource Exchange.

Preece, J. E. (1994). *An ethnographic study into the concerns and issues of participants attending a therapy group for individuals with chronic pain and/or illness*. Unpublished doctoral dissertation, Brigham Young University, Provo, UT.

Propst, L. R. (1980). The comparative efficacy of religious and nonreligious imagery for the treatment of mild depression in religious individuals. *Cognitive Therapy and Research, 4,* 167–178.

Propst, L. R. (1988). *Psychotherapy in a religious framework: Spirituality in the emotional healing process*. New York: Human Sciences Press.

Propst, L. R. (1996). Cognitive–behavioral therapy and the religious person. In E. P. Shafranske (Ed.), *Religion and the clinical practice of psychology* (pp. 391–407). Washington, DC: American Psychological Association.

Propst, L. R., Ostrom, R., Watkins, P., Dean, T., & Mashburn, D. (1992). Comparative efficacy of religious and nonreligious cognitive–behavioral therapy for the treatment of clinical depression in religious individuals. *Journal of Consulting and Clinical Psychology, 60,* 94–103.

Pruyser, P. (1971). Assessment of the patient's religious attitudes in the psychiatric case study. *Bulletin of the Menninger Clinic, 35,* 272–291.

Puchalski, C. M., & Larson, D. B. (1998). Developing curricula in spirituality and medicine. *Academic Medicine, 73,* 970–974.

Puchalski, C. M., Larson, D. B., & Lu, F. G. (2000). Spirituality courses in psychiatry residency programs. *Psychiatric Annals, 30,* 543–548.

Pyszczynski, T., Solomon, S., & Greenberg, J. (2003). *In the wake of 9/11: The psychology of terror*. Washington, DC: American Psychological Association.

Rabinowitz, A. (1999). *Judaism and psychology: Meeting points*. Northvale, NJ: Jason Aronson.

Rabinowitz, A. (2000). Psychotherapy with orthodox Jews. In P. S. Richards & A. E. Bergin (Eds.), *Handbook of psychotherapy and religious diversity* (pp. 237–258). Washington, DC: American Psychological Association.

Ramsey, J. L., & Blieszner, R. (2000). Transcending a lifetime of losses: The importance of spirituality in old age. In J. H. Harvey & E. D. Miller (Eds.), *Loss and trauma: General and close relationship perspectives* (pp. 225–236). New York: Brunner-Routledge.

Randour, M. L. (1987). *Women's psyche women's spirit*. New York: Columbia University Press.

Raphel, M. M. (2001). The status of the use of spiritual interventions in three professional mental health groups. (Doctoral dissertation, Loyola College, 2001). *Dissertation Abstracts International, 62*(2), 779A.

Ray, W. J., & Ravizza, R. (1988). *Methods: Toward a science of behavior and experience* (3rd ed.). Belmont, CA: Wadsworth.

Rayburn, C. A. (1985). Some ethical considerations in psychotherapy with religious women. *Psychotherapy, 22,* 803–812.

Rayburn, C. A. (1997). *Inventory on religiousness.* Silver Spring, MD: Author.

Rayburn, C. A., & Richmond, L. J. (1996). *Inventory on spirituality.* Silver Spring, MD: Author.

Rayburn, C. A., & Richmond, L. J. (2002). Theobiology: Interfacing theology and science. *American Behavioral Scientist, 45,* 1793–1811.

Redfield, J. (1993). *The celestine prophecy: An adventure.* New York: Warner Books.

Reichardt, C. S., & Cook, T. D. (1979). Beyond qualitative versus quantitative methods. In T. D. Cook & C. S. Reichardt (Eds.), *Qualitative and quantitative methods in evaluation research* (pp. 7–32). Beverly Hills, CA: Sage.

Remie, R. C., & Koenig, H. G. (2001). Religion and health in HIV/AIDS communities. In T. G. Plante & A. C. Sherman (Eds.), *Faith and health: Psychological perspectives* (pp. 195–212). New York: Guilford Press.

Rice, L. N., & Greenberg, L. S. (1984). *Patterns of change: Intensive analysis of psychotherapy process.* New York: Guilford Press.

Richards, D. G. (1991). The phenomenology and psychological correlates of verbal prayer. *Journal of Psychology and Theology, 19,* 354–363.

Richards, P. S. (1991). Religious devoutness in college students: Relations with emotional adjustment and psychological separation from parents. *Journal of Counseling Psychology, 38,* 189–196.

Richards, P. S. (1995). [Therapist critical incident case reports]. Unpublished raw data. Department of Educational Psychology, Brigham Young University, Provo, UT.

Richards, P. S. (1999, August 21). *Spiritual influences in healing and psychotherapy.* William C. Bier Award Invited Address, Division 36 of the American Psychological Association (Psychology of Religion), Boston, MA.

Richards, P. S. (2005). Theistic integrative psychotherapy. In L. Sperry & E. P. Shafranske (Eds.), *Spiritually oriented psychotherapy* (pp. 259–285). Washington, DC: American Psychological Association.

Richards, P. S., & Bergin, A. E. (1997). *A spiritual strategy for counseling and psychotherapy.* Washington, DC: American Psychological Association.

Richards, P. S., & Bergin, A. E. (Eds.). (2000). *Handbook of psychotherapy and religious diversity.* Washington, DC: American Psychological Association.

Richards, P. S., & Bergin, A. E. (2004). *Casebook for a spiritual strategy in counseling and psychotherapy.* Washington, DC: American Psychological Association.

Richards, P. S., & Davison, M. L. (1989). The effects of theistic and atheistic counselor values on client trust: A multidimensional scaling analysis. *Counseling and Values, 33,* 109–120.

Richards, P. S., & Davison, M. L. (1992). Religion bias in moral development research: A psychometric investigation. *Journal for the Scientific Study of Religion, 31,* 467–485.

Richards, P. S., Hardman, R. K., & Berrett, M. E. (2000). *Spiritual renewal: A journal of faith and healing*. Orem, UT: Center for Change.

Richards, P. S., Hardman, R. K., & Berrett, M. E. (2001, August 24). *Evaluating the efficacy of spiritual interventions in the treatment of eating disorder patients: An outcome study*. Paper presented at the annual convention of the American Psychological Association, San Francisco.

Richards, P. S., Hardman, R. K., Berrett, M. E., & Carter, B. (in press). *Spirituality and eating disorders: Theory, research, and practice*. Washington, DC: American Psychological Association.

Richards, P. S., Hardman, R. K., Frost, H. A., Berrett, M. E., Clark-Sly, J. B., & David, D. K. (1997). Spiritual issues and interventions in the treatment of patients with eating disorders. *Eating Disorders, 5*, 261–279.

Richards, P. S., Keller, R., Smith, T. B. (2003). Religious and spiritual diversity in the practice of psychotherapy (pp. 269–286). In T. B. Smith (Ed.), *Practicing multiculturalism: Affirming diversity in counseling and psychology*. Boston: Allyn & Bacon.

Richards, P. S., Owen, L., & Stein, S. (1993). A religiously oriented group counseling intervention for self-defeating perfectionism: A pilot study. *Counseling and Values, 37*, 96–104.

Richards, P. S., & Potts, R. (1995a). Spiritual interventions in psychotherapy: A survey of the practices and beliefs of AMCAP members. *Association of Mormon Counselors and Psychotherapists Journal, 21*, 39–68.

Richards, P. S., & Potts, R. W. (1995b). Using spiritual interventions in psychotherapy: Practices, successes, failures, and ethical concerns of Mormon psychotherapists. *Professional Psychology: Research and Practice, 26*, 163–170.

Richards, P. S., Rector, J. R., & Tjeltveit, A. C. (1999). Values, spirituality, and psychotherapy. In William R. Miller (Ed.), *Integrating spirituality in treatment: Resources for practitioners* (pp. 133–160). Washington, DC: American Psychological Association.

Richards, P. S., Smith, S. A., & Davis, L. F. (1989). Healthy and unhealthy forms of religiousness manifested by psychotherapy clients: An empirical investigation. *Journal of Research in Personality, 23*, 506–524.

Richards, P. S., Smith, T. B., Schowalter, M., Richard, M., Berrett, M. E., & Hardman, R. K. (in press). Development and validation of the Spiritual Outcome Scale. *Psychotherapy Research*.

Richardson, F. C., & Zeddies, T. J. (2001). Individualism in modern psychotherapy. In B. D. Slife (Ed.), *Critical issues in psychotherapy: Translating new ideas into practice* (pp. 147–164). Thousand Oaks, CA: Sage.

Rickman, H. P. (Ed.). (1976). *W. Dilthey selected writings*. New York: Cambridge University Press.

Rickman, H. P. (1979). *Wilhelm Dilthey: Pioneer of the human studies*. London: Paul Elek.

Ring, K. (1980). *Life at death: A scientific investigation of the near-death experience*. New York: Coward, McCann & Geoghegan.

Ring, K., & Cooper, S. (1997). Near-death and out-of-body experience in the blind: A study of apparent eyeless vision. *Journal of Near-Death Studies, 16,* 101–147.

Ring, K., & Cooper, S. (1999). *Mindsight: Near-death and out-of-body experiences in the blind.* Palo Alto, CA: William James Center/Institute of Transpersonal Psychology.

Ring, K., & Valarino, E. E. (1998). *Lessons from the light: What we can learn from the near-death experience.* New York: Insight Books.

Ringwald, C. D. (2002). *The soul of recovery: Uncovering the spiritual dimensions in the treatment of addictions.* New York: Oxford University Press.

Rivas, T. (2003). The survivalist interpretation of recent studies into the near-death experience. *Journal of Religion and Psychical Research, 26,* 27–31.

Rizzuto, A. M. (1996). Psychoanalytic treatment and the religious person. In E. P. Shafranske (Ed.), *Religion and the clinical practice of psychology* (pp. 409–431). Washington, DC: American Psychological Association.

Robinson, J. P., & Shaver, P. R. (1973). *Measures of social psychological attitudes* (Rev. ed.). Ann Arbor, MI: Survey Research Center, Institute for Social Research.

Rodegast, P., & Stanton, J. (1985). *Emmanuel's book: A manual for living comfortably in the cosmos.* New York: Bantam Books.

Rodriguez, G. M. (2001). DeAlmas Latinas (the souls of Latin women): A psycho-spiritual culturally relevant group process. *Women and Therapy, 24,* 19–33.

Rogers, C. R. (1951). *Client-centered therapy.* Boston: Houghton Mifflin.

Rogers, C. R. (1957). The necessary and sufficient conditions of therapeutic personality change. *Journal of Consulting Psychology, 21,* 95–103.

Rogers, C. R. (1959). A theory of therapy, personality, and interpersonal relationships, as developed in the client-centered framework. In S. Koch (Ed.), *Psychology: A study of a science* (Vol. 3, pp. 184–256). New York: Basic Books.

Rogers, C. R. (1961). *On becoming a person.* Boston: Houghton Mifflin.

Rogers, C. R. (1973). Some new challenges. *American Psychologist, 28,* 379–387.

Rogers, C. R. (1980). *A way of being.* Boston: Houghton Mifflin.

Ronan, C. A. (1982). *Science: Its history and development among the world's cultures.* New York: Hamlyn.

Rorty, M., Yager, J., & Rossotto, E. (1993). Why and how do women recover from bulimia nervosa? The subjective appraisals of forty women recovered for a year or more. *International Journal of Eating Disorders, 14,* 249–260.

Rosik, C. H. (2000). Utilizing religious resources in the treatment of dissociative trauma symptoms: Rationale, current status, future directions. *Journal of Trauma and Dissociation, 1*(1), 69–89.

Rubin, J. B. (1996). *Psychotherapy and Buddhism: Toward an integration.* New York: Plenum Press.

Rychlak, J. F. (1979). *Discovering free will and personal responsibility.* New York: Oxford University Press.

Rychlak, J. F. (1981). *Introduction to personality and psychotherapy: A theory-construction approach* (2nd ed.). Boston: Houghton Mifflin.

Rychlak, J. F. (1994). *Logical learning theory: A human teleology and its empirical support*. Lincoln: University of Nebraska Press.

Rye, M. S., & Pargament, K. I. (2002). Forgiveness and romantic relationships in college: Can it heal the wounded heart? *Journal of Clinical Psychology, 58*, 419–441.

Sabom, M. B. (1982). *Recollections of death: A medical investigation*. New York: Harper & Row.

Sabom, M. (1998). *Light and death: One doctor's fascinating account of near-death experiences*. Grand Rapids, MI: Zondervan.

Sagan, C. (1995). *The demon-haunted world: Science as a candle in the dark*. New York: Random House.

Sanderson, C., & Linehan, M. M. (1999). Acceptance and forgiveness. In W. R. Miller (Ed.), *Integrating spirituality into treatment: Resources for practitioners* (pp. 199–216). Washington, DC: American Psychological Association.

Sanderson, S., Vandenberg, B., & Paese, P. (1999). Authentic religious experience or insanity? *Journal of Clinical Psychology, 55*, 607–616.

Sandoz, J. (2001). The spiritual secret to alcoholism recovery. *Annals of the American Psychotherapy Association, 4*, 12–14.

Sanua, V. D. (1969). Religion, mental health, and personality: A review of empirical studies. *American Journal of Psychiatry, 125*, 1203–1213.

Sarason, S. B. (1981). *Psychology misdirected*. New York: Free Press.

Scharman, J. S. (1994). Relationship issues in LDS blended families. *Association of Mormon Counselors and Psychotherapists Journal, 20*, 15–38.

Schowalter, M., Richard, M., Senst, R., & Murken, S. (in press). Die Integration von Religiosität in der psychotherapeutischen Behandlung bei religiösen Patienten—Ein Klinikvergleich [The integration of religious elements into inpatient psychotherapy for religious patients—A comparision of two clinics]. *Zeitschrift für Klinische Psychologie, Psychiatrie und Psychotherapie*.

Schroeder, G. (2001). *The hidden face of God: Science reveals the ultimate truth*. New York: Touchstone.

Schulte, D. L., Skinner, T. A., & Claiborn, C. D. (2002). Religious and spiritual issues in counseling psychology training. *Counseling Psychologist, 30*, 118–134.

Schwartz, J. M. (1999). A role for the volition and attention in the generation of new brain activity. Toward a neurobiology of mental force. In B. Libet & A. Freeman (Eds.), *Volitional brain: Towards a neuroscience of free will* (pp. 115–142). Charlottesville, VA: Academic.

Scott, W. G., & Hart, D. K. (1989). *Organizational values in America*. New Brunswick, NJ: Transaction Books.

Sears, S. F., & Wallace, R. L. (2001). Spirituality, coping, and survival. In J. R. Rodriguez (Ed.), *Biopsychosocial perspectives on transplantation* (pp. 173–180) New York: Kluwer Academic.

Seeman, T. E., Dubin, L. F., & Seeman, M. (2003). Religiosity/spirituality and health: A critical review of the evidence for biological pathways, *American Psychologist, 58*, 53–63.

Segen, J. C. (Ed.). (1992). *The dictionary of modern medicine*. Carnforth, England: Parthenon.

Seligman, L. (1988). Invited commentary: Three contributions of a spiritual perspective to counseling, psychotherapy, and behavior change. *Counseling and Values, 33,* 55–56.

Seligman, M. E. P. (1998). Building human strength: Psychology's forgotten mission. *APA Monitor, 29*(1). Retrieved January 5, 2005, from http://www.apa.org/monitor/jan98/pres.html

Seligman, M. E. P. (2002). Positive psychology, positive prevention, and positive therapy. In C. R. Snyder & S. J. Lopez (Eds.), *Handbook of positive psychology* (pp. 3–9). New York: Oxford University Press.

Seligman, M. E. P., & Csikszentmihalyi, M. (2000). Positive psychology: An introduction. *American Psychologist, 55,* 5–14.

Shafranske, E. P. (Ed.). (1996). *Religion and the clinical practice of psychology*. Washington, DC: American Psychological Association.

Shafranske, E. P. (2000). Religious involvement and professional practices of psychiatrists and other mental health professionals. *Psychiatric Annals, 30,* 525–532.

Shafranske, E. P. (2001). The religious dimension of patient care within rehabilitation medicine: The role of religious attitudes, beliefs, and professional practices. In T. G. Plante & A. C. Sherman (Eds.), *Faith and health: Psychological perspectives* (pp. 311–335). New York: Guilford Press.

Shafranske, E. P. (2004). A psychodynamic case study. In P. S. Richards (Ed.), *Casebook for a spiritual strategy in counseling and psychotherapy* (pp. 153–170). Washington, DC: American Psychological Association.

Shafranske, E. P. (2005). A psychoanalytic approach to spiritually oriented psychotherapy. In L. Sperry & E. P. Shafranske (Eds.), *Spiritually-oriented psychotherapy* (pp. 105–130). Washington, DC: American Psychological Association.

Shafranske, E. P., & Malony, H. N. (1990). Clinical psychologists' religious and spiritual orientations and their practice of psychotherapy. *Psychotherapy, 27,* 72–78.

Shafranske, E. P., & Malony, H. N. (1996). Religion and the clinical practice of psychology: A case for inclusion. In E. P. Shafranske (Ed.), *Religion and the clinical practice of psychology* (pp. 561–586). Washington, DC: American Psychological Association.

Sharma, A. R. (2000). Psychotherapy with Hindus. In P. S. Richards & A. E. Bergin (Eds.), *Handbook of psychotherapy and religious diversity* (pp. 341–365). Washington, DC: American Psychological Association.

Sheler, J. L. (2002, May 6). Faith in America: In troubled times, how Americans' views of religion are changing. *U.S. News and World Report,* 41–49.

Shine, J. (1996, February 9–11). Religious revival on campus. *USA Weekend,* pp. 8–9.

Shrock, D. A. (1984). Suppression of women by religion. *Counseling and Values, 29,* 49–58.

Sichen, F., Targ, E., Moore, D., & Smith, H. S. (1998). A randomized double-blind study of the effect of distant healing in a population with advanced AIDS. *Western Journal of Medicine, 169,* 356–363.

Siegel, B. S. (1986). *Love, medicine & miracles: Lessons learned about self-healing from a surgeon's experience with exceptional patients.* New York: Harper & Row.

Siegel, R. K. (1980). The psychology of life after death. *American Psychologist, 35,* 911–931.

Siegelman, E. (1990). *Metaphor and meaning in psychotherapy.* New York: Guilford Press.

Silverman, W. H., Pargament, K. I., Johnson, S. M., Echemendia, R. J., & Snyder, S. (1983). Measuring member satisfaction with the church. *Journal of Applied Psychology, 68,* 664–677.

Sire, J. W. (1976). *The universe next door.* Downers Grove, IL: InterVarsity Press.

Slife, B. D. (1993). *Time and psychological explanation.* Albany: State University of New York Press.

Slife, B. D. (2004). Theoretical challenges to therapy practice and research: The constraint of naturalism. In M. J. Lambert (Ed.), *Bergin and Garfield's handbook of psychotherapy and behavior change* (5th ed., pp. 44–83). New York: Wiley.

Slife, B. D., & Gantt, E. E. (1999). Methodological pluralism: A framework for psychotherapy research. *Journal of Clinical Psychology, 55,* 1453–1465.

Slife, B., Hope, C., & Nebeker, S. (1996, August). *Examining the relationship between religious spirituality and psychological science.* Paper presented at the 104th Annual Convention of the American Psychological Association, Toronto.

Slife, B. D., Hope, C., & Nebeker, R. S. (1999). Examining the relationship between religious spirituality and psychological science. *Journal of Humanistic Psychology, 39,* 51–85.

Slife, B. D., Mitchell, L. J., & Whoolery, M. (2004). A theistic approach to therapeutic community: Non-naturalism and the Alldredge Academy. In P. S. Richards & A. E. Bergin (Eds.), *Casebook for a spiritual strategy in counseling and psychotherapy* (pp. 35–54). Washington, DC: American Psychological Association.

Slife, B. D., & Reber, J. (2001). Eclecticism in psychotherapy: Is it really the best substitute for traditional theories? In B. Slife, R. Williams, & S. Barlow (Eds.), *Critical issues in psychotherapy: Translating new ideas into practice* (pp. 213–234). Thousand Oaks, CA: Sage.

Slife, B. D., & Richards, P. S. (2001). How separable are spirituality and theology in psychotherapy? *Counseling and Values, 45,* 180–206.

Slife, B. D., & Williams, R. N. (1995). *What's behind the research? Discovering hidden assumptions in the behavioral sciences.* Thousand Oaks, CA: Sage.

Smart, N. (1983). *Worldviews: Crosscultural explorations of human beliefs.* New York: Scribner.

Smart, N. (1993). *Religions of Asia.* Englewood Cliffs, NJ: Prentice Hall.

Smart, N. (1994). *Religions of the West.* Englewood Cliffs, NJ: Prentice Hall.

Smith, A. F., & Slife, B. D. (in press). *Managing inescapable values in psychotherapy.* Thousand Oaks, CA: Sage.

Smith, F. T., Hardman, R. K., Richards, P. S., & Fischer, L. (2003). Intrinsic religiosity and spiritual well-being as predictors of treatment outcome among women with eating disorders. *Eating Disorders: Journal of Treatment and Prevention, 11,* 15–26.

Smith, J. C. (1975). Meditation as psychotherapy: A review of the literature. *Psychological Bulletin, 82,* 558–564.

Smith, L. M. (1994). Biographical method. In N. K. Denzin & Y. S. Lincoln (Eds.), *Handbook of qualitative research* (pp. 286–305). Thousand Oaks, CA: Sage.

Smith, T. B., & Richards, P. S. (2002). Multicultural counseling in spiritual and religious contexts. In J. Trusty, D. Sandhu, & J. Looby (Eds.), *Multicultural counseling: Context, theory and practice, and competence* (pp. 105–127). Huntington, NY: Nova Science.

Smith, T. B., & Richards, P. S. (2005). The integration of spiritual and religious issues in racial–cultural psychology and counseling. In R. Carter (Ed.), *Handbook of racial–cultural psychology: Theory and research* (Vol. 1, pp. 132–162). Hoboken, NJ: Wiley.

Smith, T. W. (2001). Religion and spirituality in the science and practice of health psychology: Openness, skepticism, and the agnosticism of methodology. In T. G. Plant & A. C. Sherman (Eds.), *Faith and health: Psychological perspectives* (pp. 355–380). New York: Guilford Press.

Snyder, C. R., & Lopez, S. J. (Eds.). (2002). *Handbook of positive psychology.* New York: Oxford University Press.

Solomon, R. C. (1990). *The big questions: A short introduction to philosophy* (3rd ed.). San Diego, CA: Harcourt Brace Jovanovich.

Sorokin, P. A. (1957). *Social and cultural dynamics: A study of art, truth, ethics, law, and social relationships* (Rev. and abridged). Boston: Extending Horizons Books.

Southern, S. (2002). The tie that binds: Sadomasochism in female addicted trauma survivors. *Sexual Addiction and Compulsivity, 9,* 209–229.

Spackman, M. P., & Williams, R. N. (2001). The affiliation of methodology with ontology in a scientific psychology. *Journal of Mind and Behavior, 22,* 389–406.

Sparr, L. F., & Fergueson, J. F. (2000). Moral and spiritual issues following traumatization. In J. K. Boehnlein (Ed.), *Psychiatry and religion: The convergence of mind and spirit. Issues in psychiatry* (pp. 109–123). Washington, DC: American Psychiatric Association.

Speight, S. L., Myers, L. J., Cox, C. I., & Highlen, P. S. (1991). A redefinition of multicultural counseling. *Journal of Counseling and Development, 70,* 29–36.

Spero, M. H. (Ed.). (1985). *Psychotherapy of the religious patient.* Springfield, IL: Charles C. Thomas.

Spero, M. H. (1990). Parallel dimensions of experience in psychoanalytic psychotherapy of the religious patient. *Psychotherapy: Theory, Research, and Training, 27,* 53–71.

Spero, M. H. (1992). *Religious objects as psychological structures.* Chicago: University of Chicago Press.

Sperry, L. (2001). *Spirituality in clinical practice: Incorporating the spiritual dimension in psychotherapy and counseling.* New York: Brunner/Routledge.

Sperry, L., & Giblin, P. (1996). Marital and family therapy with religious persons. In. E. P. Shafranske (Ed.), *Religion and the clinical practice of psychology* (pp. 511–532). Washington, DC: American Psychological Association.

Sperry, L., & Shafranske, E. P. (Eds.). (2005). *Spiritually oriented psychotherapy.* Washington, DC: American Psychological Association.

Sperry, R. W. (1988). Psychology's mentalist paradigm and the religion/science tension. *American Psychologist, 43,* 607–613.

Sperry, R. W. (1995). The riddle of consciousness and the changing scientific worldview. *Journal of Humanistic Psychology, 35,* 7–33.

Spiegel, D., Bloom, J. R., Kraemer, H. C., & Gottheil, E. (1989). Effect of psychosocial treatment on survival of patients with metastatic breast cancer. *Lancet, 2,* 888–891.

Spilka, B., Comp, G., & Goldsmith, W. M. (1981). Faith and behavior: Religion in introductory psychology texts of the 1950's and 1970's. *Teaching of Psychology, 8,* 158–160.

Spilka, B., Hood, R. W., Jr., & Gorsuch, R. L. (1985). *The psychology of religion: An empirical approach.* Englewood Cliffs, NJ: Prentice Hall.

Spilka, B., Hood, R. W., Jr., Hunsberger, B., & Gorsuch, R. (2003). *The psychology of religion: An empirical approach* (3rd ed.). New York: Guilford Press.

Spilka, B., Shaver, P., & Kirkpatrick, L. (1985). General attribution theory for the psychology of religion. *Journal for the Scientific Study of Religion, 24,* 1–20.

Stake, R. E. (1994). Case studies. In N. K. Denzin & Y. S. Lincoln (Eds.), *Handbook of qualitative research* (pp. 236–247). Thousand Oaks, CA: Sage.

Stanard, R. P., Sandhu, D. S., & Painter, L. C. (2000). Assessment of spirituality in counseling. *Journal of Counseling and Development, 78,* 204–210.

Stark, R. (1971). Psychopathology and religious commitment. *Review of Religious Research, 12,* 165–176.

Stark, R., & Glock, C. Y. (1968). *American piety: The nature of religious commitment.* Berkeley: University of California Press.

Staver, M. D. (1995). *Faith and freedom: A complete handbook for defending your religious rights.* Wheaton, IL: Crossway Books.

Stein, A. E. (2003). *Fragments: Coping with attention deficit disorder.* New York: Haworth Press.

Steinfeld, G. (1999). Brief therapy with postpartum depression: Integrating cognitive–behavior and through field therapies within a spiritual framework. *Journal of Psychotherapy Integration, 9,* 337–362.

Steinfeld, G. J. (2000). Spiritual psychology and psychotherapy: Is there theoretical and empirical support? *Journal of Contemporary Psychotherapy, 30,* 353–380.

Stern, E. M. (Ed.). (1985). *Psychotherapy and the religiously committed patient.* New York: Haworth Press.

Stricker, G., & Gold, J. R. (Eds.). (1993). *Comprehensive handbook of psychotherapy integration.* New York: Plenum Press.

Striegel-Moore, R. H., & Smolak, L. (2001). *Eating disorders: Innovative directions in research and practice*. Washington, DC: American Psychological Association.

Strommen, M. P. (Ed.). (1971). *Research on religious development: A comprehensive handbook*. New York: Hawthorn.

Strommen, M. P. (1984). Psychology's blind spot: A religious faith. *Counseling and Values, 28*, 150–161.

Strunk, O., Jr. (1970). Humanistic religious psychology: A new chapter in the psychology of religion. *Journal of Pastoral Care, 24*, 90–97.

Sue, D. W. (1978). Eliminating cultural oppression in counseling: A conceptual analysis. *Personnel and Guidance Journal, 55*, 422–424.

Sue, D. W. (1981). *Counseling the culturally different*. New York: Wiley.

Sue, D. W., Bergnier, J. E., Duran, A., Feinberg, L., Pedersen, P., Smith, E., et al. (1982). Position paper: Cross-cultural counseling competencies. *Counseling Psychologist, 10*, 45–52.

Sue, D. W., Bingham, R., Porche-Burke, L., & Vasquez, M. (1999). The diversification of psychology: A multicultural revolution. *American Psychologist, 54*, 1061–1069.

Sue, D. W., & Sue, D. (1977). Barriers to effective cross-cultural counseling. *Journal of Counseling Psychology, 24*, 420–429.

Sue, D. W., & Sue, D. (1990). *Counseling the culturally different: Theory and practice* (2nd ed.). New York: Wiley.

Sue, S., Zane, N., & Young, K. (1994). Research on psychotherapy with culturally diverse populations. In A. E. Bergin & S. L. Garfield (Eds.), *Handbook of psychotherapy and behavior change* (4th ed., pp. 783–817). New York: Wiley.

Sutherland, C. (1992). *Reborn in the light: Life after near-death experiences*. New York: Bantam Books.

Sweeney, D. S., & Landreth, G. (1993). Healing a child's spirituality through play therapy: A scriptural approach to treating children. *Journal of Psychology and Christianity, 12*, 351–356.

Sweet, M. J., & Johnson, C. G. (1990). Enhancing empathy: The interpersonal implications of a Buddhist meditation technique. *Psychotherapy, 27*, 19–29.

Swinton, J. (2001). *Spirituality and mental health care: Rediscovering a forgotten dimension*. London: Jessica Kingsley.

Tamminen, K. (1991). *Religious development in children and youth: An empirical study*. Helsinki, Finland: Suomalinen Tiedeakatemia.

Tan, S. Y. (1987). Cognitive–behavior therapy: A biblical approach and critique. *Journal of Psychology and Theology, 15*, 103–112.

Tan, S. Y. (1993, January). *Training in professional psychology: Diversity includes religion*. Paper presented at the National Council of Schools of Professional Psychology midwinter conference, La Jolla, CA.

Tan, S. Y. (1994). Ethical considerations in religious psychotherapy: Potential pitfalls and unique resources. *Journal of Psychology and Theology, 22*, 389–394.

Tan, S. Y. (1996). Religion in clinical practice: Implicit and explicit integration. In E. Shafranske (Ed.), *Religion and the clinical practice of psychology* (pp. 365–387). Washington, DC: American Psychological Association.

Tan, S. Y. (2003). Integrating spiritual direction into psychotherapy: Ethical issues and guidelines. *Journal of Psychology and Theology, 31,* 14–23.

Tan, S. Y., & Dong, N. J. (2000). Psychotherapy with members of Asian American churches and spiritual traditions. In P. S. Richards & A. E. Bergin (Eds.), *Handbook of psychotherapy and religious diversity* (pp. 421–444). Washington, DC: American Psychological Association.

Tan, S. Y., & Dong, N. J. (2001). Spiritual interventions in healing and wholeness. In T. G. Plante & A. C. Sherman (Eds.), *Faith and health: Psychological perspectives* (pp. 291–310). New York: Guilford Press.

Tan, S. Y., & Johnson, W. B. (2005). Spiritually oriented cognitive–behavioral therapy (pp. 77–103). In L. Sperry & E. P. Shafranske, (Eds.), *Spiritually oriented psychotherapy*. Washington, DC: American Psychological Association.

Taylor, E. (1994, November–December). Desperately seeking spirituality. *Psychology Today,* 54–68.

Templeton, J. M., & Herrmann, R. L. (1994). *Is God the only reality? Science points to a deeper meaning of the universe.* New York: Continuum.

Thomson, R. F. (2000). Zazen and psychotherapeutic presence. *American Journal of Psychotherapy, 54,* 531–548.

Thorne, B. (1998). *Person-centered counseling and Christian spirituality: The secular and the holy.* London: Whurr.

Tillich, P. (1963). *Morality and beyond.* New York: Harper & Row.

Tipler, F. J. (1994). *The physics of immortality: Modern cosmology, God and the resurrection of the dead.* New York: Doubleday.

Tjeltveit, A. C. (1986). The ethics of value conversion in psychotherapy: Appropriate and inappropriate therapist influence on client values. *Clinical Psychology Review, 6,* 515–537.

Tjeltveit, A. C. (1999). *Ethics and values in psychotherapy.* New York: Routledge.

Topper, C. (2003). *Spirituality in pastoral counseling and the community helping professions.* New York: Haworth Pastoral Press.

Toulmin, S. (1962). *Foresight and understanding.* San Francisco: Harper.

Trautmann, R. L. (2003). Psychotherapy and spirituality. *Transactional Analysis Journal, 33*(1), 32–36.

Trujillo, A. (2000). Psychotherapy with Native Americans: a view into the role of religion and spirituality. *Handbook of psychotherapy and religious diversity.* (pp. 445–466). Washington, DC: American Psychological Association.

Truzzi, M. (1980). A skeptical look at Paul Kurtz's analysis of the scientific status of parapsychology. *Journal of Parapsychology, 44,* 35–55.

Trzepacz, P. T., & Baker, R. W. (1993). *The psychiatric mental status examination.* New York: Oxford University Press.

Turner, D. J. (2002). Religion. In *2002 Britannica Book of the Year* (pp. 300–308). Chicago: Encyclopedia Britannica.

Ulrich, W. L., Richards, P. S., & Bergin, A. E. (2000). Psychotherapy with Latter-Day Saints. In P. S. Richards & A. E. Bergin (Eds.), *Handbook of psychotherapy and religious diversity* (pp. 185–209). Washington, DC: American Psychological Association.

U.S. Government Printing Office. (1997). The Constitution of the United States (19th reprint). Superintendent of Documents, Mail Stop: SSOP, Washington, DC 20402-9328. Retrieved April 16, 2005, from http://www.gpoaccess. gov/constitution/html/art2.html

U.S. Library of Congress. (1991). Book of the Month Club and Library of Congress Center for the Book survey of lifetime reading habits. Retrieved February 8, 2005, from http://www.loc.gov/loc/cfbook/booklists.html

Uzoka, A. F. (1979). The myth of the nuclear family. *American Psychologist, 34,* 1095–1106.

van Lommel, P., van Wees, R., Meyers, V., & Elfferich, I. (2001). Near-death experience in survivors of cardiac arrest: A prospective study in the Netherlands. *Lancet, 358,* 2039–2045.

Van de Kemp, H. (1996). Historical perspective: Religion and clinical psychology in America. In E. P. Shafranske (Ed.), *Religion and the clinical practice of psychology* (pp. 71–112). Washington, DC: American Psychological Association.

Vaughan, F., Wittine, B., & Walsh, R. (1996). Transpersonal psychology and the religious person. In E. P. Shafranske (Ed.), *Religion and the clinical practice of psychology* (pp. 483–509). Washington, DC: American Psychological Association.

Vernon, A. (Ed.). (1993). *Counseling children and adolescents.* Denver, CO: Love.

Viney, W., & King, D. B. (1998). *A history of psychology: Ideas and context* (2nd ed.). Boston: Allyn & Bacon.

Vitz, P. C. (1990). The use of stories in moral development: New psychological reasons for an old education method. *American Psychologist, 45,* 709–720.

Vitz, P. C. (1992a). Narratives and counseling: Part 1. From analysis of past to stories about it. *Journal of Psychology and Theology, 20,* 11–19.

Vitz, P. C. (1992b). Narratives and counseling: Part 2. From stories of the past to stories for the future. *Journal of Psychology and Theology, 20,* 20–27.

Vizzini, J. (2003). *A comparison study of puppet therapy to regular therapy in a chemical dependency twelve-step treatment model.* Unpublished doctoral dissertation, Loyola College, Columbia, MD.

Wagar, W. W. (1977). *World views: A study in comparative history.* New York: Holt, Rinehart & Winston.

Wallas, G. (1926). *The art of thought.* New York: Harcourt Brace.

Wallis, C. (1996, June 24). Faith and healing. *Time,* 58–64.

Walsh, F. (Ed.). (1999). *Spiritual resources in family therapy*. New York: Guilford Press.

Wann, T. W. (1964). *Behaviorism and phenomenology*. Chicago: University of Chicago Press.

Warner, C. T. (1986). What we are. *Brigham Young University Studies, 26,* 39–63.

Warner, C. T. (1995). *Bonds of anguish, bonds of love*. Salt Lake City, UT: Arbinger.

Warner, C. T. (2001). *Bonds that make us free: Healing our relationships, coming to ourselves*. Salt Lake City, UT: Shadow Mountain.

Warner, C. T., & Olson, T. D. (1984). Another view of family conflict and family wholeness. *Association of Mormon Counselors and Psychotherapists Journal, 10,* 15–20.

Watson, G., Batchelor, S., & Claxton, G. (Eds.). (2000). *The psychology of awakening: Buddhism, science, and our day-to-day lives*. York Beach, ME: Samuel Weiser.

Watson, J. B. (1983). *Psychology from the standpoint of a behaviorist*. Dover, NH: Frances Pinter. (Original work published 1924)

Watson, R. A. (2000). Toward union in love: The contemplative spiritual tradition and contemporary psychoanalytic theory in the formation of persons. *Journal of Psychology and Theology, 28,* 282–292.

Watts, J. A. (2000). Developing eyes to see and ears to hear: Ministering to self-injurers. *Journal of Ministry in Addiction and Recovery, 7*(1), 35–49.

Watts, R. E. (2000). Biblically based Christian spirituality and Adlerian psychotherapy. *Journal of Individual Psychology, 56,* 316–328.

Weaver, A. J., Koenig, H. G., & Larson, D. B. (1997). Marriage and family therapists and the clergy: A need for clinical collaboration, training, and research. *Journal of Marriage and Family Therapy, 23,* 13–25.

Weber, P. J. (Ed.). (1990). *Equal separation: Understanding the religion clauses of the First Amendment*. Westport, CT: Greenwood Press.

Weidlich, W. (1990). Reconciling concepts between natural science and theology. In J. Fennema & I. Paul (Eds.), *Science and religion: One world-changing perspectives on reality* (pp. 73–86). Norwell, MA: Kluwer Academic.

Wells, G. W. (1999). The context of religion in clinical child psychology. In W. K. Silverman & T. N. Ollendick (Eds.), *Developmental issues in the clinical treatment of children* (pp. 199–212). Boston: Allyn & Bacon.

Welwood, J. (2000). *Toward a psychology of awakening: Buddhism, psychotherapy, and the path of personal and spiritual transformation*. Boston: Shambhala.

Wertheimer, M. (1970). *A brief history of psychology*. New York: Holt, Rinehart & Winston.

West, W. (2000). *Psychotherapy and spirituality: Crossing the line between therapy and religion*. Thousand Oaks, CA: Sage.

West, W. (2004). Humanistic integrative spiritual psychotherapy. In P. S. Richards & A. E. Bergin (Eds.), *Casebook for a spiritual strategy in counseling and psychotherapy* (pp. 201–230). Washington, DC: American Psychological Association.

White, F. E. (2002). The lived-experience of psychospiritual integration: A qualitative study with licensed psychotherapists who actively integrate spirituality into their practice of psychotherapy (Doctoral dissertation, Institute for Transpersonal Psychology, 2002). *Dissertation Abstracts International, 63*, 2613B.

Whitehead, A. N. (1967). *Science and the modern world.* New York: Free Press. (Original work published 1925)

Whitehead, A. N. (1968). *Modes of thought.* New York: Free Press. (Original work published 1938)

Whitehead, A. N. (1968). *The function of reason.* Boston: Beacon Press. (Original work published 1929)

Whiting, J. R. S. (1983). *Religions of man.* Leckhampton, England: Stanley Thornes.

Wicks, R. J., Parsons, R. D., & Capps, D. (Eds.). (1985). *Clinical handbook of pastoral counseling.* New York: Paulist Press.

Williams, R. N. (1992). The human context of agency. *American Psychologist, 47,* 752–760.

Williams, R. N. (2005). Agency: Philosophical and spiritual foundations for applied psychology. In L. Fischer & A. P. Jackson (Eds.), *Turning Freud upside down: Latter-Day Saint perspectives in psychology and psychotherapy* (pp. 150–176). Provo, UT: Brigham Young University Press.

Wilson, J. P., & Moran, T. A. (1998). Psychological trauma: Posttraumatic stress disorder and spirituality. *Journal of Psychology and Theology, 26*(2), 168–178.

Woodward, K. L., & Underwood, A. (1993, December 27). Angels. *Newsweek,* 52–57.

Woolfolk, R. (1998). *The cure of souls: Science, values, and psychotherapy.* San Francisco: Jossey-Bass.

Worthington, E. L., Jr. (1986). Religious counseling: A review of published empirical research. *Journal of Counseling and Development, 64,* 421–431.

Worthington, E. L., Jr. (1988). Understanding the values of religious clients: A model and its application to counseling. *Journal of Counseling Psychology, 35,* 166–174.

Worthington, E. L., Jr. (1989a). Religious faith across the life span: Implications for counseling and research. *Counseling Psychologist, 17,* 555–612.

Worthington, E. L., Jr. (1989b). *Marriage counseling: A Christian approach to counseling couples.* Downers Grove, IL: InterVarsity Press.

Worthington, E. L., Jr. (1990). Marriage counseling: A Christian approach to counseling couples. *Counseling and Values, 35,* 3–15.

Worthington, E. L., Jr. (1998). *Dimensions of forgiveness: Psychological research and theological perspectives.* Philadelphia: Templeton Foundation Press.

Worthington, E. L., Berry, J. W., & Parrott, L. (2001). Unforgiveness, forgiveness, and health. In T. G. Plante & A. C. Sherman (Eds.), *Faith and health: Psychological perspectives* (pp. 107–138) New York: Guilford Press.

Worthington, E. L., & Drinkard, D. T. (2000). Promoting reconciliation through psychoeducational and therapeutic interventions. *Journal of Marital and Family Therapy*. 26(1), 93–101.

Worthington, E. L., Jr., Dupont, P. D., Berry, J. T., & Duncan, L. A. (1988). Christian therapists' and clients' perceptions of religious psychotherapy in private and agency settings. *Journal of Psychology and Theology*, 16, 282–293.

Worthington, E. L., Jr., Kurusu, T. A., McCullough, M. E., & Sandage, S. J. (1996). Empirical research on religion and psychotherapeutic processes and outcomes: A ten-year review and research prospectus. *Psychological Bulletin*, 119, 448–487.

Worthington, E. L., Jr., & Sandage, S. J. (2001a). Religion and spirituality. *Psychotherapy*, 38, 473–478.

Worthington, E. L., Jr., & Sandage, S. J. (2001b). Religion and spirituality. In J. C. Norcross (Ed.), *Psychotherapy relationships that work* (pp. 371–387). New York: Oxford University Press.

Worthington, E. L., Jr., & Scott, G. G. (1983). Goal selection for counseling with potentially religious clients by professional and student counselors in explicitly Christian or secular settings. *Journal of Psychology and Theology*, 11, 318–319.

Worthington, E. L. Jr., Wade, N. E., Hight, T. L., Ripley, J. S., McCullough, M. E., Berry, J. W., et al. (2003). The Religious Commitment Inventory—10: Development, refinement, and validation of a brief scale for research and counseling. *Journal of Counseling Psychology*, 50, 84–96.

Wray, I. (1986). Buddhism and psychotherapy: A Buddhist perspective. In G. Claxton (Ed.), *Beyond therapy: The impact of eastern religions on psychological theory and practice* (pp. 123–138). London: Wisdom.

Wulff, D. M. (1991). *Psychology of religion: Classic and contemporary views*. New York: Wiley.

Wulff, D. M. (1997). *Psychology of religion: Classic and contemporary views* (2nd ed.). New York: Wiley.

Wulff, D. M. (2000). Mystical experience. In E. Cardena, S. J. Lynn, & S. Krippner (Eds.), *Varieties of anomalous experience: Examining the scientific evidence* (pp. 397–440). Washington, DC: American Psychological Association.

Yalom, I. D. (1980). *Existential psychotherapy*. New York: Basic Books.

Yalom, I. D. (1995). *The theory and practice of group psychotherapy* (4th ed.). New York: Basic Books.

Yarhouse, M. A., & Fisher, W. (2002). Levels of training to address religion in clinical practice. *Psychotherapy*, 39, 171–176.

Yarhouse, M. A., & VanOrman, B. T. (1999). When psychologists work with religious clients: Applications of the general principles of ethical conduct. *Professional Psychology: Research and Practice*, 30, 557–562.

Young, J. S., Cashwell, C., Wiggins-Frame, M., & Belaire, C. (2002). Spiritual and religious competencies: A national survey of CACREP-accredited programs. *Counseling and Values, 47*, 22–33.

Younggren, J. N. (1993). Ethical issues in religious psychotherapy. *Register Report, 19*, 7–8.

Zilboorg, G., & Henry, G. W. (1941). *A history of medical psychology*. New York: Norton.

Zinnbauer, B. J., Pargament, K. I., & Scott, A. B. (1999). The emerging meanings of religiousness and spirituality: Problems and prospects. *Journal of Personality, 67*, 889–919.

AUTHOR INDEX

Numbers in italics refer to listings in the reference section.

Wolterstorff, N., 68, *382*
Woodward, K. L., *397*
Woolfolk, R. L., 52, 279, *376, 397*
Worthen, D., 297, *352*
Worthington, E. L., Jr., 7, 47, 61, 67,
    69, 159–160, 163, 165, 187,
    206, 215, 225, 241–242, 246,
    253, 256, 260, 262, 264, 266,
    268, 273, 286, 294, 297–298,
    305–306, 308, 329, 335, 337–
    338, 340, *356, 375–376,*
    397–398
Wray, I., 305, *398*
Wulff, D. M., 38, 144, 206–207, 228,
    398

Yager, J., 304, *386*
Yalom, I. D., 40, 107, 220, *398*
Yarhouse, M. A., 68, 183, 217, *398*
Yerxa, D. A., 52, *364*
Young, J. S., 205, 344, 346, *399*
Young, K., 64, 155, *392*
Younggren, J. N., *399*
Yu, D. C., 258, *375*

Zane, N., 64, 155, *392*
Zeddies, T. J., 106, *385*
Zilboorg, G., 55, *399*
Zinnbauer, B. J., 21, 339, *399*
Zuttermeister, P., 241, 244, *369*

SUBJECT INDEX

Cultural background. *See also*
    Multiculturalism
    naturalism and, 46–47, 54–55
    worldview and, 77, 220
Cultural community, 126

Death-related visions, 137n, 139–143
Deception, 121–122
Deity, concept of
    comparison of worldviews, 94–95
    Eastern and naturalistic worldviews,
        92–93, 96
    God image, 228–229
    in scientific theism, 97, 100
    theistic worldview and, 84, 85
Delinquency, 133, 134
Demographic data on religious adherents,
    8, 80–81
Denominational interventions, 18–19,
    290–291
Denominational therapeutic stance,
    158–159
Depression, 132, 134
Determinism, 32, 42, 46, 103–104
Development. *See* Human development
    and functioning
Dilthey, Wilhelm, 74, 77
Discovery-oriented research design, 331,
    332
Divine inspiration, 101, 102, 321–322
Doctrinal knowledge, 229, 232
Drug abuse, 133, 134
Dual relationships, 184–188, 254, 269

Eastern spiritual worldview, 78, 92–93,
    94, 96. *See also* Eastern world
    religions
Eastern world religions
    commonalities, 93, 94–95, 96
    conflict with naturalism, 46–47
    major religious traditions, 78,
        89–92
    meditation and, 255–256
    sacred writings, 258–259
Eating disorders, 304–305
Ecclesiastical authority, 188–193
Eclecticism. *See* Integrative psychology
Ecumenical assessment, 236–239
Ecumenical interventions, 290–291

Ecumenical therapeutic stance, 18,
    155–158
Empathy, 173–175, 220, 245
Empirically supported treatments, 46
Empiricism, 16–17, 34, 43, 316
Epistemology, 315–318. *See also* Ways of
    knowing
    assumptions of modernistic science,
        33–34, 54
    theistic view of, 318, 322–324
Eternal spiritual identity, 116–119,
    227–228
Ethical hedonism
    altruism contrasted with, 107, 326
    defined, 33
    influence on psychotherapy, 39, 43,
        45, 65–66
    religious conflicts with, 47
Ethical issues in therapy, 183–209
    competence, 204–207
    dual relationships, 184–188
    imposition of religious values,
        193–199
    and religious affiliation, 216–217
    usurpation of religious authority,
        188–193
    work setting boundaries violation,
        199–204
Ethical relativism
    defined, 33, 42
    vs. moral responsibility, 120–121
    psychology's adoption of, 39, 66
    religious conflicts with, 47
    in therapy, 166
Ethical values. *See* Values
Ethnographic research design, 332–335
Evolution, theory of, 35, 37, 39
Existential psychology. *See* Humanistic–
    existential psychology
Experimental control, 147–148

Faithful intimacy, 124–125
Family kinship, 125
Family systems psychotherapy, 283
Family therapy, 214–215, 297–298
Fellowship, 270–273
Festivals, 267
Fidelity, 124–125
First Amendment, U.S. Constitution,
    199–200

Forgiveness, 9, 263–266
Freedom of choice. *See* Agency
Freud, Sigmund, 37–39

George Washington Institute for
    Spirituality and Health (GWish),
    57
Goals and values, worldview impact on,
    75–77
Goals of psychotherapy, 154
God
    communication with, 114
    concept of, in scientific theism, 97,
        100
    inspiration by, 101, 102, 321–322
    personal relationship with, 106–
        107
God image, 228–229
Governmental settings, therapy in,
    199–204
Graduate training programs. *See*
    Training/training programs
Grounded theory research design,
    332–335
Group therapy, 214–215, 294, 296

Hard determinism, 32
Healing experiences, 139, 145
Healing power of love, 177–178
Healing, stages of, 265
Health. *See* Mental health; Physical
    health
Health psychology, 347
Heart disease, and Type A personality,
    301–303
Hedonism. *See* Ethical hedonism
Hermeneutics, 327
Hinduism, 89, 258
Holism, 46, 102–103, 326
Human development and functioning,
    115–126
    agency vs. impairment, 119–120
    benevolent power vs.
        authoritarianism, 122–124
    eternal spiritual identity vs.
        mortal overlay, 116–119
    faithful intimacy vs. infidelity
        and self-focus, 124–125
    integrity vs. deception, 121–122

marriage, family, and community
    vs. alienation and isolation,
    125–126
moral responsibility vs. relativism
    and uncertainty, 120–121
progression vs. stagnation, 126
theistic view of, 113
theories of, 105, 120
Humanistic–existential psychology, 40,
    62, 63, 283
Human nature
    comparison of worldviews on, 94–95
    morality and, 105–106
    naturalistic view of, 19, 41, 44–45
    in theistic personality theory,
        111–115
    theistic worldview and, 19, 84, 86

Idealism of freedom. *See* Subjective
    idealistic worldview
Identity, 116–119, 227–228
Impairment vs. agency, 119–120
Individualism, 106
Infidelity, 124–125
Informed consent, 161, 162
Inpatient treatment settings, 215–216
In-session interventions, 289–290
Inspiration/intuition
    in scientific discovery, 101, 102,
        319–322
    in therapy, 171, 173–175, 253–254
    as way of knowing, 317–318
Integrative psychology, 16, 17–18, 63–65,
    179–181, 293–294
Integrity, 121–122
Interactionism, nondualistic, 58
International Association for Near-Death
    Studies, 139
International Center for the Integration
    of Health and Spirituality
    (ICIHS), 56
Interpersonal relationships
    theistic perspective, 16, 106–107
    worldview impact on, 75–77
Interpersonal spiritual interventions,
    292–293
Interventions. *See* Spiritual interventions
Interview and assessment guide, 230–231
Intimacy, faithful, 124–125
Intuition. *See* Inspiration/intuition

Islam, 82–83, 85–88, 258
Isolation, 124–125

Jainism, 90–91, 258–259
James, William, 40
Judaism, 79, 82, 85–88, 257
Jung, Carl G., 40

Knowing, ways of, 136–138, 315–318.
    See also Epistemology

Legal–mechanical worldview, 34–35
Life after death. *See* Afterlife
Lifestyle
    congruence with values, 229,
        230–231
    theistic approach's impact on,
        347–348
    worldview impact on, 75–77
Love, healing power of, 177–178

Mainstream traditions of psychology
    integration with, 11–12, 293–294
    theistic psychotherapy compared to,
        19, 283
Managed care, 46
Manualized treatment programs, 215–216
Marital instability, 133, 134
Marriage, in human functioning,
    125–126
Marriage therapy, 297–298
Materialism, 33, 36, 42, 45, 46, 326
Mature spiritual orientation, 232–234
Measures of religiosity/spirituality,
    239–244
Measures of religious/spiritual outcomes,
    246–249
Mechanism, 32–33, 34–35, 42, 46
Medical profession, influences from,
    55–57
Medieval Christianity, 31
Meditation, 255–257, 302–303
Mental health
    morality and, 120
    prayer and, 252–253
    religion and, 59–60, 129–136,
        220–221

values and, 66–67, 167–171, 276
    worldview impact on, 75–77
Meta-empathy, 173–175, 245
Metaphysical worldview. *See* Worldview
Methodological flaws in research studies,
    148–149
Methodological naturalism, 32
Methodological pluralism, 101–102,
    324–329
Mind–body connection, 49, 301–303
Mind/Body Institute, 56
Mind–body medicine, 56–57
Minority groups. *See* Multiculturalism
Miracles, 114
Modernistic science. *See also* Naturalism
    constraints of, 45–46
    development of, 11–12
    philosophical assumptions of, 31–34,
        42–43, 324–327
    psychology's adoption of, 37–39, 48
    religious conflicts with, 46–47
    view of human nature, 41, 44–45
Monotheistic world religions
    commonalities, 84–88
    conflict with naturalism, 46–47
    major religious traditions, 31, 78,
        79–84, 257–259
Monotheistic worldview. *See also*
        Monotheistic world religions
    compared to other worldviews, 78,
        92–96
    implications of, 19–20
    in theistic spiritual strategy, 14
Moral absolutism, 104
Moral development, 105, 120. *See also*
        Human development and
        functioning
Moral instruction, 275–279
Morality. *See also* Values
    Eastern spiritual worldview, 93, 94
    human nature and, 105–106
    naturalistic scientific worldview, 95
    theistic worldview, 84, 87, 94
    in therapy, 166–171
Moral responsibility, 120–121
Moral universalism, 98, 104–106
Mortal overlay, 116–119, 127
Multiculturalism
    education in, 341–346
    religion and, 64–65, 157, 341
    research on, 338–339

in therapy, 155–158, 220, 305
worldview and, 77, 220
Multidimensional assessment of
outcomes, 245–249
Multisystemic assessment, 234–236
Mystical experiences, 114, 143–145

Naive methodological pluralism, 328
National Institute for Healthcare
Research (NIHR), 56
National Institute of Mental Health, 60
Naturalism
constraints of, 19, 45–46
impact of, 48
philosophical assumptions of, 32,
34–37, 42–43, 315, 326
reexamination of, 68
religious conflicts with, 46–47
as theology, 74n
trends in opposition to, 39–41, 49–
50, 60–65
view of human nature, 41, 44–45
Naturalistic theism, 97, 314
Naturalistic universalism, 32, 42, 45, 108,
327
Naturalistic worldview
challenges to, 49–50
compared to other worldviews, 77–
79, 93, 95, 96
domination of psychotherapy, 37–
39, 48, 78–79
problematic aspects of, 19
spiritual experiences and, 147
Near-death experiences, 137n, 139,
140–142
Newton, Isaac, 35, 323
Nondualistic interactionism, 58
Nontranscendent interventions, 291–
292

Objective idealistic worldview, 77–78.
See also Eastern spiritual
worldview
Objectivism, 43, 45, 326
Orthodoxy, 225–226
Outcomes assessment, 245–249
Outcomes, naturalistic limitation of
options, 45, 46
Out-of-session interventions, 289–290

Pantheism, 89. See also Eastern world
religions
Pastoral counseling, 40, 349
Pathological religious experiences, 234
Personality theory, 14, 111–129. See also
Human development and
functioning
psychospiritual themes of, 230–231
view of human nature, 111–115
view of therapeutic change, 113,
127–129
Personality traits, 133
Phenomenological research design,
332–335
Philosophical foundations of theistic
psychotherapy, 14, 97–109
agency, 98, 103–104
altruism, 99, 107–108
contextuality, 99, 108
moral universalism, 98, 104–106
scientific theism, 97–102
theistic holism, 98, 102–103
theistic relationism, 99, 106–107
Philosophy of science. See Naturalism;
Scientific philosophical
assumptions
Physical health. See also Mind–body
connection
prayer and, 252
religion and, 129–136, 220
worldview impact on, 75–77
Physics, 20th-century developments,
50
Pilgrimages, 267
Places of worship, 267
Pluralism of scientific theism, 101–102,
324–329
Polytheism, 89. See also Eastern world
religions
Positive psychology movement, 49,
60–61
Positivism, 33–34, 324, 325
Postmodernism, 52–53, 101–102, 324–
325, 328
Power, use of, 122–124
Prayer
and health, 252–253
in therapy, 171–172, 252–255,
269
Premonitions of death, 139, 142
Problem-solving styles, 226–227

Process of religious–spiritual assessment, 234–245
  ecumenical approach (level 1), 235–239
  focused approach (level 2), 235–236, 239–244
  general suggestions, 211–216
  meta-empathy in, 173–175, 245
  multilevel multisystemic strategy, 234–236
Process options, naturalistic limitation of, 45, 46
Process variables, 211, 213
Progression vs. stagnation, 126
Psychodynamic psychotherapy, 15, 283
Psychological adjustment, religion and, 130, 134
Psychology. *See also specific schools of psychology*
  alienation from religion, 6–7, 29–31, 47, 78–79, 159–161
  impact of modernistic science, 37–39, 48
  philosophical influences, 52–53
  problems with naturalistic approach, 41, 44–47
  public distrust of, 159–161
  public influence on, 54–55
  spiritually oriented approaches, 6–7, 67–68
  trends opposing naturalism, 39–41, 49–50, 60–65
Psychology of religion, 29–31, 339, 343–344
Psychosis, 133, 134
Psychotherapists. *See* Therapists
Psychotherapy. *See also* Therapist, role of
  assessment in. *See* Religious–spiritual assessment
  outcomes assessment, 245–249
  process. *See* Process of religious–spiritual assessment
  purpose and goals of, 154
Public attitudes on religion and spirituality, 5–6, 49, 54–55
Purpose of life, and worldview, 84, 86, 93, 94–95

Qualitative inquiry, 101–102, 148, 324–325, 328–329

Qualitative research designs, 332–335
Quantitative inquiry, 101–102, 324–329
Quantitative research design, 329–332
Quantum theory, 50

Racial background, 77, 305
Realism, 34, 43, 53, 97, 102, 314
Reality, questions on nature of, 74
Reason, as way of knowing, 317
Reconciliation, 265
Reductionism, 32, 42, 47
Relationism, theistic, 99, 106–107
Relationships
  dual, 184–188, 254, 269
  in human functioning, 125–126
  theistic perspective, 106–107
  therapeutic, 177–179
  use of power in, 122–124
  worldview impact on, 75–77
Relativism. *See* Ethical relativism
Relativity, theory of, 50
Relaxation response, 56, 256
Religion. *See also* Spirituality
  alienation from psychology, 6–7, 29–31, 47, 78–79, 159–161
  conflict with naturalism, 46–47
  defined, 21–22
  dialogue with science, 49, 51–52, 319–322
  mental health and, 59–60, 129–136, 220–221
  negative portrayal of, 38, 59, 163
  psychology of, 29–31, 339, 343–344
  public interest in, 5–6, 49, 54–55
  research on, 29–30, 55–57, 313–314
  schism with medicine, 55–57
  sensitivity to, in therapy, 156–158, 220. *See also* Multiculturalism
Religious adherents, demographic data, 8, 80–81
Religious affiliation, 225
Religious and spiritual practices as interventions, 251–279
  contemplation and meditation, 255–257
  fellowship and service, 270–273
  implementation of, 165–166
  moral instruction, 275–279
  prayer, 171–172, 252–255, 269
  reading sacred writings, 257–262

Scientific philosophical assumptions. *See also* Naturalism
  adoption of naturalism, 34–37
  late-20th-century philosophy and, 52–54
  medical research and, 52–54, 57–59
  modernistic science influences, 31–34, 42–43
  recent trends challenging, 49–50, 60–65, 68–69
  religion–mental health research and, 59–60
  societal and public influences, 54–55
Scientific process, theistic view of, 319–322
Scientific theism
  epistemology, 318, 322–324
  methodological pluralism, 324–329
  philosophical foundations, 97–102
  scientific process, view of, 319–322
Scientists, belief in God by, 11, 35, 321–322
Scriptures, 257–262, 260n
Secular psychotherapy traditions, 179–181
Self-help groups, 126
Selfishness, 107
Self-love, 107
Seligman, M. E. P., 60–61
Sensationism, 34, 36, 43
Sense experience, 316. *See also* Empiricism
Service, altruistic, 270–273
Sexual intimacy, in therapeutic relationship, 178–179
Shinto, 91
Sikhism, 83–84, 85–88, 258
Single-subject research design, 331, 332
Social adjustment, religion and, 134, 220–221
Social support, 270–273. *See also* Religious communities
Societal influences on psychology, 49, 54–55
Soul, 58
Spirit of Truth, 112, 114, 122
Spiritual aspect of personality, 114–115
Spiritual assessment. *See* Religious–spiritual assessment

Spiritual direction, seeking, 273–275
Spiritual experiences, 136–150
  abnormal, 234
  caveats and countercritique, 146–149
  core, index of, 244
  death-related visions, 137n, 139–143
  healing experiences, 139, 145
  mystical experiences, 114, 143–145
  naturalistic worldview and, 147
  recognition of in therapy, 175–176
  as way of knowing, 136–138
Spiritual guidance, in therapy, 171
Spiritual identity, 116–119, 227–228
Spiritual imagery, 255–257
Spiritual interventions. *See also* Religious and spiritual practices as interventions
  application to clinical issues, 299–305
  categories of, 286–293
  client selection for, 222
  contraindications for, 209, 222
  implementation of, 165–166
  integration with mainstream orientations, 11–12, 293–294
  mainstream compared to, 283
  necessity for, 13
  purpose of, 282–284
  research on, 305–308, 337–341
  special populations applications, 299–305
  therapeutic modalities applications, 294–299
  variety and prevalence of, 284–286, 287–288
Spirituality. *See also* Religion
  comparison of worldviews, 94–95
  conflict with naturalism, 46–47
  defined, 21–22
  health and, 129–136, 220–221
  public interest in, 5–6, 49, 54–55
  research on, 29–30, 55–57, 313–314
  theistic worldview and, 84, 87
Spiritual leaders. *See* Religious leaders
Spiritually oriented psychotherapy, 67–68, 305–308, 337–341. *See also* Theistic psychotherapy
Spiritual maturity, 232–234
Spiritual needs of clients, 222–223

ABOUT THE AUTHORS

P. Scott Richards received his PhD in counseling psychology in 1988 from the University of Minnesota. He has been a faculty member at Brigham Young University since 1990, where he is a professor in the Department of Counseling Psychology and Special Education. He is coauthor of *A Spiritual Strategy for Counseling and Psychotherapy* (American Psychological Association [APA], 1997), coeditor of the *Handbook of Psychotherapy and Religious Diversity* (APA, 2000), and coeditor of *Casebook for a Spiritual Strategy in Counseling and Psychotherapy* (APA, 2004). He was given the Dissertation of the Year award in 1990 from Division 5 of the APA (Evaluation, Measurement, and Statistics) for his psychometric investigation of religious bias in moral development research. In 1999, he was awarded the William C. Bier Award from Division 36 of the APA (Psychology of Religion). He currently serves as president of Division 36 (2004–2005). He is also a licensed psychologist and maintains a small private psychotherapy practice at the Center for Change in Orem, Utah.

Allen E. Bergin received his PhD in clinical psychology in 1960 from Stanford University. He was a faculty member at Teachers College, Columbia University, from 1961 to 1972. He was a professor of psychology at Brigham Young University (BYU) from 1972 until his retirement in 2001. While at BYU, he served as the director of the Values Institute (1976–1978) and director of the doctoral program in clinical psychology (1989–1993). He is past president of the Society for Psychotherapy Research and coeditor of the classic *Handbook of Psychotherapy and Behavior Change* (1994). He is coauthor of *A Spiritual Strategy for Counseling and Psychotherapy* (American Psychological Association [APA], 1997), coeditor of the *Handbook of Psychotherapy and Religious Diversity* (APA, 2000), and coeditor of *Casebook for a*

Spiritual Strategy in Counseling and Psychotherapy (APA, 2004). In 1989 he received the Award for Distinguished Professional Contributions to Knowledge from the APA. In 1990, Division 36 of the APA (Psychology of Religion) presented him with the William James Award for Psychology of Religion Research. He has also received the Society for Psychotherapy Research's Distinguished Career Award (1998) and the American Psychiatric Association's Oskar Pfister Award in Psychiatry and Religion (1998).